ISSUES IN DEMOCRATIC
CONSOLIDATION

Issues in Democratic Consolidation:

The New South American Democracies in Comparative Perspective

Edited by
Scott Mainwaring
Guillermo O'Donnell
and J. Samuel Valenzuela

Published for the Helen Kellogg Institute for International Studies by

UNIVERSITY OF NOTRE DAME PRESS
NOTRE DAME, INDIANA 46556

Library of Congress Cataloging-in-Publication Data

Issues in democratic consolidation : the new South
    American democracies in comparative perspective /
    edited by Scott Mainwaring, Guillermo O'Donnell,
    and J. Samuel Valenzuela.
        p.   cm.
    Includes index.
    ISBN 0-268-01210-5
    1. South America—Politics and government—
1980–   2. Democracy—South America—History—
20th century.   I. Mainwaring, Scott, 1954–   .
II. O'Donnell, Guillermo A.   III. Valenzuela, J.
Samuel (Julio Samuel)
F2237.I87   1992
320.98—dc20   91-50566
                                                CIP

Manufactured in the United States of America

Contents

Acknowledgments

The Kellogg Institute has provided a stimulating and hospitable environment for this project, above all because it has afforded us the opportunity to work closely with each other over a period of several years. Since its inception in 1983, the Institute has been committed to sponsoring research on democracy and democratization, especially in Latin America. This volume is an expression of that commitment.

We are above all grateful to the Executive Director of the Institute, Ernest Bartell, C.S.C., for his continuing support for our individual and collective projects. We are also thankful to our other colleagues at the Institute, Roberto Da Matta, Alejandro Foxley, and Timothy Scully, for their stimulation and encouragement.

James Langford, Director of the Notre Dame Press, nurtured the project in a variety of ways. Timothy Power translated the chapter by Guillermo O'Donnell, and Caroline Domingo helped edit several chapters. Rosario Bell, Dolores Fairley, and Daphne Shutts provided good cheer and assistance with word processing.

Introduction

Scott Mainwaring, Guillermo O'Donnell,
and J. Samuel Valenzuela

The last decade and a half has been marked by an unprecedented extension in the number of countries that have adopted democracy as their form of government. More people than ever before in the two-hundred-year history of experimentation with modern representative government now exercise the basic voting and other rights of citizenship under formally democratic national political institutions. The wave of change away from various forms of dictatorial rule began in the mid–1970s in Southern Europe, resulting in the now consolidated democracies of Spain, Portugal, and Greece. It continued in the late 1970s and throughout the 1980s in Latin America as the authoritarian regimes that had taken hold in much of the region gave way to elected governments. At the same time Ferdinand Marcos was unseated in the Philippines, and the South Korean military regime successfully orchestrated its own transformation by submitting its chosen candidate for the presidency to the verdict of the electorate. Then most swiftly in 1989 a tidal wave of transitions to democracy swept through Central and Eastern Europe, enabled by prior changes in the Soviet Union that led to the breakdown of the postwar geopolitical boundaries. At each setting overtaken by democratic openings, new as well as old and long-suppressed sentiments, collectivities, organizations, and institutions came to the fore in a precarious and at times conflictual mix that may, we hope, have the potential to generate lasting democratic regimes.

The earlier Southern European and Latin American regime transitions spawned an ample literature during the late 1970s and 1980s. This literature examined in detail what Guillermo O'Donnell calls in his contribution to this volume the first of two transitions from

1

authoritarian rule to democracy. This first transition begins with the initial stirrings of crisis under authoritarian rule that generate some form of political opening and greater respect for basic civil rights, and it ends with the establishment of a government elected in an open competitive contest, with universal adult franchise and effective guarantees for the respect of traditional democratic rights and liberties.

Although the degree of harshness and repressiveness of authoritarian regimes varied considerably, the first transition was punctuated with hardships that exacted their toll of suffering. Many people died in the struggle for democracy. Others were jailed, tortured, persecuted, exiled, and/or fired from their jobs. Ordinary citizens endured affronts to their dignity and livelihood in situations where little recourse was available against established authorities holding arbitrary and often whimsical power. It took a great deal of courage to demand respect for the most elementary rights that citizens in established democracies take for granted. Opposition activities also required the often hard-to-sustain hope that a democratic outcome was in the end possible. The very inception of the first transition was seemingly out of the question for a long time in many cases, notably in most of the Warsaw Pact countries as well as in Chile. In other instances, particularly in Brazil and in Poland, the course of the first transition was very protracted, and everywhere its successful conclusion was by no means certain at each of its most critical moments.[1] But eventually, in sequences that differed from one case to the next, through small changes or dramatic and breathtaking events, authoritarian rule gave way to democratic elections to constitute national governments and the first phase was complete.

The articles in this book contain repeated references and analyses of the varied modalities and complex processes related to the first transition, but their primary concern is with the second one. This transition begins with the inauguration of a democratic government and ends — if all goes well — with the establishment of a consolidated democratic regime.

The dividing line between these two transitions is not always easy to identify precisely. This is especially true where a new democratizing government was not chosen through a clear-cut national electoral contest but was constituted, nonetheless, by individuals who were identified at the moment of change with the opposition to authoritarian rule. Analysts may debate, for example, if in Brazil the second transition began with the presidency of José Sarney or that of Fernando Collor de Mello. Sarney was unexpectedly elected vice-president in 1985 on an opposition list led by Tancredo Neves that defeated the military government's candidate in an electoral college devised to favor an official victory, and he became president when Neves died shortly before taking office; by contrast, Collor was elected on the basis of a national popular election. A parallel difficulty can be observed in cases where leaders associated with the authoritarian regime were able to win national elections in which, despite some irregularities, voters had a choice. In South Korea, Paraguay, and Bulgaria this was to a variable extent the case. In such ambiguous situations, the second transition may be said to have begun as long as the new authorities respect all human and democratic rights of citizenship, commit themselves to an electoral process which local oppositions view as fair, and govern following constitutional procedures that correspond to the broad outlines of democratic practice. Following these criteria, the second transition in Brazil began with the Sarney government, in South Korea with Ro, in Paraguay with Rodríguez, but the June 1990 elections in Bulgaria did not complete the first transition.

It is similarly not easy to establish when the second phase, that of democratic consolidation, reaches closure. And yet a notable characteristic distinguishes transitional democracies from consolidated ones: while in the latter all major political actors take for granted the fact that democratic procedures dictate government renewal, the elected governments of transitional democracies operate in a political environment in which democratic continuity is still uncertain. They face actors who are unwilling to submit fully to democratic rules of the game and who can use their access to state or other resources to issue credible threats of destabilization and thereby block policy initiatives. Given these circumstances, both the democratic empowerment of those who are elected as well as the democratic accountability of political actors are incomplete. The political leaders and informed publics therefore lack the conviction that the democratic method to form governments will last long into the future, a conviction that is essential for democratic consolidation. Consequently, it is impossible to hinge the closure of the second phase on a specific event or formula (such as the second transfer of power from one elected government to another). But the qualitative difference between transitional and consolidated regimes is such that ana-

lysts should be able to determine whether specific cases are one or
the other.

Despite the many ways that the first transition impinges on the
second one — as the chapters in this volume note repeatedly — the
issues and problems of each phase differ. The literature on the first
transition focuses on the development of social and political oppositions to the authoritarian regime, the emergence of splits between
hard-liners and soft-liners within the circles of power, the ultimately
unsuccessful attempts by authoritarian rulers to legitimize their rule
by liberalizing rather than democratizing, the formation of coalitions pressing for democratic change between different and sometimes formerly divided political and social forces, the reactivation
of social and political life that results from the waning of the repressiveness of authoritarian rule, and so on. This literature stresses
the difficulty and reversibility of democratization, but its main focus is on the process of termination of authoritarian rule.

Writings on the second transition must still focus on the possible reversibility of democratization, but other problems having to
do with the construction of democratic institutions are added to the
agenda. The following are some of the questions raised: Does the
lifting of authoritarian repression allow for the resurfacing of old
and intractable problems and conflicts that may have led to democratic crisis in the past? To what extent have the political and other
leaders learned from past mistakes that led to crisis situations and
to authoritarian rule? Do the authoritarian regime's political figures
and other actors retain important positions of power and do they
have disloyal attitudes towards the new regime? Is the military subordinate to elected governments? What kind of alliances and new
cleavages emerge in the course of creating or recreating democratic
procedures? Is civil society adequately connected through political
parties and other channels of representation to the evolving political debates? Are the political institutions adequate to ensure inclusiveness and stability? How able and honest are the new democratic
political leaders? What are the effects of economic success, stagnation, or recession — whichever the case may be — on the legitimation
of the new governmental institutions? To what extent does such legitimation depend on adequate policy performance by the democratic government? How far can the new authorities press for redistribution and other social measures where there is a legacy of
gross neglect of the poor by authoritarian regimes? Can, in sum,
fully democratic and long sustainable political institutions emerge

and can these offer the possibility of successfully addressing economic and social problems?

While the essays in this book attach their conception of democratic consolidation to a minimal and procedural definition of democracy, the politics of the second transition — precisely because it permits and even fosters public debates over issues — raises problems that are broader than those that pertain in a strict sense to the transformation of the political regime. These broader problems cannot be ignored because their complex and often unexpected ramifications may affect the long term viability of even such minimally conceived democratic political institutions. Hence the literature on the second transition focuses on a wider array of issues than that on the first. It also contains a more pessimistic tone. The multiple shortcomings that need to be addressed only magnify the sense that the second transition is far from ideally complete and is therefore precarious. The literature on the second phase of democratization parallels to a certain extent the inevitable *desencanto* (disenchantment) that follows the initial joyous period of victory that corresponds to the instauration of the democratic governments. Such governments are bound to fall short of the expectations and hopes that are raised by the mobilization against authoritarian rule. The disenchantment may develop more rapidly and be more widespread and more deeply felt in some cases than in others; therefore it affects the second transition to different degrees. The literature on the specific cases usually reflects such variations as well. A comparative assessment should temper this pessimism in some cases; thus, although the very notion of *desencanto* first emerged in democratizing Spain, from a Latin American viewpoint the second transition in Spain was a resounding success.

This book deals with some of the issues and problems confronted in the course of the second transition and illustrates dominant themes in the analysis of still inconclusive democratic transitions. While the authors of the chapters often draw on broader comparisons, the primary substantive focus here is on new South American democracies.

Democratization in South America

The wave of first transitions to democracy was notably extensive in South America. In 1978 the only democracies in the subcontinent were Venezuela and Colombia (although in the latter case the record of respect for human rights and free and fair electoral competition was questionable).[2] By 1990, every country in the region had an elected government (although the presidential election in Paraguay was not a fair one, in Peru the Sendero Luminoso insurrection has curtailed electoral participation and stimulated widespread violations of human rights, Guyana has yet to complete the first transition, and Surinam oscillates between direct and indirect military rule). The 1980s were overall the best decade ever in terms of formal political democracy in South America.

The breadth of the democratic expansion in the 1980s has given rise to hopes that this new wave would not be, like previous more limited ones, a short-lived part of a cycle rather than a more enduring phenomenon. The literature on Latin American politics of the 1950s to mid–1970s emphasized the difficulties of establishing a stable political regime of any kind—whether authoritarian or democratic—in much of the region.[3] Will the current transitional democracies continue to be afflicted by the weakness and instability that were characteristic of prior democratic experiences in most of the subcontinent? Are there still multiple power currencies aside from elections (which must be only currency to constitute governments in consolidated democracies) such that the new South American democracies still fit the "living museum" image Charles Anderson applied to Latin American politics?[4]

Most observers initially greeted the new elected governments with guarded optimism and believed, not without reason, that the current wave of democratization has occurred under more auspicious circumstances than previous ones. Liberal democratic principles are today the main legitimating formula after the defeat of fascism in the Second World War and the decline of Communism more recently. (Perhaps authoritarianism based on religious fundamentalism is still an alternative, particularly in the Islamic world.) Throughout Latin America there is a new commitment to democracy among political actors and intellectuals. This is especially true of those on the left of the ideological spectrum, who no longer view the Cuban model as a positive example to the same extent as before—if at all. The prior experience of unsuccessful revolutionary attempts, years of harsh authoritarian military rule, and the realization of the multiple failures and denial of liberties under Communist rule have prompted a renewed valuing of the importance of liberal democracy not only as a means for political change, but also as a fundamental end in itself.[5] Only in Peru is a chiliastic insurrectionary Left, one which is notably involuted and isolated from current trends, gaining ground.

On the right, the recent wave of authoritarian governments proved so destructive in many countries that the military and its allies hold little optimism that another round of coups would resolve the outstanding problems of the region. In most cases — Brazil, Ecuador, and Chile being partial exceptions — the militaries failed to construct efficient governments. As a result, the armed forces have become less sanguine that they hold the answers to their countries' destinies, and their civilian supporters are searching for new ways to exert their influence. Even in Peru, where the current situation of economic collapse, insurrection, and national disintegration is most acute, the military has so far refrained from a coup, quite possibly in this case given the very extremity of the national crisis, while the civilian right has been able to press successfully for the adoption of neoconservative policies.

Current trends in the Catholic Church favor democracy as well. While the Church in Latin America sometimes supported the overthrow of elected governments with which it had significant conflicts, the salience of the issues that led to such conflicts has declined. Moreover, there is today greater consensus over the value of democracy among both conservative and progressive segments within the Church than at any prior moment. Conservative groups until the 1950s and even 1960s felt comfortable with authoritarian governments that drew some of their discourse from orthodox variants of Catholic social doctrine. But the failures of military governments, their human rights abuses, and overall trends in international Catholicism since the end of the Second World War have led to a growing rejection of such positions. For its part the Catholic Left has turned away from the Marxist critiques of liberal democracy that it had absorbed to a greater or lesser extent in the late 1960s and 1970s during the heyday of liberation theology.

The United States' policy towards Latin America is also more favorable toward political democracy than at any time in the past. The end of the Cold War reduced anti-Communism as a pressing concern that led United States policy makers to lend unwarranted and in many cases tragic support to antidemocratic forces. Conflicts over issues such as U.S. investments in Latin America do not appear likely to acquire the same intensity as in previous circumstances;

Latin American policy makers are currently more pragmatic and U.S. private interests more sophisticated in their business practices. Thus, the U.S. government, which historically proved to be more a foe than a friend of democracy in Latin America, does not appear likely to bolster or even lend tacit support to military conspiracies to replace elected governments. In fact, the most recent record is rather one of active U.S. support for democratic procedures.

The disposition of these various actors produces a conjuncture that favors the continuity of democratic governments to a greater extent than had been the case at any time in this century in South America. But such continuity, while necessary, is not enough to ensure democratic consolidation, and very serious obstacles and challenges to its prospects remain. The second transition promises, if anything, to be more difficult in some cases than the first. Its main short term problems lie in the enormous socioeconomic constraints, dismal policy performances, and inadequate leaderships to construct and extend democratic institutions by feckless civilian governments. As the 1990s begin, except for Chile and Uruguay which show greater promise, the new South American democracies are fragile ones that neither fall at the hands of new military dictatorships or revolutionary movements, nor move decisively toward democratic consolidation.

The right and the military, exceptions aside, have not been converted into authentic believers in democracy. In several countries the right is disadvantaged in playing the electoral game given its historic inability to build effective mass political parties, and a coup option looms still in the background as a recourse of last resort. Civilian supremacy over the military has also yet to be accomplished in all of the new South American democracies. Military revolts have been a menacing reality most notably in Ecuador and Argentina, and remonstrations by the military against the Chilean government have been the main sore point of its first year in power.

The current wave of South American democratization occurs, with the exception of Chile, in a context of severe economic distress. For many countries the 1980s have been the worst decade in terms of economic performance in this century. Virtually nobody anticipated how poorly most of the new civilian governments would perform on a wide variety of dimensions. The economic and social record is a particularly telling indicator of failures. Four countries in the region (Argentina, Bolivia, Brazil, Peru) hit inflation rates of four or five digits per year. Living standards have fallen in most countries, and income inequalities have simultaneously grown worse. The debt crisis looms on the horizon, with no end in sight. Economic adjustment to improve competitiveness in international markets and fiscal and monetary restraint to fight inflation are hardly compatible with the political agenda of democratic consolidation. The latter is not impossible, but is all the more difficult at a time when unions are in the process of recreating their organizations, new collective bargaining practices are being established, parties are extending their reach to formerly disenfranchised social sectors, legislatures are or should be asserting their participation in fundamental policy decisions and debates, capitalists ought to be investing in job producing growth, and expenditures on social services should be rising to meet the expectations raised by democratic change. In a nutshell, policy performance by new democratic governments should be positive for the sake of legitimating democracy, but the context of severe crisis makes such an outcome doubtful. Not surprisingly the parlous state of most South American economies has weakened the legitimacy of democratic governments, though paradoxically the economic crisis may also have restrained prospective authoritarian elites from overthrowing them lest they themselves must shoulder the burden for improving the economic situation. Although stable democracies can be built in periods of economic downturn,[6] there are probably no cases of successful democratic consolidation in economic conditions as devastating as those facing most Latin American countries today.

Similarly, on the political front, in most countries disappointments, frustrations, and poor performance have been a telling reminder that the tasks of democratic consolidation are far from easy. There have been many instances of egregious corruption and clientelism leading to an erosion of democratic legitimacy. In Brazil and Peru, Presidents Sarney and García staggered to the end of their presidential terms bereft of much public support or credibility. In Argentina, President Alfonsín left office early, overwhelmed by hyperinflation, policy paralysis, and the erosion of the Radical Party.

With the poor performances of the new democracies, the public mood in most countries has turned to pessimism and cynicism. Even in Uruguay, which can probably boast more successes — or perhaps it would be more appropriate to say fewer failures — than any of the other new democracies that began half a decade ago, public opinion has soured.[7] In Argentina and Brazil, public opinion surveys show staggering cynicism about politicians and parties. Democracy has suffered from the combination of poor policy performance and graft.

Outside of Chile and Uruguay, political parties and legislatures remain fragile. Parties and legislatures are major channels for organizing, articulating, and even reducing the expression of societal demands and interests, and as such play an important role in democracies.[8] Although parties need not be well established at the beginning of democracy, if they do not become institutionalized over time, prospects for developing effective mechanisms to express and channel interests are limited, and legitimacy and governability are likely to suffer. For this reason, it is troubling that parties and legislatures in most of the new democracies of South America have shown no signs of becoming more effective in the 1980s; indeed, they were often discredited by their association with inept governments. The widespread proclivity of presidents to undermine parties and legislatures has had deleterious consequences on institution building.

In most of the region, presidential systems have encouraged populism, zero-sum competition, made building stable legislative alliances more precarious, and rendered effective policy formulation more difficult. Prospects for changing to semi-presidential or parliamentary systems are not good. The era of television politics has made it possible for political outsiders, such as Alberto Fujimori in Peru, to sweep to presidential victory, but has made it even more difficult for parties to establish deeper roots in society. The weakness of institutional channels facilitates the ascendancy of populist leaders who promise a great deal but lack the institutional bases of support to accomplish their objectives, not to speak of urging restraint by the population when needed.

In sum, while the current circumstances favor the continuation of the fragile South American democracies, the complex tasks of building democratic institutions and consolidating them still lie ahead. If the difficult processes of the second transition are not realized, then a reversion to military interventions and authoritarian rule become more likely in the future. If this were to be, tragically, the case, the extensive South American democratization will turn out to be just a stronger cycle — but a cycle nonetheless. An auspicious moment will have been lost. At present, the transitions in Chile and Uruguay show the greatest potential for reaching closure; both countries had consolidated democracies in the past, and this facilitates the second transition.

The Essays in This Book

The analysis of the second transition poses such a broad range of intellectual and political problems that it would be impossible to cover all of them in a single volume. Thus, this book addresses some of the basic conceptual groundwork for the study of the post-authoritarian phase of democratic transitions, takes stock of the recent literature on transitions, and discusses a selection of key issues pertaining to the process. These issues include the effects of the modalities of the first transition on the second, the challenges to subordinating the military to civilian government control, the problematic continuities of political personnel from the authoritarian to the democratic period, the weakness of interest group connections to parties and policy making in state bureaucracies and legislatures, the difficulties in building proper channels for political representation and accountability, and the inadequacy of the evolving political institutions to ensure both the continuity as well as the "democraticness" of the new regimes. A major theme running through this collection is that transitions may be arrested by the multiple political, economic, and even social constraints under which they occur, and that the resulting "stunted" regimes are more prone to reversal. And yet the authors of this book agree that notwithstanding the constraints imposed by the past and by the nature of the transitions, choices matter. Future outcomes are not uniquely determined by past constraints; if they were, there would be very few democracies in the world, since all countries had to overcome important hurdles to achieve democratic regimes.

Although the essays have as a primary reference the new democracies of South America, there are frequent brief comparative references to other cases that serve mainly to highlight the peculiarities of the former. However, the reader should not expect to find here a complete descriptive coverage of the new South American democracies. This book has not been framed by such an attempt; rather, its authors have approached their topics thematically.

The opening contribution to this volume is that of Guillermo O'Donnell. In addition to laying out the distinction between the first and the second transitions that has been noted above, he presents the difference between transitions where there is an excessive emphasis on accords or pacts, including those with authoritarian actors, as opposed to those in which there is too much competition between democratic actors who lose sight of their need to retain a strategic alliance against authoritarian forces. The first are prone to reversals by a successive limitation of the room for elected officials to formulate and implement policies, or by what he calls "slow death," whereas the second are subject to reversal by military coup or "sudden death." O'Donnell also discusses the effects of the relative economic success and repressiveness of authoritarian regimes over the prospects for democratic continuity after the transition. In what he calls the "paradox of success" he notes that second transitions are favored by the authoritarian regime's failures, destructiveness, and higher repressiveness insofar as they strengthen the antiauthoritarian sentiments in the population. The main substantive focus of his chapter is on Brazil, whose transition he sees as laden with difficulties. These stem in large measure from the relative success of the military regime, from the continuities of both the political class and of a certain "style of doing politics" despite the transition, from the weight of social inequalities and the embryonic nature of popular sector organizations and parties. Brazil's new democracy is prone to populism, clientelism and prebendalism. It lacks norms and institutions that will establish a clear distinction between public and private and create proper channels for political representation and accountability. O'Donnell also provides in the closing section of his essay a definition of democratic consolidation.

Beginning with the observation that the notion of democratic consolidation has been used all too loosely in the recent discussions of transitions, Samuel Valenzuela's essay attempts to provide a more delimited conception. Linking it to a minimal formal definition of democracy, he identifies four problem areas that typically undermine its full development in transitional settings: first, the existence of nondemocratic "tutelary powers" that attempt to retain the capacity to oversee the decisions of elected governments; second, the presence of "reserved domains" of policy from which democratic governments are excluded despite their desire to control them; third, the operation of an electoral system that is deliberately designed with egregious biases to minimize the influence of specific sectors of opinion; and fourth, the widespread sense among political actors and informed publics that the electoral system may not be the *only* means to renew governments. Valenzuela then characterizes the process of democratic consolidation as a series of confrontations between actors in which these impediments to the minimal workings of a formal democracy are removed, resulting in the generalized perception that the new regime will continue well into the foreseeable future. The chapter concludes with a detailed discussion of facilitating conditions for the process of consolidation. These have to do with the modalities through which the first transitions to democratic governments took place, the influence of historical memories of alternative regimes, the degree of moderation of political conflict, the management of socioeconomic conflict, and the subordination of the military to the democratic government.

Based on a familiarity with a wide range of transitions in Southern and Eastern Europe and South America, Adam Przeworski's chapter provides an abstract, almost game-theoretic approach to the logic of transitions to democracy. Transitions begin with a process of authoritarian regime liberalization, which Przeworski argues comes about from a mutual interaction between schisms within the authoritarian regime and organization of the opposition. Yet liberalization is inherently unstable, for once it is unleashed, either the opposition conquers growing space leading ultimately to the demise of authoritarianism, or the regime must repress, leading to the marginalization of the regime factions that initially proposed liberalization. Przeworski argues that successful transitions to democracy are necessarily conservatizing, because only institutional arrangements that make radical social and economic changes difficult provide the security that induces actors to play by democratic rules of the game. For democracy to be established, it must protect to some degree the interests of the forces capable of subverting it, above all capitalists and the armed forces.

Felipe Agüero's contribution addresses the difficulties encountered by the new South American democracies in subordinating the military to civilian government control. He notes that while claiming to represent the enduring and essential interests of the nation and state, all the military establishments in the new democracies have retained high degrees of autonomy from elected governments in what he calls "protective entrenchment," and they all seek to extend their influence to non-military spheres of policy in what he characterizes as "expansive entrenchment." This unusually autonomous and strong

position of the military stems in part, Agüero argues, from the fact
that the South American authoritarian regimes were military ones
which withdrew from power while retaining considerable ability to
negotiate the terms of the transition. Agüero also notes that the international environment is not as conducive to placing the military
under civilian democratic government control as is the case in the
Southern European context from which he draws frequent comparative observations. Moreover, civilian political institutions and leaderships have been too weak to be able to deal authoritatively with the
military. As a result, they have preferred to let the military define
the terms of its involvement in the state.

Catherine Conaghan's chapter focuses on the attitudes of business leaders towards democratization in the new Andean democracies. She notes that business leaders advocated a return to civilian
rule because they were dissatisfied with the access they had to military
governments. They also were concerned that the military in government would lose too much credibility and prestige, thereby creating
more favorable political conditions for a leftist insurrection. And
yet the new democratic governments did not give business — which
frequently advocates state-business dialogues exclusive of labor —
any greater access to the new technocratic economic policy-making
teams. Business organizations also have poor connections to the parties of the right, which continue to be weak in these countries. Moreover, business leaders appear not to be genuinely prodemocratic,
for they seek to retain the option of advocating or provoking a military coup if the political circumstances, in their view, require it.

Frances Hagopian's chapter examines how traditional political leaders that supported authoritarian rule ensconced themselves
in positions of power in Brazil's new democracy during the transition process. Induced by incentives from opposition leaders and by
the erosion of military rule, traditional political leaders abandoned
the military regime between 1982 and 1985. In so doing they made
possible a transition to democracy in 1985, but they also won control of key policy-making positions, assumed leadership within several former opposition parties, thwarted progressive reforms, bolstered pervasive clientelism, fought successfully to retain political
institutions that favor conservative actors, and perpetrated nondemocratic practices in the new democracy. Because the practices of these
traditional political elites are regressive and nondemocratic, their
prominence compromises the prospects for democratic consolidation.

Finally, Scott Mainwaring's chapter is a review of some of the major themes, debates, and disagreements in the burgeoning literature on democratic transitions and consolidation. He begins with a discussion of the notion of democracy, which has been used excessively loosely in some quarters. Some analysts have equated democracy with the holding of competitive elections, thereby establishing a subminimal procedural definition. Most analysts have seen splits in the authoritarian coalition as the starting point of liberalization and eventual democratization, but such processes often involve complex interactions between regime and opposition forces from an early stage. Although leaders are the most important actors in most transitions, mass action and elite-mass linkages can be of crucial importance. Recent scholarship has often seen democracy as a second-best solution, an unintended consequence that emerged when political leaders sought other objectives, but the historical record suggests that in Latin America democracy has worked only where political leaders saw it as a best solution. The chapter also argues, contrary to those who have highlighted the uncertainty of democracy, that in important regards democracy provides greater certainty than other political regimes.

Written around different themes, collectively these essays contribute to our understanding of processes of democratic consolidation. They also provide a broad if disturbing analysis of the problems confronting the new democracies in contemporary South America.

NOTES

We are grateful to Abraham Lowenthal for his helpful suggestions.
1. On uncertainty as a central feature in transitions to democracy, see Guillermo O'Donnell and Philippe Schmitter, "Tentative Conclusions about Uncertain Democracies," Part IV of Guillermo O'Donnell, Philippe Schmitter, and Laurence Whitehead, eds., *Transitions from Authoritarian Rule: Prospects for Democracy* (Baltimore: Johns Hopkins University Press, 1986).
2. See Jonathan Hartlyn, *The Politics of Coalition Rule in Colombia* (New York: Cambridge University Press, 1988), especially chapter 7.
3. See especially Douglas Chalmers, "The Politicized State in Latin America," in James M. Malloy, ed., *Authoritarianism and Corporatism*

in Latin America (Pittsburgh: University of Pittsburgh Press, 1977). See also Merle Kling, "Toward a Theory of Power and Instability in Latin America," *Western Political Quarterly* 9, no. 7 (March 1956), pp. 21–35.

4. Charles Anderson, *Politics and Economic Change in Latin America* (Toronto: Van Nostrand, 1967), p. 92. See also Eldon Kenworthy, "Coalitions in the Political Development of Latin America," in Sven Groennings, E. W. Kelley and Michael Leiserson, eds., *The Study of Coalition Behavior: Theoretical Perspectives from Four Continents* (New York: Holt, Rinehart, and Winston, 1970).

5. For a forceful expression of this new commitment see Francisco Weffort, *Por que democracia* (São Paulo: Brasiliense, 1984). See also Robert Packenham, "The Changing Political Discourse in Brazil," in Wayne Selcher, ed., *Political Liberalization in Brazil: Dynamics, Dilemmas, and Future Prospects* (Boulder: Westview, 1986). The change of perspective in the Left is particularly noticeable in the Chilean Socialist Party.

6. Juan Linz and Alfred Stepan argue that this was the case in Spain. See their "Political Crafting of Democratic Consolidation or Destruction: European and South American Comparisons," in Robert Pastor, ed., *Democracy in the Americas: Stopping the Pendulum* (New York: Holmes and Meier, 1989), pp. 43–45.

7. Luis Eduardo González and Andrés Rius, "La opinión pública montevideana a cuatro años de la restauración democrática," unpublished paper, Montevideo, 1989. At the end of the first year of democratic government in Chile, public opinion polls were highly favorable to the new government. However, the Chilean transition, while promising, is still too new to draw a valid comparison with other countries.

8. On the importance of parties in democratic politics see Giovanni Sartori, *Parties and Party Systems: A Framework for Analysis* (New York: Cambridge University Press, 1976).

Transitions, Continuities, and Paradoxes

Guillermo O'Donnell

Introduction

In the recent history of Latin American countries, the struggles against authoritarianism were hard-fought and filled with uncertainty. These struggles contained a strong ethical element, driven by indignation over the atrocities committed by the authoritarian regimes: not only the violations of basic human rights, but also the responsibility of these regimes for the aggravation of a grossly unequal distribution of all types of resources. These struggles were not only against authoritarian regimes; they were also for democracy. We viewed democracy not only as a desirable arrangement for the articulation of political life, but also as an adequate (though likely slow) path to the establishment of more just and egalitarian societies.

Today, several years after the inauguration of democratic governments, it has become evident that these paths will be more lengthy and difficult (and even reversible) than we had imagined in our most pessimistic predictions during the antiauthoritarian struggles. The obstacles are varied and imposing. There is great dissatisfaction among many who enthusiastically welcomed the end of the authoritarian regimes; the democratic forces seem at times to weary or to lose their way.

Many friends and *compañeros* of the antiauthoritarian struggles today occupy high positions in government or in party leadership in Brazil, Argentina, Chile, and Uruguay. They belong to weak governments, beset by countless problems, both domestic and foreign, and threatened by powerful authoritarian actors. It is clear to them, as it is to those who chose to remain in intellectual life, that these weak and incomplete democracies must be nurtured and defended from the very real risks of an authoritarian regression.

17

In a sense, the authoritarian period was easier than the current situation. We knew then why and against whom we were fighting, in a solidarity stitched together as much from the critique of that domination as from the democratic wager which we were making. Now we must find an answer to the question of how to make a democratic critique of democracy—particularly when this democracy is so incomplete and threatened by our old enemies. The answer is not easy. An embittered critique which foregoes the analysis of constraints and circumstances is unsatisfactory. So too is silence, whether it is based on misguided benevolence or on the eternal impulse not to displease those in power.[1]

The above implies the ongoing construction of a necessary dimension of democracy: that of space for a democratic critique of democracy which warns about obstacles, points out risks, and criticizes acts and omissions which appear as hindrances not only for the survival of these democracies but also for their consolidation and expansion into certain areas—economy, society, and culture—in which so little progress has been made to date. As will be seen in the following pages, this critical analysis varies from Brazil to Argentina. But the concerns and values that drive the analysis are the same.

1. The Two Transitions: A Strategic Perspective

It is useful to conceptualize the processes of democratization as actually implying two transitions. The first is the transition from the previous authoritarian regime to the installation of a democratic government. The second transition is from this government to the consolidation of democracy or, in other words, to the effective functioning of a *democratic regime*. The democracy to which I refer is political democracy (or polyarchy, according to the definition of Robert Dahl),[2] which may coexist with varying degrees of democratization in the economic, social, and cultural spheres. There are two reasons why it is important to make this distinction: first, because the conquest of political democracy is worthwhile in its own right; and second, because the distinction between political democracy on the one hand and socioeconomic and cultural democratization on the other is precisely what allows us to explore the various relationships between the two.

In Brazil, the first transition was unusually long.[3] For the Latin

American countries which have recently completed the first transition (Brazil, Argentina, Chile, Uruguay, Peru, Ecuador, and the Dominican Republic), it has already become clear that the second transition will be not any less arduous nor any less lengthy; the paths that lead from a democratic government to a democratic regime are uncertain and complex, and the possibilities of authoritarian regression are numerous.[4] The first condition (obvious, but still important) for the path leading to a democratic regime to be accessible is that there be no authoritarian regression. This regression can occur through a "sudden death," via a classic military coup. It can also occur through a "slow death," in which there is a progressive diminution of existing spaces for the exercise of civilian power and the effectiveness of the classic guarantees of liberal constitutionalism. Here we would have that which in the previously cited work with Schmitter we called *democradura* or a "civilian government with military sovereignty." In either of these two scenarios — one swift and spectacular, the other slow and at times opaque — the second transition would be aborted.

This is the crux of the strategic problem facing democratic actors: on the one hand, to avoid regression, while on the other to push the process in such a way that — despite unsteady speed and numerous uncertainties — it moves forward to the consolidation of democracy. There are serious obstacles to this process. Among them we need refer to the persistence of decidedly authoritarian actors who control important resources of power; the attitude, widespread among other actors, of neutrality or indifference regarding the type of political regime in place; and the prevalence in many social spheres of profoundly authoritarian patterns of domination. These are usual obstacles to all transitions. Today, in our cases, we must add to these the consequences of a deep economic crisis and the aggravation of social inequalities.

In light of these obstacles, it would be convenient if there were a majority of democrats among the population (I define as democrats those individuals who understand, accept, and practice the rules of political democracy). But that is not the case. The existence of a majority (or at least a strong and conscious minority) of democrats in the sense defined above is a consequence of the existence — over a sufficiently long period of widespread practice — of political democracy. It is not a cause which precedes and explains the emergence of political democracy. If it were, then no democracy would ever have emerged anywhere in the world; in no known case does there appear to have been a majority of democrats before the advent of political democracy.

Furthermore, it appears that the acquisition through repeated practice of a set of democratic attitudes — in politics as well as in other spheres — tends to spill over from its point of origin in the direction of other patterns of authority. Here there exists a complex dialectic between politics and other spheres of social life that allows for various extensions of socioeconomic and cultural democratization. The acquisition of democratic beliefs and attitudes seems to be contagious: if we practice them in certain types of activities, it is likely that we will extend them to others and/or support those who attempt to do so. The emergence of a rich social fabric of institutions and of patterns of democratic (or, at least, nondespotic and nonarchaic) authority is facilitated by the observance of the guarantees and freedoms typical of political democracy; on the other hand, the consolidation of democracy is greatly assisted by the progressive (although not linear) expansion of that fabric. This is one reason why the road before us is long, complicated, and subject to dangerous impasses and possible reversals. But this teaches us that the only way to further the process of democratic construction is to practice democracy in the political sphere and — at the very least — to fight against despotic patterns of authority at all levels of society.

One of the great enigmas (and indicators of difficulty) of the second transition is that the truly democratic actors are a minority in a situation where they seek to move toward consolidation of a political regime based on the principle of majority rule, at least as regards the selection of those who will govern. When the problem is framed in this way, there seems to be little reason for optimism. However, contemporary South American democratic actors have certain factors working to their advantage. The first is the *antiauthoritarian position* of the greater part of the population. The population may not be familiar with or understand the premises and operational mechanisms of political democracy, and may follow authoritarian practices in various spheres of social life. But what it does know is that it does not want the return of *that* authoritarian regime or military regime (whatever it was called) which it recently had to endure. This is the source of the main political asset of democratic actors: the existence of an electoral majority which is antiauthoritarian although not strictly democratic.

The second factor is the current prestige of democratic discourses, and conversely, the weakness of openly authoritarian *political* discourses. This is a crucial innovation of the current wave of democratization in South America. In early periods, the prestige of more or less fascist "solutions" or of populist or traditional authoritarianism, as well as the (at best) ambivalent attitude of the left toward political democracy, virtually guaranteed that democratic discourses would not prevail. Currently, in part as a consequence of the global ideological climate, and particularly as a consequence of the hard lessons learned since the 1960s with the series of bureaucratic-authoritarian regimes in South America, few voices openly challenge political democracy.[5] This does not exclude the great (and growing) influence of conservative ideologies in the socioeconomic sphere, nor the opportunistic calculus of those who have decided to wait for the right moment to reveal their authoritarian positions, nor the extensive penetration of authoritarian patterns of domination in the economy, in society, in culture, and in family relationships. But the above-mentioned innovation is real, and although it is limited to the political sphere, it functions at precisely the central level for the construction of a regime of political democracy. Like the existence of an antiauthoritarian but not necessarily democratic majority, the current supremacy of prodemocratic political discourses is not ideally suited to navigate the precarious pathways of the second transition; it would be much better if this supremacy were extended to other patterns of authority. Furthermore, both factors are subject to withering by the passage of time: the antiauthoritarian orientation depends on clear and intense memories of the authoritarian regime, and the influence of democratic discourses depends in part upon those same memories and in part on their capacity to be translated into concrete meanings for the majority of the population.

In order to advance toward the consolidation of democracy, we see that democratic actors must at least: (a) neutralize those actors who are unconditionally authoritarian, either by isolating them politically or by turning them into fragmented sects which cannot threaten the survival of the regime, and (b) in regard to neutral actors, promote preferences or at least practices which are compatible with the functioning of democracy. I refer to "practices," because it is not necessary (although it is of course desirable) that these actors become "democrats" themselves. It is enough for them to believe that the democratic game will continue indefinitely (in this sense, the passage of time works in favor of democratization) and/or to conclude that any alternative political regime is too uncertain or risky for them, although they may prefer it in principle.[6] As regards the antiauthoritarian majority, democratic actors must (c) in the first place increase the numbers and intensity of strictly democratic actors, and secondly, cause the sphere in which that majority really counts (the electoral sphere) to become a critical locus of decision making as regards the important issues facing the nation. Summarizing the preceding points, democratic actors must go on creating a fabric of institutions which can carry out the mediation of the interests, identities, and conflicts mobilized in a given period. This task of building representative institutions, which I shall discuss later, is fundamental. It is the crucial thread which leads to a consolidated democracy; without it, any degree of democratization achieved is precarious and potentially explosive.

Due to their very nature, democratic actors are pluralistic and different, not homogeneous. They compete among themselves, both in the electoral arena as well as in the area of the diverse interests which they represent or invoke. At the same time, however, during the uncertain trajectory from a democratic government to a democratic regime, these actors must recall that their real quarrel is with the camp of authoritarian actors, because of the risks which the latter themselves represent and because of their capacity to eventually wrest the neutral actors to support an authoritarian regression. It is with this calculus in mind that, during the second transition, democratic actors should agree to subordinate their strategies (including competition among themselves) to the imperative of not facilitating a return to authoritarianism. This is the great accord or pact of the second transition. In most cases it is an accord (implicit, neither public nor formal), or sometimes a pact (explicit, and almost always public and formalized) of a specifically *political* nature. Although it may include clauses of another kind (normally intended to resolve an economic crisis), the basic content of the accord or pact entails an attempt: first, to try to delimit the set of properly democratic actors, and second, to cooperate on certain acts and omissions as a way of reducing the danger of an authoritarian regression. However, even if these actors come together in good faith, their accord or pact — which henceforth I will call a "democratizing accord" — gives rise to important ambivalences. One of them has to do with who can be and who should be the pact makers. Another relates to the decisions (and non–decisions) which some pact makers view as necessary in order to avoid a sudden death of the process of democratization and which others may consider instead to be steps toward a slow death of the process.

For these reasons, among others (chief among them the inevitable disagreements about what *kind* of democracy the second transition should produce), during this period the interactions among democratic actors usually are a complex and changing combination of antiauthoritarian accords and of competition within the democratic camp. Even at this abstract level, it is already apparent that on the one hand, an exaggeration of "accordism" could liquidate that element of competitiveness without which democracy simply does not exist; on the other hand, a degree of competition which loses sight of the shared interest of democratic actors in the continuation of the process may irresponsibly aggravate the risks of authoritarian regression. Note that at this point in the argument an asymmetry appears. It is unlikely that excessive accordism will provoke a dramatic rupture (it looks more like the road to a slow death of the second transition); contrarily, excessive competition threatens to provoke a sudden death by means of a classic military coup.

Within the camp of democratic actors, there is a very important subset: politicians. Their personal vocation and professional activity, in a regime which is or which tries to be representative, consists of seeking to get elected in order to occupy important government positions. The main capability (and hence responsibility) of leading the transition from a democratic government to a democratic regime belongs to them. Certainly they are not the only democratic leadership, nor are they the only potential participants in the democratizing accord; other democratic actors in various societal organizations are also important. But it is politicians who must make the most important decisions — especially those which, from within or outside government, affect the building and strengthening of those institutions specific to democracy — regarding the fate of the second transition. Even more than the fate of the first transition or that of an already consolidated democracy, the fate of the second transition depends on the quality of democratic (professional) politicians — those who are supposed to both desire and understand the meaning of the institutionalized practice of political democracy.

It is worthwhile to state now some rather obvious propositions

about these actors. The first is that a democratic politician, both
out of personal conviction as well as for pragmatic reasons relating
to the preservation of his/her role, has an overarching interest (in
the short term) in the maintenance of democracy and (in the long
term) in the eventual consolidation of that process. The second propo-
sition is that, in principle, a politician wants to get elected, and in
order to do so, must be previously elected or designated as a candidate by his/her party. The third is that in order to be a candidate
that politician must play the game being played by most other politicians — in other words, s/he must adjust to (or at least not deviate
too much from) the style of politics which is prevalent among his/
her colleagues. We may now move on to more concrete issues.

2. Authoritarian Regimes and Transitions

Let us now make a brief reference to the recent authoritarian
past. Simplifying, within the "family" of bureaucratic-authoritarian
regimes,[7] we can identify those which were economically destructive
and highly repressive — Argentina, Uruguay, and on several occasions Bolivia, and Greece under the colonels. The economic destructiveness in these cases is evident in the severe recessions, deindustrialization, and unemployment which they provoked. Although
a large part of the bourgeoisie and the middle classes tended to support the implantation of authoritarianism, it did not take long for
them to realize that (apart from a few sectors mostly concentrated
in financial capital and the upper middle class) economically they
were severely harmed by these regimes. As regards repressiveness,
these cases came closest to a true state terrorism. Not only was there
a large number of victims of unspeakable horrors, there were relatively few people who felt entirely safe from terror; insecurity and
fear affected broad sectors of the population, including many who
supported the implantation of these regimes.[8] With one exception
(Uruguay), these regimes ended in collapse,[9] due to an explosion
of internal conflicts which was facilitated by massive (although often
silenced for long periods by repression) opposition. In some cases,
these regimes brought about their own collapse by projecting their
internal problems outward and embarking upon a warlike adventure (like the Cyprus intervention in the Greek case or the Falklands/
Malvinas War in the Argentine case). The collapse led to transitions
in which the authoritarian rulers were unable to control the agenda

of issues to be negotiated with the opposition and the results thereof (in these cases, note the typically failed attempts to impose an extensive institutionalized role for the armed forces in the future civilian government).

This type of transition saddles the new democracy with tremendous problems resulting both from a wrecked economy and from the deep political and psychosocial wounds caused by the recent, extensive repression. On the other hand, due to the economic destructiveness of the authoritarian regime, its incumbents and principal supporters—including the armed forces—suffer an acute and generalized loss of prestige. This leads to a comparatively high degree of demilitarization under the new democratic government. The armed forces occupy few institutional spaces within the new government, they lose a good deal of the civilian state apparatus which they normally take over during the authoritarian regime, and they lose their capability to formulate or veto policies (except for those which refer to the military institution). This allows relatively broad degrees of freedom for the new democratic government, which is less subject than in more militarized situations to intervention and vetoes by the armed forces in diverse areas of public policy. However, in this type of transition the new democratic leadership encounters enormous restrictions resulting from the severe economic and social crisis caused by destructiveness of the outgoing authoritarian regime. Furthermore, the greater degrees of freedom which these governments gain in relation to the armed forces has the important tradeoff of many military sectors' being profoundly hostile to the government and alienated from civilian rule. In other words, these new democracies are under the threat of sudden death by a coup.

Let us now outline the second type of cases. In these, the authoritarian regimes were relatively successful economically and, although they indeed applied repression, this repression was significantly less extensive and systematic than in the cases discussed above. In contemporary Latin America, the cases which can be placed in this category are Brazil and Ecuador, as well as Chile, with some caveats which I cannot elaborate in the present text, written before the installation of a democratic government in this country. In Europe, Spain also corresponds to this category, although with some qualifications which I discuss below. This is a comparative judgment: as regards Brazil, I am not unfamiliar with the economic crisis which accompanied the final years of the authoritarian regime, nor with the intensely income-concentrating nature of the economic growth that was achieved, nor with the severe repression brought to bear, especially between 1969 and 1971. But this repression was less massive, less continuous, and less systematic than in the first group of cases, and it affected to a far lesser degree the sense of personal security of entrepreneurs and middle sectors. On the other hand, the rapid economic growth achieved by the countries of the second group contrasts with the economic destruction and deindustrialization experienced by the countries of the first (which also suffered sharp income concentration).

These characteristics have consequences which are worth exploring. First, in this second type of cases thanks to the periods of strong economic expansion important sectors of the entrepreneurial and middle classes are products of the authoritarian regime. Although many of these actors moved to the opposition during the transition,[10] they harbor more positive memories of the authoritarian regime than in the cases of strong repression and economic destruction. Second, to the extent that the authoritarian regime was more successful in terms of (at least) economic growth, the loss of prestige and attendant unpopularity of the armed forces tend to be less than in the other cases.

The transitions in these regimes do not result from collapse; they are transitions which usually are processed through a series of accords or pacts.[11] In contrast to the other cases, incumbents of authoritarian regimes which were economically successful and relatively nonrepressive achieve a high degree of control (although this declines over time) over the rhythm and agenda of the transition. In both types of transition there may be accords and eventually formalized pacts; but only in the cases at hand are authoritarian rulers able to force a good deal of their agenda upon the opposition. In addition, when the authoritarian regime is based around the armed forces, the high degree of bargaining power which they retain gives rise to accords in which they receive firm guarantees that "the past will be overlooked," and in which they secure broad participation in the new civilian government. As Alfred Stepan has pointed out,[12] Brazil is an extreme case in this sense; later we shall see that Brazil is unique in other respects as well.

Leaving aside Ecuador,[13] which would make this text too lengthy, I will proceed to examine the cases of Brazil and Spain. The literature has insisted, correctly, on the important similarities between these two cases.[14] But perhaps more insight could be gained by focusing on some of the differences. To begin with, although it was pacted and largely under the control of the regime, the Spanish first transition was far shorter than the Brazilian; it lasted less than two years, compared to Brazil's eleven. On top of that, the Spanish transition began by declaring unequivocally that its goal was political democracy, not, as in Brazil, a liberalized form of authoritarianism to be achieved in "slow, gradual, and secure" fashion. With such a goal in mind, certain rapid measures were taken by Adolfo Suárez and King Juan Carlos: the formation of the Union of the Democratic Center (UCD), under the leadership of Suárez; the negotiations with the Spanish Socialist Workers Party (PSOE) and the Spanish Communist Party (PCE), which, to the outrage of the Franquist hardliners, resulted in the legalization of both parties; the brilliant maneuvering by the King and Suárez to obtain the self-dissolution of the Cortes (the rubber-stamp Franquist legislature based on corporativist representation); direct elections which confirmed Suárez as the premier civilian constitutional authority in the new democracy; and elections for a Constituent Assembly which produced a superb charter, negotiated by the above parties and acceptable to all three.

Certain characteristics of Franquism were absent in the Brazilian bureaucratic-authoritarian regime and created a more favorable situation in Spain than in Brazil (or, for that matter, any other country in Latin America). First was the still-vivid memory of the Civil War and fear of its repetition, which provided the impulse for accords and convergences among the parties. Second was the death of Franco in the absence of institutionalized mechanisms of succession for the various factions (or "families," as they were known) which made up the regime. Third, these difficulties led the King to embrace the democratic solution as the most effective channel for finding institutional formulas which would not cause dramatic ruptures or stir up the ghosts of the Civil War. Fourth, in the latter period of Franquism the armed forces made up only one of the families of the regime, whereas they retained a much more central role in the Latin American cases.[15] Finally, the geopolitical situation of Spain encouraged important support from the European Economic Community, from various European governments, and from various European political parties (notably the Social Democrats) with a view to a rapid, democratic conclusion of the transition, as well as to

guaranteeing the authenticity of the promises of the principal Spanish leftist parties to accept the rules of the democratic game and
to abandon revolutionary and/or Leninist lines. In contrast, Latin
American countries are subject to the principal — and often inconsistent — influence of several agencies (including military agencies)
of the United States government.[16]

In another contrast with Brazil, the electoral victory of Suárez
came through a party, the Union of the Democratic Center (UCD),
which, true to its name, constituted a real democratic center (although the party disappeared within a few years). To its left were
the PSOE, the PCE, and other, smaller parties (mostly regionalist).
To its extreme right the UCD had *Fuerza Nueva,* headed by Blas
Piñar, which represented the most fascist tendencies of Franquism
and which had almost no electoral support. To its right, the UCD
had the Popular Alliance (AP), led by Carlos Fraga Iribarne. Before the transition, Suárez held a second-tier position in Franquism
as the leader of the Falange, the lifeless *Movimiento* with which
Franco had hoped to supplant the political parties. With few exceptions, the rest of the UCD directorate (within which Suárez exercised important leadership) was made up of persons with similar
origins, by leaders of small provincial parties or by *técnicos* with
no previous political experience. In contrast, the AP was the vehicle
for the notables of the Franquist regime, beginning with Fraga Iribarne himself. As David Gilmore points out, with one exception
"not one of Fraga's new allies had been an advocate of political
reform. Indeed, (until the formation of AP), they had been among
the most vigorous opponents of democracy. . . ."[17] Clearly, like their
Brazilian counterparts, these individuals would have preferred a
slow, gradual, and secure liberalization of the regime, not the political democracy in which they found themselves obliged (with obvious misgivings) to compete, due to what they perceived as Suárez's
"treasonous" opening of the game to the PSOE and the PCE. The
continuity with Franquism represented by the AP was made clear
during the campaign for the first general elections in June 1977:
"There were a lot of *franquistas* masquerading as democrats. Almost half of AP's successful candidates had been ministers in Franco's governments. . . . Fraga had constructed a party that was un-
ashamedly *franquista* and appealed — at a time of international
recession — to the nostalgia of the economic success of the sixties."[18]
In those elections, won by the UCD with the PSOE a close second,

the AP obtained a respectable percentage (8.2%) of the vote—but this was insufficient to prevent the UCD, the PSOE, and the PCE from forming the axis of the new political game. The democratizing accord (prior to the famous Moncloa Pacts, which were based on the preceding understandings) was reached between the UCD and the PSOE, and to a lesser degree with the PCE (due in part to its declining electoral strength and to its competition with the PSOE for a similar electoral constituency).

The tendency which was clearly disloyal to democracy, the *Fuerza Nueva,* was marginalized; and the AP—the party of Franquist notables as well as of the bureaucratic and social interests which they embodied—remained outside of the democratizing accord and, during that period, a minor force in the electoral arena. Another important consequence of this strategy of transition was the high degree of turnover in the upper echelons of the Spanish political class. To quote once again from Gilmore's useful study, as a result of the 1977 elections, "All of the older politicians who, one year earlier, might have been expected to play an important role in the transition had been left either without seats or in charge of minor parties without much influence."[19] In this way, although facing serious obstacles (acute regional problems, the violence of ETA and of a few extreme rightist groups, the scare caused by Colonel Tejero's *putsch,* and serious economic problems—although these pale in comparison with ours), Spanish democracy marched onward to its consolidation, which occurred when in 1982 the PSOE defeated the UCD and Felipe González formed his government in accord with the Constitution.

The contrasts with Brazil are readily apparent. It is sufficient to note the following: (1) In Brazil the transition was far longer and was tightly controlled by the regime; furthermore, its military element, along with the numerous political and institutional inflexibilities which this tends to introduce, was much stronger than in Spain. (2) Until practically the last minute, the intentions of the regime and of the armed forces were ambiguous regarding the instauration of a political democracy or only some liberalization. (3) The huge campaigns for direct elections pushed in the direction of a truly democratic solution, but were not enough to prevent the transition from proceeding within the preexisting institutional framework; that is, in an Electoral College which, thanks to its rigged composition, seemed to guarantee the victory of the regime's presidential candidate no matter who he was. (4) The political disintegration of the regime, expressed by and at the same time accelerated by the victory of Paulo Maluf (a political outsider who worried many of the regime's notables) as the candidate of *continuismo,* gave rise to negotiations with the leader of the most conciliatory (and conservative) segments of the opposition, Tancredo Neves. (5) Although there is no concrete proof of this, it is almost certain that Tancredo made a crucial accord with the armed forces, guaranteeing to them that "the past would be overlooked" as well as a large role in the next government. (6) Another pact was reached with certain notables of the regime, who by then were dissenting from the direction the regime was taking (especially in regard to the candidacy of Maluf); that pact, which gave birth to the "Democratic Alliance," was announced to the public through the *Compromisso com a Nação* (Commitment to the Nation) document of August 1984, signed by the Brazilian Democratic Movement Party (PMDB) and by the aforementioned notables, who soon formed the Party of the Liberal Front (PFL). (7) In contrast to the accords of the Spanish transition, the Brazilian accords were *not* an agreement to compete electorally for the highest government positions in the country, but rather to resolve this question through the alliance created in the Electoral College. (8) It may be that Tancredo's accord with the armed forces, as well as the pact with "trustworthy" (in the eyes of the military) individuals—the notables of the regime—eliminated the risk of a coup. (9) These notables controlled Electoral College votes without which the PMDB's presidential candidate could not have been elected. (10) Both of these circumstances gave the PFL leaders a degree of bargaining power which was far greater than the proportion of votes they would have received in a direct election; hence a large number of these notables were vaulted by the Democratic Alliance into highly important government positions, including the vice-presidency and several federal ministries.[20] (11) This process was accompanied by a typical bandwagon effect. The evidence that a majority was being formed around the candidacy of Tancredo Neves led even more regime politicians to abandon Maluf and support the former, so much so that by the time of the Electoral College balloting, Tancredo emerged victorious by a hefty margin.

The great unanswered question is to what degree the pressures by the armed forces and the notables of the regime were a bluff which could have been exposed by continuing the mobilization of the *Diretas*

Já (Direct Elections Now) campaign. But the fact is that the opposition leadership, beginning with a cautious and conservative politician like Tancredo, preferred not to run the (no doubt important)
risks of a strategy which could have led to a much clearer alignment
of the democratic forces, and which would have left the regime's
notables in a position not unlike that of Fraga Iribarne and the
Popular Alliance. It is also true that in Brazil there was no King
Juan Carlos nor an Adolfo Suárez who — although they emerged from
within the authoritarian regime — opted early, unequivocally and
efficaciously for democratization. Also, in Brazil, unlike in Spain,
there were no opposition parties with long-standing social roots and
the resulting capacity for representing and controlling their social
bases. The Brazilian transition was channelled through an accord
of "all for all" to *not* resolve the transition by competing electorally
with one another. The important continuities which owe their origin
to this are the confining conditions[21] within which the second transition, currently underway, develops. None of this is necessarily better or worse than in other transitions; but most of them, including
the Spanish case, display elements of discontinuity which are much
more pronounced than in the Brazilian transition.

3. The Paradoxes of Success

I believe that the severe difficulties of consolidating democracy
in Brazil are due primarily — and quite paradoxically — to the relative economic success and low degree of repressiveness of the preceding bureaucratic-authoritarian regime, as well to some unique
characteristics of that regime and of the transition which ended it.
Moreover, the factors which underlie this apparent paradox simultaneously illustrate and reinforce certain characteristics which, while
certainly visible in other countries, are present to an extreme degree
in Brazil: enormous social inequalities combined with a dynamic
economy and with archaic and repressive patterns of authority, including those which link state and society and the several classes
and social sectors therein.

With few exceptions,[22] the studies of transitions from authoritarian regimes depart from the assumption that the second group
of cases discussed above would have more favorable conditions than
the first group for the consolidation of democracy. Basically, the
inheritance of a ruined economy, the numerous wounds and hate

sowed in the social fabric by the high degree of repression and violence, and the presence of armed forces who are politically defeated
in a transition through collapse and thus are likely hostile to the
new democracy, all appear to make the consolidation (or the simple
survival) of these democracies less likely than in the cases of economic success, relatively low repressiveness, and negotiated transition. In the latter, the expansion of productive forces occurring under the authoritarian regime should make it easier to govern the
economy and at least to assuage the most burning social issues. Furthermore, a repression which was less severe and more circumscribed,
the numerous contacts and mutual understandings between the incumbents of the regime and the opposition typical of a negotiated
transition, and armed forces less alienated from the new government (although as I have noted, at the cost of having them deeply
ensconced within that government), also appear more favorable to
democratic consolidation.

With regard to Brazil, it has been seen as an additional advantage that the bureaucratic-authoritarian regime did not eliminate the
legislature (although it subordinated it, and often intervened arbi-
trarily therein) at the national level as well as at the state and municipal levels, and that it maintained the existence of political parties (although these were parties that the regime had created). This
contrasts with the elimination of Congress and the banning of political parties which, with the exception of Paraguay, characterizes
the other South American authoritarian regimes. It also contrasts
with the authoritarian regimes of interwar Europe and the recent
cases of Portugal, Greece and Turkey. This peculiarity of Brazil would
seem to improve even more the chances for democratic consolidation, in that the survival and subsequent revitalization of these institutions would constitute an institutional framework within which
to process (more effectively and with less uncertainty than in the
cases where that framework was suppressed) the multiple conflicts
and uncertainties of both transitions.

It is time to rethink these assumptions and opinions. Obviously,
this is not as simple as turning one hundred and eighty degrees
and discovering that the second group of cases—to which Brazil
belongs—is really the one that presents the most serious difficulties
for the consolidation of democracy; the problems of cases emerging from economic destruction and very severe repression are sufficiently arduous to support that conclusion. The objective here is
to understand some complex comparative questions.

To begin with, we should note that the high-risk scenarios for the cases in the first group hinge on the assumption that the end of the process of democratization is likely to arrive swiftly and spectacularly, through a coup. But there exists a second possibility, whose end result may not be very different from the first: the slow death brought about by the progressive reduction of civilian authority, until it is no more than a façade for a highly repressive regime centered on the armed forces (a recent example is the presidency of Bordaberry in Uruguay.) These processes are driven by the aggravation of social and economic crises, by the consequent perception of powerlessness of the civilian government, and by the bourgeoisie's (often joined in this by sectors of the middle class) assessment that its basic class interests are being threatened. In situations such as Brazil's today, where the armed forces are firmly entrenched (and where, for the same reasons, the conservative interests which were linked to the authoritarian regime also have a strong presence in the government), if these processes are unleashed, a more likely scenario than a coup is a less spectacular process of successive authoritarian advances to the point of what I earlier termed a *democradura*.

The most important question at hand, however, is: In what sense do the seeming advantages of the preceding authoritarian regime and of a first transition like the one in Brazil actually complicate the consolidation of democracy? The difficulties appear on several levels. One of them is the existence, in such cases, of a memory of the authoritarian regime which is less negative than in the cases of high repression and democratic destruction. This may diminish the extent and the intensity of the antiauthoritarian position which, as we have seen, is one basic resource supporting the strategies of democratic actors. The policy constraints and failures which are usual in situations as complicated as these transitions, along with severe economic and social crises, normally cause a strong drop in the enthusiasm and support which accompanies the first moments of these democracies. But this phenomenon, which in Spain was labeled *desencanto* (disenchantment), may have various degrees. In cases of authoritarian regimes which were economically destructive and highly repressive, probably more policy failures, a deeper economic crisis, and more time are necessary for the adoption of an attitude of generalized indifference in relation to the survival of the civilian government and to the process of democratization. In contrast, in the cases which were economically successful and less repressive, the camp of authoritarian actors may be nourished more rapidly and more easily by many of those who originally supported the inauguration of the democratic government.

Another difficulty—in reality, part of the preceding—is that the initial neutrality on the part of the bourgeoisie and a good part of the middle class can, in cases like the Brazilian one, be converted into support for (or at least passive consent to) an authoritarian regression. Although the bourgeoisie and the middle classes had many conflicts with the preceding regime, a large part of them benefitted enormously from that regime, and many segments of those classes owe their very existence to it. In contrast, due to the economic destructiveness and the profoundly irrational decision making of the other kind of authoritarian regime, in these cases there would probably have to be greater degrees of crisis and social threat before those actors would opt for an authoritarian "solution." Although there is some historical and comparative evidence which is consistent with these speculations,[23] they continue to be just that: themes which merit further comparative investigation.

Another difficulty stems from the political stratum itself. This has been another blind spot in the literature. We have occupied ourselves with the varying degrees of continuity in the role and influence of the armed forces in relation to the new democracies. This, indeed, is a very important theme, but we have given little attention to another theme which is perhaps no less important: that of the continuities in the political personnel of the authoritarian regime. Surely the reason for this oversight is that in the majority of transitions this problem was resolved almost by itself. With authoritarian regimes which were economically destructive and highly repressive, and/or those regimes which dragged their countries into disastrous wars (like the European Fascist regimes), this problem practically does not emerge. Regardless of the continuities in the armed forces and in certain bureaucratic segments of the state, these political personnel are simply out of the game in the democratic period. The reasons for this are various, and can be combined in different ways: legal proscription of these politicians and their parties (as in most of Europe following the war); the steep loss of prestige by the authoritarian regime, which ensures that these politicians cannot win votes in the democratic period (as in the cases of transition by collapse); and, in almost all cases, the suppression of parties and parliament by the authoritarian regime (or the introduction of nonelectoral forms of corporativist representation in Spain and Portugal), which means that these notables lack experience in electoral politics and territorially-based constituencies. This includes the (Fascist) cases, where the authoritarian regimes were terminated by defeat in a foreign war, and the occupying forces were determined to install political democracy; the Southern European and Latin American cases of transition through collapse accelerated by failure in a foreign military action (Greece and Argentina after 1976, and, in a more complicated way, Portugal); the cases of collapse through endogenous reasons (Argentina 1969–1973 and Bolivia on several occasions); and one case (Uruguay) in which the authoritarian regime initially retained important bargaining power, despite having been economically destructive and highly repressive.

In this regard, once again the most similar case to Brazil is that of Spain. But in Spain, as I have noted, the parties embodying the highest degree of continuity with the Franquist regime were left outside the democratizing accords and the new government. If Brazil, to recall Stepan's observations, is the case of greatest continuity from the authoritarian regime to the civilian regime in terms of the armed forces, then comparatively speaking this continuity is even greater in relation to the civilian politicians of the authoritarian regime.[24] This is important in understanding the second Brazilian transition and its current difficulties. The theme is complex and should be elaborated.

Most people tend to project the future as a lineal projection of the past. Thus, if the preceding authoritarian regime was relatively not repressive and economically successful, it is likely that, if an authoritarian regression is foreseen, many will predict that the new regime will repeat those characteristics. This common–sense projection of the past into the future probably also operates among politicians. If a highly repressive regime threw them out of the game (and this high repressiveness also implies death, imprisonment, and exile to many of them), they will tend to fear that a possible authoritarian regression will have similar characteristics. Because of this, these politicians feel that they stand on the brink of an abyss — and they can only preserve their role with the continuation of the democratic process.

On the other hand, if the regime was relatively nonrepressive, and although having exercised repression against certain politicians was benevolent to the majority of them, it is likely that predictions about a possible authoritarian regression will be based on what happened in the past. If on top of this the national Congress continued to function (although subordinated to the executive branch), and especially if the state and local chambers (along with numerous clientelistic avenues to the state apparatus in those jurisdictions) were maintained, then during the authoritarian regime a large part of the political stratum continued to practice the same kind of politics that it practiced before. This brings us to another dimension in which Brazil displays a degree of continuity which is very high in relation to successful democratizations completed since the Second World War: the dimension that I will call "the predominant style of doing politics."[25]

If this is the situation of most of the political stratum (and if we also recall that other converging factors will probably weaken the antiauthoritarian positions of some voters), then a problem is apparent: it is possible that the advantages of a regime which is authoritarian yet economically successful and less repressive will be paid for with problems in defining who are the properly democratic actors. In this case many politicians do not feel they are on the brink of the abyss: they may imagine that a turn to authoritarianism, like the previous one, will not suppress their role nor fundamentally alter the way in which they do politics. At a given time, for varying combinations of personal conviction and opportunism, all may speak favorably of democracy—but how to distinguish the democratic actors from those who have only a mild and conditional preference for the preservation and consolidation of democracy? Who are, in this case, the legitimate parties to a democratizing accord or pact, and who are "the others" of that pact—the nondemocratic adversaries without whom the pact itself is meaningless?

The high degree of continuity of the Brazilian bureaucratic-authoritarian regime may now present a serious obstacle to democratic consolidation. A political style which is predominantly clientelistic and prebendalist (a term which I shall elaborate below) may be normal in an oligarchical republic based on a predominantly agrarian society, where capitalist social relations are not widespread, and where there is little organization and mobilization of the popular sector. The politics practiced in such contexts consists of "conversations among gentlemen,"[26] which scarcely conceive of party discipline. Relations with the subordinated classes are clientelistic. With regard to the state apparatus, these relations are based on the distribution or appropriation of sinecures; relations among politicians consist basically of the exchange of support and "favors" for the (mostly regionalist) interests which they embody.[27] This oligarchical style was the predominant style of politics practiced in Brazil prior to the coup of 1964. It is still the case today. The maintenance of parliamentary activities during the authoritarian regime, as well as the relative benevolence of this regime with regard to the segments of the political stratum which had less national and more parochial perspectives and linkages, seems to have contributed greatly to the maintaining of the predominance of this style of doing politics.

Perhaps this argument can be better understood by noting the contrasts with highly repressive authoritarian regimes. With the proscription of political parties and the closing of the legislature at all levels (which are typically among the first decisions taken by these regimes), the political stratum finds itself, to put it simply, unemployed. When representative institutions are suppressed and the political parties proscribed, politicians are prevented from continuing to play the politics they practiced before the advent of the authoritarian regime. Judging from what I could observe during the recent authoritarian experiences in Argentina and Uruguay, some politicians attempt to maintain their former lifestyle through elaborate denials of their unemployment. Others use the free time imposed upon them to acquire new contacts, to reflect upon the past and their role in it, to ask new questions about the future, and to read avidly. Still others are imprisoned or exiled; in the latter case, they have the opportunity to meet politicians who practice other styles, as well as to observe the actual functioning of democratic regimes. We know that not all learn from this, but some do. In this way an opportunity is opened up which is less available in the cases of high continuity: that of the appearance of important innovations in the leadership, discourses, and style of the political class. If there is able leadership, and if an important segment of the political stratum becomes receptive to new practices and discourses, then the probability of consolidating democracy is enhanced. This set of circumstances obtained in the postwar democratizations in Europe, and again recently in Spain, Portugal, and Greece. The same phenomenon was also apparent in the two older contemporary Latin American regimes which can be classified as indisputably democratic: Venezuela and Costa Rica.

4. Democracy and Republic

It is worthwhile to recapitulate those aspects in which Brazil displays a comparatively high degree of continuity vis-à-vis the preceding authoritarian regime.[28] The first relates to the influence and institutional presence of the armed forces. The second has to do with the notables of the authoritarian regime. The third relates to the prevailing political style. Let us now examine some aspects of these continuities.

Although its origins are not the same as those of liberal democracy, there is one dimension without which contemporary democracies, with their web of individual, associative, and political rights and guarantees, could not exist. This is the tradition of republic (etymologically, *res publica,* the public realm). The republic is based upon a careful distinction between what is public and what is private or personal. From the republic comes the idea that the ruler is the servant of the citizens, in whose name he or she administers the public interest. This, in turn, is the basis of the state of law, which affirms the distinction between the public sphere and the private sphere, subordinates government decisions to its rules, and sanctions any violations thereof. The rulers and officials are not, in the republican conception, "above" the law; to the contrary, they have a special obligation to subject themselves to it. This is related to the idea of accountability (a term which, perhaps not accidentally, has no direct equivalent in Spanish or Portuguese), which consists of two main aspects: one, already mentioned, is the obligation of rulers and officials to subordinate their actions to the law; the other is the responsibility of the ruler to render an account of his/her actions, with enough transparency so that citizens may evaluate his/her rule and, ultimately, ratify it or reject it in fair and competitive elections.[29] Citizenship presupposes a government which is not only democratic but also republican. The republican element is indispensable for the effective guarantee of the rights of political democracy.

Non-republican rule is ultimately nondemocratic. The roots of this can be discovered in the inability — typical of archaic social and political relations of domination — to distinguish between the public sphere and the private sphere, or to establish representative institutions for the collective subjects of those relations. Max Weber is relevant here:

A patrimonial position above all lacks the bureaucratic distinction between the 'private' and the official spheres. . . . Therefore, on all properly political occasions, the purely personal desires (of the ruler) determine the limits of his personnel's tasks. . . . The loyalty of a patrimonial servant is not an objective loyalty to perform objective tasks limited in their scope and content by specified norms, but rather the personal loyalty of a servant who is personally tied to his master. . . . The separation between public and private matters, between public and private goods, disappears as a system of prebends and appropriations grows.[30]

Although contemporary Brazil is obviously very different from the ancient societies which Weber had in mind,[31] the continuities discussed above indicate a strong element of patrimonialism (and consequently of clientelism, personalism, and prebendalism as well) not only in the style of doing politics but also in the style of governing. With regard to the legislature, that style was made visible by the inability of the Congress to constitute itself as one of the key centers of discussion and decision making on important national issues. As for the executive branch, the predominance of the patrimonialist style generates a curious blend of omnipotence and impotence. Omnipotence can be seen in the frequent handing down of decisions which are not subject to the institutional and legal procedures of a constitutional system. Impotence is evident in that these measures frequently fail as effective regulations of national life. A consequence is that this impotence eats away not only at the prestige of certain politicians and rulers, but also at the prestige and authority of political institutions. Nor is it helpful that the vacuum generated by this is often attempted to be filled by wild swings between blatantly technocratic and populist styles of government. All of this aggravates one of Brazil's most serious problems: the existence of few and fragile institutional mediations between politics and society, a situation which both expresses and reinforces the enormous gaps which separate the "elites" from the overwhelming majority of the population.[32]

Despite important individual exceptions, the cumulative effect of the continuities cited above is to maintain the predominance of the patrimonialist politicians, who are often in an alliance (born of the conservatism inherent in their respective styles and world views) with blatantly authoritarian politicians. Perhaps the greatest cause for concern is that during the first years of the Brazilian second transition, this predominance was unshaken. On the other hand, the surprising silences and ambiguities on the part of the democratic and republican politicians[33] may be due to the fact that they face the "dilemma of candidacy" which I outlined in the first section. Because these politicians do not make up a critical mass (and/or because no leader has emerged from their ranks to create this critical mass or overcome its absence), and because they wish to continue to play the game of politics, then in order to obtain positions of sufficient influence to modify the game, they must be designated or elected by their parties to run for important positions — and to this end, it is wise not to malign or threaten the continuity of the predominant style of politics.

These references to certain styles of practicing politics and governing draw our attention toward factors which are more historical and structural than those introduced up till now. A detailed examination of these factors is beyond the reach of this chapter. In the meanwhile, it is helpful to address some of these factors and their interrelationships; otherwise the analysis made here would lie floating in a seemingly (and deceivingly) indeterminate social world. This is the objective of the following pages.

5. Gaps and Contrasts

Compared to the rest of Latin America, Brazilian capitalism is quite dynamic. Although it may be less evident (at least to a good many of the Brazilians with whom I have discussed the topic), from my perspective what comes to mind is the more bourgeois nature of this capitalism: it is more productive, less speculative, and more oriented toward the accumulation of capital in its own market than most countries of Spanish America.[34] The latter, with their long history of crises and recessions (and nowadays many of them with ruined productive structures), currently pose a crucial enigma. How to resolve within capitalist parameters the problems of capital accumulation and growth, when a sluggish and impoverished state apparatus (to say nothing of the limitations imposed by the external debt, which in almost all the other countries is relatively more burdensome than in the Brazilian case) can hardly serve as the dynamic axis, and when the bourgeoisie is hardly involved in productive activities, and is so subordinated to (or merged with) financial and speculative capital? Under these circumstances, what policies and projects for capital accumulation can be reformulated in the short and medium run, and be supported by sufficiently broad sectors of the population? What opportunities for survival would remain for these new democracies, and what painful adjustments of individual and collective expectations would be necessary?

Regarding this issue, there are important differences between Brazil and most of the rest of Latin America. Although Brazil is far from overcoming the problems of capital accumulation and growth (as is evident in the current crisis), it has the important advantage of a rather dynamic and diversified productive structure. Another difference is subjective, but no less important: at least until recently, the Brazilian population (beginning with the bourgeoisie itself) thought it likely that the economy's dynamic behavior would continue into the future. Both aspects contrast with the enormous difficulties of growth faced by most of the other Latin American economies. From these difficulties arise behaviors and expectations, and from these in turn arise different opportunities; in a considerable part of Spanish America the behavior of the bourgeoisie is predominantly speculative, if not predatory. In Brazil, on the other hand, although the recent crisis has generated worrisome speculative tendencies, the bourgeoisie (while much more dependent than in the central capitalist countries on support and sinecures from the state) has tended to focus on productive activities.[35]

But we must also look at the other side of the coin. On the other side lie the extreme inequalities in Brazil, which are accompanied by the archaic and repressive social relations which sustain the system of social domination. From the very beginning, the great capacity for accumulation and for productive modernization of Brazilian capitalism has been based on particularly repressive relations of exploitation and domination of the workers. Slavery, a high degree of social and regional heterogeneity, an abundant labor supply, the statist corporatism implanted by the *Estado Novo* and left intact by all subsequent regimes, and the resulting fragmentation and lack of organization of the popular sector are all part of a long and complex list of factors. As a result of these factors, and at the same time reinforcing them, Brazil is — like no other country in Latin America — a country of phenomenal contrasts, especially in the wake of the rapid capital accumulation (variously described as savage, unequal, internationalizing, etc., but accumulation nonetheless) of the past few decades.

Of course, all of Latin America—in some countries more sharply, in others less so—is marked by the contrasts between the very rich and the very poor. But in Brazil, that contrast is part of a panorama which is more complicated and more spectacular. I refer here to the contrast between, on the one hand, overwhelming poverty (the sorry common patrimony of Latin America), and on the other hand, factories, commerce, and services which are the hallmark of a dynamic economic modernity which none of the other countries approach. There is something here which is more incongruent (and scandalous) than the contrasts visible in other countries long punished by a history of crises and recessions, in which there is misery as horrendous as that of Brazil but where the productive structures are less rich and modern.

The above cannot be understood without taking into account the archaic nature of labor relations, as well as, more generally, the deep authoritarianism which marks the relationships of many segments of the bourgeoisie and of the state apparatus (and of other actors as well) with all those who are seen as "socially inferior." In "E eu com isso?"[36] I argued that this authoritarianism sails the open seas of a sociocultural tradition in which the subjective distance between classes (and the substratum of its objective inequalities) is extraordinarily great. With the partial exception of the years immediately preceding the coup of 1964, the above has generated dominant classes which are socially and politically more secure than their counterparts in Spanish America. The Spanish American dominant classes, although in different ways and through diverse processes, have repeatedly felt threatened in their viability as agents of capital accumulation, and on occasion, even in their very existence as a class. In Brazil, in contrast, the result of the complex historical processes which I have referred to[37] has been a bourgeoisie which is politically and socially more secure, and which is also more capable and more predisposed to accumulate as a national social class than the other Latin American bourgeoisies.

However, these advantages on the productive and economic side have an important counterpoint. Democratic advances in the capitalist societies never resulted from unilateral concessions on the part of the bourgeoisie. Instead, they resulted from the organization, struggles, and pressures of the popular sector (especially, though not exclusively, the urban workers), which in the end convinced the bourgeoisie and/or governments of the convenience of ratifying those democratizing advances. Generally, these "pressures from below" were not sufficient but were, in almost all cases, necessary for the achievement of those advances.[38] In most of Western Europe, the theme of these struggles was not only universal suffrage and the legalization of the parties which claimed to represent the previously excluded. Other themes were the rights of organization and representation of the labor force and of its access to the public services of the state, not as objects of an enlightened benevolence, but as rights to which all citizens — because they were citizens — could legitimately stake a claim.

The names given to certain social subjects ("bourgeoisie," for example) point to certain similarities at a high level of abstraction. However, in order to understand historical processes, we must remember that these subjects are constituted through their interrelationships with other social subjects. In this sense, the long-standing absence of the popular sector as a social and political actor defined the historical mode of existence of the Brazilian bourgeoisie: it is a class which economically has achieved great successes, but which was constituted as a profoundly authoritarian social and political subject — as were all bourgeoisies before the growing organization and political presence of the popular sector led them down the road of negotiations and democratizing concessions. Until the present years of uncertain democratization there are very few other historical cases of a bourgeoisie which has economically been so successful and yet socially and politically so little challenged.

Political conduct which is pluralist (although not necessarily democratic) derives from the recognition of the legitimacy of difference, from the acceptance of the "other" as a subject having valid interests and rights beyond the will of the ego. The bourgeoisie's "other," precisely in order to define itself as such, tends to constitute itself as a collective subject.[39] Throughout the history of capitalism, workers' struggles to be recognized by the state and by the bourgeoisie as a collective actor drove the extension of democratic rights in the sphere of political citzenship, as well as (though more incompletely so) in the sphere of labor relations and relations with the state. The victories and defeats along that road determined that the bourgeoisie and workers would mutually constitute themselves as social and political subjects. On the workers' side, the pro-

cess was led principally by the unions and parties, whose right to
exist and to speak for their constituents was not granted out of
kindness: often it was won only after long conflicts and drawn-out
negotiations. If on the one hand the price of this was the increasing
inability of the parties to limit themselves to classist appeals, as well
as their disavowal of the goal of doing away with the capitalist parameters of society,[40] on the other hand the bourgeoisie had to accept the collective representativeness of the workers' organizations
— and had to negotiate with them the extension of a whole range
of rights.

In contrast to this, in an archaic relationship there is no recognition of collective actors. Instead, there is the rule of those individuals who, by virtue of their traditionally dominant position,
in exchange for "favors" expect continued loyalty from their subordinates. This, of course, is the anatomy of clientelism. To the extent
that this type of relationship prevails, both a requisite and a result
of it is the fragmentation of the popular sector, as well as a fierce
resistance to any effort on the part of the subordinated classes to
organize as collective subjects and to be represented as such. In Brazil, this phenomenon colors numerous social relationships which embody a colossal degree of negation of the "other" who is seen as
socially inferior. One thinks of the abuse of violence by police in
poor neighborhoods;[41] of the treatment meted out to a *popular* who
appears without a sponsor at a public agency; of the criminal disregard of pedestrians by those driving automobiles; and of the conditions of semi-slavery under which most domestic servants toil.
Behind all of this is the bossy grimace of one who puts the *inferior*
in "his place."[42] A society burdened with the heritage of slavery, and
in which for such a long period the bourgeoisie was not subjected
to the civilizing experience of having to face and negotiate with its
class counterpart, finds enormous difficulties in all spheres — including the political one — in recognizing and institutionalizing the identity of others.

Regarding these issues, I can only sketch out some consequences
of direct relevance here. The first is the enormous benefit which the
bourgeoisie derives from the reproduction of archaic and repressive
labor relations, whether or not these occur in the most productive
and modern regions and sectors.[43] Second, the condition which makes
that benefit possible is the reproduction of the organizational weakness and the diffuse social and political identities of the workers.

Third, this type of relationship is intrinsically anti-institutional. It is based on the nonrecognition of collective identities and interests,[44] which can only be made viable through mechanisms of representation. In other words, this is a social world crisscrossed by the power derived from personal relations among very unequal actors; it is a world almost without institutions or representation. For this reason, the modern and the archaic are not in a dichotomous relationship (as in the "two Brazils" which were once the subject of so much discussion); they are mutually interpenetrating, even within the most dynamic regions and economic activities.

Until now I have discussed some aspects of social and economic relations. It is now appropriate to examine some political dimensions. It is significant that the high economic growth experienced by Brazil in the past few decades, as well as the enormous social changes which have moved this country toward a highly complex and differentiated society,[45] have occurred in a severe (and ever more noticeable) vacuum of social and political institutions capable of processing these changes. The bureaucratic-authoritarian regime could not but be hostile to the establishment of representative institutional mediations for the popular sector; however, as I have just argued, the causes of this vacuum seem to me older and deeper, and little progress has been achieved after the termination of that regime. In the following section we shall examine some of these questions.

6. Political Mediations and Institutions

The paths of Brazilian history have obstructed the emergence of reasonably autonomous organizations and identities within the popular sector. The enormous socioeconomic distance between the dominant classes and the dominated classes is easily transposed to the existing political distance between the *elites* and the *povo*. Both gaps reinforce one another, and together they hamper that which is most necessary in order to achieve and consolidate the political institutions specific to democracy. By this I mean the emergence of regularized and predictable practices which are generally and habitually respected, which are embodied in public organizations capable of processing the demands of politically active sectors of society with little or no disruption or violence, and which are in line with rules of the competitive game which prohibit suppressing that com-

petitiveness. Another way to put this is to note that in any attempt
to build democracy, there are two fundamental issues to be considered. The first is the issue of representation. Who will be represented,
by whom, and how; and who will be (or continue to be) excluded?
The second issue is that of the characteristics of the institutions
through which that representation would be channelled. This is not
just a question of the overall effectiveness of these institutions, but
also of the degree to which they allow themselves to express the voice[46]
of those who choose to claim their right to citizenship. For reasons
outlined above, I believe that this issue is paramount in Brazil today. The type of outright exclusion of the popular sector common
in Latin America's past seems to be no longer possible — at least not
without an authoritarian regression — in the great neo-oligarchical
holdover which is the political system of this socially complex and
economically dynamic nation.

    Currently, the demands to modernize social and political rela-
tionships are numerous and growing. But resistance is enormous.
As these demands are made in such a socially authoritarian and politically elitist context, some are absorbed through clientelistic mechanisms, while others are splintered and disaggregated without anchor-
ing in collective subjects strong enough to hold their own in national
politics. For this reason, many of these demands are seen as un-
acceptable or even "subversive."[47] The dynamic which unfolds in
this way may be a trap not only for authentically democratic actors,
but also for those who, while seeing themselves as heirs to the liberal tradition,[48] in practice deny the popular sector its place in the
sun of Brazilian politics. Even democratic politicians with a modern and republican understanding of politics, perhaps faced with
the "dilemma of candidacy," seem to be stuck in excessive dedica-
tion to an "elite politics" which is as penetrable to the interests which
always had access to it as it is distant from the concerns and aspirations of the majority of the population. As for Leonel Brizola, his
discourse purports to eliminate these practices; but *brizolismo* and
other forms of populism are no less elitist in their assumptions and
their conception of leadership, nor are they any less hostile to the
emergence of autonomous organizations and identities within the
popular sector. The *Partido dos Trabalhadores* (PT), on the other
hand, aligns itself against all of this, but does this so forcefully that
it tends to distrust even its own leaders who achieve some electoral
success. The PT also harbors rigidly dogmatic lines, and thus has

serious difficulties in practicing the inevitable share of negotiation and compromise implicit in democratic politics.

In preceding pages I noted that in Brazil the predominant political style is typical of the "parties-in-parliament" of an oligarchical republic, where clientelism, the preeminence of personal relationships, strong regionalism, highly diffuse ideologies, and little or no party discipline predominate. The basic assumption is that the only existing politics is that which is practiced by the gentlemen in parliament and the executive; most of the population is excluded from political life. Mirroring the social world, this style of practicing politics creates a world with no mediations; in it, the logic of representation[49] functions at best very intermittently. Without representation, the dimension which presupposes it — accountability — also disappears, and no advances are made in creating and strengthening the institutions which could challenge the predominance of patrimonialism and clientelism. Left untouched are the sinecures, which range from cases of simple nepotism to colossal waste of public resources; the blend of arbitrary omnipotence and recurrent impotence which evince many government decisions; and the frequent violation of the patterns of governmental behavior which could lead to the establishment of the effective rule of law, to cite only a few. As a result of the above, the distinction between the public sphere and the private sphere is too often lost.

This has multiple consequences, some of which I have mentioned and to which I will now add a few more. One is that after several years of democratic life, it is difficult not to give poor marks to the role played by the National Congress and the state legislatures. Although there are some important exceptions, Congress appears to be the place where the aforementioned characteristics are most concentrated and visible. Politicians of the most traditional (and worst) stripe, clearly incapable of transcending narrow local or sectoral interests; massive clientelism and *empreguismo;** a high level of absenteeism in legislative sessions; poor standards of debate; an incapacity for legislative initiative, which means that many important decisions are made by decree or through bills sent "ready-

---

Empreguismo refers to the practice of securing or creating jobs in the state bureaucracy for political allies and constituencies, with no or little consideration of the individual's merits or for whether the position is even necessary. (Translator's note)

made" from the executive while the progressive and liberalizing initiatives of some legislators get bogged down in the conservatism typical of this style of politics. Furthermore, Congress is the best place to observe one of the most serious problems of institutional weakness: the extraordinary plasticity of almost all of its parties.[50] Important (and unimportant) politicians change parties, whether at the national or local level, at the slightest change in the official winds or as a result of personal conflicts in which ideological positions or interests seem to have no importance whatsoever. This plasticity, along with other factors mentioned earlier, reinforces (even if only by creating enormous cognitive obstacles to making sense of what goes on in politics) the extremely low levels of political information and party identification of the population[51] as well as the great volatility of voting patterns evident in recent elections. It also reinforces the skepticism of the many who think that "the politicians" only look after personal interests. If in the near future there are no clear and consistent signals that these tendencies will diminish, then I fear that the *desencanto* I referred to earlier will exhaust dangerously the two great resources of democratic actors: the size and intensity of the antiauthoritarian majority, and the influence of democratic discourses.

7. A Stalled Transition?

The reader will have noticed that to this point I have not defined "democratic consolidation" or, equivalently, the attainment of a democratic regime. I understand a consolidated democracy or a democratic regime as one: (1) where there is political democracy (or polyarchy, to recall the definition of Robert Dahl) in which democratic actors no longer have as one of their central concerns the avoidance of a (sudden or slow) authoritarian regression, and consequently do not subordinate their decisions (and omissions) to such a concern; (2) where social and political actors who control significant power resources (even if they may not all be strictly democratic) habitually subject their interrelations to the institutions specific to political democracy by means of practices compatible with the reproduction of these institutions — institutions which, whether they like it or not, these actors calculate will last indefinitely; (3) where the habitual nature of these practices and the strengthening of these institutions (which succeed in establishing themselves as important, though not exclusive, loci of national power) sustain the "procedural consensus" which Schmitter and I discussed in our cited work, and promote the uncertain nature of outcomes[52] of fair and competitive elections; (4) where this set of political relationships is increasingly consistent with the extension of similarly democratic (or at least non-despotic and non-archaic) relations into other spheres of social life; (5) where rulers and officialdom subject themselves to the distinction between the public and the private and there exist reasonably effective mechanisms to sanction anti-republican actions on their part.

This set of statements is enough to show how far away our countries are from consolidated democracy and how difficult is the road ahead. But, as I have argued, the problems are not the same in each country, and their relative seriousness in different dimensions shows important variations from case to case. In Brazil the principal challenge is that of overcoming its high levels of patrimonialism and elitism. If my arguments are correct, the road to a solution winds through more than just the realm of politics. One reason for this is that overcoming the dominant political style implies criticizing its narrow understanding of the proper place for politics in a democracy. Another reason is that to the extent that political elitism and patrimonialism are closely related to the aspects of social domination which I have noted in this chapter, one conclusion seems to follow: in Brazil as in few other countries, the task of building democracy includes that of attaining some reasonable levels (which cannot be specified with any precision, but which certainly would be significantly more advanced than the current ones) of modernization and democratization of many social — not just political — relations, and redefining a role for the state consistent with these advances.

From the comparative perspective in which I have analyzed the Brazilian case, one of the few problems *not* faced by other transitions beset by enormous difficulties (some of which are more serious than those in Brazil) is that of determining who can and should be the participants in the democratizing accord. In other cases, whether due to ideological conviction or to the instinct for self-preservation of a political stratum which has just suffered a much more traumatic experience than in Brazil, the lines are reasonably clearly drawn between the democratic actors and their adversaries. This is a "coalition of some against others"; on one side, the democratic actors, and on the other side, the authoritarian (or ambivalent regarding democratization, as in the case of the *Alianza Popular* in Spain) segments of the political stratum. The alliance of the former achieves its great political victory when painting the latter as "the others" in the process of democratization.

In contrast to the above, the second Brazilian transition has appeared to be the work of a coalition of anyone and everyone. Perhaps it is more accurate to say "almost everyone," given that the alliance which realized the first transition often defined "the others" as the PT and Brizola's PDT. Regardless of one's opinions about these two parties, from a democratic perspective this is a perfect illustration of the degree to which the axes of the political game were thrown out of whack. In the resulting confusion, democratic actors are blended in complex fashion with patrimonialist or decidedly authoritarian actors. This does not necessarily have to do with party affiliations or personal backgrounds. As was demonstrated in Spain by Adolfo Suárez and his *franquista* past or in Greece by Constantin Caramanlis (a leader emerging from a sternly conservative right wing party), some of these individuals may become democratic actors of great importance. On the other hand, as is borne out by several examples in Brazil, even some of the most distinguished opponents of the authoritarian regime have arrived to the second transition without having changed in the least their patrimonialist styles of politics and rulership. This suggests that if it is true, as I have argued, that the main issue is one of politically defeating not only authoritarianism but also archaic patrimonialism (and indeed, the ideological dogmatism of other actors as well), then this problem goes to the heart of practically all Brazilian parties, as well as of its national, state and municipal governments. Perhaps this is the clearest indicator of the difficulty of the challenge ahead.

NOTES

This chapter is an abridged and revised version of a text published in Fábio Wanderley Reis and Guillermo O'Donnell, eds., *A democracia no Brasil: dilemas e perspectivas* (São Paulo: Edições Vértice, 1988).

1. On this theme, see Luciano Martins, "Armação da crise e desarme da crítica," *Folha de São Paulo,* March 23, 1987, p. 3A.

2. Robert Dahl, *Polyarchy: Participation and Opposition* (New Haven: Yale University Press, 1971). The "minimal" conditions for polyarchy (or political democracy) are, according to Dahl, that "all full citizens must have unimpaired opportunities: (1) to formulate their preferences; (2) to signify their preferences to their fellow citizens and the government by individual and collective action; (3) to have their preferences weighed equally in the conduct of the government, that is, weighted with no discrimination because of the content or source of the preference." *Polyarchy,* p. 2.

3. On this theme, see Guillermo O'Donnell and Philippe Schmitter, *Transitions from Authoritarian Rule: Tentative Conclusions about Uncertain Democracies* (Baltimore: Johns Hopkins University Press, 1986).

4. A partial exception is Uruguay, the country of recent transition which has advanced the furthest in the consolidation of its democracy. But it is significant that this, along with Chile, is the only case of *re*democratization. The Uruguay of today can look back on a long democratic tradition, unlike the other cases mentioned in the text.

5. On this theme, see Francisco Weffort, *Por que Democracia* (São Paulo: Brasiliense, 1984) and Guillermo O'Donnell, "The United States, Latin America, and Democracy: Variations on a Very Old Theme," in Kevin Middlebrook and Carlos Rico, eds., *The United States and Latin America in the 1980s: Contending Perspectives on a Decade of Crisis* (Pittsburgh: University of Pittsburgh Press, 1986).

6. Since (at least) Max Weber, we have known that the reasons for acting coherently and regularly according to certain rules may be quite different from the belief in their validity or innate justifiability. In a pioneering essay Dankwart Rustow insisted on the strictly pragmatic reasons for which an actor may accept, as a "second best" solution, the advent of democracy. See his "Transitions to Democracy: Toward a Dynamic Model," *Comparative Politics* 2, no. 3 (April 1970): 337–363. In our work cited above in note 3, we review and expand this argument.

7. My most recent discussion of this theme is found in Guillermo O'Donnell, *Bureaucratic Authoritarianism: Argentina, 1966–1973, in Comparative Perspective* (Berkeley: University of California Press, 1988).

8. Regarding the 1976–1982 period in Argentina, these issues are elaborated in Guillermo O'Donnell, *Contrapuntos: autoritarismo e democratização* (São Paulo: Edições Vértice, 1986) and in "Democracia en la Argentina: micro y macro," Working Paper no. 2, Helen Kellogg Institute for International Studies (December 1983).

9. O'Donnell and Schmitter, *Tentative Conclusions about Uncertain Democracies.*

10. On this opposition, Sebastião Velasco e Cruz, "Empresários, economistas, e perspectivas da democratização no Brasil," in Guillermo

O'Donnell and Fábio Wanderley Reis, eds., *A democracia no Brasil: dilemas e perspectivas* (São Paulo: Edições Vértice, 1988), and the same author's "Os empresários e o regime: a campanha contra a estatização" (Ph.D. diss., University of São Paulo, 1984). Also see Fernando Henrique Cardoso, "Entrepreneurs and the Transition Process: The Brazilian Case," in O'Donnell, Schmitter, and Whitehead, eds., *Transitions from Authoritarian Rule,* Part III, pp. 137–153.

11. Donald Share and Scott Mainwaring, "Transitions through Transaction: Democratization in Brazil and Spain," in Wayne Selcher, ed., *Political Liberalization in Brazil: Dynamics, Dilemmas, and Future Prospects* (Boulder: Westview Press, 1986), pp. 175–215; and O'Donnell and Schmitter, *Tentative Conclusions about Uncertain Democracies.*

12. Alfred Stepan, *Rethinking Military Politics: Brazil and the Southern Cone* (Princeton: Princeton University Press, 1988).

13. On this case, see Anita Isaacs, "Dancing with the People: The Politics of Military Rule in Ecuador, 1972–1979" (Ph.D. diss., Oxford University, 1986). I am indebted to this work for drawing to my attention the paradoxes and tradeoffs inherent in cases such as Ecuador and Brazil.

14. Some exceptions to this, which are attentive to the differences between the cases, are José Alvaro Moisés, "A transição política ou o longo percurso dentro do túnel," in *Ciências Sociais Hoje-1985,* pp. 8–35, and Share and Mainwaring, "Transitions through Transaction."

15. On these and other relevant characteristics of Franquism, see Juan Linz, "Oppositions to and under an Authoritarian Regime: The Case of Spain," in Robert Dahl, ed., *Regimes and Oppositions* (New Haven: Yale University Press, 1973), pp. 171–259, and José A. Biescas and Manuel T. de Lara, *España bajo la dictadura franquista, 1939–1975* (Barcelona: Editorial Labor, 1980). From the abundant literature on the Spanish transition, see especially José Antonio Maravall and Julián Santamaría, "Political Change in Spain and the Prospects for Democracy," in Guillermo O'Donnell, Philippe C. Schmitter and Laurence Whitehead, eds., *Transitions from Authoritarian Rule: Prospects for Democracy* (Baltimore: Johns Hopkins University Press, 1986), Part I, pp. 71–108; Raymond Carr and Juan Pablo Fusi, *Spain: Dictatorship to Democracy* (London: Allen and Unwin, 1981); Jorge de Esteban and Luis López Guerra, *De la dictadura a la democracia: diario político de un período constituyente* (Madrid: Universidad Complutense, Facultad de Derecho, 1979); Donald Share, *The Making of Spanish Democracy* (New York: Praeger, 1986); and David Gilmore, *The Transformation of Spain: From Franco to the Constitutional Monarchy* (London: Quartet Books, 1985).

16. A fine treatment of this theme can be found in Laurence Whitehead, "International Aspects of Democratization," in O'Donnell, Schmit-

ter, and Whitehead, eds., *Transitions from Authoritarian Rule,* Part III, pp. 3–46.

17. Gilmore, *The Transformation of Spain,* p. 169 ff.

18. Gilmore, p. 182.

19. Gilmore, p. 185.

20. Eunice Durham puts it well in "Salvadores e bodes expiatórios," *Folha de São Paulo,* July 21, 1987, p. 3A: "Tancredo Neves had ensured his own election in the manner of traditional politics: by distributing the ministries and handing out jobs in clever maneuvers designed to satisfy the interests of some and neutralize the opposition of others."

21. See the classic article by Otto Kirchheimer, "Confining Conditions and Revolutionary Breakthroughs," in F. S. Burin and K. L. Schell, eds., *Politics, Law, and Some Exchanges: Selected Essays of Otto Kirchheimer* (New York: Columbia University Press, 1969), pp. 385–407.

22. An exception, which analyzes the problems and costs resulting from a type of transition like the Brazilian one, is Luciano Martins, "The Liberalization of Authoritarian Rule in Brazil," in O'Donnell, Schmitter, and Whitehead, eds., *Transitions from Authoritarian Rule,* Part II, pp. 72–94.

23. See Anita Isaacs, "Dancing with the People."

24. On this and related themes, see Frances Hagopian and Scott Mainwaring, "Democracy in Brazil: Problems and Prospects," *World Policy Journal* IV, no. 3 (Summer 1987), pp. 485–514; Leôncio Martins Rodrigues, *Quem é quem na Constituinte: uma análise sócio-política dos partidos e deputados* (São Paulo: OESP–Maltese, 1987); and Timothy Power, "A direita política: Discurso e comportamento, 1987–1990," paper presented at the "Seminário Nacional sobre Comportamento Político," Universidade Federal de Santa Catarina, Florianópolis, March 12–14, 1990.

25. On this concept see Marcelo Cavarozzi, "Political Cycles in Argentina since 1955," in O'Donnell, Schmitter, and Whitehead, eds., *Transitions from Authoritarian Rule,* Part II, pp. 19–48, and "Los partidos argentinos: subculturas fuertes, sistema débil" (unpublished manuscript, CEDES, Buenos Aires, 1985).

26. It is not accidental that this expression is of Colombian origin. See Alexander Wilde, "Conversations Among Gentlemen: Oligarchical Democracy in Colombia," in Juan Linz and Alfred Stepan, eds., *The Breakdown of Democratic Regimes: Latin America* (Baltimore: Johns Hopkins University Press, 1978).

27. On these and related matters, see Frances Hagopian's contribution to this volume.

28. My argument here obtains notwithstanding the high rate of turnover in Brazilian congressional elections, especially those of 1986, for two reasons: first, because I am referring mainly to the notables, the highest

ranking civilian politicians of the authoritarian regime, and second, because a large number of the new legislators, especially those from the less developed regions, can boast of long political careers at the state and municipal levels — exactly those levels at which the political practices antedating the bureaucratic-authoritarian regime were least affected by it. On these topics, see the works cited in footnote 24.

29. See esp., Gianfranco Poggi, *The Development of the Modern State: A Sociological Introduction* (Stanford: Stanford University Press, 1978). Of course the accountability and transparency of existing democratic governments only partially approximate the ideal. This is, once again, a question of degree. Any advances on this score must be measured against the current situation in most of Latin America (which squares with a long tradition) in which there is an extremely high degree of opacity and impunity as relates to rulers and their actions. See the interesting discussion by Norberto Bobbio: "What is democracy if not a set of rules (the so-called rules of the game) for resolving conflict in non-violent ways? What is a good democratic government if not above all one that respects the law? . . . . Democracy is, par excellence, government by laws. When a democratic government loses sight of its foundational principle, it quickly becomes the opposite, a form of autocratic government." *Il futuro della democrazia* (Torino: Einaudi, 1984), p. 170. See also Bobbio's *Estado, governo, sociedade* (São Paulo: Paz e Terra, 1987) for an analysis of this and other related themes.

30. Max Weber, *Economía y sociedad* (Mexico City: Fondo de Cultura Económica), Vol. II, pp. 774, 776, 784.

31. In preparing this chapter I reread Simon Schwartzman's *Bases do autoritarismo brasileiro* (Rio de Janeiro: Editora Campus, 1982). Building on Weber, the author submits an interesting general interpretation of Brazil in terms of the category of neo-patrimonialism. Although I do not agree with every element of his interpretation, many of the themes that Schwartzman develops are essential for introducing and understanding issues which more current analyses do not fully capture.

32. From a similar angle, and anticipating some themes which I discuss in the following pages, Alain Touraine writes in "As possibilidades da democracia na América Latina" (*Revista Brasileira de Ciências Sociais* 1, no. 1, 1986) that: "Patrimonialism is an obstacle to democracy in that it does not recognize the autonomy of political processes in effecting change" (p. 6). The jurists of the eighteenth and nineteenth centuries, [and] Machiavelli and Jean Bodin during the Renaissance, shaped the concepts of rule of law and of institutions. Against the power of the feudal lords was set the rule of law; rather than a juridical formalism, it was a condition for public order and civic peace. Conflicts could no longer be resolved through private means, by force, corruption, or negotiation (among

private actors): they had to be submitted to institutions and political norms established by the central power. . . . A politics of *representation* . . . presupposes the unlinking of those elements forged in the complex unity of the national popular system, the formation of a more statelike State, of more 'social' actors, and of a more representative political system" (p. 13, italics in original). The weekly *Senhor,* commenting on the refusal of a number of ministers implicated in scandals to resign their posts, asks how this could occur: "The answer is simple: because they conceive of power as their personal property. In this they hardly differ from most of the mighty of our medieval plague. They administer public affairs like the *fazendeiro* runs his estate" (May 19, 1987, p. 22).

33. As noted by Francisco Weffort in "Transição à deriva," *Folha de São Paulo,* April 17, 1987, p. 3A.

34. I am making a comparison between Brazil and the rest of Latin America. Clearly, if the point of reference were core capitalism, then the evaluation would be different.

35. Although the available estimates are very rough, a good indicator of the differences I am emphasizing is the lower rate of capital flight from Brazil than is the case elsewhere in Latin America.

36. In Guillermo O'Donnell, *Contrapontos: Autoritarismo e democratização* (São Paulo: Edições Vértice, 1986).

37. For a comparative analysis of these processes, see O'Donnell, *Bureaucratic Authoritarianism.*

38. See especially Goran Therborn, "The Rule of Capital and the Rise of Democracy," *New Left Review* 103 (1977): 251–271, and John Stephens, "Democratic Transition and Breakdown in Europe, 1870–1939: A Test of the Moore Thesis," University of Notre Dame, Kellogg Institute, Working Paper no. 101 (November 1987).

39. Claus Offe and Helmut Wiesenthal, "Two Logics of Collective Action," in Claus Offe, *Disorganized Capitalism* (Cambridge: MIT Press, 1985), pp. 170–220.

40. Adam Przeworski, *Capitalism and Social Democracy* (Cambridge: Cambridge University Press, 1985).

41. See Paulo Sérgio Pinheiro, *Escritos indignados* (São Paulo: Brasiliense, 1984), and Roberto DaMatta, ed., *A violência brasileira* (São Paulo: Brasiliense, 1982).

42. See the analysis of Roberto DaMatta in "Do You Know Who You're Talking to?" in his *Carnivals, Rogues, and Heroes* (Notre Dame, Ind.: University of Notre Dame Press, 1991; Portuguese edition: 1980). I have undertaken some similar speculations in "E eu com isso?"

43. As emphasized by Francisco de Oliveira in his "A opera bufa, again" (unpublished manuscript, CEBRAP, São Paulo, 1986).

44. On this theme see Fábio W. Reis, "Partidos, ideología e con-

solidação democrática," in Fábio W. Reis and Guillermo O'Donnell, eds., *A democracia no Brasil.*

45. On these social changes see Wanderley Guilherme dos Santos, "A pós-revolução brasileira," in Hélio Jaguaribe, et al., *Brasil, sociedade democrática* (Rio de Janeiro: José Olympio Editora, 1985), and Vilmar Faria, "Desenvolvimento, urbanização e mudanças na estrutura do emprego: a experiência brasileira dos últimos trinta anos," in Bernardo Sorj and Maria Hermínia Tavares de Almeida, eds., *Sociedade e política no Brasil pós-64* (São Paulo: Brasiliense, 1983). On the subject of economic transformation, see, among other sources, José Serra, "Ciclos e mudanças estruturais na economia brasileira de após-guerra," *Revista de Economia Política* 2/3 no. 7 (1988), pp. 111–135, and Luiz Carlos Bresser Pereira, *Development and Crisis in Brazil, 1930–1983* (Boulder: Westview Press, 1984). On the social costs of these processes see especially Sérgio Abranches, *Os despossuídos: crescimento e pobreza no país do milagre* (Rio de Janeiro: Jorge Zahar Editor, 1985).

46. In the sense employed by Albert Hirschman in *Exit, Voice, and Loyalty: Responses to Decline in Firms, Organizations, and States* (Cambridge: Harvard University Press, 1970).

47. Luciano Martins has correctly insisted on this point in "Armação da crise e desarme da crítica."

48. On the profound ambiguities of the liberal tradition in Brazil (and actually, in all of Latin America), see especially Hélgio Trindade, "Bases da democracia brasileira: Lógica liberal e práxis autoritária," in Alain Rouquié, Bolivar Lamounier, and Jorge Schvarzer, eds., *Como renascem as democracias* (São Paulo: Brasiliense, 1985), pp. 46–72.

49. On the negation of the logic of representation and its consequences, apart from the works already cited, I also refer the reader to José Murilo de Carvalho and Aspásia Camargo, "A Constituinte e a nova ordem liberal no Brasil: A Constituição e a organização do Estado," *Cadernos de Conjuntura* no. 8 (November 1986), IUPERJ, Rio de Janeiro.

50. In their *Partidos políticos e consolidação democrática* (São Paulo: Brasiliense, 1986), Bolivar Lamounier and Rachel Meneguello emphasize this aspect as crucial to the construction of democracy in Brazil. See also Scott Mainwaring, "Brazilian Party Underdevelopment in Comparative Perspective," *Political Science Quarterly,* forthcoming.

51. On these issues see Reis, "Partidos, ideologia e consolidação democrática," as well as the works cited therein.

52. Adam Przeworski "Some Problems in the Study of the Transition to Democracy," in O'Donnell, Schmitter, and Whitehead, eds., *Transitions from Authoritarian Rule,* Part III, pp. 47–63.

Democratic Consolidation in Post-Transitional Settings: Notion, Process, and Facilitating Conditions

J. Samuel Valenzuela

As the new democracies that replaced authoritarian rule in country after country during the seventies and eighties grow out of infancy, social science observers have shifted their focus from the analysis of transitions from authoritarian rule to problems of democratic consolidation. Much of the previous scholarly discussion was anchored on examinations of the political processes occurring in the closing phases of authoritarian rule and on the manner in which the change to the democratically elected governments occurs. Current queries center on how really democratic the post-transition political institutions are and on their long-term prospects, i.e., whether they are prone to succumb to a new round of authoritarian rule or whether they will prove to be stable or "consolidated." The modalities assumed by the transition, the way in which political actors are organized, and the various political institutions that emerge or re-emerge during the course of the transition are understood to make a significant difference for the long-term viability of newly democratized regimes.[1]

However, this is simply a shift in perspective and not of the basic question being addressed; for both the old and the new discussions are ultimately about the broader problem of the transition from authoritarian to democratic regimes. This process is obviously not over when democratically elected authorities assume power, because this does not *ipso facto* necessarily inaugurate — journalistic labels applied to nations where such political leaders have constituted governments notwithstanding — a democratic regime. The overall change from an authoritarian to a democratic regime contains, as Guillermo

57

O'Donnell notes, not one but two transitions: the first leads to the "installation of a democratic government," and the second to the "consolidation of democracy," or to "the effective functioning of a democratic regime."[2] There is a complex relationship of continuity and discontinuity between the first and the second transitions. The building of a consolidated democracy involves in part an affirmation and strengthening of certain institutions, such as the electoral system, revitalized or newly created parties, judicial independence and respect for human rights, which have been created or recreated during the course of the first transition. In this sense the process of change from one transition to the other is a lineal one. But in many ways there is no such linearity; building a consolidated democracy very often requires abandoning or altering arrangements, agreements, and institutions that may have facilitated the first transition (by providing guarantees to authoritarian rulers and the forces backing them) but that are inimical to the second. Such is the case with legislatures that include nondemocratically generated representation, with military autonomy from the executive, or with supreme councils empowered to review the actions of democratic governments. Hence, some of the obstacles to surmount on the new course towards consolidation are set by the characteristics of the earlier transition phase.

While the scholarly production referring to problems of democratic consolidation continues to increase significantly, the term itself has often been used in a haphazard, uncritical way, as if its meaning were clear and its closure self-evident. Hence, this chapter suggests a more clearly delimited conception of democratic consolidation, to which task it turns first. It then indicates the manner in which the process of consolidation unfolds after the first transition from authoritarian rule to a democratic government, and concludes with a lengthy discussion of a series of conditions that can facilitate or, inversely, detract from its realization. The chapter illustrates its points by drawing its examples mainly from recent cases of transition.

The Notion of Democratic Consolidation

The juxtaposition of "consolidated" with "democracy" induces uses of the combined term that are misleading for the study of transitions. Since something that is "consolidated" has the quality of being seemingly immune to disintegration, there is a tendency to associate "consolidated democracies" with their stability and, by extension, to convert the passage of time with no regime reversals and the absence of potentially destabilizing factors into the basic criteria for democratic consolidation.

While the durability of a democratic regime is an attribute of consolidation, this characteristic does not provide in itself an adequate basis to ground the notion of consolidation. The retention of democratic government after a process of transition does not necessarily ensure the consolidation of a democratic regime. In some instances it is possible that democratically elected governments may succeed one another for a considerable time without reversals simply as a result of the caution of its leadership in not challenging actors whose power escapes democratic accountability.[3] In this case the resulting stability cannot be equated with progress towards creating a fully democratic regime; what enhances stability may detract from the democratic quality of a regime. The process of democratic consolidation would require redefinitions, sometimes at considerable risk, of the regime's institutions and/or of the relations among political actors. Moreover, consolidated democracies are not necessarily free of destabilizing conditions such as presence of sharp ideological differences among major parties and political leaders, armed separatist or terrorist movements, social unrest that percolates through urban riots, or racial and ethnic tensions leading to violent confrontations; requiring all of these to wither away before presuming democratic consolidation in new or reestablished democracies would be an excessively stringent test. Consolidated democracies are also not immune to processes of breakdown. In fact, they may be vulnerable to the very perception of their solidity by democratic elites that take the existence of democratic institutions for granted, even in situations of crisis, and therefore do not reach the necessary accommodations to prevent their demise.[4] In sum, the absence of political crisis, of destabilizing elements, and the durability of a newly democratic setting are in one sense an insufficient test and in another an excessively demanding one for the notion of democratic consolidation. Additional criteria are needed to assess whether destabilizing factors prevent democratic consolidation.

Similarly, all discussions of democratic consolidation carry an explicit or implicit definition of what democracy is, and analysts are not predisposed to assigning the "consolidated democracy" label to a political system that does not meet all of their criteria for what a democracy should be. This produces a tendency to push the conception of democracy in discussions of democratic consolidation towards an ideal, well-structured and comprehensive institutional system that can hardly be attained.[5] Even long established democracies rarely have all the attributes that can ideally be associated with such regimes. Whether it is low levels of informed citizen participation (and participation *tout court* in the case of the United States), political leaders who are divisive and personalistic, parties that are rigidly ideological or not programmatic enough, the influence of funding hidden from public scrutiny in electoral coffers, the growing sophistication of misleading political marketing as the key strategy for capturing the vote, legislatures that are insufficiently influential or that concentrate on petty issues while state bureaucracies go unchecked, the cozy accommodations between private interests and their supposed state regulators, excessive social inequality and inadequate welfare institutions, the insufficient organization of the working class and other popular sectors, inadequate mechanisms for negotiations between capital and labor, and so on, it is always possible to deplore one deficiency or another. If such and other assorted ills can be found in democracies whose "consolidation" is not at issue, situations that have recently made the transit out of authoritarian rule should hardly be held to strict and comprehensive standards either. Otherwise no democratic regime is truly "consolidated" for the lack of an ingredient deemed essential, and it is impossible to assign a reasonable closure to the second transition process.

The notion of democratic consolidation should therefore be linked, as has been suggested by O'Donnell, to a minimalist, not a maximalist, conception of democracy.[6] There is considerable consensus over what constitutes, as O'Donnell and Schmitter put it, the "procedural minimum" of democracies — namely, "secret balloting, universal adult suffrage, regular elections, partisan competition, associational recognition and access, and executive accountability."[7] Similarly, Robert Dahl lists a series of eight "institutional requirements" for the existence of a democracy, which are: "(1) freedom to form and join organizations; (2) freedom of expression; (3) right to vote; (4) eligibility for public office; (5) right of political leaders to compete for support [and votes]; (6) alternative sources of information; (7) free and fair elections; and (8) institutions for making government policies depend on votes and other expressions of preference."[8] These conceptions refer to the formal and procedural aspects of democracy at a nation-state level, rather than to any substantive or social considerations or to the presence of democratic forms in entities at the subnational level.[9] They are also based on an admittedly narrow notion of citizenship and formal legal and political equality, rather than on a more comprehensive conception of equality, the development of which is in any case not precluded.[10] The associational freedoms that accompany formal democracies can lead as well to the development of corporate interest groups and mechanisms of corporatist interest intermediation.[11] But without the above-noted formal democratic procedures at the nation-state level a democracy cannot be said to exist no matter how egalitarian the society, how progressive the social policies, how advanced the democratic procedures at the subnational level, or how developed the expression of interest representation through corporatist intermediation. The notion of democratic consolidation should refer to this procedural minimum.

Nonetheless, attaching a minimal definition of democracy to the conception of democratic consolidation is only a first step towards elucidating what a consolidated democracy is. This latter notion requires further elaboration.

The minimal procedures of a democracy presuppose, despite their minimality, the development of a complex institutionalization, the skeletal outlines of which are generally formally established, i.e., written, in constitutional and other laws. It includes the separation of powers, without which there is no executive accountability nor protection for the rights of citizens, and also more specific matters such as the rules for carrying out elections or streamlining the legislative process. This democratic institutional edifice permits, even fosters and shapes, the development of organizations, such as parties, interest groups, and lobbies, and a mass media through which a variety of opinions can be expressed, all of which articulate and channel societal political demands. Their access to and intervention in the policy-making process is very often not formally established, but becomes nonetheless part of the recurrent and accepted set of institutionalized procedures of the democratic system, even though its appropriateness may occasionally be challenged and publicly debated. Both the impact of the democratic institutional edifice on the formation of such organizations as well as the latter's influence over the elaboration of policy, including policy decisions regarding the formal outlines of the institutional edifice itself, attest to the characteristic blurring of the lines of separation between the state and civil society in a democracy. The daily workings of these institutions, both formal and informal, and of their associated societal organizations, configure what can be called a *virtuous* institutionalization insofar as they permit the reproduction of the minimal procedures of a democracy. Yet to hinge the consolidation label only onto a system that has developed an adequate set of such virtuous institutional mechanisms, even if such adequacy could be determined correctly with due consideration for the great variety of forms they assume in different types of democracies, would stretch the notion of consolidation needlessly and make it highly ambiguous. It would once again link, perhaps unwittingly, the conception of democratic consolidation to an institutional ideal of what it should be.

Therefore, instead of focusing on the institutionalization, both formal and informal, that is compatible with — and even buttresses — the workings of a democracy, it is better to look at that which tends to undermine its operation — or at what can be called *perverse* institutionalization. Following this analysis, a consolidated democracy would be one that does not have perverse elements undermining its basic characteristics, although the list of such perversities cannot be extended endlessly; otherwise, the conception of consolidation runs the risk of being anchored, again perhaps unwittingly, on the presence or absence of what in the last instance can be viewed as potentially destabilizing elements. To retain a delimited conception of democratic consolidation, the perverse patterns must be closely anchored on the minimal conception of democracy.

Since in essence a democratic regime is one in which governments are formed by individuals who win national elections, the possible perversions are those that can undermine the end of the democratic process, i.e. the authority of democratically elected governments, and can detract from its means, i.e., from the fairness as well as the centrality of the electoral mechanism as a route to form governments. While the list of perverse elements could probably be extended, the following four are the principal ones that can be identified.

To begin with those that undermine government authority, a first perverse element is the existence of nondemocratically generated *tutelary powers*. They attempt to exercise broad oversight of the government and its policy decisions while claiming to represent vaguely formulated fundamental and enduring interests of the nation-state. A regime cannot be considered a consolidated democracy if those who win government-forming elections are placed in state power and policy-making positions that are subordinate in this manner to those of nonelected elites. Obviously, no democratic government is above the law, and all are therefore subjected to oversight by the courts and other specialized bodies (such as accounting offices); but these forms of overview are specific to executive accountability, serve to review government and or legislative compliance with the constitution and other basic laws, to protect human rights, and to guard against corruption and abuses of power. A tutelary power is quite different: its limits are ill-defined. Part of the process of building European democracies in the nineteenth and early twentieth centuries was to eliminate the tutelary power held by monarchs, making cabinets and prime ministers accountable only to elected parliaments, and armies subordinate to decisions taken by the government rather than the crown. In recent transition settings, the military have often sought to place themselves in such a tutelary role. This can occur through the creation of formal institutions, as illustrated notably by the military-dominated Council of the Revolution enshrined in the Portuguese constitution of 1974, or through ambiguous constitutional references to the role of the Armed Forces as "guarantors" of the constitution and the laws. It can also exist informally as a result, for instance, of military self-definitions as the "permanent institution" of the state (i.e., as opposed to "transient" ones such as governments) that can therefore best interpret and uphold the "general interests of the nation." Hence, where the individuals who win government-forming elections are subjected to such tutelary power, they do not unambiguously "acquire the power to decide," to use Schumpeter's expression.[12] And the various political forces whose policy preferences most closely coincide with those holding such tutelary power will be tempted to use the latters' possible intervention in the political process as a threat to obtain what they want, thereby undercutting democratic arenas of negotiation and compromise.

A clear attempt by the outgoing authoritarian regime to establish the institutional and organizational basis for exercising military tutelarity over the democratic process occurred in the Chilean transition. The 1980 Constitution, enacted by General Pinochet, stipulates that the Armed Forces "guarantee the institutional order of the Republic."[13] There is no explanation as to how this function is to be exercised, nor what the term "guarantee" means in this context. And yet top military officers do not lack the means to make their views known in the institutions of the new constitutional order. They occupy four (including, in addition to the heads of the Army, Navy, and Air Force, the head of the National Police) of eight seats in a "National Security Council" whose objectives are, in addition to overseeing national security, to examine any matter that may "gravely undermine the bases of the institutional system," for which they may demand information from any government or state official.[14] Two of the nonmilitary members of the National Security Council were also named, indirectly, by General Pinochet before leaving the Presidency. Moreover, the transitory articles of the 1980 Constitution allow General Pinochet to remain the Commander in Chief of the Army for eight years after the initiation of the first democratically elected presidential term of office. President Patricio Aylwin, whose term began in March of 1990, asked Pinochet to resign despite the legal stipulations, since "it would be more convenient for the country," but the latter refused.[15] Hence, although the constitution also stipulates that the head of the Army is subordinate to the President, the most fundamental element of that subordination, the power of appointment and removal, is absent for a lengthy period after the transition to an elected government. Pinochet's attempt to place himself in a tutelary position over the democratic process was reaffirmed by his creation of a so-called Political-Strategic Advisory Committee, whose officially announced role is to assist him in carrying out his duties as a member of the National Security Council. The Committee, which has roughly 50 staff members, is designed to keep tabs on every aspect of national policy.[16]

A second element that prevents full governmental empowerment is the existence of what can be called *reserved domains* of authority and policy making. In contrast to the ambiguous and generalized tutelary power, the reserved domains remove specific areas of governmental authority and substantive policy making from the purview of elected officials. Again, there are many instances in which policy areas are excluded from elected government officials' control or from the scope of electoral majorities in regimes that can be considered, nonetheless, democratic. Democracies that are strongly consociational or consensual, as Arend Lijphart has argued, deliberately restrain the influence of electoral majorities in areas of policy that are of specific interest to minority segments of the political community.[17] Even in democracies that are strongly majoritarian, key policy areas may be insulated from the influence of elected officials; a good case in point is the Federal Reserve Bank of the United States. Such insulation may be the product of informal agreements or formal pacts, and may be enshrined in constitutions, laws, or in the statutes of autonomous state agencies. In still other settings areas of policy may be left by elected officials for discussion and agreement among, and/or with, corporatist interests, as happens particularly in small European democracies with strong forms of sectoral corporatism.[18]

The problematic reserved domains of democratic transitional settings are different. They pertain to areas of policy that elected government officials would like to control in order to assert governmental authority or carry out their programs, but are prevented from controlling by veiled or explicit menaces of a return to authoritarian rule.[19] The reserved domains are products of impositions by political actors — such as the military, the monarch, the judicature, the high civil service, and/or nonstate actors such as capitalists — who are not themselves subjected to electoral accountability but have privileged access to crucial elements of state power to make credible their threat of destabilization. By contrast, policy insulation in democracies results from arrangements reached by negotiation and agreement among political actors who are empowered to enter these arrangements by virtue of their recognized leadership and/or representation of a segment of the political community. As is the case with tutelary powers, the reserved domains may be the product of tacit or explicit "understandings" the margins of which may be unclear, or they may be formally established. In either case they may have facilitated the first transition by providing assurances to powerful nonelectoral actors or electoral minority ones related to the authoritarian regime that their interests would not be affected by democratically elected authorities. This is one important instance in which the second transition to a consolidated democracy has to undo what was wrought to facilitate the first transition to a democratic government. What may have eased the first constrains the second transition.

The Chilean transition furnishes, once again, convenient examples of these reserved domains, in this case of a highly institutionalized nature. The most important is the armed forces and military policy. The legal apparatus legated by the authoritarian regime permits the armed forces to derive automatically a large portion of its own income—which in no case should fall below 1989 levels in real terms—from the sales of copper by the state-owned Corporación del Cobre. Democratic government officials cannot determine the use of the military budgets, acquisitions of armaments, have limited say over officer promotions and appointments, even for foreign service assignments, and are barred from changing military doctrine and the curricula in the respective academies. Control over military intelligence is also left entirely in officers' hands. The departing Pinochet regime also created—and named the first board members to lengthy terms—an autonomous Central Bank that has control over monetary, credit, and exchange policies, and an autonomous council to oversee radio and television programming and licensing of stations.[20] In addition, by offering financial incentives it induced older justices to retire and thereby appointed about half of the members of a Supreme Court with expanded powers; it named all but 16 of the nation's 325 mayors; and it legally prohibited the new democratic government from appointing all but the top officials at all levels of the state administration, effectively granting tenure to all civil servants—even those who previously held only temporary positions. The democratically elected Congress is also barred by a special law from exercising its constitutionally established prerogative of investigating and judging malfeasance by previous government officials, and an amnesty law protects the military from prosecution for human rights abuses.

Turning to the means of selecting those who will form governments (as well as occupy legislative seats), a third way in which the operation of minimal democratic procedures can be vitiated is through major discriminations in the electoral process.[21] Surely, most electoral systems in democracies are biased in the sense of underrepresenting minority parties and candidates. This is particularly the case with the simple plurality system in single member districts, which normally produces substantial legislative majorities for parties that obtain a minority of the national vote.[22] Some discrimination against such minority representation is, nonetheless, helpful to ensure proper democratic governance: this facilitates building legislative majorities (with or without coalitions), and minimizes the possible tyranny of the minority that can come from having fringe elements in the political community hold the balance of power between larger blocs.[23]

And yet, situations of transition may be, again, different from these. The electoral rules may be deliberately designed by actors who hold power at key moments of the first transition to underrepresent grossly significant sectors of opinion, while overrepresenting others (even though these rules may not always work as they are intended to by their framers). This may be done through the vote counting procedures or through an electoral apportionment that creates glaring inequities in the weight of individual votes. In addition, as often occurs in the first elections after authoritarian rule, party choices of candidates for office and voter preferences may be guided by calculations (correct or incorrect) regarding who can best ensure the continued stability of the new democratic system. While this may indeed bolster that stability, this form of choice by no means reflects democratic consolidation. In some cases, certain candidates may be expressly prohibited from running, or may feel physically threatened if they do. These settings are only questionably democratic.

The Chilean transition also illustrates the egregious discriminations that can occur in situations of transition with congressional representations and electoral laws. Pinochet's 1980 Constitution reserves nine senate seats to be filled by individuals appointed by the president or by other state organs, such as the Supreme Court, that have been closely connected with the authoritarian regime. All of these appointments were made before the transfer of power to the democratically elected government. Moreover, the electoral law was deliberately and successfully crafted to furnish the right with the largest possible contingent of members of Congress in both houses.[24] As a result, with its nine designated senators and its representation greatly favored by the electoral system, the right has, with a minority of the popular vote, a majority in the Senate and a sizeable segment of 48 seats in a 120 member House.[25] With its Senate majority, the right can, if it wants, block legislation and all efforts to reform the constitution dictated by the military regime, which it generally views as one of the latter's most important legacies.

Finally, a fourth problem pertains to the centrality of the electoral means to constitute governments. Free elections must indeed be *the only* means through which it is possible to do so. Democratic consolidation cannot occur if military coups or insurrections are also seen by significant political actors as possible means to substitute governments. This is the basic linchpin underlying all the other elements that detract from the consolidation process, for tutelary powers, reserved domains, and electoral discriminations would be impossible to maintain in the long run were it not for the threat of overthrowing democratically elected authorities. These are tactics applied by powerful — but nonelectoral or electorally minoritarian — political forces to safeguard their interests. The actors who are committed to the electoral procedures and who generally stand to gain from them are likely, given the threat of a complete reversal of the democratic process, to feel compelled to acquiesce to their opponents' institutional and substantive demands. The democratic method is thereby subverted to a large extent even when regularly scheduled elections are not interrupted, i.e., when there are no coups or successful insurrections. This then generates a vicious cycle of perverse institutionalization. Success yields repetitions of successful strategies, thereby strengthening the importance of the rules of the political game that violate the democratic method, which then further enhances their importance and use. While powerful nonelectoral or electorally minoritarian actors could develop an organizational capacity to protect and pursue their interests through venues that are potentially compatible with democracy (such as creating new parties or establishing privileged links with preexisting ones, forging coalitions, appealing to public opinion, lobbying with legislators, quietly or publicly petitioning the executive, and/or participating in corporatist forms of interest intermediation) they may still rely on their capacity to threaten an interruption of the democratic process in order to increase their ability to obtain preferred policy options through the normal democratic venues. They will therefore seek to retain that potentially subversive option alive.

Virtuous and perverse institutionalizations can coexist, but their conjunction is perverse. Disaffected capitalists who disinvest, workers who strike and demonstrate in the streets, farmers who clog capital cities with their tractors, truck drivers who block highways, and military officers who remonstrate all know, even if they also try to influence the outcome of elections, that there is in the last instance the possibility of stimulating a military coup.[26] Eventually, this situation can lead to widespread disaffection with what becomes an inadequate democracy by those segments of the population that would ordinarily prefer the continued existence of the democratic regime.

This may enhance the prospects of more radical or populist appeals, and further exacerbate, as a result, the tendency of the opposing political forces to seek protection from the application of the democratic method to form governments.

By contrast, a system in which elections are the only means to form governments obliges the significant political actors to design their political strategies in ways that are consistent with the democratic procedures. This permits a cycle of virtuous institutionalization: the more the various actors develop an effective organizational political capacity to advance their goals, protect their interests, and preserve their values in the democratic institutional environment, the more secure will be their commitment, in general, to that environment. For this effect to occur, the democratic system must of course permit all major politically active segments of the population a voice: democracy must be inclusive. In this environment, groups flexing their particular nonelectoral "power capabilities," to use Charles Anderson's term, will assess their actions in different terms from those available in the perverse cycle setting.[27] Thus, unions and working-class parties will try to calculate the effects of strikes on the possibility of gaining or losing middle-class votes; capitalists know that if they disinvest, the resulting sluggish economic performance can be blamed on incumbents in the next elections; and military leaders who remonstrate know that they simply jeopardize their careers, as they do not have a chance to set in motion a coup and therefore cannot count on pursuing their goals by threatening insubordination. The difference between the perverse and the virtuous cycles does not lie in the fact that various social groups will resort to *entirely* different strategies in seeking to press for their policy options or protect their interests. The difference lies in the presence or absence of additional means, aside from the electoral one, to form governments.

Democratic consolidation occurs with the clear predominance of the virtuous cycle depicted above. Or, to state it with the terms used here, a democracy is consolidated when elections following procedures devoid of egregious and deliberate distortions designed to underrepresent systematically a certain segment of opinion are perceived by all significant political forces to be unambiguously the only means to create governments well into the foreseeable future, and when the latter are not subjected to tutelary oversight or constrained by the presence of reserved domains of state policy formulation.[28]

Other nonminimalist features of such democratic systems can flow from the prevalence over time of these basic conditions; thus, parties, interest groups, issue-specific movements of opinion, a more or less informative mass media, a political culture of compromise and negotiation, concertation among opposing organized interests, respect for individual rights, and other organizational and institutional features that buttress democracy may develop—to a greater or lesser extent—in what can become quite different types of democracies. The term democratic regime should, strictly speaking, be reserved for such consolidated democracies. The expression "proto-democracies" or simply "nonconsolidated democracies" can be used to refer to political systems where the formalities of a democracy exist, namely, periodic elections with universal suffrage, freedoms of expression and organization, and so on, but the electoral process is not viewed unambiguously as the only means to create governments, and/or where tutelary powers, electoral discriminations, and/or important "reserved domains" of policy making exist.

The Process of Democratic Consolidation

Once the first transition has been accomplished, the process of reaching democratic consolidation consists of eliminating the institutions, procedures, and expectations that are incompatible with the minimal workings of a democratic regime, thereby permitting the beneficent ones that are created or recreated with the transition to a democratic government to develop further. It reaches closure, following the basic conception presented above, when the authority of fairly elected government and legislative officials is properly established (i.e., not limited as noted) and when major political actors as well as the public at large expect the democratic regime to last well into the foreseeable future. Given favorable conditions—to be noted below—and barring all reversals, this kind of closure can occur relatively rapidly in some cases, as happened in Spain, but in others it may take decades, as was the case with the French Third Republic.

The establishment or reestablishment of the procedures consonant with democratic governance multiplies the numbers of political and social actors who actively participate in politics. The new institutions generate a new political balance of forces, as some actors win and others lose relative shares of power, authority, and influence when compared to the balance that prevailed under the previous regime. The attempts to preserve tutelary oversight, reserved domains, egregious discriminations in the electoral system, and the notion that a nonelectoral route to create the national government is always possible, constitute formal or informal institutional mechanisms for some actors to retain power capabilities they would otherwise not have given the exclusive operation of forms of empowerment compatible with democracy. Thus, while democratic consolidation is basically about the elimination of formal and informal institutions that are inimical to democracy, it takes the form of a struggle between actors who benefit — or think they could benefit at a certain point — from those institutions' existence, and those who do not.

The process of consolidation, or its derailment, thereby unfolds through precedent-setting political confrontations that alter or revalidate the institutional and procedural environment in its perverse or beneficent aspects.[29] When perverse aspects are formally instituted in the constitution, in laws, or in statutes, some of these confrontations will necessarily be over their elimination. Democratic consolidation is impossible without undoing (by deliberate changes or by converting the offending items into dead letter) the formally established institutions that conflict with the minimal workings of a democracy. Other confrontations can be over incidents, notably coup attempts, in which the continuation of the transition itself is at stake and in which the most perverse of the polity's informal institutions — the notion that governments can be created through coups — is displayed. But most confrontations are over specific issues, be they whether to prosecute military officers for past human rights violations, increase wages, alter the tax burden, reduce defense spending, change the judicial system, reform labor legislation, reorganize the administration of schools, revamp municipal government, etc. These events contain a text (the overt issue being debated or the specific incident being resolved) and a subtext which is far more significant for the purposes of analyzing democratic consolidation. It has to do with whether or not the debate and resolution (if any) of the issue enhances, sustains, reduces, or eliminates the perverse formal or informal institutions that impair democratic consolidation. Has the issue led, say, to challenging the tutelary power of the military or trodden into one of its reserved domains in a manner that makes it less able — by revealing divisions among top officers, a lack of support from civilian leaders for military pretensions, or some such circumstance—to exercise effectively such power or reserve such domain in the future? Has the debate led certain political forces to seek military support for their aspirations in a way that shows their ability—or their inability—to use a threat of destabilization as a prop to obtain the policies they favor? Has the confrontation shown that elected officials in the government and in Congress have the authority to resolve key questions of policy, or has it been deflected to another formal or informal institutional arena? The discussion if not resolution of these issues may not only set important precedents that manifest the extent to which the beneficent institutions of a democracy are in operation but, more significantly, it may also advance the citizens' and political actors' change of expectations regarding their long-term durability. As a result, the process of consolidation may either be advanced, held on hold, or derailed in what can be seen in retrospect—but hardly ever in anticipation—as a concatenation of critical events that progressively mold the institutional and organizational environment as well as the actors' perceptions of it, increasing or deflating in the process the relative preeminence of the various political actors.[30]

The process of consolidation is not necessarily advanced by the prodemocratic forces' setting a deliberate agenda of "consolidation" and by their singleminded pursuit of its goals. (Such a prodemocratic agenda can be established for reaching the formal institutions of a democracy, but accomplishing the necessary changes to attain that goal is not equal to, nor does it necessarily guarantee, democratic consolidation.) In fact, announcing the existence of such an agenda will in most cases be self-defeating. Openly discussing whether or not a certain measure advances consolidation or whether consolidation has been reached may detract from its advancement by raising it as a questionable rather than a taken-for-granted and therefore moot issue. Once democratic institutions are in place, consolidation is reached, in the final analysis, only when most political actors perceive them to be in place unproblematically well into the future. Consolidation occurs as a post factum realization. The debate and, if possible, resolution of the issues leading to the various confrontations present opportunities to—so to speak—"use" the complex institutions of a democracy, and in the process—hopefully—to disarticulate those that are inimical to it. It is the double combination of such use and such purging that eventually should generate the desired sense that the democratic institutions are durable indeed.

In the course of the confrontations over issues, most political actors, whether they prefer democratization, its limitation, or renewed forms of authoritarianism, will pursue short-term gains over their opponents without much regard for the long-term consequences for consolidation of their actions. On occasion, those favoring democratic consolidation as a long-term goal may pursue short-run gains — perhaps as a result of their strife with other prodemocratic forces over policy issues — that in retrospect prove injurious to that goal; there may even be at times no immediate clarity regarding the long-term consequences of their actions. Similarly, actors preferring a re-edition of the authoritarian regime may well press successfully for short-term gains whose long-term consequences are, when examined in retrospect, beneficial to democratic consolidation. For example, in preserving the unity of the Armed Forces under his command — a key to retaining his own power — General Pinochet could be indirectly contributing to democratic consolidation in Chile. Such consolidation is unlikely if the Army is a fractious one. Hence, while it is reasonable to expect that the short-run failures of actors seeking to preserve perverse procedures and the short-run successes of those hoping to eliminate them will benefit democratic consolidation in the long term, it is difficult to determine unambiguously that all their actions will have these results. The historical agenda of the consolidation process is subject to many contingencies.

Conditions Affecting Democratic Consolidation

Despite the contingencies in the process of consolidation, a comparison of transition settings should permit the abstraction of a proximate roster of conditions that facilitate consolidation. What follows is an illustrative presentation of some of these facilitating features. Although these are elements that can help determine the outcome, none of them should be viewed as necessary to it. Otherwise, the analysis of consolidation could be construed to hinge once again on a stringent list of ideal conditions.

A. The Modalities of the First Transition, and the Attitudes of the Principal Authoritarian Regime Elites towards Democratization

The manner in which any new regime, whether authoritarian or democratic, is inaugurated has a significant effect over the re-

gime's subsequent evolution. In cases of democratization, it should
be possible to point to the inaugural conditions that are most conducive to initiating a rapid process of democratic consolidation.

The quite varied modalities assumed by the transitions out of
authoritarianism have led analysts to propose typologies to discrimi-
nate among them. After usefully reviewing the various types, Scott
Mainwaring suggests that a threefold typology is the best way to
distinguish such transitions. Some transitions occur through a "defeat" or "collapse" of the authoritarian regime; others give way to
democratization through "transaction"; while others, those that lie
somewhere between these polar types, undergo transition by "extrication." This typology essentially adds a third intermediary category to the overall distinction between *reforma* and *ruptura* that
emerged from the stark contrast presented by the initiations of the
Spanish and Portuguese transitions of the mid–1970s. It is necessary, as Mainwaring notes, to accommodate the many cases that do
not fit well in either.[31]

Further clarification of the differences among the three categories could enhance their usefulness by turning the intermediate
one into a distinct type rather than the middle segment of a con-
tinuum.

A basic distinguishing feature of transitions that occur by "extrication" or by "transaction" from those that begin through a "defeat" of the authoritarian regime is the relative ability, in the former
cases, of the outgoing rulers to hold on to power for a significant
length of time beyond the onset of the crisis that sets in motion the
process of transition. Rulers who have this capacity can threaten
to stretch it out further, and are therefore able to specify some conditions to their eventual transfer of power. While this distinction
separates "defeat" or "collapse" from "extrication" and "transaction"
fairly well, the difference between the latter two categories, which
rests implicitly on the degree to which outgoing authoritarian rulers
can stipulate their departing conditions, is not drawn sharply enough.
Presumably in cases of "transaction" this capacity is maximal, but
it is hard to make categoric judgments with such differences of degree. Hence, adding an additional criterion, namely, whether the
first transition occurs with or without breaking the formal rules of
the authoritarian regime, can assist in establishing the difference between cases in which authoritarian rule does not simply "collapse."
These rules can be enshrined in a constitution or basic document,

in special acts, or simply in a selective but circumscribed and predictable use of aspects of a preexisting, even democratic, constitution. Transitions through "extrication"—no matter how long they take—would refer to those in which such rules are broken, and transitions through "transaction"—again, no matter how long they take—would be reserved for transitions occurring without having broken the formal framework of the prior authoritarian regime. Authoritarian rulers can generally be presumed to have greater capacity to impose conditions—to "transact" in a way favorable to them—over their oppositions in "transaction" (*reform* may still be the better term to use) rather than "extrication" situations. In all transitions by "collapse" the rules of the authoritarian regime are violated, but its rulers are unable to impose any conditions to their leaving power—otherwise the transition would occur by "extrication."

Still, these categories need to be supplemented by others before they can usefully distinguish among the dynamics of various transitions. For instance, both the Spanish and the Chilean transitions occurred through reform, i.e., without violating the formal rules of the authoritarian regimes, but this similarity is of little interest in what have been such different cases. What must be added to the above discussed types is a dimension that captures the attitudes of the *last* ruling elites of the authoritarian regime towards democratization. Some favor it, as did King Juan Carlos and Adolfo Suárez in Spain and, more recently, the authorities in Hungary, Czechoslovakia, East Germany, and Lithuania. Others may have an ambivalent attitude towards democratization, confusing it with the liberalization of the authoritarian regime and revealing considerable wariness over its extension, as was the case in Brazil, in South Korea, and perhaps in Poland and the Soviet Union. And still others may be fundamentally opposed to it. Such was the case with General Augusto Pinochet, who repeatedly rejected democracy by associating it with assorted ills he saw in the Chilean past, such as demagogic politicians, chaos, Marxist infiltration, and so on. His explicit intention was to create a "protected" democracy, a euphemism for the continuation of an authoritarian regime under his direction.

The combination of both dimensions, i.e., the modalities of the transition with the attitudes of the exiting authoritarian rulers towards democratization, generates a variety of types which are exemplified with approximate national examples in Figure 1. There is no space here to discuss each one as a prototypical first transition. What is important to highlight is that the first transitions that are most likely to generate the least problematic processes of democratic consolidation are those in which the last ruling elites of the authoritarian regime favor democratization. Such situations occur after the triumph within the authoritarian regime of what could be called, borrowing in part from Guillermo O'Donnell's classic statement of the "soft-liner" versus "hard-liner" split, as the super-soft-liners, i.e., those who not only favor the liberalization of authoritarian rule but are committed to democratization.[32] Moreover, transitions led by such super-soft-liners that occur, in addition, through reform, are more likely to permit the same political leaders who carry out the transition to retain leading positions in the new democratic context. As such, their first to second transitions have greater continuity. These transitions are only threatened by the ability of hard-liners to stage a revolt against them, but hard-liner success in these cases is limited by the fact that the super-soft-liners have already emerged by defeating them from within the regime; hence it is not surprising that Alexander Dubcek's Czechoslovakia and Imre Nagy's Hungary, two cases that led to authoritarian reversion, required external support for it.

Other cases of transition are less favorable for the successful resolution of the process of consolidation. While transitions that occur through the collapse or defeat of entrenched "hard-line" rulers opposed to democracy have the advantage of generating a largely clean slate upon which to build new institutions, as first transitions to democracy these are extremely risky, since it is not at all clear that those who take power in such convulsed situations will be committed to building a genuine democracy, or whether the social and political forces that supported the authoritarian regime will be allowed, or even willing, to participate in it. The second transition in these cases will have a greater probability of success and will occur more smoothly if the outgoing authoritarian regime elites are highly isolated from the nation's social and political forces, if political leadership willing to participate (and have its opponents participate) in a democratic framework is available for all major segments of opinion, and if the authoritarian regime collapses swiftly in the absence of civil war or much internal violence. The Greek transition was therefore much easier than that of most other cases such as Portugal or Nicaragua. The Portuguese transition required the elimination of the Grand Council of the Revolution, a body designed

Figure 1
MODALITIES OF TRANSITION TO DEMOCRACY FROM AUTHORITARIAN RULE
Change Occurs Through:

ATTITUDES OF THE LAST MAIN AUTHORITARIAN REGIME ELITES TOWARDS DEMOCRACY	Collapse, Defeat or Withdrawal[1]	Extrication[2]	Reform[3]
Favor full democratization	Czechoslovakia 1989	East Germany 1990 Peru 1980 Brazil 1945	Spain 1975–76 Hungary 1989
Prefer liberalized authoritarian regime but will accept democratization	Argentina 1983 Colombia 1958	Venezuela 1958 Argentina 1973	Poland 1989 Brazil 1980s South Korea 1987
Opposed to democratization	Greece 1974 Portugal 1975 Germany and Japan 1945 Italy 1945 Romania 1989	Uruguay 1985	Chile 1990

[1] Rules of the authoritarian regime are abandoned, and rulers cannot or opt not to negotiate conditions for leaving power.
[2] Rules of the authoritarian regime are abandoned, but rulers negotiate leaving power.
[3] Transition occurs without breaking the rules of the old regime.

to protect the new regime from the influence of forces supporting the old order. In Nicaragua, the commitment of the Sandinistas and of their opponents to democratic consolidation was questionable, and the mutual suspicions and resentments were aggravated by the fact that in the aftermath of civil war the Sandinista–controlled army became the Nicaraguan Armed Forces. That army has become, after the transfer of power to President Violeta Chamorro, a "reserved domain" of Sandinista control.

Among the remaining situations, the most unusual is the one combining a first transition through reform with a hard–line authoritarian regime leadership opposed to democracy, i.e., the Chilean case in Figure 1.[33] This type of first transition poses unique and difficult problems for the subsequent consolidation of democracy. As a transition through reform, it permits a great deal of continuity in the political elites and state officials who remain in place from the authoritarian regime to the democratic situation. And given that in the main such elites are basically opposed to a democratic regime (at best some accept it conditionally), the transition through reform allows them the capacity to create formal (i.e., legally based) institutions and the organizational basis for exerting tutelage and for reserving domains while ceding the way to what then becomes a highly bounded transition. The second transition must then proceed unavoidably through reform as well. Its success depends on a favorable relative balance of political forces within the new institutional strictures, and the opportunities they offer to accomplish the necessary reforms without abandoning their formal procedures.

B. Regime Comparisons, Historical Memories, and Legitimacy

All transitions stimulate collective memories of past political symbols, institutions, leaders, parties, and social organizations, creating images of what must be restituted, newly created, avoided, and eliminated. These memories are associated with past regimes, inviting most importantly comparisons among the evolving transitional democratic situation, the prior authoritarian regime, and the regime or regimes (depending on the specific experiences) that preceded the latter.

The leaders of regime changes often stimulate comparisons to the immediately preceding regime by appealing to what can be called "inverse legitimation," i.e., attempts to validate the new regime and even garner support for it by pointing to real or exaggerated faults of the previous one.[34] Referring to these comparisons, Guillermo O'Donnell suggests that democratic consolidation is favored by widespread highly negative experiences of the population with repression and economic failure under the authoritarian regime.[35] If this is the case, there may well be greater public resistance to any attempts to overthrow the democratic regime when it faces difficulties, as well as greater reluctance on the part of political elites favoring authoritarianism to make them.[36] As a result, the notion that the electoral route is the only viable one to form governments would be enhanced.

O'Donnell also suggests that, in general, cases that involve redemocratization, i.e., those in which there already was a consolidated democracy in the not so remote past, have significant advantages over those in which the current transition represents a case of constructing a democratic regime for the first time.[37] Parties and a party system are usually more readily reconstituted to operate in a democracy in such cases, and other political institutions, such as the organization of legislatures, the operation of the electoral system, the restoration of civic ceremonies associated with a prior democracy, and so on, all fall more easily into place. Similarly, the new democratic situation appears to be a continuity of something that existed in the past rather than a new and unknown departure, a notion that is all the more important and favorable for a reconsolidation of democracy if the prior democratic regime was in addition tied to feelings of national identity and pride.[38] Such cases of redemocratization are only hampered by returning images of the crisis that led to their breakdown, which opponents of the democratic process will usually attempt to emphasize. Successful redemocratizations therefore require a deliberate effort on the part of the democratizing elites to avoid resurrecting symbols, images, conducts, and political programs associated with the conflicts leading to prior breakdown.[39]

In cases where the past democratic referent is to democratic situations that contained one or more of the perverse institutional elements delineated above (tutelage or coup politics for example), the reconstitutive tendency in the new transitional process may lead to a reassertion of the same perverse elements, adding considerable difficulties to the prospects for democratic consolidation. Past democratic episodes in many Latin American countries have been of this nature; in Peru, Ecuador, and Bolivia, most notably, civilian and

military elites usually retained an undercurrent of coup politics behind the formalities of the democratic process, and in Brazil—again
most notably—the military somehow retained the sense that it is
entitled to exercise the old *poder moderador* of the emperor, thereby
leading to pretensions of tutelage. In these cases, democratic consolidation requires a decisive break on the part of the democratizing elites (hopefully both civilian and military) with such past practices. A widespread sense that they led to profound failures may
stimulate this change.

A central difficulty with collective memories of regimes, political figures, and symbols is that they can be a source of significant
division among different segments of the population. One of the
main problems of democratic consolidation in the French Third
Republic was that the political elites were divided in their regime
preferences, and each sector had its past regime referent and its associated symbols to invoke.[40] Thus, democratic consolidation is
favored by situations in which the evaluations of the past by the
different sectors all lead, somehow, to attitudes favorable to an accommodation among political forces. This accommodation requires
the various sectors to view positively those elements in their favored
past regimes that other segments do not find too objectionable, and
reject or at least criticize those that were most divisive. An example
of the latter from the Spanish case is the rejection by the current
Left of the extreme and rabid anticlericalism of its forebears during
the Spanish Second Republic. Accommodation also requires a search
for unifying national symbols. If each sector relentlessly insists on
changing the name of every plaza and street to commemorate past
figures and dates that are highly divisive, and if anniversaries of past
events that have entirely different meanings for the various communities are observed, then political symbols and regime comparisons
will retain the currency of past conflicts. Similarly, democratic consolidation is favored if the various sectors agree that a democratic
regime would be, following Juan Linz's minimal definition of legitimacy, if not the most favored then the "least evil" among the
alternatives.[41]

The initial period of transition can itself stimulate such perceptions. For this, it is best if, to use Juan Linz's terms again, the new
democratic government is relatively efficacious and effective, and its
leadership is perceived to be relatively honest and able.[42] At a time
in which the democratic institutions are fragile because they are new

or have been recently recreated, it is best if the policies and leaders that emanate from their workings be given relatively high marks; otherwise, the public (and especially the politically organized and active segments) may associate negative performances with the regime and its alternatives may appear preferable. This does not necessarily mean that overall economic and social conditions must be favorable for a successful transition. Rather, the basic point is that democratic political leaders and governments be widely viewed as doing the best that can be done given the circumstances, even if the transition coincides with difficult times.[43]

Unfortunately, as noted briefly by Linz, such public perceptions can be more difficult to attain in a democratic context given its greater openness and the expectations it often raises.[44] By broadening the arena for discussion of national issues (in legislatures, television debates, universities, and so on) and by stimulating political competition for votes, the public's awareness and exposure to problems can easily expand, thereby increasing the sense that the government is inadequate to resolve them. Democratic guarantees to freedom of expression also raise the extent of public scrutiny of political leaders, and while this is a necessary and welcome development, it exposes leaders to the barbs of unethical opponents who may succeed in distorting the public's perception of them. If the political change raises popular expectations that longstanding problems and privations associated with the authoritarian regime will be overcome, the gap between such expectations and the possibilities of meeting them even with the best of policies may be unbridgeable.

Democratic consolidation would therefore be favored by government leaders who try to lower public expectations while at the same time undertaking policies that deliver results that exceed their own rhetoric; by a relative absence of government corruption; by the development of a truthful but responsible press that is not strictly tied to partisan alignments; and by the presence of a restrained, nondemagogic democratic opposition. The Spanish transition, despite the negative economic context in which it occurred, exemplifies well this combination of favorable perceptions and responsible press as well as opposition behavior. Such conditions are a tall order, but approximating them is all the more important if the prior authoritarian regime has an aura of success and probity, whatever the actual facts.

C. The Moderation of Political Conflict

It is hardly novel to assert that the moderation of political conflict would serve to advance democratic consolidation. Nothing is more destructive of democracy than frequent confrontations in the streets, the legislature, the state administration, and elsewhere between groups who view themselves as engaged in zero-sum conflict. The lifting of authoritarian repression and the return of democratic liberties to organize, petition, and demonstrate should not lead to widespread disorder and violence. The establishment of democratic constitutional processes should not lead to either policy stalemates for want of compromises among different forces, or to what politically organized minorities view as a complete disregard for their interests and values (or of course for their democratic rights — but if these are violated the new regime is not a democracy). Hence, the greater the degree of consensus among political forces, the easier it is to consolidate democracy. Attempts to retain tutelary power, reserved domains, electoral discriminations, and the use of coup or insurrection politics are in the final analysis expressions of distrust by powerful actors of the consequences they perceive would flow from the electoral victories of their opponents.

Giovanni Sartori has usefully broken down the notion of consensus into three possible meanings: firstly, that over "ultimate values"; secondly, over "rules of the game, or procedures"; and finally, over "specific governmental policies." He notes that the first is a "facilitating" but not an indispensable condition for the existence of a democracy, while the second is indeed a fundamental prerequisite; he adds that discussion and dissensus in the third sense is part of the essence of democratic governance.[45]

Following the first sense, political conflict would certainly take on moderate contours if there were a relatively small ideological distance among the major sectors of the polity, and if the national community were not divided into different linguistic, religious, racial, or ethnic segments that distrust each other and have a history of conflict. However, countries that have experienced democratic breakdown in the past or that only recently made transitions to democracy generally do not have the kind of ultimate value consensus that can be found in Scandinavia or the United States. Hence, this facilitating condition is generally lacking. Nonetheless, consolidation would be favored if the transition coincides with a decline in ideological distance (as has occurred in countries with a strong Marxist Left as a result of the rise of Eurocommunism and, more recently, the collapse of the Communist model); with a surge in support for pragmatic center parties and moderate leaders, old or new, and a decline in that for the extremes; and/or with a new willingness on the part of political leaderships, both top and middle-level, to forge agreements and understandings that safeguard the value commitments and interests of their respective constituencies or communities. This latter point is particularly important. Political conflict is often stimulated by the more extremist views of the leaders and militants of different segments of societies, and their willingness to resort to negotiations and compromises in fact will in these cases not place them beyond but more in line with the sentiments of their constituencies. Such moderation is the likely result of what political leaders see with new clarity as the costs and sacrifices imposed by the outgoing authoritarian regime, and of the current development of a new or renewed appreciation for the democratic system and its rights.

Sartori's second dimension of consensus, that over procedures, amounts, when reached, to a minimization of what Linz would call disloyalty and semi-loyalty.[46] It is certainly an important component of democratic consolidation, for it buttresses the notion that democracy will continue indefinitely.

But several comments are in order: first, despite the analytical usefulness of Sartori's distinctions, this dimension of consensus is not completely detached from the former one. The procedures will be accepted as long as the various political forces view them as being fair. This consensus will prove to be elusive if the procedures are not inclusive of all political forces, or are viewed by some as giving undue advantages to others, resulting in policy outcomes that are perceived to be unacceptably injurious to some segment's values or interests. Hence, procedural consensuses are more readily reached if the participants in the democratic process do not expect to lose all the time, and think that no dire consequences will follow when they do lose. The more the political community is sharply divided, as Sartori notes, the more the democratic majority principle has to be tempered with respect for minority positions.[47] The procedures must also be molded to the specificities of national societies, yielding different types of democracies. Such procedures serve to structure a particular balance of power among the various segments of the political community, and this balance should not be viewed as grossly out of kilter with the size and importance of the segments' various social bases. Second, the consensus over procedures cannot include what I have labelled here the perverse formal and informal institutions. Not only does their existence prevent democratic governance, but they may also derail the second transition in the long run by stimulating conflict over the procedures, the alienation of the political forces that are disadvantaged by them, and eventually the "slow death" of democracy—to follow O'Donnell's expression.[48] Thirdly, some procedures are quite simply better than others. Despite a consensus over the procedures, their actual workings may lead to unnecessary rigidities, conflicts, and even breakdowns. Generally speaking, procedures that lead to staging zero-sum forms of conflict can be detrimental to democratic consolidation. By avoiding one important winner-take-all form of confrontation, namely presidential elections, parliamentary regimes are, for instance, more suitable to the transit to a consolidated democracy than presidential ones.[49] Semi-presidential systems are no better. Their potential for generating two heads of state (when the president does not belong to the same majority as the prime minister who enjoys the confidence of the legislature) is an open recipe for conflict that could have dire consequences unless the leaders in question reach the necessary accommodations, based normally on who has the most recent electoral majority. While any system can only work adequately, in the final analysis, given the willingness of political leaders to avoid pushing it to crisis limits, the adoption of procedures that can stimulate debates over competencies or that call for zero-sum confrontations will not favor consolidation.

Finally, while disagreements and discussions over policy are part of the essence of democracy, democratic governments—especially transition governments—should not pursue single-mindedly policies that reflect divisive positions. Moreover, as noted earlier, policies that maximize efficacy and effectiveness can enhance the ability of the transition government to consolidate the democratic process.

D. The Management of Social Conflict

The consolidation of democracy is also favored by the creation of the proper frameworks for channeling and resolving social conflict. Guillermo O'Donnell and Philippe Schmitter have noted that the transition to democracy leads to a broad "resurrection of civil society."[50] Many groups take advantage of the new political circumstances to create (or recreate) and expand their organizations and articulate their grievances, some of which may have been suppressed by the authoritarian regime.[51] The new organizing may lead to confrontations among social groups, "resurrecting" as well old animosities among communities — as shown by the resurgence of regional nationalisms most dramatically in Central Europe and in the Soviet Union.

Obviously, political and social conflicts are intimately related. During the authoritarian regime, the absence or inadequacy of institutions (such as national elections and democratically generated legislatures) through which opponents of the regime can express their views and programs leads them to center their opposition activities in a variety of loci in civil society (such as churches, the labor and student movements, sports clubs, etc.).[52] The resulting confrontations between authoritarian regimes and social movements and organizations can help undermine authoritarian rule by continually demonstrating its essential illegitimacy. During the course of the first transition, as O'Donnell and Schmitter argue, the willingness and ability of social organizations to show restraint may prove to be an important contribution to ensuring that it will not be derailed by a reassertion of the possibly still powerful hard-line forces of the outgoing authoritarian regime.[53] But a successful second transition requires the elimination of this form of politically motivated restraint, and this by definition: even if such restraint can help ensure the stability of the transitional form of democracy, it is a reflection of the fact that important social and political actors do not lend credence to its endurance into the foreseeable future.

Yet the release of this restraint (or its absence in certain transitions) should not lead to broadscale confrontations among social groups. If this were the case, the consolidation of democracy may well be delayed or questioned anew. The resulting overload of issues difficult to resolve and public disorder as demonstrations and possibly violent confrontations among groups spill into the streets can foster doubts about the ability of the fledgling democratic process to address national problems and can rekindle sentiments in favor of renewed authoritarian rule. Although the financial capacity of the state and overall economic conditions will hardly, if ever, suffice to satisfy all demands, this is not the crucial point regarding these challenges. Rather, the key lies in the creation of what can be called adequate "social demand–processing settlements."

Such settlements include the creation, change, or expansion

of a variety of arrangements. They may entail, first, setting up new state institutions (or restructuring old ones) that will receive and process social demands; second, the establishment, expansion, or recreation of popular and other associations to voice demands and negotiate some resolution to them, with leaders who have the necessary legitimacy and support to be able to call off demonstrations and other collective actions;[54] third, the development of mutually agreeable procedures that social groups who confront each other regularly (such as labor and business) can follow to settle their differences, with or without state assistance; and fourth, the existence of the proper links between social groups and the political leaders in parliament if not also in the executive to ensure that legislation and other state actions affecting the features of the settlement and its subsequent changes result, as far as possible, from a parallel political as well as social consensus.

These settlements are most adequate to facilitate democratic consolidation when they are perceived by all those concerned to operate with a minimum of politicization. In other words, when state institutions are responsive to social group demands through their normal bureaucratic operation, without provoking drawn-out collective action against them given the widespread perception of their insensitivity or unfairness; when the leadership of social groups is viewed as acting primarily in the best interests of its members, however defined for the short, medium and/or long term, and not primarily in response to the national strategies of the parties they may be affiliated to; when the procedures to be followed in negotiating differences are not continually put into question by the relevant actors; when it is unclear who are the proper actors to resolve the issues at hand; or when social demands and disputes continually become part of a national political debate given the intervention of legislators, cabinet members, or party leaders, thereby interfering with the "normal" conflict resolution procedures and making the outcome hinge in part on the national balance of political interests and forces. This form of politicization can result from the lack of congruity (produced by the operation of the electoral system and/or the high degree of segmentation of party constituencies) between the strength of a party or parties in the formal institutions of the political arena and the extent and intensity of its or their support within social movements and organizations.

In brief, democratic consolidation is favored if social conflicts and demands are handled through predictable and broadly accepted procedures that are inclusive of all the relevant groups but are, at the same time, insulated within the narrowest possible boundaries in terms of the specificity of the issues and the state, political, and social actors who are involved. But "social settlements" with these characteristics do not occur automatically in the immediate aftermath of the first transition, a point at which social conflicts and demands will inevitably be highly politicized as a result of the regime transition. An important aspect of the second transition is the construction of new social demand and conflict processing settlements, and its success depends at least in part on their adequacy. It may not always be possible to reach proper arrangements to deal with them, in which case the new democratic system may continue to be perceived as fragile.[55]

E. Subordinating the Military to the Democratic Government

Placing the military under the authority of the elected government is a key facilitating condition for democratic consolidation. Insofar as elected government officials are unsuccessful in their attempts to subordinate the military, the resulting military autonomy is contrary to the consolidation of democracy since it would be, following the above indicated conception, a reserved domain containing a fundamental ingredient of state power: force of arms. In this case reducing military autonomy is an indispensable ingredient for consolidation. In its most extreme form, military autonomy contains the following elements: fixed budgetary lines that provide the basic sources of funding for the armed forces but cannot be reviewed by democratic government officials; exclusive military control over the expenditures of its budget; no (or only pro forma) review of officer promotions by elected authorities or their representatives; designation of the top ranking officers strictly following the lines of seniority; no civilian governmental review of training programs and military doctrine; exclusive military control over the deployment of units, and over intelligence gathering and storing of information; the existence of a military justice system to try all cases involving officers regardless of the nature of the offense; and a ghettoization of military life, including family life, through the development of separate housing units for officers, hospitals, schools, clubs, and credit unions.

Let us suppose that democratically elected government officials and their civilian political opponents have no interest in exerting any control over military policies and other such matters, readily agreeing to let this aspect of the state remain in the hands of officers. This is an implausible scenario, for even where elected government officials seemingly express no interest in seeking control over the military it is not clear whether such inaction results from impotence or from conviction. Be this as it may, in this case military autonomy would not constitute, following the definition noted above, a reserved domain.

And yet, even in the unlikely event that military autonomy would not constitute a reserved domain, it would still be inimical to democratic consolidation. Such autonomy tends to engender, if it is not already present, military tutelage over the political system, as officers have the independent organizational basis, plus the force of arms, to question government policies. For the same reason it also tends to generate an undercurrent of coup politics as officers can sooner or later be perceived by civilian opponents of the government to be available, given appropriate conditions, to overthrow it. Elections would not then be the only means to constitute governments, in which case the democratic process would hardly be consolidated.

Hence, a fully democratic regime should contain in constitutional and other basic laws the formal outlines of military subordination to elected government officials, exclusive of any provisions suggesting military tutelage. And yet, prescribing this subordination in statutory terms by no means ensures it in practice, as demonstrated by Alfonsín's Argentina, nor does it prevent retrogression of government control over the military where it appears to present few difficulties during the course of the first transition, as was the case in Spain and could still perhaps be in Central and Eastern Europe. Consequently, the key question for democratic consolidation is whether or not the second transition succeeds in removing or preventing the emergence of the specter of coup politics.

There is broad consensus in the specialized literature that successful military coups occur when there appears to be considerable civilian support for them, and that coup politics therefore involves both civilian and military elites.[56] In this form of politics, civilian opponents of the government seek to maximize their capacity to use the threat of a military coup to further their political ends. This involves establishing and retaining close links to important officers and/or the ability to initiate civil unrest and other forms of destabilization that will induce the military to intervene. To counter opposition efforts the government cannot let its relations to the military deteriorate. As a result, it is bound to be receptive to the military's demands, whatever they may be, and eager to demonstrate to its opponents that it has a good working relationship with the military. As part of this effort, some heads of government may appoint military officers to important positions where they can serve, depending on the circumstances, in a "neutral" and "technical" capacity or in a way that deliberately expresses the military's support for the government's policies (or vice versa, in effect). The end result is to continually buttress, paradoxically, the autonomy and politicization of the military. The military can obtain from the government what it wants as long as it is courted by civilian forces that are never far from playing coup politics, but it is forced, in order to continue the game, to make itself available as the ultimate political arbiter. This form of politically induced autonomy leads to military tutelage over the political process, and can be exercised on a more or less continuous basis without resorting frequently to actually staging a coup. Needless to say, democratic consolidation under these circumstances is hardly possible. Through the actions of both civilians and the military, the democratic government remains under a thinly tethered sword of Damocles. Ironically, governments that are able to tether the sword more tightly by properly playing coup avoidance may also reaffirm the sword's place in the political system; engaging in the rules of perverse institutions is a vicious circle.

Discarding coup politics requires changes both in the military establishment and in the civilian political forces. The military's disposition and ability to interject itself in the overall political process and couple its corporative demands with the implicit threat of using its arms against the government must somehow be drastically reduced. It should no longer be available to civilian forces pressing the government with their alternative policy agendas. Civilian political elites should also end all attempts to use contact with the military or appeals to the military as trump cards to enhance their power capabilities. Change must occur at both levels for a long-term resolution of this problem. Any hint of military availability to act against elected authorities will eventually generate civilian forces willing to use it to buttress their positions, and no military establishment can refrain permanently from continuous courting by civilian forces in both the opposition and the government seeking to score political gain in an atmosphere that — given precisely the existence of civilians courting the military — will stimulate perceptions of national political crisis.

Second transitions differ regarding whether or not the specter of coup politics will become a significant problem. The variations are related to the following points.

Regarding the military side of the coup politics equation, cases of transition differ in the military's proximity to and identification with the outgoing authoritarian regime. These differences can have a significant impact on the military's autonomy from and attitudes towards the new democratic government when coupled, in particular, with the modalities assumed by the transition. Where the military has been very proximate to the authoritarian regime (as in cases of military government) and the officers identified strongly with its objectives, military autonomy and the development of coup politics are likely to be higher than in other situations unless the modality of the transition permits a thorough reorganization or refounding of the armed forces under a new leadership committed to democratic norms. This refounding occurred, for example, in postwar Germany and Japan under the influence of the allied and American occupation forces, and in Costa Rica under the aegis of the successful 1948 insurrection led by José Figueres. Such reorganizations spring from transitions through defeat or collapse rather than reform or extrication, but not all such defeats lead to the complete revamping of the armed forces. While the Argentine transition of 1982–83 in many respects occurred through a collapse of the authoritarian military regime, it did not lead to a profound transformation of the military institution despite President Alfonsín's reforms.[57]

In the absence of these transitions through collapse and military refounding, the creation of a military establishment that is unavailable to civilian coup-mongers and plotters can nonetheless be obtained through the reorientation of the armed forces under new political-military leadership. King Juan Carlos made a critical difference in the Spanish transition through his decisive leadership against military insubordination — most dramatically during the February 23–24, 1981 coup attempt — thereby permitting the civilian transitional governments to restructure the armed forces. Although Franco's regime was not a military one, the armed forces were virtually the only segment in the Spanish post-transition that continued to have strong Franquist sentiments and identity.[58] In Portugal General Eanes played an important role in pressing the military to regain its discipline and return to the barracks. Subsequently, military tutelarity over the government as expressed through the military-dominated Council of the Revolution was terminated through the constitutional reforms approved in 1982 under Eanes's presidency.[59] Individual idiosyncrasies of actors placed in key positions and other fortuitous circumstances can have important unexpected effects on key processes of the transition, and military subordination to civilian authority is no exception. No observers would have expected King Juan Carlos, Franco's hand–picked successor through a monarchical restoration that passed over Juan Carlos's father, to play such a decisive democratizing role.

The unavailability of the military for coup politics is also enhanced if its military doctrine — i.e., the conception of its role in the state and national society, of its actual or potential enemies, of the nature of war, and the definitions of national security that flow from these — focuses primarily on external threats to national territorial integrity. Such a doctrine minimizes the internal political involvement of the military, even if defensive planning requires paying attention to the internal economic and social conditions that buttress it. It also generates military organization, armament and deployment that are less conducive to internal political intelligence and to the logistics of staging coups. Internal security matters should be in the hands of specialized police units under the Ministries of the Interior. Such an externally focused doctrine will be easier to develop in the absence of serious internal insurrectionary threats against the state. And, as noted by Alfred Stepan, military doctrine and national security definitions should be elaborated primarily by civilians and should result in a civil-military consensus with military involvement in an advisory capacity.[60] Such consensus is, again, easier to retain when the object of military doctrine rests on external threats.

Unfortunately, as has occurred most significantly in Latin America, military doctrine has been in many cases elaborated exclusively by the armed forces. Moreover, its emphasis outside a few arenas of likely international conflagration has been on what are perceived to be internal threats to the security of the state. Genaro Arriagada has shown that this internal focus began in the Southern Cone with the confrontations between the military and striking workers — and the emerging radical Left — in the early twentieth century.[61] It expanded with the rise of the Cold War and the new role of the Armed Forces as bulwarks against the spread of Communism, which led to a greater focus on internal "subversion" in all areas of national societies, including the churches, unions, and educational institutions.[62] This led to a great expansion of internal intelligence gathering as military professionalism led officers to a direct involvement with internal political control and repression. Although the end of the Cold War should facilitate change in military doctrine, military establishments are bound to view with great suspicion any attempt by civilians in transition governments to alter its components, conceptions, and training programs.

Given a military-civilian consensus over the role of the armed forces, governments should try to furnish the military with the necessary means to accomplish it, which includes proper channels for the military to express its corporative needs. Officer discontent over salaries, assignments, and promotions should be avoided, as long as these are consistent with forms of professionalism compatible with democratic governance.[63] Any military rebellions motivated by officer discontent over institutional and career problems can set the kindling for the initiation of coup politics. No matter how circumscribed officer demands may be to military problems, such rebellions can lead civilian opponents of the government to side with them in order to gain military contacts that can subsequently enhance their power capabilities or even generate a coup coalition. Officer rebellions can therefore signal to civilian elites their availability to engage in coup politics. The principal difficulty in many cases is that there is no civilian-military consensus over the military's mission. Hence, officer discontent and rebellions against civilian authorities may be a manifestation of attempts to impose, or retain, definitions of the military's mission that are rejected by civilians.

Turning to the civilian side of coup politics, such politics are avoided if the civilian political forces develop the necessary consensus — preferably over fundamental ends, but at least over procedures — including the agreement that none will attempt to develop a military trump card to enhance power capabilities. Such an agreement, explicit or implicit, may be difficult to obtain in some situations. It is facilitated by a context that includes significant international pressures in its favor; that contains a negative assessment of the previous military interventions or governments; that permits civilian forces close to the military to voice their demands effectively following the democratic procedures; and in which the political leadership — civilian or military — of the outgoing authoritarian regime develops a favorable attitude towards democracy. The result should be a total political isolation of rebellious military officers, such as in Spain where only the far rightist fringe had sympathy for them. It is likely that had this not been the case, the King alone would not have been able to take such effective action to confront military insubordination. Given the Latin American military's overdimensioned definition of its mission and its willingness to act against governments repeatedly in the past, a firm consensus among civilian leaders to reject any involvement with rebellious military officers or to strike privileged relations with the military is the main recourse to eliminate or prevent the emergence of coup politics. Among the Latin American cases the Uruguayan comes closest to having attained this important consensus.

Conclusions

This paper has attempted to present a delimited notion of democratic consolidation. Such consolidation can be said to have been achieved when most significant political actors and informed publics expect the democratic process to last indefinitely, and when it is basically free of what have been called "perverse institutions," namely, tutelary powers, reserved domains of policy, egregious and deliberate distortions of the electoral system and political representation, and the existence of the widespread belief that nonelectoral means are possible to form the national government. These "perverse" elements are conceptually anchored on a minimal formal definition of the democracy. While the procedures that comprise the democratic process lead to a complex institutionalization of a "virtuous" sort since it buttresses a reproduction of that process, the notion of democratic consolidation cannot be left to rest on an analysis of these institutions because it will unavoidably tie consolidation to an ideal conception of democratic polities. Were this the case, few democracies would have that attribute. The conceptual link to elements that detract from the minimal workings of the democratic process is strict enough; in fact, by its measure no democracy in Latin America can presently be considered consolidated. Moreover, consolidated democracies have been a rarity in Latin America: Costa

Rica since the 1950s, Venezuela since the 1960s, Chile from the mid-1930s to 1973, Uruguay from the mid-1930s to the Bordaberry presidency, and perhaps Argentina in the mid–1920s.

This paper has also noted that the process of democratic consolidation unfolds through a series of political confrontations which either buttress or remove the perverse elements that detract from the minimal democratic process. These confrontations can be over reforms of the political institutions themselves or over substantive policies. While actors favoring democratic consolidation and those opposing it will generally act in ways that advance their preferences, both can actually contribute to the process or detract from it given short-run calculations of gain, miscalculations, or unanticipated consequences. Consolidation is reached as an ex post facto realization; any deliberate plan to advance it will, by virtue of its stated goal, indicate to all those concerned its absence.

While keeping the notion of democratic consolidation tied strictly to a procedural skeleton, this paper has also analyzed some conditions that can facilitate (or detract) from its advancement. Other facilitating conditions could be added to those that were mentioned, as this seems to be a particularly fruitful venue for further comparative research.

NOTES

This paper began as a "think piece" entitled "Some Thoughts on the Consolidation of Democracies" written for a workshop on processes of democratic consolidation in Western Europe and Latin America, organized by Guillermo O'Donnell and Philippe Schmitter and held at the Kellogg Institute in April 1987. I thank both organizers of that workshop for their reactions, and Guillermo O'Donnell for the conversations held over the course of two years that helped to clarify my thinking on the topic. The paper also benefitted from comments on a second version by David Collier, Arend Lijphart, Philippe Schmitter, Alfred Stepan, and Carlos Waisman. My appreciation as well to Guillermo O'Donnell, Scott Mainwaring, Timothy Scully, and Raimundo Valenzuela for their encouragement and observations on this version, while I take responsibility for the deficiencies that remain.

1. An illustration of this trend is the argument made by Juan Linz regarding the superiority and greater stability of parliamentary over presi-

dential constitutional arrangements for democracies. See his "Democracy, Presidential or Parliamentary: Does It Make a Difference?" paper written for the project "The Role of Political Parties in the Return to Democracy in the Southern Cone," sponsored by the Latin American Program of the Woodrow Wilson International Center for Scholars, the Smithsonian Institution, and the World Peace Foundation, July 1985. The argument that a parliamentary regime would be best for Chile is made forcefully by Arturo Valenzuela, "Origins and Characteristics of the Chilean Party System: A Proposal for a Parliamentary Form of Government," a paper prepared for the same project. Revised and translated versions of these papers appear in Oscar Godoy Arcaya, ed., *Hacia una democracia moderna: la opción parlamentaria* (Santiago: Ediciones de la Universidad Católica de Chile, 1990), while an abridged version of Juan Linz's paper appears as "The Perils of Presidentialism," *Journal of Democracy,* 1, no. 1 (Winter 1990), pp. 51–59. Similar institutional and political process arguments are contained in Juan Linz and Alfred Stepan, "Political Crafting of Democratic Consolidation or Destruction: European and South American Comparisons" in Robert A. Pastor, ed., *Democracy in the Americas: Stopping the Pendulum* (New York and London: Holmes and Meier, 1989). For a review of the literature on presidentialism in Latin America, see Scott Mainwaring, "Presidentialism in Latin America," *Latin American Research Review,* 25, no. 1 (1990), pp. 157–179.

2. Guillermo O'Donnell, "Transições, continuidades e alguns paradoxos" in Fábio Wanderley Reis and Guillermo O'Donnell, eds., *A Democracia no Brasil: Dilemas e Perspectivas* (São Paulo: Vértice, 1988), p. 43. A revised English version of this paper appears as chapter 1 of this volume.

3. This can lead to what Guillermo O'Donnell calls the "slow death" of democracy; Vinicio Cerezo's Guatemala is a case in point. See O'Donnell's contribution to this volume.

4. Juan Linz, in *The Breakdown of Democratic Regimes: Crisis, Breakdown, and Reequilibration* (Baltimore: Johns Hopkins University Press, 1978), notes that democratic breakdowns are more the result of the unwillingness or inability of the regime's defenders to agree among each other than the effect of challenges by antidemocratic forces. The Chilean and Uruguayan democracies can be said to have been consolidated in the terms to be noted below prior to their 1973 breakdowns. Major Chilean political leaders of the left, center, and even right, including President Aylwin, have noted that in retrospect they regret the actions they took during the Allende government, given their effect in producing the breakdown of Chilean democracy. None foresaw the eventual outcome; even those who eventually favored military intervention expected it to lead to a rapid restoration of democratic government. For an analysis of the breakdown of

Chilean democracy, see Arturo Valenzuela, *The Breakdown of Democratic Regimes: Chile* (Baltimore: Johns Hopkins University Press, 1978).

5. This is what happens in José Nun's "La teoría política y la transición democrática," in José Nun and Juan Carlos Portantiero, eds., *Ensayos sobre la transición democrática en la Argentina* (Buenos Aires: Puntosur Editores, 1987), where the notion of democratic consolidation refers to a broad project of building all kinds of political and social relations and institutions. A similar problem can be seen in Manuel Antonio Garretón's *Reconstruir la política: Transición y consolidación democrática en Chile* (Santiago: Editorial Andante, 1987), pp. 53–55, where democratic consolidation refers to a model of socioeconomic development that is compatible with democracy, to an increased autonomy but adequate interrelationships among the state, the political system, and civil society, and to an inclusive and well-established party system.

6. Guillermo O'Donnell in "Notes for the Study of Democratic Consolidation in Contemporary Latin America," paper presented at a meeting on "Dilemmas and Opportunities of Democratic Consolidation in Contemporary Latin America" held at CEBRAP, São Paulo, December 16–17, 1985, pp. 2, 4.

7. Guillermo O'Donnell and Philippe Schmitter, "Tentative Conclusions about Uncertain Democracies" in Guillermo O'Donnell, Philippe Schmitter, and Laurence Whitehead, eds., *Transitions from Authoritarian Rule: Prospects for Democracy* (Baltimore: Johns Hopkins University Press, 1986), p. 8.

8. Robert Dahl, *Polyarchy* (New Haven: Yale University Press, 1971), p. 3.

9. Formal definitions of democracy owe much to Joseph Schumpeter's discussion of the concept. See his *Capitalism, Socialism and Democracy,* (New York: Harper Torchbooks, 1962, third edition), part V. For a discussion of some of the limitations of his definition of democracy see J. Samuel Valenzuela, *Democratización vía reforma: La expansión del sufragio en Chile* (Buenos Aires: Ediciones del IDES, 1985), pp. 22–35. For a radically different, and in my view inadequate, "participatory" conception of democracy see C. B. Macpherson, *The Life and Times of Liberal Democracy* (New York: Oxford University Press, 1977), chapter 5. See also Carole Pateman, *Participation and Democratic Theory* (New York: Cambridge University Press, 1970) for a critique of formal democratic conceptions from the perspective of effective participation by ordinary people in the affairs of government as well as at the subnational level.

10. For critique of this narrow conception of equality and a discussion of democracy from a broader perspective of this notion see David Held, *Models of Democracy* (Stanford: Stanford University Press, 1987), especially chapter 9.

11. For a discussion of the endurance of corporatism in democracies

see Philippe Schmitter, "Still the Century of Corporatism?" in, among other sources, Philippe C. Schmitter and Gerhard Lehmbruch, eds., *Trends toward Corporatist Intermediation* (Beverly Hills: Sage Publications, 1979). See also Philippe C. Schmitter, "Democratic Theory and Neo–Corporatist Practice," *Social Research* 50, no. 4 (Winter 1983).

12. Schumpeter, p. 269. The quote is drawn from his well-known definition of democracy.

13. *Constitución Política de la República de Chile: 1980* (Santiago: Editorial Jurídica, 1985) article 90. General Pinochet attributes great significance to this clause. In a speech given on August 23, 1989, on the relation between the Armed Forces and the transition, he stressed this clause as one of the main innovations of the 1980 Constitution, one that finally recognizes a "natural function of the Armed Forces and Police," that is, recognizes "their political function." He went on to list a long number of policies that civilian authorities must follow in the future to remain in agreement not only with the letter but also the "spirit" of the Constitution. Among these he included no change in the Amnesty Law of 1978 that exempted all military officers from prosecution for human rights violations. See *La Epoca,* 24 August 1989, p. 13.

The Brazilian Constitution of 1988, although it was drafted after the first transition, also places the Armed Forces in a guarantorship role. It notes that they "guarantee constitutional powers and, by the initiative of any one of these powers, law and order." *Constituição da República Federativa do Brasil, 1988* (Brasília: Centro Gráfico do Senado Federal, 1988), article 142.

14. *Constitución Política de la República de Chile: 1980,* articles 95 and 96. These articles were modified to some extent in mid–1989. The modifications appear in *La Epoca,* 2 June 1989, and the text above incorporates them.

15. See *El Mercurio,* December 24, 1989, p. D1, for an account of the first meeting between General Pinochet and president-elect Aylwin, in which the latter asked him to resign.

16. A description of the so-called *Comité Asesor Político y Estratégico* appears in *Hoy,* no. 679 (23–29 July 1990), pp. 11–13.

17. On such democracies, see Arend Lijphart, *Democracy in Plural Societies: A Comparative Exploration* (New Haven and London: Yale University Press, 1977); and Arend Lijphart, *Democracies: Patterns of Majoritarian and Consensus Government in Twenty-One Countries* (New Haven and London: Yale University Press, 1984).

18. See Gerhard Lehmbruch, "Concertation and the Structure of Corporatist Networks" in John Goldthorpe, ed., *Order and Conflict in Contemporary Capitalism* (Oxford: Clarendon Press, 1984) for a development of the concept of "sectoral corporatism."

19. Manuel Antonio Garretón has used the terms "authoritarian en-

claves" or "residues" to refer generally to what I have called reserved domains. These are misnomers. Enclaves are separate entities within, but not connected to, others; the reserved domains are, by contrast, at the center of the political problematic of the second transition. Residues are trace elements that do not affect their environment; again, this is not the case with the reserved domains of transitional settings. See Manuel Antonio Garretón, *La posibilidad democrática en Chile* (Santiago: FLACSO, 1989), pp. 51–63.

20. In the case of the Central Bank, the Pinochet government appointed some board members sympathetic to the democratic opposition in what was viewed as a major concession.

21. This discussion assumes transitions to mass suffrage democracies, since all democratic transitions at this point in time lead to universal access to the vote by adult citizens. It also glosses over important differences between presidential and parliamentary systems.

22. Elections in Great Britain are generally singled out as an example. The majoritarian effect is exacerbated in this case by the existence of well structured parties. For a brief analysis of the broad variety of electoral systems and their mathematical properties in generating representation see Robert A. Newland, *Comparative Electoral Systems* (London: The Arthur McDougall Fund, 1982).

23. The Israeli electoral system, while among the least biased of all systems with its proportional representation in a single nationwide district with only a 1 percent threshold for representation, in fact makes democratic governance more difficult by over-empowering the small parties that hold the balance of power between Likud and Labor.

24. The electoral system devised by the Pinochet government is unique in the annals of elections. It can best be labelled as a binominal majority list system. It is binominal because each district (whether senatorial or for the lower house) elects two representatives; in addition, the law requires that each list present not more than two candidates per district. The votes are then added by list to determine a first and a second place winning list. If the second winning list has less than half the vote total of the first, then the first list elects its two candidates to fill the district representation. If the second list has half plus one or more of the votes obtained by the first, then the candidates who obtained the highest vote totals on each of the two lists are elected, regardless of whether the runner-up candidate in the first winning list has more votes than those of the best placed candidate on the second list.

25. The right's "Democracy and Progress" pact, from which all the right's representatives to the congress were elected, obtained 33.28 percent of the vote in the Senate races and elected 42 percent of the seats that were disputed; and with 33.35 percent of the vote in the lower house elections

it elected 40 percent of the total seats (figures calculated from *La Segunda,* 15 December 1989). These electoral percentages do not include the votes for other extreme right and right lists. To figure them into the calculation of the relation between votes and seats is incorrect because it is not clear how many votes the main list of the right would have lost had those fringe candidates been included in it.

26. This is what Samuel Huntington called "mass praetorianism." See his *Political Order in Changing Societies* (New Haven and London: Yale University Press, 1968), chapter 3.

27. Anderson thought the perverse cycle setting described the "Latin American political system." But he failed to note that individuals in established democracies also use their peculiar "power capabilities" to score political points; the difference is that the perverse cycle settings include, quite simply, the possibility of a military coup or insurrection while the consolidated democratic ones (even when they are Latin American cases) do not. He also ties his conception to a modernization approach. He assumed that the "Latin American political system" would decline as the countries of the region increased their development. This is a very questionable assumption. See Charles Anderson, *Politics and Economic Change in Latin America* (Toronto: Van Nostrand, 1967), chap. 4.

28. A parenthetical note on the qualifier "significant" in the above definition: conspiratorial antisystem groups, such as terrorist elements or putschist nuclei in the armed forces, may exist in consolidated democracies as long as they are isolated from other political forces, are composed of small minorities, and are viewed as incapable of disrupting the democratic system by the participants in the democratic political game. Thus, French, Italian, German, and even Spanish (post–1981) democracies can be viewed as consolidated despite the presence of terrorist groups at various points. Peruvian democracy facing the Sendero Luminoso insurrection cannot.

Can British democracy be faulted for distortions in its electoral procedures that would lead to questioning its consolidation given the definition above? My answer is a firm no. The same electoral procedures have been in place ever since the United Kingdom began democratic elections; they are not the product of the deliberate distortions noted in the definition. The American South before the civil rights legislation is a more problematic case. In fact, given its denial of voting rights to large numbers of blacks the South can hardly be considered to have had democratic local and state governments.

29. Guillermo O'Donnell has presented the process of democratic consolidation as a struggle between forces that favor democracy and those that prefer authoritarianism, a struggle that is played out in part by these forces' seeking to capture the support of the larger segments of the body

politic that are indifferent, or neutral, as to the existence of one or another regime. See his "Notes for the Study of Democratic Consolidation in Contemporary Latin America," as well as his contribution to this volume, where this theme is presented briefly. While benefitting from this insight, the analysis here presents this confrontation as one that is about preserving or eliminating the formal and informal procedures that are incompatible with democracy. In these confrontations, actors who are basically democratic do not always take positions — given short-run calculations — that advance consolidation, nor do those who are pro-authoritarian consistently advocate institutional arrangements that detract from it. This represents a shift in focus which is, nonetheless, consistent with much of O'Donnell's analysis.

30. One of the most dramatic examples of a confrontation that had a consolidating effect was the failed coup of 23 February 1981 in Spain. It was the most serious event involving the military, elements of which had previously remonstrated against the civilian government authorities. The defeat of the uprising through the active intervention of the King, in whose support the conspirators mistakenly had placed their hopes, became the death knell of this nondemocratic option to constitute the Spanish government. Not all cases are so dramatic or so successful. The defeat of several military insurrections in Alfonsín's Argentina did not have the effect of eliminating the notion that military coups are an option in the future. Rendering the mechanics of military coups inoperable may take years of constantly reasserting civilian supremacy over the military, and repeated unsuccessful coups may, given the specific context, keep this option alive rather than show its ineffectiveness.

In the use of the notion of a "concatenation of critical events" I am repeating my analysis in *Democratización vía reforma,* pp. 132–133.

31. See Scott Mainwaring's contribution to this volume. He refers explicitly to "most recent transitions in Latin America" as examples that do not fit.

32. Guillermo O'Donnell, "Notas para el estudio del proceso de democratización política a partir del estado burocrático autoritario," *Desarrollo Económico,* 22, no. 86 (July–September 1982).

33. There is no space in this paper to explain the paradoxical combination of a first transition through reform in which the main helmsman of the authoritarian regime is opposed to democratization. It has to do with the fact that the Pinochet regime made the 1980 Constitution a centerpiece of its political legacy, but the democratic opposition was able to defeat Pinochet following its procedures. The latter could then not abandon the legal apparatus he had created, but chose to bind it with additional strictures diminishing the authority of the democratic government.

34. Arturo Valenzuela and I first used the notion of "inverse legitima-

tion" to point to the deliberate attempts by the then new military government in Chile to validate its rule by referring to the failures of the previous government and the democratic past in general; in J. Samuel Valenzuela and Arturo Valenzuela, "A Regime in the Making? Post-Coup Politics in Chile," paper presented at the World Congress of Sociology, Toronto, 19–24 August 1974, at a Political Sociology Research Committee session chaired by Juan Linz, p. 43.

Juan Linz's "minimal definition of legitimacy" incorporates the notion of comparisons: "a legitimate government is one considered to be the least evil of the forms of government" in Juan Linz, *The Breakdown of Democratic Regimes: Crisis, Breakdown, and Reequilibration* (Baltimore: Johns Hopkins University Press, 1978), p. 18.

35. See O'Donnell's chapter in this volume.

36. From this perspective, the widespread perception of economic and political failure of Communist regimes in Central and Eastern Europe is an important advantage for democratic elites. Similarly, for Spanish political elites and public opinion the successful model of democracy and development in the European Economic Community served as powerful proof that both were possible at the same time, and that the Franco regime stood in the way of an integration into Europe.

37. O'Donnell, "Notes for the Study of Democratic Consolidation in Latin America," p. 9.

38. Such was the case in Latin America, especially in Chile and Uruguay.

39. In Chile and Uruguay this has been done quite consciously by the main political elites of the democratic transition, and constitutes a hopeful sign for democratic consolidation. Spain also furnishes a good example of this purposive avoidance of associations with problematic elements from the past.

40. Paradoxically, the inability of the various elites to come to agreements over the form the regime should take and over which should be the national colors permitted, by default, the inception of the Third Republic. See Jean-Marie Mayeur, *Les débuts de la IIIe République, 1871–1898* (Paris: Editions du Seuil, 1973), chapter 1.

41. Linz, *The Breakdown of Democratic Regimes,* p. 18.

42. Efficacy refers to the ability of the government to articulate policies and goals that will resolve national problems, while effectiveness refers to the capacity to actually implement such policies and goals. High marks on both counts are important in enhancing, as Linz notes, the legitimacy of democratic institutions. Linz, *The Breakdown of Democratic Regimes,* pp. 16–23.

43. Juan Linz and Alfred Stepan, "Political Crafting of Democratic Consolidation or Destruction," note that the Spanish consolidation oc-

curred despite coinciding with economic difficulties; see especially pp. 43, 46.

44. Linz, *The Breakdown of Democratic Regimes,* p. 22.

45. Giovanni Sartori, *The Theory of Democracy Revisited. Part One: The Contemporary Debate* (Chatham, N.J.: Chatham House, 1987), pp. 90–91.

46. Juan Linz, *The Breakdown of Democratic Regimes,* pp. 27–38.

47. Sartori, p. 240. This in fact occurs in most democracies, not only in consociational ones, as Dahl shows in his discussion of Lijphart's model of consociationalism. See Robert Dahl, *Democracy and its Critics* (New Haven: Yale University Press, 1989) pp. 156–162.

48. See O'Donnell's contribution to this volume.

49. See footnote 1 above.

50. Guillermo O'Donnell and Philippe Schmitter, "Tentative Conclusions," pp. 48–56.

51. For a discussion of labor movements in the context of the first transition to democracy see J. Samuel Valenzuela, "Labor Movements in Transitions to Democracy: A Framework for Analysis, *Comparative Politics* 21, no. 4 (July 1989).

52. José María Maravall, *Dictatorship and Political Dissent* (London: Tavistock, 1978), p. 166, notes this point in his discussion of the connection between the parties of the Spanish Left and the worker and student movements. It is elaborated and illustrated with the Chilean case in Arturo Valenzuela and J. Samuel Valenzuela, "Party Oppositions under the Chilean Authoritarian Regime" in J. Samuel Valenzuela and Arturo Valenzuela, eds., *Military Rule in Chile: Dictatorship and Oppositions* (Baltimore: Johns Hopkins University Press, 1986), especially pp. 213–219.

53. O'Donnell and Schmitter, pp. 26–27.

54. The capacity to call off collective actions is a key component of labor movement formation. See J. Samuel Valenzuela, "Uno schema teorico per l'analisi della formazione del movimento operaio" in *Stato e Mercato* 1, no. 3 (December 1981), p. 467. Such a notion can be extended to other organizations that engage in collective action.

55. One of the social settlements that always needs to be addressed in democratic transitions is that of labor-management relations. Authoritarian regimes invariably interfere with the industrial relations system given labor's potential to become a locus of opposition organizing. The transition does not permit the survival of the authoritarian regime's labor containment schemes, and a new settlement must be reached. Forging it will prove easiest and most conducive to democratic consolidation when both labor and employer organizations can rapidly develop (if they do not already have them) broadly accepted leaderships, and when these leaders are able to devise the new procedures by mutual consent with a minimum of state interference.

Other conflicts and demands can vary widely across national societies. In some, the existence of peripheral or regional identities or nationalisms can be a vexing problem that surfaces strongly with the lifting of the authoritarian regime's repression. The creation of the Spanish *autonomías,* which for some regions such as Castilla and León meant the development of somewhat artificial units, can be seen in retrospect to have been an excellent way to settle the centrifugal regionalisms of that divided national society. The settlements must be tailor-made to the specificities of each situation. In the Soviet Union, which may not be a viable unit under a democratic system, the Spanish solution of limited sovereignty would probably only accelerate national disintegration. In other transitions one of the most difficult issues can result from demands for redress of the authoritarian regime's human rights violations. This problem has particularly acute consequences in situations where the forces associated with the authoritarian regime retain powerful positions in the new democratic context.

56. This is one of the points elaborated in Alfred Stepan, *The Military in Politics: Changing Patterns in Brazil* (Princeton: Princeton University Press, 1971). For other sources that develop this notion see Felipe Agüero's contribution to this volume, note 1. It should be noted that such appearance of support for a military coup has nothing to do with majority opinions in the population as expressed in elections or in reliable surveys. It pertains more to a certain "climate of opinion" generated by newspaper editorials and public comments by political and other elites.

57. For a discussion of the Argentine military in the aftermath of the transition see Andrés Fontana, "La política militar del gobierno constitucional argentino" in Nun and Portantiero, eds., *Ensayos sobre la transición democrática en la Argentina.* In Fontana's estimation, the changes did not "destroy completely (although they did affect) the institutional bases of military autonomy and corporative consciousness" (p. 382).

58. The relationship between the military and the Spanish transition is discussed in Felipe Agüero, "Gobierno y Fuerzas Armadas en la España posfranquista," unpublished paper, August 1989.

59. Although General Ramalho Eanes was not particularly pleased with the diminution of presidential power in the 1982 reforms, he supported the abolition of the Council of the Revolution and other features that assured the subordination of the military to the elected government. For a general discussion of these matters see Walter C. Opello, Jr., *Portugal's Political Development: A Comparative Approach* (Boulder, Colorado: Westview, 1985), p. 74 and chapter 7. For a general treatment of the Portuguese transition see Thomas C. Bruneau, *Politics and Nationhood: Post-Revolutionary Portugal* (New York: Praeger, 1984).

60. Alfred Stepan, *Rethinking Military Politics: Brazil and the Southern Cone* (Princeton: Princeton University Press, 1988), p. 141.

61. See Genaro Arriagada Herrera, *El pensamiento político de los*

militares: estudios sobre Chile, Argentina, Brazil y Uruguay (Santiago: Centro de Investigaciones Socioeconómicas, 1984).

62. In addition to Genaro Arriagada's discussion of this process, see Alfred Stepan, "The New Professionalism of Internal Warfare and Military Role Expansion" in Alfred Stepan, ed., *Authoritarian Brazil: Origins, Policies, and Future* (New Haven: Yale University Press, 1973).

63. See Stepan, *Rethinking Military Politics,* p. 132, where he cites what J. Samuel Fitch calls "democratic professionalism" as one such form that is compatible with the democratic process.

The Games of Transition

Adam Przeworski

1. Introduction

The strategic problem of transition is how to get to democracy without either being starved by those who control productive resources or killed by those who have arms. As this very formulation suggests, the path to democracy is mined. And the final destination depends on the path. In most countries where democracy has been consolidated, it turned out to be economically quite conservative, and for this very reason fragile. And in some countries, transitions seem to have gotten stuck.

The central question concerning transitions is whether they lead to self-sustaining democracy, that is, a system in which the politically relevant forces (1) subject their values and interests to the uncertain interplay of democratic institutions and (2) comply with outcomes of the democratic process. Self-sustaining democracy is established when most conflicts are processed through democratic institutions, when nobody can control the outcomes of the political process ex post, the results are not predetermined ex ante, they matter within some predictable limits and they evoke compliance of the relevant political forces.[1] In less abstract terms, a transition to democracy is complete when: (1) there is a real possibility of partisan alternation in office, (2) reversible policy changes can result from alternation in office, and (3) effective civilian control has been established over the military.[2]

Note that a breakdown of an authoritarian regime may be reversed, as it was in Czechoslovakia in 1968, in Brazil in 1974, or in Poland in 1981, or it may lead to a new dictatorship, as in Iran. And even if the outcome is not the old or a new dictatorship, the transitions can get stuck somewhere along the way, in noncompeti-

105

tive regimes that limit contestation or suffer from an organized threat of military intervention. Finally, note that even if democracy is established, it need not be self-sustaining: democratic institutions may systematically generate outcomes that cause some politically important forces to opt for authoritarianism.[3] Hence, self-sustaining democracy is only one among the possible outcomes of breakdowns of authoritarian regimes.

If democracy is to be consolidated, four problems must be resolved along the way: (1) An institutional framework for contestation, to use Dahl's (1971) term, must be constructed. (2) A competitive representative regime must be established. (3) Economic conflicts must be channelled into the democratic institutions. (4) The military must be tucked under civilian control. These problems are discussed in turn, preceded by a prologue—the breakdown of the authoritarian regimes—and followed by brief conclusions.

First, however, a brief note on the method. The approach I utilize entails a particular image of transitions to democracy. They are a process, the states of which consist of strategic situations which I will also call "conjunctures." Each strategic situation is characterized by the presence of particular political forces endowed with interests which involve different mixtures of conflict and coordination, by conditions which have been generated by earlier actions and by conditions that are exogenous. Change from one conjuncture to another occurs as an outcome of actions pursued by the actors.[4] One can thus think of the entire process in terms of a logical tree, in which the knots are the particular conjunctures and branches represent the possibilities inherent in each conjuncture. Transitions are not simply games in extensive form because one of the characteristics of this process is that the players need not be the same in successive conjunctures: they tend to be reconstituted as the result of the game itself. Nevertheless, several concepts of the game-theoretic apparatus can be applied to the analysis of this process.

To ask how and where transitions can go and where they can end is to inquire about the equilibria of this process: conjunctures such that once entered into will not be departed from unless some exogenous conditions change. Such equilibria provide the answer to our question. Yet we need to distinguish them further: some equilibria are stable once and only once the process has entered them, while other states tend to attract the process. Thus, we can distinguish three types of conjunctures: (1) those that cannot last, including democracies that are self-destructive, (2) "traps" or locally stable equilibria, and (3) "attractors," to which the process tends and where it remains, once having reached them.

This approach generates hypotheses of a comparative nature: hypotheses which specify the consequences of conflicts among actors endowed with particular interests and values as a function of the conditions independent of their will. These hypotheses should be tested by recourse to comparative evidence. And as the events in Eastern Europe unfold, we are for the first time on the verge of having enough cases to test them systematically, perhaps even statistically. Yet I only suggest, not test, such hypotheses here.

2. Liberalization

A common feature of all dictatorships, whatever mix of inducements and constraints they utilize, is that they cannot and do not tolerate independent organizations.[5] The reason is the following: as long as no collective alternatives are available, individual attitudes toward the regime matter little for its stability.[6] Even Weber (1968, I:214) observed that "people may submit from individual weakness and helplessness because there is no acceptable alternative." What is threatening to authoritarian regimes is not the breakdown of legitimacy but the organization of counter-hegemony: collective projects for an alternative future.[7] Only when collective alternatives are available, political choice becomes available to isolated individuals.[8] This is why authoritarian regimes abhor independent organizations: they either incorporate them under centralized control or repress them by force.[9] This is why they are so afraid of words, even if these words convey what everyone knows anyway, for it is the fact of uttering them, not their content, that has the mobilizing potential.[10]

How does it happen then that at some moment a group within the authoritarian power establishment decides to tolerate autonomous organization of the civil society? The Spanish regime stopped at one time repressing the *Comisiones Obreras;* Pinochet allowed the reemergence of political parties; Jaruzelski passed in July 1986 an amnesty law for political activities that did not include a recidivism clause, thus signalling a de facto legalization of the opposition; Krenz accepted the existence of the embryonic Neues Forum. Such moments signal fissures within the authoritarian power bloc and they indicate to the civil society that at least some forms of autonomous organization would not be repressed. They mark the onset of "liberalization."[11]

Explanations of such decisions fall into two categories: "from above" and "from below." To some extent these explanations reflect real differences. Hungary, for example, is generally viewed as an almost pure case of divisions within the authoritarian power bloc. In the words of Karoly Grosz, "the party was shuttered not by her opponents but — paradoxically — by the leadership."[12] East Germany represents the other extreme: there were no indications of a split within the power bloc until hundreds of thousands of people occupied the streets of Leipzig. Yet a striking aspect of the case study literature is that often different causes are cited to explain the same events: with regard to Brazil, for example, Cardoso (1979) saw the *distensão* as a result of a long-standing division within the military, while Lamounier (1979) as a consequence of popular mobilization. Indeed, the "top-down" and the "bottom-up" models often compete to explain liberalization.

The reason for these analytical difficulties is that the model that simply distinguishes the two directions is too crude. Short of a real revolution — a mass uprising which leads to the disintegration of all the apparatuses of repression[13] — decisions to liberalize combine elements from above and from below. For even in those cases where divisions within the authoritarian regime became visible well before any popular mobilization, the question is why did the regime crack at a particular moment. And a part of the answer always is that the Liberalizers within the regime saw the possibility of an alliance with some forces that up to then remained unorganized. Conversely, in the cases in which mass mobilization antedated visible splits within the regime, the question remains as to why the Liberalizers decided not to repress it by force. Those in power are in power because they control guns: why would they be no longer willing or able to use them in order to repress the attempts at organization? Liberalization is a result of an interaction between splits within the authoritarian regime and autonomous organization of the civil society. Popular mobilization signals to the potential Liberalizers the possibility of an alliance that could change the relations of forces within the power bloc to their advantage; visible splits within the power bloc indicate to the civil society that political space may have been opened for autonomous organization. Hence, popular mobilization and splits within the regime feed on each other.

Whether visible splits or popular mobilization occur first, the logic of liberalization is the same. What is different is its pace. Popular mobilization dictates the rhythm of transformations since it propels the regime to decide whether to repress, coopt, or devolve power. Yet whether liberalization lasts years, months or days, the regime and the opposition face the same sequence of choices.

Projects of liberalization launched by forces within the authoritarian power establishment are invariably intended as controlled openings of the political space. They typically result from divisions within the authoritarian bloc sparked by various signals which portend an imminent crisis of some sorts, including signs of popular unrest. The project of Liberalizers is to relax social tension and to strengthen their position within the power bloc by broadening the social base of the regime: to allow some autonomous organization of the civil society and to incorporate the new groups into the authoritarian institutions. In the light of this project, liberalization is to be continually contingent on the compatibility of its outcomes with the interests or values of the authoritarian bloc. Thus liberalizations are referred to as "opening" (*abertura*), "decompression" (*distensão*), "renewal" (*odnowa*), or "reconstruction" (*perestroika,* "remodeling," as of a house). All these are terms with strong connotations of limits to reform.

Yet liberalization is inherently unstable. What normally happens is what Ilya Ehrenburg called in 1954 *The Thaw* (*ottepel*): a melting of the iceberg of civil society which overflows the dams of the authoritarian regime. Once repression declines, for whatever reasons, the first reaction is an outburst of autonomous organizations within the civil society. Student associations, unions, and proto-parties are formed almost overnight. In Brazil, lawyers, journalists and students organized first, followed by the *comunidades de base*. In Poland, 10 million people joined Solidarność within a few weeks in September 1980. Even organizations founded and controlled by the regime declared themselves independent: not only the professional associations but even the Tourism and Sightseeing Society and the Stamp Collectors' Association. The situation is still more controlled in the Soviet Union, where many new groups try to become "official" by attaching themselves to pre-existing organizations, but even there, after five years of *perestroika* as many as sixty thousand autonomous groups, clubs, associations, circles and federations explore the limits of the political space.[14]

As these organizations form, they declare themselves independent of the regime; they proclaim their goals, interests and projects. Yet the regime has centralized, noncompetitive institutions which incorporate only those groups which accept centralized direction and which control the outcomes of any political process ex post. Thus, on the one hand, autonomous organizations emerge within the civil society while, on the other hand, there are no institutions where these organizations could present their views and negotiate their interests. Because of this *décalage* between the autonomous organization of the civil society and the closed character of state institutions, the only place where the newly organized groups can eventually struggle for their values and interests are the streets. Inevitably, the struggle assumes a mass character and spills onto the streets.[15]

Once that happens, liberalization can no longer continue. The tear gas that shrouds the streets and stings the eyes of Liberalizers, the eruption of mass movements, the unrest and disorder, constitute the evidence that the policy of liberalization has failed. Since liberalization is always intended as a process controlled from the above, the emergence of autonomous movements constitutes the proof that liberalization is not, or at least no longer, a viable project. Street demonstrations are the proof that the most sacrosanct of authoritarian values, "order" itself, has been violated.[16] Mass eruptions undermine the position of Liberalizers within the authoritarian bloc.

In China, student demonstrations forced the Liberalizers to beat a retreat in 1987 and cost them the leadership of the Party. Repression increased again. In South Korea, however, similar demonstrations led to a break within the regime and transformed Liberalizers into democratizers. These are indeed the alternatives: either to incorporate the few groups that can be incorporated and to repress everyone else, returning to the authoritarian stasis, or to open the political agenda to the problem of institutions, that is, of democracy.[17] Liberalizations are either reversed, leading to grim periods euphemistically termed "normalization,"[18] or they continue on to democratization.

The perplexing fact is that so many authoritarian politicians believe that they will succeed where others have failed and they go on to fail. The Brazilian case is classical: as Smith (1987:207) observed, "The difference between liberalization and democratization was clear for Golbery: if implemented properly, careful doses of liberalization could substitute for genuine democratization, thereby maintaining the political exclusion of subaltern groups and preempting meaningful demands for real reform of the economic model."[19] In Poland, the Jaruzelski regime came as close as one can to squaring the circle: the strategy was to create democratic institutions, such as the Administrative Court, the Constitutional Tribunal, self-management councils and independent unions, the Consultative Council to the Government, and an Office of the Ombudsman . . . and to retain power.[20] Even in those cases in which liberalization occurred only under the intense pressure of mass demonstrations, in East Germany and Czechoslovakia, the first project of the liberalizing leadership was to suck the dissent into the authoritarian system: Krenz encouraged "the people" to share their grievances with the Party and promised the "authorities" would listen; Vladyslav Adamec handpicked some non-communists for his first cabinet, and both had hoped that the mobilization would be diffused by these measures. Yet they all erred in their expectations and they were all eventually forced to accept democratization. Why?

Examine the situation from the point of view of proto-Liberalizers, at the moment when the choice of opening the regime appears on the horizon. The proto-Liberalizers can maintain their present position within the power bloc and then the result is status quo, denoted in Figure 1 as SDIC (status quo dictatorship). Or they can decide to issue signals that they are willing to tolerate some autonomous organization outside the power bloc: to "open." If the organized forces within the civil society decide to "enter" into the new organizational forms created by the regime, typically some "Front of National Unity," and no further autonomous mobilization occurs, the result is BDIC (broadened dictatorship): the liberalization strategy is successful. If the civil society continues to organize autonomously, Liberalizers face the choice of going back to the fold and agreeing to repress popular mobilization or of continuing onto TRANSITION to democracy. Repression, however, may be ineffective: if it succeeds, the outcome is NDIC (narrower dictatorship) in which the Liberalizers find themselves at the mercy of the executors of repression; if it fails, the outcome is an INSURRECTION. Assume that Liberalizers attach the probability r to successful repression.

Note immediately that the process of liberalization can be launched only if some groups within the authoritarian regime prefer broader dictatorship to the status quo. Liberalizers prefer BDIC

Figure 1

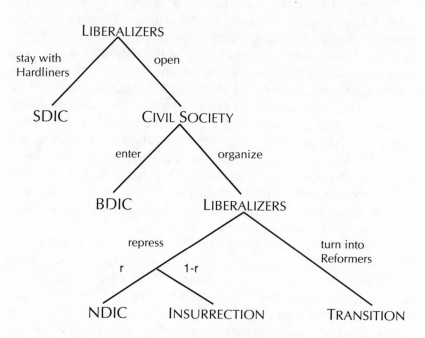

to SDIC because broadening the social base strengthens the regime as a whole and because the groups which enter the regime constitute natural allies for Liberalizers vis-à-vis Hardliners. INSURRECTION is the worst outcome for everyone within the regime.

Now, if everyone knows everything and everyone knows the same, then the only possible outcomes of this game are either the status-quo or broadened dictatorship: liberalization occurs only when it will be successful. Suppose that the preferences of Liberalizers are BDIC > SDIC > TRANSITION > NDIC > INSURRECTION. Then Liberalizers will know that if the society organizes, they will have to turn into Reformers. So does the civil society. Hence, if Liberalizers open, society organizes. But Liberalizers prefer SDIC to TRANSITION. Hence, they never open. In turn, suppose that the preferences of Liberalizers are BDIC > SDIC > NDIC > TRANSITION >

INSURRECTION and that Liberalizers attach a high probability to the success of repression. Then Liberalizers know that they will choose repression if society organizes. So does the civil society. Since for the society BDIC > NDIC, civil society enters knowing that Liberalizers would opt for repression if they organize. And since for Liberalizers BDIC > SDIC, they open. The outcome is thus BDIC.

How then can the process ever arrive at TRANSITION? I see two possible explanations, both relying on mistaken assumptions by someone.

(1) Suppose Liberalizers are in fact proto-democratizers, that is, their preferences are BDIC > TRANSITION > SDIC > NDIC > INSURRECTION.[21] Yet Liberalizers have to reveal their preferences strategically, given that Hardliners within the regime would never accede to liberalization if they knew that Liberalizers are prepared to go all the way. Hence Liberalizers announce that they prefer BDIC > SDIC > NDIC > TRANSITION and Hardliners believe them.

Now suppose that the decision to open depends on the consent of Hardliners: if Liberalizers propose to open, Hardliners decide whether to agree, in which case the rest of the game ensues, or not to permit the opening, in which case the outcome is status quo. Now, assume that (1) Hardliners prefer NDIC to SDIC and that (2) Hardliners believe that the society mistakenly believes that Liberalizers are in fact proto-democratizers. Then Hardliners analyze the situation as follows: If they agree to open, the society, believing that Liberalizers will not opt for repression, will organize. Yet Liberalizers prefer the outcome expected as a consequence of repression. Hence, Hardliners think the result of opening will be NDIC. They agree to open. But given the true preferences of the Liberalizers, the outcome is TRANSITION.

This explanation assumes that Liberalizers know all along what they are doing and deliberately mislead Hardliners while sending correct signals to the society. It is difficult to evaluate the plausibility of this story, precisely because under this scenario Liberalizers are forced to reveal their preferences strategically. Hence, we have to decide whether Liberalizers are sincere when they claim that they want only to invigorate the regime by broadening its base.[22] Given their public statements, either they are very good liars or this is not a plausible story.

(2) Suppose that the preferences of Liberalizers are BDIC > SDIC > NDIC > TRANSITION > INSURRECTION and their prior es-

timate of successful repression is high, which implies that the outcome will be BDIC. Hardliners play no role in this story: perhaps
the regime is not divided or the Liberalizers control arms. Liberalizers open, expecting the society to enter. But the society has a lower
estimate of successful repression and believes that Liberalizers have
the same estimate. Hence, society organizes. Once Liberalizers observe that the society continues to organize, they downgrade their
estimate of successful repression, to the point that they prefer TRAN-
SITION to the outcome expected under repression. Hence, civil society organizes and Liberalizers update their beliefs about the effectiveness of repression as they watch the streets.

These assumptions seem plausible. As the 82-year-old head of
the East German security apparatus, Erich Mielke, is alleged to have
said to Honecker, "Erich, we can't beat up hundreds of thousands
of people": a statement I interpret as a technical, not a moral, ad-
monition (*New York Times,* 19 November 1989, p. 15). If popular
mobilization increases in spite of beatings and jailings, the regime
revises downward its beliefs about the effectiveness of shooting. Moreover, at one moment the stakes become enormous: not enlisting in
the repression is an act of treason, for which a Romanian general
was forced to commit "suicide" as Ceausescu's last act in power,[23]
but joining repression that failed landed Prague's Party Secretary
in jail just a couple of weeks later. Under such conditions, jumping
sides seems as good a way to save one's skin as shooting.[24]

These two explanations assume that preferences are fixed and
that actors are rational, even if ill informed. But two more explanations are plausible.

One is sociological. As the organization of the civil society
crystallizes, its leadership becomes known and personal contacts
become established, the Liberalizers learn that the opposition is not
as threatening as they had thought. Here is General Jaruzelski, in-
terviewed already as the elected President, by Adam Michnik, now
the editor-in-chief of the pro-Solidarity daily newspaper, on the eighth
anniversary of the repression of 1981: "Gradually our view of the
world was changing. Today we see it differently. But we had to arrive there, we had to bump our head. All of us had to. In any case,
why look far? For several years you passed in my eyes, and not only
mine, as a particularly demonical personage."[25] Negotiations show
that the opposition is willing to listen and to make concessions; personal contacts bring rapprochement among individuals. Gradually,

transition appears as less of a chasm and repression seems simply uncivilized. Liberalizers change their preferences endogenously, as a result of bargaining with the opposition.

The second one is psychological. Liberalizers may not be rational. Rational actors form their beliefs based on the information they receive and act upon their desires given these beliefs. Indeed, if they are truly rational, they use beliefs to temper desires. Irrational actors let their desires affect their beliefs and screen out undesirable information. Suppose that the regime has no choice but to open. Foreign pressure, "economic and political strangulation," may leave no choice but to liberalize: Nicaragua is a clear case here. Popular mobilization may be uncontainable, as it was in Poland. Under such conditions, the Liberalizers are likely to persuade themselves that the opening will be successful, even that they will win competitive elections if they proceed all the way to democracy.

If any of these hypotheses is true, the spectacle of Liberalizers who venture into an infeasible project and turn coats in mid-course becomes intelligible: either Liberalizers were in fact ready to proceed to democracy to begin with but they had to hide their true intentions, or they discovered in mid-course that repression is unlikely to succeed, or they found that they do not have as much to lose as they had thought at the beginning, or they had no choice and were just putting on a good face.

But liberalization does not always lead to transition, as the tragic events in Tiananmen Square have reminded us. When will the outcome of liberalization be repression and a narrower dictatorship in which Liberalizers are eliminated? We already know that this outcome is not possible if everyone knows everything and they know the same. Suppose that (1) Liberalizers want only to broaden the regime, (2) Liberalizers believe that the society knows that they prefer BDIC to TRANSITION and that they are ready to repress if need be, and (3) the society mistakenly believes that Liberalizers are in fact democratizers or that they would not opt for repression because they believe it to be ineffective. Then Liberalizers open, expecting the society to enter; the society believes that if it continues to organize, Liberalizers will opt for transition, but Liberalizers opt for repression.

Hence, liberalization — an opening that results in the broadening of the social base of the regime without changing its structure — is not a feasible project unless everyone has full and accurate knowledge about everybody else's preferences and the probability of successful repression. Some misperceptions lead liberalization to transition, others to repression. Yet whatever its outcome, liberalization is not a feasible project. The perennial tragedy of liberalizers was described already by Marx in 1851: they want democracy that would keep them in power and they are stung when it turns against them. They try to hold on as long as they can, but at one point they must decide whether to go backward to authoritarian restoration or forward to democratic emancipation.

3. Democratization

3.1 Introduction

The problem that thrusts itself at this moment to the center of the political agenda is whether any institutions that would allow an open-ended, even if limited, contestation will be accepted by the relevant political forces. And as soon as these institutions are in place, the question arises whether they will evoke spontaneous compliance, that is, absorb the relevant political forces as participants willing to subject their interests to uncertain competition and to accept the outcomes.

The image that the campaign for democracy as a struggle of "the society" against "the state" is a useful fiction during the first period of transition, as a unifying slogan of all forces opposed to the current authoritarian regime. But societies are divided in many ways and the very essence of democracy is the competition among political forces with conflicting interests. This situation creates a dilemma: to bring about democracy, antiauthoritarian forces must unite against authoritarianism, but to be victorious under democracy, they must compete with each other. Hence, the struggle for democracy always takes place on two fronts: against the authoritarian regime for democracy and against one's allies for the best place under democracy.

Thus, even if they may coincide temporally in some cases, it is useful to focus separately on the two different aspects of democratization: the "extrication" from the authoritarian regime and the "constitution" of a democratic one. The relative importance of the aspects of extrication and constitution depends on the place within the authoritarian regime of those political forces which control the apparatus of repression, most often the "armed forces."[26] Wherever the military remains a cohesive and autonomous actor, elements of extrication dominate the process of transition. Chile and Poland are the paradigmatic cases of extrication but the aspect of extrication also overshadowed transition in Spain, Brazil, Uruguay and South Korea. In contrast, wherever military cohesion disintegrated as a result of a failed foreign adventure — Greece, Portugal and Argentina — and in those regimes where the military were effectively subjected to civilian control — all the Eastern European countries except Poland — extrication and constitution were intertwined.

3.2 Extrication

Since extrication has been extensively studied, I proceed schematically. First, let me follow O'Donnell (1979) and O'Donnell and Schmitter (1986) in distinguishing four political actors: Hardliners and Reformers (who may or may not have been Liberalizers) within the authoritarian bloc and Moderates and Radicals within the opposition. Hardliners tend to be found among the repressive cores of the authoritarian bloc: police, the legal bureaucracy, censors, some journalists, etc. Reformers tend to be recruited among politicians of the regime and some groups outside the state apparatus: sectors of the bourgeoisie under capitalism, economic managers under socialism.[27] Moderates and Radicals need not represent different interests. Indeed, relations between interests and tactical positions tend to be fluid during transition.[28] They may be distinguished only by risk aversion. Moderates may be those who fear Hardliners, not necessarily those who have less radical goals, as evidenced by this statement of Santiago Carrillo, then the General Secretary of the Spanish Communist Party: "One should have the courage to explain to the working class that it is better to pay surplus value to this bourgeois sector than to create a situation that may turn against them" (Carrillo, 1974:187).

Extrication can result only from understandings between Reformers and Moderates. Extrication is possible only if (1) an agreement can be reached between Reformers and Moderates to establish institutions under which the social forces they represent would have a significant political presence, (2) Reformers can deliver the consent of Hardliners or neutralize them, and (3) Moderates can control Radicals.

The last two conditions are logically prior since they determine the set of possible solutions for Reformers and Moderates. Whatever agreement they reach, it must (1) induce Hardliners to go along with Reformers and (2) dissuade Radicals from mobilizing for more profound transformations. When can these conditions be satisfied?

The first condition depends obviously on the identity of the Hardliners. If the armed forces resist extrication, they must be cajoled into passivity by Reformers. Moderates must pay the price of this persuasion. Just consider the price extorted by Pinochet for his consent to free elections: (1) permanence of the current commanders-in-chief of the armed forces and the police, (2) protection of the prestige of members of the military and the police, (3) energetic struggle against terrorism, (4) respect for the opinions of the national security council to be formed by four military and four civilians, (5) maintenance of the amnesty covering political crimes committed between 1973 and 1978, (6) abstention by the political authorities from intervening in the definition and application of defense policies, including not modifying the powers of the military courts, the command structure, and military budget allocations and not interfering in the promotion of generals (normally a presidential prerogative), (7) the right to name nine members of the Senate, (8) autonomy of the Central Bank, the president of which is to be chosen by the military, and (9) acceptance of privatizations conducted during the last months of the military regime, without investigation into how they were conducted. If the armed forces themselves are the Reformers and the resistance comes from bureaucrats, the situation is simpler, even if at moments dramatic.[29] Yet note that in Poland, where the impetus for reforms came from the head of the Armed Forces, the Hardliners also succeeded in exacting a number of guarantees: (1) the Communist Party was guaranteed 35 percent of seats in the lower, and more important, house of the Parliament (*Sejm*) and its then allies were given another 30 percent (in principle, ample support to form a government); (2) the regime was given to understand that the opposition would not block the election of General Jaruzelski as President; and (3) matters of external defense and internal order were left under the control of Communists.

If Reformers are a viable interlocutor for the Moderates only when they can control or deliver the Hardliners, Moderates have no political importance unless they can restrain Radicals. Cravatted moderate gentlemen may lead civilized negotiations in government

palaces but if streets are filled with crowds or factories are occupied
by workers calling for the necks of their interlocutors, their moderation is irrelevant. As Reformers must negotiate a deal acceptable
to Hardliners, Moderates must deliver terms tolerable for Radicals.
And if they cannot obtain such terms from Reformers, their only
solution is to leave enough power in the hands of the apparatus of
repression to intimidate the Radicals. On the one hand, Moderates
need Radicals to be able to put the pressure on Reformers; on the
other hand, Moderates fear that Radicals will not consent to the
deal they work out with Reformers. No wonder the feasible set is
often empty.

When can an agreement that satisfies all these constraints be
reached? Reformers face a strategic choice of remaining within the
authoritarian alliance with Hardliners or of seeking a democratic
alliance with Moderates. Moderates, in turn, can seek an all-out destruction of the political forces organized under the authoritarian
regime by allying with Radicals or they can seek an accommodation by negotiating with Reformers. Suppose the structure of the
situation is as follows:[30]

Figure 2

		MODERATES ally with	
		RADICALS	REFORMERS
	HARDLINERS	Authoritarian regime survives in old form: 2,1	Authoritarian regime holds with concessions: 4,2
REFORMERS ally with	MODERATES	Democracy without guarantees: 1,4	Democracy with guarantees: 3,3

Under such conditions Reformers have a dominant strategy,
namely, to ally always with Hardliners. If Moderates ally with Radicals, the opposition is defeated and the authoritarian bloc survives
intact, which is better than democracy brought about by a coalition

of Moderates and Radicals which offers no guarantees for Reformers. If Moderates seek an alliance with Reformers, some concessions are made at the cost of Hardliners. These concessions are better for Reformers than democracy even with guarantees. Hence, potential Reformers are always better off defending the authoritarian regime in alliance with the Hardliners.

The defining feature of this situation is that Reformers have no political strength of their own and thus no prospects to be politically successful under democracy. Without special guarantees they would do very badly under democracy and even with guarantees they are still better off under the protection of their authoritarian allies. This was the case of Poland in 1981.[31] The reformist sectors within the Party were a viable interlocutor for the opposition only because they relied on the repressive apparats of the state. No competitive institutions could compensate for the lack of political support for the Communist (Polish United Workers) Party, which in clandestine polls was getting 3 to 5 percent of the eventual vote. Under such conditions, Reformers cannot venture into a democratic alliance with Moderates.

Suppose that Reformers do have sufficient political strength to be able to compete under democratic conditions if they are given institutional guarantees. Is this sufficient for them to opt for democracy? Consider the following situation:

Figure 3

| | **MODERATES** ally with | |
	RADICALS	REFORMERS
HARDLINERS	Authoritarian regime survives in old form: 2,1	Authoritarian regime holds with concessions: 3,2
REFORMERS ally with **MODERATES**	Democracy without guarantees: 1,4	Democracy with guarantees: 4,3

Here Reformers have political weight independently of Hardliners: they can actually get some support under competitive conditions and they prefer democracy with guarantees over all other alternatives. Yet the outcome for Reformers depends on the actions of
Moderates: if Moderates opt for guarantees, Reformers are better
off under democracy but if Moderates ally with Radicals, Reformers lose. And Moderates prefer democracy without guarantees. Examine this structure of conflict in extensive form, that is, assume
that Reformers decide first what to do, anticipating the reaction of
Moderates:

Figure 4

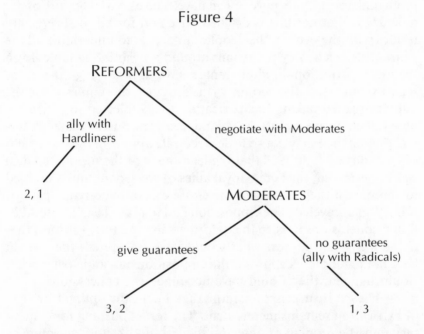

Reformers analyze the situation as follows: if they ally with Hardliners, the result will be the status quo, which is the second best outcome. They would be better off under democracy with guarantees.
But if they decide to negotiate with Moderates, the latter will opt
for an alliance with Radicals, resulting in the worst outcome for Reformers. Hence, Reformers stay within the regime.

When is then a negotiated extrication possible? If everyone analyzes the situation correctly, either of two conditions is sufficient:
(1) the Moderates prefer a democracy which protects the interests
of some forces allied with the authoritarian regime over one that

promotes interests of Radicals, or (2) the Reformers are the ones who control the armed forces. If Reformers have some political strength of their own and if Moderates prefer an institutional arrangement in which the forces associated with the authoritarian regime remain as a counter-balance to the demands of Radicals, then Reformers have nothing to fear from democracy.[32] Alternatively, even if Moderates prefer a more radical form of democracy, Reformers need not fear extrication as long as they control the apparatus of repression.

Clearly, this entire analysis assumes more knowledge than the protagonists normally have or can have. The essential feature of democracy is that nothing is decided once and for all: if sovereignty resides with the people, the people can decide to undermine all the guarantees reached by politicians around a negotiating table. Even the most institutionalized guarantees give at best a high degree of security but never the certainty. In Uruguay, the amnesty for the military passed during the extrication was subjected to a referendum (albeit unsuccessful). In Poland, everyone miscalculated at several points: the Party got so little electoral support in the first round of elections of June 1989 that the legitimacy of the negotiated deal was undermined, the hereto loyal allies of the Communists decided to venture on their own, and the entire carefully designed plan of transition unraveled. The Opposition had to make last minute additional concessions to keep the Reformers in the game. I suspect that if the Party had known what would have transpired, they would have not agreed to elections; if the Opposition had anticipated what would happen, they would have not made the concessions.[33]

Yet even if surprises are more than likely, the optimal strategy of extrication remains inconsistent. The forces pushing for democracy must be prudent ex ante and they would like to be resolute ex post. But the decisions made ex ante create conditions that are difficult to reverse ex post, since they preserve the power of the forces associated with the *ancien régime*. Ex post the democratic forces regret their prudence but ex ante they have no choice but to be prudent.[34]

3.3 Constitution

All transitions to democracy are negotiated: some with representatives of the old regime and some only among the prodemocratic forces seeking to form the new system. Negotiations are not always needed to extricate the society from the authoritarian regime but they are necessary to constitute democratic institutions.

The groups seeking to establish democratic institutions confront two generic problems: substance versus procedure and agreement versus competition. To what extent should social and economic outcomes be left open-ended and to what measure should some of them be guaranteed and protected regardless of the outcomes of the competitive interplay? Among recent experiences, the Spanish Constitution of 1977 came nearest to a classical liberal constitution that specifies only the rules of the game and says almost nothing about outcomes (except private property), while the Brazilian Constitution of 1988 went to the other extreme, listing detailed social and economic rights.[35] Which decisions should be made by agreement and which should be subject to competition? Must some institutions, such as constitutional tribunals, armed forces or heads of state, stand as arbiters above the competitive process or should they all be subject to periodic electoral verdicts? To what extent and by what means should the society bind itself to prevent some future transformations?[36] These are the issues inherent in establishing democratic institutions.

But there is one additional aspect to consider. Following O'Donnell (1987) we need to make a distinction between democratization of government and of regime. The first process concerns institutions; the second the relations between state institutions and the civil society.

Since a concept of representation underlies the argument that follows, let me summarize how I see a representative regime. A representative system is one in which: (1) there exist autonomous organizations; (2) they are stratified internally into leaders and followers; (3) leaders have the capacity to (a) invoke collective identities, (b) control the strategic behavior of followers and (c) sanction defections; (4) leaders are representatives, that is, they participate in representative institutions; and (5) representation makes a difference for the well-being of their followers.[37] To participate is to act as if strategies chosen from a particular set of institutionally defined alternatives mattered for the realization of interests. Autonomous organizations participate if and only if outcomes of conflicts processed within the representative institutions do depend on the strategies of participants and the differences among outcomes significantly affect the well-being of their constituents. On the one hand, if participation does offer opportunities for improving the well-being of their followers, all independent organizations must participate or vanish. On the other hand, if participation has no consequences then autonomous organizations turn against the regime.[38]

Each of the forces struggling against authoritarianism must also consider its future position under democracy. They must all stand united against dictatorship but they must divide against each other.[39] If they divide too early, the outcome is likely to repeat the experience of South Korea, where the rivalry between two anti-authoritarian presidential candidates — rivalry which is personal but also regional and economic — permitted electoral victory of the candidate associated with the dictatorship. If they do not divide at all, the new regime will be a mirror image of the old one: not representative, not competitive. This is the danger facing Eastern Europe: that the revolution will end being only anti-communist, not democratic.[40]

One solution to this dilemma is political pacts: agreements among leaders of political parties (or proto-parties) to (1) divide government offices among themselves independently of election results, (2) fix basic policy orientations, and (3) exclude (and if need be repress) outsiders.[41] Such pacts have a long tradition of what used to be called *trasformismo* in Italy, Spain and Uruguay. The Venezuelan 1958 pact of Punto Fijo is the model of such agreements. According to this pact, three parties would divide government posts, pursuing policies committed to developmentalist goals under private property and excluding Communists from the political system. This pact has been highly successful in organizing democratic alternations in office, even if it cost Venezuela the largest guerilla movement in Latin America.

Note that partners to such pacts extract private benefits from democracy and that they protect their rents by excluding outsiders from competition. Democracy turns out to be a private project of leaders of some political parties and corporatist associations, an oligopoly in which leaders of some organizations collude to prevent outsiders from entering.

The same dilemma appears in a modified form after democratic institutions are in place. The classical problem of any opposition under democracy is how much to oppose and by what means. If the opposition does not oppose, does not present alternatives and does not struggle energetically for these alternatives, then the representative power of political institutions, their capacity to mobilize and to incorporate, is weak. Democracy is anemic. But if the opposition does oppose vigorously, democracy may be threatened. Particularly under difficult economic conditions, intransigent opposition may create an ungovernable situation. If every time a party loses an election or every time a government adopts an unpopular policy, the opposition launches a general strike, it may weaken democratic institutions and create conditions for the military to intervene.

Perhaps the clearest place to observe this dilemma was within the Peronist movement in Argentina. The *Renovadores* wanted to become an electoral party and to reduce tactics to electoral and parliamentary struggles, while the orthodox wing wanted to remain a "movement" and to struggle for "social justice" by all means. Thus Ubaldini did not think that losing elections should prevent the CGT from general strikes while Peronist deputies in the Congress absented themselves whenever they thought they would lose, thus undermining the quorum.

Again, one way out of the dilemma, is a *pacto político*. The ostensible purpose of such pacts is to protect embryonic democratic institutions by reducing the level of conflict over policies and personnel. While institutional pacts establish the rules of the game and leave the rest to competition, these are substantive pacts, intended to remove major policy issues from the competitive process.[42] Such pacts are offered as necessary to protect the democratic institutions from pressures to which they cannot respond, but the danger is that they become cartels of incumbents against contenders: cartels that restrict competition, bar access, and distribute benefits of political power among the insiders. While entrepreneurial profits may be an inevitable private reward to those who undertake the democratic project, the role of democratic competition is to dissipate such profits rather than to turn them into permanent rents.

The fear of divisions is motivated not only by the specter of authoritarian restoration. It is inherent in democracy, as evidenced in the perpetual ambiguity of democratic theory. Both Rousseau and Madison feared interests, passions, and the "factions" to which they give rise; both saw democracy as a mechanism to reach an agreement, to discover the common good. Differences of opinion, conflicts of interest, procedural wrangling are often seen as obstacles to rationality. Yet conflicts of values and of interests are inherent in all societies. Democracy is needed precisely because we cannot agree. Democracy is a system of processing conflicts without killing one another: it is a system in which there are differences, conflicts, winners and losers. Conflicts are absent only in authoritarian systems: no country in which a party wins 60 percent of the vote twice is a democracy.

3.4 Conclusion

Whether democracy results from negotiated extrication or only negotiated constitution, democratic institutions must either protect or suppress the basic interests of all the political forces that are capable of subverting democracy. They must either open sufficient opportunities for promoting group specific interests to incite all major social forces into participation or they must close access and repress extra-institutional manners of political struggle.

Whenever extrication is negotiated, guarantees must be given to forces associated with the *ancien régime*. Negotiated extrications are possible only if some sectors within the dictatorship expect to have a significant political presence under democratic conditions but even under such conditions democratic compromise may require additional institutional guarantees for these sectors.

But even when extrication results from a distintegration of the repressive apparats, the democratic institutions resulting from negotiated constitution must be conservatizing: institutions that emerge from transitions are designed in such a way as to minimize the responsiveness of policy to movements of public opinion. They include separations of powers, double chambers, strong constitutionalism, protection of minorities, and even substantive norms, for example, the commitment to private property in the Spanish Constitution of 1977.

Conflicting political forces agree to a particular institutional system if this system protects their interests and values better than the available alternatives. And only institutional systems which make radical economic and social changes difficult protect conflicting interests and values.

4. Institutionalization of Economic Conflicts

Democracy opens to individuals the possibility to organize, and to the already existing parties, unions, and other associations, an arena to struggle for the improvement of material conditions.

Democratic institutions offer those who are poor, oppressed, or otherwise miserable as a consequence of their economic situation an opportunity to find redress via collective action, directed at employers or the state. Hence the advent of democracy is accompanied by an explosion of expectations: for most people democratization promises not only political rights but also social transformations.

Yet if democracy is to be consolidated, distributive conflicts must be institutionalized: all major political forces must channel their economic demands through the democratic institutions and abjure other tactics. Regardless how pressing their needs may be, politically relevant groups must be willing to subject their interests to the interplay of democratic institutions. They must be willing to accept defeats and to wait, confident that the democratic institutions would continue to offer opportunities the next time around. They must adopt the institutional calendar as the temporal horizon for their actions: they must think in terms of forthcoming elections, contract negotiations or at least fiscal years.[43] They must assume the stance put forth by John McGurk, the Chairman of the British Labour Party, in 1919: "We are either constitutionalists or we are not constitutionalists. If we are constitutionalists, if we believe in the efficacy of the political weapon (and we do, or why do we have a Labour Party?) then it is both unwise and undemocratic because we fail to get a majority at the polls to turn around and demand that we should substitute industrial action" (quoted in Miliband, 1975:69).

Democratic institutions can evoke such self-restraint only if the outcomes of the democratic process remain within two limits: on the one hand, some groups do improve their material situation as a result of their participation in the democratic competition, either in terms of policy outputs or by acquiring new rights, and, on the other hand, the gains in immediate consumption do not threaten investment which, whether it remains in private or public, national or foreign hands, is guided by criteria of profitability. Needless to say, these are narrow limits.

The unprecedented proportions of the economic crisis facing a number of countries raise fears that this crisis will undermine the nascent democracies and bring back the repression. Perhaps the most dramatic scenario has been painted by Flisfisch (1985:25): "(i) under democratic conditions, there is a tendency on the part of all actors to use strategies of social pressure; (ii) under conditions of acute stagnation, the generalized use of strategies of social pressure reinforces and prolongs the stagnation; (iii) when it is sufficiently long, a situation of acute stagnation generates destabilizing political effects; (iv) the most likely result is an initiation of a new cycle of militarization, possibly with even more repression than previously." Note that this conclusion is based on two assumptions: that democracy unleashes economic conflicts and that the effect of a prolonged economic crisis is to destabilize the democratic institutions and to cause a new cycle of military dictatorships.[44]

I think that we do not know whether in general democracy inhibits economic development, promotes it, or is irrelevant one way or the other. The statistical evidence, whatever it is worth, is mixed.[45] The already developed democracies tend to have growth rates higher than many, although not all, less developed dictatorships. Moreover, the experience of the developed countries shows that democracies which have strong unions and left-wing governments exhibit, on the one hand, low strike rates, slower wage growth, lower labor share of value added, and, on the other hand, higher investment, more rapid economic growth, more welfare spending and a more equal distribution of income. In the developed countries, strong unions and political parties representing the poorer segments of the population are willing to moderate their pressures for immediate consumption in order to induce firms to invest and employ. They are willing to offer wage restraint because they expect that firms will invest in exchange and because they feel sufficiently strong politically to be confident that they will share in the benefits of growth.[46] Hence, with strong unions and left-wing parties, democracy need not cause uncontrollable distributional pressures.

Yet several conditions which restrain the pressures for immediate consumption on the part of unionized wage earners and capitalists in the developed democracies appear absent in the less developed countries. One reason may be that the pressures for immediate consumption are caused by absolute deprivation: people who are starving cannot wait. Another hypothesis, which I find more persuasive,[47] is that the unequal distribution of income provides much greater opportunities for redistribution. Just within the manufacturing sector, the differences in the share of net income consumed by capitalists are enormous: in 1985 this share ranged from about 10 percent in Austria and Norway to well under 40 percent in Greece, Spain and the United States to 62 percent in Brazil and 69 percent in Argentina.[48] In Brazil, the top quintile of households gets 67 percent of income, in Turkey 57 percent, Venezuela 54 percent, Argentina 50 percent, the United States and Spain 40 percent, in Belgium 36 percent.[49] Hence, there is much to gain in the short run by pressing for redistribution, even if the rates of investment are already low and would fall even more under redistributive pressures. Finally, the third hypothesis is that the uncertainty characteristic of many less developed countries makes any sacrifices of present consumption too risky to be rational. Here again the evidence is dramatic: the fluctuations of exchange rates, interest rates, inflation rates and the purchasing power of households are often staggering.

The new democratic regimes face these pressures for immediate consumption under an exceptionally unfavorable international economic conjuncture, often under the burden of debt and with economic systems ridden with inefficiencies inherited from the authoritarian era. They must cope with powerful inflationary pressures as they seek to reform the economic system. The determinants and the remedies are the same in many countries, South and East. States are financially on the verge of bankruptcy, public bureaucracies are overgrown, financial markets do not exist, firms are overprotected. States have been weak in the South and the East: they are vulnerable to predatory pressures from large firms, public or private, incapable to collect taxes, ineffective in evoking compliance with rules. No wonder the remedy is the same: it is no accident that a title in a Polish newspaper read "Menem like Balcerowicz."[50]

While sharing the direction of economic reforms, the new democratic governments seem to have been pursuing two contrasting political strategies to control economic conflicts, relying alternatively on decrees or on concertation and sometimes vacillating between *decretismo* and *pactismo*. As a former Argentine Vice-Minister of the Economy observed, requirements of participation conflict with requirements of competence.[51]

In Argentina and Brazil, where the inflationary pressures have been strong, governments resorted to repeated shocks, freezing wages and prices and adopting or at least announcing a series of accompanying measures. From the political point of view this is a strategy of control from above: the shocks were ideas of technicians, by their very nature they had to be adopted without consultations and announced by surprise. This policy could have been successful only if it did not involve broad participation. At the same time, the shocks were only a stop-gap measure: longer-term success of this policy required using the interim period to introduce structural reforms. But these reforms — a reduction of public spending and an, at least selective, opening of the economy — have intolerable political costs and cannot be imposed without broad consultations. Hence, this strategy is internally contradictory in political terms: it combines measures which can be successful only without external consultation with other measures that require broad consent.

The contrasting strategy is to involve unions and employers' associations in economic policy making.[52] The "social pacts" that result from concertation typically consist of an exchange of wage restraint on the part of the unions for some welfare programs as well as for economic policies that control inflation and encourage investment and employment. Both in Venezuela and in Spain the first of such pacts established the rudiments of the industrial relations system while subsequent accords, with varying degrees of success, attempted to regulate specific wage and employment targets.[53] Yet there are several reasons why such pacts seem unlikely to succeed in most new democracies:

(1) "Social pacts" are always exclusive: Schmitter (1984:365) correctly incorporates this feature into their very definition. Unionized workers represent only a part of the popular sectors in Latin America (Grossi and dos Santos, 1983:143). "Can the union movement, based in the sphere of production," Lechner (1985:30) asks rhetorically, "represent popular movements, founded in the context of reproduction?"

(2) Unions will participate in such pacts only if they are strong: encompassing, centralized and influential politically. Otherwise, they have no reasons to expect that they would benefit in the future from the present underutilization of their power. Yet, while employers may be favorably disposed to make immediate concessions, they fear strong unions and fight against extending to unions the rights that might be used against them in the future.

(3) The state may not conform to the terms of a pact both because under democracy any government must be concerned with interests broader than those of unions and employers and because members of the state apparatus, politicians and bureaucrats, have interests of their own. Hence, the terms of pacts between unions and employers often come in conflict with the economic policy preferred and actually followed by the government.

(4) Even if unions in the private sector may be willing to participate in a pact, public sector unions have no incentives to do so. In the for-profit sector, unions trade wage restraint for employment and investment but neither the employment nor investment in public services depends on the wage rates of their employees. Hence, public sector unions face neither the stick of unemployment nor the carrot of investment. In turn, social pacts involving the for-profit sector normally include commitments to reduce public spending, a threat to the public sector unions.

These obstacles seem so overwhelming that the strategy of concertation does not seem either feasible nor effective in regulating distributional conflicts. Yet the idea of resolving conflicts by an agreement is so tempting that the issue of social pacts never quite disappears from the political agenda of the new democracies.

If this analysis is correct, neither the reliance on decrees nor on pacts offers an effective strategy for dealing with economic conflicts. As a result, many governments vacillate between these two extremes: they promise concertation and shock the eventual partners with decrees. In the end, the state ends up being perceived both by employers and by unions as the principal source of economic instability.[54]

5. Imposition of Civilian Control over the Military

Except for Poland, the Communist systems of Eastern Europe constituted civilian regimes.[55] The military and most of the forces of order were subject to minute political control, which extended even to operational matters.[56] Hence, it should not be surprising that in the conflicts over the leading role of the Communist Parties the armed forces in all Eastern European countries placed themselves squarely on the side of those who wanted to abolish the communist monopoly of power. "The army wants to serve not a party but the nation": this has been the paradigmatic declaration of generals. Yet from a Latin American perspective, this noble sentiment sounds ominous: not as a pledge to democratic values but as an assertion of independence.

In Latin America, the military have preserved their autonomy and have continued to exercise tutelage over the political system: not only in those countries where transition to democracy was a result of negotiations but even in Argentina, where they suffered a humiliating external defeat. The specter of military intervention is a permanent constraint on the political process and the eventual re-action by the military is a consideration that permeates everyday political life in such new democracies. Among the recent transitions to democracy, Spain and Greece are the only countries where democratic governments succeeded in establishing effective civilian control over the military and freed themselves from this tutelage.

Why would not democratic governments seek to impose civilian control over the military? Why would they tolerate military autonomy, the prospects of intervention, and often public humiliations?[57] The Argentine experience is particularly poignant, since the impunity enjoyed by kidnappers, torturers and murderers has a profound demoralizing effect on the nation's political life.

One obvious answer is that democratic governments fear that any attempt to impose civilian control would immediately provoke exactly that which it is intended to eliminate in the future: military intervention. The strategic calculus involved in this decision must be the following. First, the probability of an immediate coup in case of an attempt to establish civilian control must be seen as higher than when the military is left alone. Hence, even if once established civilian control would greatly reduce the likelihood of military intervention, the probability that the coup would ever occur is lower without civilian control. Consider the following table:

Table 1

**Probability that a
coup would occur**

	immediately	eventually but not now
With tutelage	0.20	0.60
With civilian control	0.80	0.01

Under such conditions, the probability that the military would step in now or in the future if they continue to exercise tutelage over the political system is 68 percent while the probability that they would make a coup if the government seeks to impose civilian control is 80.2 percent.[58]

This is not the end of the difficulty, since not all coups are the same. One argument for punishing violations of human rights is that the effect of such punishment would be dissuasive: military officers would think twice before stepping in again because they would know that once out of power, they would be punished. That may be true but if this argument is valid then it also implies that if the military is not deterred from stepping in by the threat of punishment then it will be less likely to ever give up power because of this threat. Thus imposition of civilian control may lower the probability of a coup but it may increase the conditional probability that once it occurs, the coup will be highly repressive, a *golpe duro*.

Thus if a government is intent on not provoking a coup and not risking repression, it may swallow its moral outrage and its democratic ideals and accept the limits set by the military tutelage.[59] But I suspect that this reasoning is not sufficient to explain the behavior of civilian politicians with regard to the military. There are two reasons why democratic politicians may not want to dismantle the threat from the military even if they could.

First, Fontana (1984:121) observed that in 1981 the Argentine political parties feared that if the threat from the military is removed, a new wave of popular mobilization would push them, like in 1973, farther to the left than they would wish to go and could cost political leaders their jobs. To paraphrase an expression Ernest Bevin once used with regard to the Labour Party, they "did not want to be put in position of having to listen to their own people." If the military can be counted on to repress popular mobilizations, then their tutelage is a bulwark for established political parties. Military tutelage is necessary to protect the regime from demands for greater representativeness.[60]

Secondly, the problem in many countries with long traditions of military intervention is the absence of institutional structures and even of models for institutions through which the civilian control over the military could be exercised.[61] Through their chain of command, the military are responsible directly to the president, rather than to parliamentary committees and civilian bureaus that would supervise the particular aspects of their conduct. Without such an apparatus of civilian control, the choice faced by democratic governments may be one of either tolerating military autonomy or destroying the military altogether.[62] And here, I suspect, nationalism plays a role: no president can afford to commit himself or herself to actions that would undermine the "defensive capacity of the nation." Perhaps when the choice of strategy vis-à-vis the military appears as one of leaving it intact or dismantling it altogether, the perpetuation of military domination turns out to be a lesser evil for nationalistic politicians.

The issue about the civilian control over the military is not only whether it is prudent to attempt it but also who wants to have it.[63]

8. Conclusions

An institutional framework that permits social and economic transformations, a regime that is competitive and representative, and the military tucked under civilian control: these are the essential conditions for democracy to be self-sustaining. Yet nothing guarantees that these conditions will be established in the process of transition: many transitions get stuck somewhere along the way.

By the first criterion, probably all democracies are incomplete: while there is some evidence that partisan control does have consequences for economic performance, including unemployment, inflation, investment and income distribution, the range of economic and social transformations resulting from the democratic process seems quite narrow. And there are good reasons to think that the binding constraints are institutional, not economic. Democratic institutions are likely to be economically and socially conservatizing: this is simply the price which democrats must pay.

Yet transitions can be arrested even earlier, as a result of collusion among politicians to keep important issues out of the competitive process or as a consequence of military tutelage. Consider the possible cases:

(1) Some countries, Spain and Greece specifically, have arrived at competitive regimes with civilian control over the military. They have thus completed the transition.

(2) Some countries, such as Argentina and the Philippines, have competitive regimes but do not control the military. This combination is an unstable one. The competitive political process allows organization of forces and articulation of viewpoints that are intolerable to the military or some groups thereof. Moreover, the potential of a military intervention affects the behavior of political forces within the competitive process since it opens the possibility of blackmailing others with praetorian strategies (Huntington, 1968) such as "if you do not moderate your demands, we will ask the military

to intervene" or "if you do not concede to our demands, we will create a disorder which will provoke the military to intervene." Competitive political processes in the presence of autonomous military creates a permanent possibility of military intervention.

(3) In some cases, notably in post-1958 Venezuela and in the mid-1980s in Brazil, politicians collude, fearing that a more competitive political process would turn against them. Such arrangements can be quite stable, even if they are vulnerable to pressure from the sectors excluded from effective political participation as well as from the military who enforce them.

The general answer to the question motivating this paper, therefore, is twofold. Economic and social conservatism of the new democratic institutions is not just a result of the constraints under which negotiated extrications occur. Democracy is a compromise, a second best for all the political forces that are capable of subverting it, and for this very reason it must protect to some minimal degree each of the multiple and conflicting interests. Moreover, transitions can get arrested along the way to democracy, in regimes that combine collusive pacts among politicians with military tutelage. Otherwise, either when the regime is competitive but the military conserve their capacity to intervene or when politicians collude but their pacts are not protected by a threat of repression, the situation continues to be volatile.[64]

What does this analysis suggest about the future course of events in Eastern Europe? I see two implications: (1) political developments will not be different than in those countries where the transition to democracy is already more advanced, and (2) economic transformations will stop far short of their current blueprints.

This text is written in January 1990, as Eastern Europe is still in turmoil. Thus far only in Poland has a partial transfer of power occurred as a verdict of the polls; in other countries governments are run by caretakers, awaiting elections under the watchful eye of the streets. Institutions that organize contestation and participation remain to be built; regimes representing divergent interests and values are yet to emerge. Thus far, the revolution in Eastern Europe has been only anticommunist; not yet democratic. And the danger is that this change will get stuck in non-contestatory, non-representative political cartels among politicians who led the antiauthoritarian transformations, implicit or explicit political pacts among the current incumbents.

When the anticommunist euphoria fades away and conflicts of interests become politically organized, politics in Eastern — I should now say "Central" — Europe will assume a form characteristic of poor capitalism. There are no reasons to believe that conditions in Bulgaria, Hungary or Poland should be different from those of Argentina, Chile or Brazil. States are weak as organizations, economies are overprotected and dominated by monopolistic firms, public bureaucracies are overgrown, welfare services are fragmentary and rudimentary,[65] agriculture is inefficient, political parties and other associations are weak. And such conditions breed governments vulnerable to political and economic pressures from large firms, populist movements of doubtful commitment to democratic institutions, armed forces that menacingly wait on the sidelines, church hierarchies torn between authoritarianism and a commitment to social justice, nationalistic sentiments susceptible to xenophobia.

Some conditions do work in favor of Central European countries: they have much less income inequality,[66] a stronger working class, a legacy of egalitarian and welfarist value systems.[67] Moreover, the geographical accident that Central Europe is in Europe will generate pressures to adhere to democratic institutions. Yet the factors that work in favor of democracy will also work against economic reforms, already in progress in Hungary, Poland and Yugoslavia and envisioned in other countries. These reforms promise to be not only radical — no less than a transition from socialism to capitalism — but also exceptionally painful. In 1990, per capita consumption is expected to decline by at least 20 percent in Hungary and Poland, there will be a drastic shift in relative incomes in the direction of inequality and massive unemployment. And the experience of other countries shows that such reforms are difficult to accomplish under democratic conditions. They mobilize the resistance of those who have most to lose: managers of protected or subsidized firms, workers who face unemployment and masses of people who fear the reduction of expenditures on income maintenance and welfare. As a result, anti-inflationary shocks are politically easier to administer than structural reforms. For better or worse, democracy has a conservatizing effect on economic systems: structural reforms grind rather than glide under democratic conditions.

Obviously, this is not to say that the future of all these countries will be identical: conditions only structure conflicts, they do not make choices. But the structure of choices is the same.

NOTES

This is a revision of a paper presented at the Conference on "A Transição Pactada. Os Casos do Brasil e da Espanha," University of São Paulo, October 17–24, 1987, and at the Conference on Internationalization of Political Democracy, Université de Montréal, September 28 to October 2, 1988. In addition to participants in these meetings, I learned from comments by Christopher Achen and Luiz Carlos Bresser Pereira. Several ideas developed below resulted from discussions with Norbert Lechner, Guillermo O'Donnell, Philippe Schmitter, Jerzy J. Wiatr, and Francisco Weffort, as well as with my students.

1. For an elaboration of the theory of democracy which underlies this formulation, see Przeworski, 1984, 1985, chapter 5 and forthcoming, chapter 1.

2. I realize that this statement is in many ways heroic. First, no government in the world completely controls the various apparats: the CIAs, KGBs, DSGEs, and the Ms somehow always succeed in pulling tricks that surprise their civilian supervisors. Secondly, it would have been easier to say that a country has reached democracy when an alternation in office has in fact occurred but then we would have to exclude Italy. Thirdly, to assess whether government policies depend on results of elections we need to know what is possible; not an easy problem.

Note that instead of framing the question the way we did, one could explore definitions instead. What is democracy? Perhaps there are just different types of democracy and the relevant question is why the process of transition arrives at one type and not another. The classical distinctions are between the "Westminster" and the consociational democracies (Lijphart, 1975), between systems relying on corporatist versus parliamentary representation (Schmitter, 1974) and between presidential and parliamentary institutions (recently Linz, 1985). Yet I believe that the combination of participation and contestation (Dahl, 1971) is a necessary and sufficient feature of any system identifiable as a democracy, regardless of the particular institutional arrangements.

3. Even if we are speaking about the transition from authoritarianism to democracy we need not think that these end states constitute equilibria themselves, that is, that once established, they continue until and unless some conditions change that are independent of anyone's will. In O'Donnell's (1978) analysis of Argentina democracy and authoritarianism are inherently unstable and they succeed each other cyclically. Hence, democracy need not be self-sustaining.

4. I am thus adopting a "micro" approach, in which actors have choices and their choices matter. Following the seminal book by Moore (1964), there developed an enormous literature in "macro-historical com-

parative sociology," in which the method is to associate inductively out-comes, such as democracy or fascism, with conditions, such as agrarian class structure. In this formulation the outcome is uniquely determined by conditions and history goes on without anyone ever doing anything. While I believe that some conditions given exogenously do importantly constrain actions, I find this approach largely irrelevant, not only because of its empiricism but mainly because of its political impotence.

5. Obviously, not all dictatorships are the same. According to a Soviet scholar (Migranyan, 1988:31), totalitarian regimes require individuals to participate actively in supporting the regime, while authoritarian regimes strike an implicit deal: "the regime reveals its willingness not to meddle in the internal life of those individuals who do not take a public stand against the authority and its official dogmas."

Moreover, some regimes tolerate no autonomous organizations of any kind: even the Animal Protection Society is organized from above and is a part of the Association of Associations, which is a part of the Front of National Unity, run out of the Ministry of Order. Other dictatorships are more selective: they ban unions and parties but they tolerate stamp collectors' societies, churches, or some producers' associations. But no dictatorship permits autonomous organization of political forces.

6. This is why explanations of regime breakdown in terms of legitimacy are either tautological or false. If by "legitimacy" we understand the appearance of collectively organized alternatives, they are tautological since the fact that these alternatives are collectively organized means that the regime has broken down. If we see "legitimacy" in terms of individual attitudes, in Lamounier's (1979:13) terms, as "acquiescence motivated by subjective agreement with given norms and values," they are false. Some authoritarian regimes have been illegitimate since their inception and they have been around for forty years.

Note that the contribution of survey studies to the understanding of regime transitions has been negligible. In Hungary in 1985, 88 percent of respondents declared confidence in the national leadership (57.3 percent "fully"), 81 percent in the parliament, 66 percent in the Party, 62 percent in trade unions (Bruszt, 1988) and yet the regime unravelled easier than in Poland, where various surveys conducted between 1981 and 1986 showed about 25 percent supporting the leadership, only about 12 percent "strongly" (Frentzel-Zagórska, 1988). Finally, note that in Spain surveys have shown that the same people who supported Franco tended to support democracy.

7. The Gramscian inspiration of these hypotheses is obvious, but Gramsci's framework, with its duality of coercion and consent, is not sufficiently specific institutionally to serve as a guide to the problem at hand. In particular, Gramsci failed to distinguish concessions given by someone

who controls the political system from realizations of interests achieved through an open–ended, even if limited, competition.

8. Demonstration effects play an important role in transitions to democracy. Here is a Brazilian joke, dating to the twilight of the dictatorship: In a crowded Rio bus, a man slaps the face of a military officer standing next to him. Another man does the same. From the back of the bus, a *mulatinho* pushes his way through and administers the third slap. The bus stops, surrounded by the police. The first man is asked: "Why did you hit the officer on the face?" "He offended the honor of my daughter, I had to react," is the answer. The second man is interrogated: "He offended the honor of my niece, I had to react," he joins. Finally, the question is directed to the *mulatinho*. "When I saw them hitting the officer, I thought the dictatorship fell," he explains.

As someone observed, the breakdown of the communist monopoly of power took ten years in Poland, ten months in Hungary, ten weeks in East Germany and ten days in Czechoslovakia. The events in Poland and Hungary demonstrated to East Germans the very possibility of this breakdown; the spectacle of the crumbling wall signalled to individual Czechs the feasibility of regime transformation.

A crucial factor in breaking individual isolation is the safety of numbers: Poles discovered the strength of the opposition when the visit of the Pope in June 1978 brought two million people to the street; in Bulgaria, the first autonomous demonstration on 17 November, 1989 grew out of one organized by the new government of Mladenov in his support; the same occurred in Romania when Ceausescu returned from Iran; in East Germany, the mass movement was released when trains carrying refugees were crossing from Czechoslovakia to West Germany.

9. A Soviet samizdat, *Chronicle-Express* (17 November 1987), made public a document of *Komsomol* entitled "To strengthen the work in the autonomous youth associations." This document observes that "the recent extension of democracy resulted in the appearance of a growing number of autonomous sociopolitical youth associations. . . . The range of their interests is extremely broad, from international information, ecology and protection of historical monuments, to a shameful speculation on not yet surpassed difficulties of the reconstruction." The document goes on to distinguish good and bad associations. In the case of the good ones, Komsomol organizations should extend their cooperation and should send their "best militants to play the role of *commissars.*" In the case of the less good ones, their leaders should be bribed or, textually, "should be offered in private concrete ways of realizing their capacities." Finally, the document goes on, if this strategy fails, the Komsomol should be prepared "to create its own alternative association."

10. A man is distributing leaflets at the Red Square. He is stopped

by a policeman, who notices that the leaflets are blank. "What is it? What
are you spreading? Nothing is written," the surprised guardian of order
exclaims. "Why bother?" the man responds. "Everyone knows."

11. I am using the terminology of O'Donnell (1979:8) according to
whom "liberalization consists of measures which, although entailing a significant opening of the previous bureaucratic authoritarian regime (such
as effective judicial guarantees of some individual rights or introduction
of parliamentary forms not based on free electoral competition), remain
short of what could be called political democracy."

12. Interview with Karoly Grosz, former First Secretary of the Hungarian (Socialist Workers') Communist Party, in *Przegląd Tygodniowy*,
No. 51 (403) Warsaw, 22 December 1989, p. 15.

13. Even Romania does not represent the case of a true revolution.
There seems to be much we still do not know about the background of
these tragic events but note that the Romanian army survived intact, with
its structure of command, the destruction of the Ceausescu regime.

14. According to a story by K. S. Karol in *Le Nouvel Observateur*
(No. 1200, Paris, 6 November 1987), the first autonomous group established in Gorbachev's Soviet Union may have been the "Spartakists," meaning obviously fans of the Moscow soccer club, Spartak. By 1987, there were
already 30,000 independent groups and they held a national congress. The
number in the text was cited after *Pravda,* 10 December 1989.

One does not know to what extent these estimates can be trusted,
but here are some numbers concerning Bulgaria: on 13 November 1989
the subtitle in the *New York Times* is "Bulgarians are passive," on 28 December the independent union, Podkrepa, is said by the *Times* to have 5,000
members, on 16 January 1990, the Paris *Libération* reports Podkrepa has
100,000 members.

15. The Brazilian experience does not contradict this general propo-
sition. It is true that in Brazil the struggle for democracy did not reach
the streets until the *diretas, já* campaign of 1984 but the reason, I think,
is that the *distensão* of 1974 was immediately transformed into electoral
competition: the institutional framework to channel opposition was available. The project of liberalization got into trouble anyway, because of the
unexpected electoral success of MDB.

Similarly, in the Soviet Union, liberalization did not lead to mass
demonstrations in the Russian part of the country, I think, for two reasons. First, popular mobilization was in fact encouraged by Gorbachev,
who attempted to develop a traditional Russian coalition of the tsar and
the people against the bureaucracy. (See explicit statements to this effect
in his *Perestroika*). Secondly, the Supreme Soviet was transformed overnight into a fairly contestatory institution, which witnesses sharp confrontations and passes laws with small majorities. Hence, the institutional

framework has been transformed de facto, to correspond to its status de jure.

16. Hence, according to the *New York Times,* 21 November 1989, Milos Jakes, the hardline First Secretary of the Czechoslovak Communist Party, accused the organizers of the demonstrations in Prague of "seeking to create chaos and anarchy." So did Honecker. All these reactions have been predicted by Marx in his writings on France between 1848 and 1851: the party which defends dictatorship is the Party of Order, for which democracy represents "chaos and anarchy."

17. The Polish events of 1955–1957 are a classical case of liberalization that ended up in normalization: after a period of autonomous organization, Workers' Councils were incorporated into the regime while the student movement was repressed. In Brazil, the failed liberalization attempt of 1974 was followed during 1975–1977 by a mixture of intensified repression and welfare measures. See Andrade (1980). For some reason, several Brazilian writers found it surprising that the liberalization project did not quite work the way it was intended and they went on to distinguish "the project" from "the process" (Diniz, 1986). They must not know Perez's third law of decompression: "Things always get out of hand."

18. These were best summarized by Milan Kundera: "A man is vomiting on the Venceslaus Square. A passerby approaches: 'Do not worry. I understand you,' he says." (I do not remember from which novel this story comes.)

19. A fascinating document outlining plans for liberalization is the speech given by General Golbery do Couto e Silva in 1980 (Golbery, 1981). Karoly Grosz summarized his earlier stance as follows: "My position was the following: let us move forward, with courage but also prudence, so that the nation would understand us and follow us. . . . I thought that a single party, having lost its two radical wings, will be able to overcome the difficulties." See the interview cited above.

20. A nice statement of this strategy is an article by Leszek Gontarski, entitled "Are we afraid of democracy?" ("Czy boimy sie demokracji?") *Życie Warszawy,* No. 291, Warsaw, 12–13 December 1987, p. 3.

21. Or perhaps even democratizers in sheep's skin, with TRANSITION > BDIC > SDIC > NDIC > INSURRECTION.

22. O'Donnell (1979:13) noted with regard to the liberalizations initiated by Lanusse (1971–1973) in Argentina and Geisel (1975–1979) in Brazil, that in each case they threatened that they would "be obliged" to stop the process if things go too far. But they were too committed to stop: a reversal of liberalization would be a victory of hardliners over the *blandos.*

23. From what we know thus far, it appears that the Minister of Defense, the Minister of Interior and the Chief of Secret Police did not comply with Ceausescu's initial order to arm their forces. When harangued

by Ceausescu during the last meeting of the Political Bureau, the last two made a sufficiently convincing show of obeisance and survived, only to try to jump sides a few days later. For the minutes of this meeting, see Jean-Paul Mari, "La dernière colère de Ceausescu," *Le Nouvel Observateur,* 11 January 1990, pp. 42–45.

24. See Przeworski (1986) for a more formal treatment of such situations.

A comment is needed here on the theory of collective action. The main weakness of Olson's (1971) view is his assumption of a "pre-strategic" status quo: in his theory individuals have a choice between doing nothing or acting to bring about a public good. But, as Sartre (1960) observed, there are situations in which the choice is only between acting for or acting against: when the royal troops were searching for arms in the houses along the street leading to the Bastille, the inhabitants who were hiding them had only the choice of either finding themselves in the Bastille or destroying it. Under these conditions, the "collective action problem" is not a prisoners' dilemma.

25. "Z generałem Jaruzelskim o stanie wojennym," *Gazeta* (Warsaw), 18 December 1989, pp. 5–6. General Kiszczak, in turn, remarked that "agents of the MSW [Ministry of Interior, i.e., police] were getting used gradually to the perspective of the coexistence with the opposition, of the inevitability of the Polish compromise. Had they not been prepared, today there might have been resistances and tensions." "Przewrót niewykonywalny," interview with General Czesław Kiszczak, *Gazeta* (Warsaw), 11 September 1989, p. 4.

26. These need not be monolithic. Note that in Eastern Europe, as a legacy of the Stalin era, there have been two organized forces of repression: the external defense armed forces, under the control of the Ministry of Defense, and the internal order army, under the control of the Ministry of Interior. The autonomy of secret police varied from country to country and period to period.

27. The attitudes of the bourgeoisie toward authoritarian regimes belie facile generalizations. In Brazil, they have been volatile and heterogeneous but it seems that by 1978 the leading sectors of the *paulista* bourgeoisie saw the military regime as a threat because of the growth of state sector. Thus, at least in Brazil the antiauthoritarian posture arose from economic liberalism. For interpretations of this posture see Bresser Pereira (1978) and Cardoso (1983). In Ecuador, in turn, it seems that the autonomy of the technobureaucrats, the "style" rather than the "substance" of economic policy making according to Conaghan (1985), turned the bourgeoisie against the military government.

28. Note that the fluid relation between interests and strategies does not of itself mean that class analysis is irrelevant to the understanding of

processes of transition. Strategies follow perceptions of success, not only interests, and these perceptions are exceedingly volatile at moments. See Przeworski (1986).

29. The program of political reforms proposed by General Jaruzelski at the Party plenum in January 1989 failed to win a majority. At this moment, the General (who was the Commander-in-Chief), the Minister of Defense, and the Minister of Interior, both also generals, offered their resignation and walked out of the meeting. Only then did the Central Committee deem desirable the turn toward negotiations with the opposition.

30. The first number in each cell represents the value of this outcome to Reformers, the second number to Moderates and 4 is better than 3, than 2, than 1. These numbers are not interpersonally comparable: they only rank the alternatives. Hence, Moderates may be miserable under their second worst option, while Reformers may be quite happy with theirs.

31. The Polish situation was analyzed in game theoretic terms by Stefan Nowak in *Polityka* (Warsaw), September 1981.

32. Just reverse the payoffs to Moderates under the two forms of democracy in Figure 4.

33. Party strategists cited all kinds of reasons why Solidarity would do badly in the elections of June 1989: an eminent reformer predicted that Party candidates would win a majority in the elections to the Senate! But the other side was equally surprised. When asked whether the political developments followed his plan, Walesa responded: "My project was different from what happened. With regard to politics, I wanted to stop at the conquests of the roundtable: make a pause and occupy ourselves with the economy and the society. But, by a stroke of bad luck, we won the elections." Interview in the *Figaro,* Paris, 26 September 1989, p. 4.

34. Since democracy has been consolidated in a number of countries, some North American intellectuals now advise that the protagonists in the struggles against authoritarianism should have been more radical in pushing for social and economic transformations. For a typical fantasy of this kind, see Cumings (1989).

35. On the tension between procedural and substantive aspects of constitutions see Casper (1989).

36. On this topic see essays in Jon Elster and Rune Slagstad, eds. (1988).

37. Note the following: (1) Organizations that participate in representative institutions must be stratified into leaders and followers—by definition, these institutions seat individuals, not masses. Sociology is thus not needed to explain why mass movements become "oligarchical" once they enter representative institutions: Luxemburg's analysis is more penetrating than Michels's. (2) Under many circumstances, whenever individual interests place individuals in competition with one another, leaders can-

not represent individual interests, only those interests that are collectively optimal but individually inferior. Hence, to prevent free riding, leaders must provide selective incentives or coerce followers. At the same time, it should be expected that followers will be normally dissatisfied with leaders: they do not represent individual interests.

38. This summary is based on Przeworski (1985), chapter 4.

39. Thus the pre-negotiations about the shape of the negotiating table are not just a squabble. The regime in place has good reasons to fear a two-sided division, since this arrangement unites the opposition. The Polish solution was to make the table "round": no sides. The Hungarian way was to make it triangular but octagonal solutions were entertained.

40. The situation in Eastern Europe is particularly complicated for the following reason. The natural division of interests and opinions runs along the Right-Left dimension, even if peasants may stand apart in some countries. The difficulty is that any new party of the Left would have to include some former communists but an alliance with them would be a kiss of death for any political party. In Poland, some Catholic groups within the anticommunist coalition are trying to force the Left into an alliance with reformed communists, precisely because they know the electoral consequences. See the editorial in *Tygodnik Solidarność* (Warsaw), 22 December 1989.

Note that in Brazil, it took five years before PMDB divided into its ideological currents. Established originally to provide window dressing for the authoritarian regime, the MDB was the only cover for a legal opposition activity and as such it became an umbrella for all kinds of political forces. Everyone was certain that this artificial creature would fall apart into its natural parts the day political parties could legally exist—and it briefly did when the right wing separated as the *Partido Popular.* Yet the separation did not last long, and in its new incarnation the PMDB turned into the largest party in the country, developed local machines, and continued to win elections until 1989.

41. Wiatr (1983) proposed a similar arrangement for Poland, under the name of "contractual democracy."

42. Impatient that the *Sejm* might be unable to process eleven important pieces of economic legislation in seven days, Walesa proposed that the government be given power to rule by decree, a suggestion supported by 53 percent of the population.

43. This notion of "institutional time" is due to Norbert Lechner (personal communication).

44. The notion that democracy intensifies class conflict is as old as the first modern democratic institutions. Macalay, Ricardo and Marx agreed that universal suffrage would be used by those who do not own property to expropriate the riches. In Marx's view, democracy inevitably "unchains

the class struggle." The poor threaten the rich and the rich abandon democracy, typically by "abdicating" political power to the permanently organized armed forces. For Marx, as well as for his contemporaries at the other end of the political spectrum, the combination of democracy with capitalism was thus an inherently unstable form of organization of society, "only the political form of revolution of bourgeois society and not its conservative form of life" (1934:18), "only a spasmodic, exceptional state of things . . . impossible as a normal form of society" (1971:198).

45. Adelman and Morris (1967:202), Huntington and Domínguez (1975:61), Marsh (1979:240) found that democracy inhibits economic growth and Weede (1983) discovered that this effect is particularly strong among the countries where the state spends above 20 percent of the GNP. Przeworski (1966) found that between 1949 and 1963 mobilizing dictatorships beginning at medium levels of development grew most rapidly, followed by the already developed democracies, followed by exclusive dictatorships and the least developed countries in general. Finally, Dick (1974) did not find any of these effects. Since I can find a major flaw in each of these studies, I do not think that the current statistical evidence should be taken as conclusive.

46. For the logic of this exchange see Przeworski (1988).

47. I am often struck that the widely shared intuition according to which pressures for immediate consumption are higher under bad economic conditions has no economic micro-foundations. For if it is true that the poor cannot wait, it is also true that they have more to gain by waiting.

48. I calculated these numbers using data on the share of wages and investment in net value added from the *World Bank Development Report,* diskette version. The share of consumption out of profits is calculated by assuming that wage earners get no income from capital in Argentina and Brazil and one half of it in Austria and Norway.

49. Data for all countries other than Belgium are from *Veja,* Rio de Janeiro, 1 November 1989, p. 39. For Belgium the data are from the World Bank, diskette version.

50. Balcerowicz was the economic tsar of the Mazowiecki government in Poland. *Gazeta* (Warsaw), 13 December 1989, p. 6.

51. Juan Carlos Torre, speaking at the symposium on the *Transição Política: Necessidade e Limites da Negociação,* São Paulo, June 1987 (Albuquerque and Durham, 1987).

52. In a personal communication, Bresser Pereira pointed out that these strategies need not contrast, citing the case of Israel. This is true, but in Israel the Hisdatrut owns half of the country and the shock package was assisted by two billion dollars from the United States. Poland may repeat the experience of Israel: the union movement is politically strong and a one billion dollar stabilization fund has been collected. At this mo-

ment, at least, the union says "We may not like the variant [of the economic plan] but we like the direction and we have full confidence in the government."

53. A useful descriptive comparison of the Venezuelan and the Spanish experience with social pacts is given by Córdova (1985). On Spain see García (1984), González (1985), Pérez-Díaz (1986). Venezuela, I think, is a case apart because of the rent income derived from oil. Karl (1987) and McCoy (1987) offer contrasting analyses of social pacts in Venezuela but in my view the first one exaggerates and the second one underrates the role of oil. The best analysis of social pacts in Latin America is in my view Lechner's (1985) article. For a review of Latin American experiences with concertation see dos Santos, editor (1987).

54. The second *Plano Bresser* was announced on the eve of a meeting that was designed to investigate the feasibility of a social pact at the personal instigation of President Sarney. For the complaints at the inconstancy of government policies see the presentations by both the representatives of employers' associations and union leaders during the São Paulo seminar on social pacts (Albuquerque and Durham, 1987).

55. Poland was different. The declaration of the state of war on 13 December 1981 was a coup d'état directed against the Communist Party. The coup made it evident that the communist system as we had known it broke down, since the Party was no longer capable of ruling on its own. The dictatorship that followed 1981 was a military regime and, as we have seen above, the pattern of extrication in Poland was typical of such regimes.

56. Secret police is a different matter: conflicts between secret police and communist parties punctuated much of the political life of communist regimes. Secret police is the group that had most to lose from the dismantling of Communism and it was the target of popular ire in several countries.

57. In October 1987, the Brazilian government raised military pay by more than one hundred percent overnight in reaction to a takeover of the local city hall by a small military unit stationed in a provincial town: all this after the Minister of Finance had publicly committed himself not to do it.

58. Let p be the probability of an immediate coup under tutelage and t the probability of an eventual coup in this case. Let q be the probability of an immediate coup if the government imposes civilian control and c the probability of an eventual coup. Then the total probability of a coup under tutelage is $p + (1-p)t$ and under attempted civilian control it is $q + (1-q)c$.

59. In an 1987 article, entitled "La política militar del gobierno constitucional argentino," Fontana stresses that in 1983 the government did not have a good picture of the situation within the armed forces, that it

believed erroneously that the military would purify itself if given a chance, and that it repeatedly underestimated the solidarity among military generations. All of this may be true, but what strikes me is that the article fails to demonstrate that the government had any military policy.

60. José Antonio Cheibub (personal communication) offered the following criticism of this hypothesis: "the explanation based on the elite's fear of popular mobilization is not good for two reasons. First, because leaders of countries that face a problem of civilian control over the military learned (or should have learned) that the protection the military offers (from one perspective) is also a threat (from another perspective). In other words, their job as politicians is also threatened by the very tutelage they want to maintain to protect them from popular mobilization. . . . Second, it seems to me that this explanation may be . . . transformed into an argument that assumes the political elite in those countries to be inherently, intrinsically conservative; that it always prefers the risk of a military coup to a greater representativeness of the regime."

61. This observation is due to José Murilo de Carvalho.

62. For example, Delich (1984:135) presents as follows the choice available to the Argentine democratic government: since the atrocities committed by the military constituted acts sanctioned by the military as an institution, under written orders and under control by the military command, the democratic government can only either condemn the totality of the Armed Forces or forget everything.

63. This is how in October 1987 José Murilo de Carvalho (1987:18) characterized the attitudes of the Brazilian political forces in the Constituent Assembly: "it is more difficult to visualize a surge of a solid political will to construct the hegemony of civil power. As we have seen, such a will certainly does not exist in the political action of the current occupant of the presidency of the Republic and it does not manifest itself in an unambivalent way in the majority party, the PMDB. It is not even necessary to say that there are no traces of such will in the PFL, the PTB, etc. Whoever observes the political scene in the New Republic has the impression that military tutelage is something normal and that it should continue to be exercised."

It should not be surprising, therefore, that the *Latin American Weekly Report* of 15 September 1988 (WR–88–36) could report, under the title "Brazil's military gain quietly what Pinochet demands loudly," that "As some Brazilian military men have readily admitted in private, whereas elsewhere civilians have worried how much autonomy they could or should grant the military, in Brazil the military have carefully dosed the autonomy of the civilians."

64. The main difficulty with these assertions comes from the United States, where electoral politics constitutes the most protected industry in

the country, where the representative power of political parties is minimal, and where no third party broke into the system during the twentieth century—all that in the face of relatively low levels of repression. One might be tempted to make sense of this anomaly by making the claim which some Brazilians (Andrade, 1981; Moisés, 1986) make with regard to their country, namely, that their civil society is "weak," which I take to mean, "unable to organize to push its way into the representative system." But civil society in the United States appears extremely strong, at least if we believe various measures of political participation other than voting.

65. This assertion may seem surprising given the widespread view that the Communist systems "at least" provided welfare services. But, first, the level of welfare services deteriorated rapidly since the early seventies. And, secondly, whatever there is left of the welfare system, it is being rapidly dismantled as the central command system disintegrates. Welfare services under central command economies were distributed in the same way as everything else: the planner distributed iron ore, shoes, potatoes, medical visits, places in schools and vacations. As markets replace central allocation, the welfare system must be built from scratch in a completely new form: as an insurance against bad chance in an autonomous and thus far unpredictable mechanism. And the state must be completely transformed to deliver welfare services: it must now collect revenues from those who do well in the market and distribute it according to needs.

66. Relative to Latin America, not necessarily to Western European or Far Eastern countries.

67. I hesitate to put much stake in the normative traditions since, at least in Poland, they seem to be rapidly eroding. In 1980, 70.6 percent of respondents accepted without reservations the principle of limiting highest incomes. In 1981 this proportion fell to 50.7, in 1984 to 29.6 and by 1988 it reached 27.5. Moreover, inter-group differences became profound: in 1981, 68.8 percent of specialists with higher education accepted this principle, against 71.6 percent of skilled workers. By 1988, only 37.0 percent of specialists supported limits on highest incomes against 63.0 percent of skilled and 70.0 percent of unskilled workers. Results concerning the norm of full employment show the same dynamic. See Kolarska-Bobińska (1989).

REFERENCES

Adelman, Irma, and Cynthia T. Morris. 1967. *Society, Politics, and Economic Development.* Baltimore: Johns Hopkins University Press.
Albuquerque, José Augusto C., and Eunice R. Durham, eds., 1987. *Tran-*

sição política: Necessidade e limites da negociação. São Paulo: Universidade de São Paulo.

Andrade, Regis de Castro. 1980. "Política social e normalização institucional no Brasil." In Luis Maira et al., *América Latina: Novas estratégias de dominação.* Petrópolis: Editora Vozes.

Bruszt, László. 1988. "'Without Us but For Us'? Political Orientation in Hungary in the Period of Late Paternalism." *Social Research* 55:43–77.

Cardoso, Fernando Henrique. 1983. "O papel dos empresarios no processo de transição: O caso brasileiro." *Dados* 26:9–27.

Carrillo, Santiago. 1974. *Demain l'Espagne.* Paris: Seuil.

Casper, Gerhard. 1989. "Changing Concepts of Constitutionalism: 18th to 20th Century." Manuscript, University of Chicago.

Conaghan, Catherine. 1983. "Industrialists and the Reformist Interregnum: Dominant Class Political Behavior and Ideology in Ecuador, 1972–1979." Ph.D. dissertation, Yale University.

Córdova, Efren. 1985. *Pactos sociais: Experiência internacional, tipologia e modelos.* São Paulo: IBRART.

Crain, W. Mark. 1977. "On the Structure and Stability of Political Markets." *Journal of Political Economy* 85:829–842.

Cumings, Bruce. 1989. "The Abortive Abertura: South Korea in the Light of Latin American Experience." *New Left Review* 173:5–33.

Dahl, Robert E. 1971. *Polyarchy.* New Haven: Yale University Press.

Delich, Francisco. 1984. "Estado, sociedad y Fuerzas Armadas en la transición argentina." In Augusto Varas, ed., *Transición a la democracia.* Santiago: Associación Chilena de Investigaciones para la Paz.

Dick, William G. 1974. "Authoritarian versus Nonauthoritarian Approaches to Economic Development." *Journal of Political Economy* 82:817–827.

Diniz, Eli. 1986. "The Political Transition in Brazil: A Reappraisal of the Dynamics of the Political Opening." *Studies in Comparative International Development* 21:63–73.

Elster, Jon, and Rune Slagstad, eds. 1988. *Constitutionalism and Democracy.* Cambridge: Cambridge University Press.

Flisfisch, Angel. 1985. "Reflexiones algo oblícuas sobre el tema de la concertación." In Mario R. dos Santos et al., *Concertación social y democracia.* Santiago: Centro de Estudios del Desarrollo.

Fontana, Andrés. 1984. "Fuerzas Armadas, partidos políticos y transición a la democracia en Argentina." In Augusto Varas, ed., *Transición a la democracia.* Santiago: Associación Chilena de Investigaciones para la Paz.

———. 1987. "La política militar del gobierno constitucional argentino." In José Nun and Juan Carlos Portantiero, eds., *Ensayos sobre la tránsición democrática en la Argentina.* Buenos Aires: Puntosur Editores.

Frentzel-Zagórska, Janina. 1988. "Civil Society in Poland and Hungary." Manuscript, Australian National University.

García, Manuel Alonso. 1984. "En torno a una política de relaciones laborales." *Papeles de Economía Española* 22:265–281.

Golbery do Couto e Silva. 1981. *Conjuntura política nacional: O poder executivo e geopolítica no Brasil.* Rio de Janeiro: Livraria José Olympio.

González, Fernando Suárez. 1985. "El marco institucional de las relaciones laborales." *Papeles de Economía Española* 22:265–281.

Grossi, María, and Mario R. dos Santos. 1983. "La concertación social: una perspectiva sobre instrumentos de regulación económico-social en procesos de democratización." *Crítica y Utopía* 9.

Huntington, Samuel P. 1968. *Political Order in Changing Societies.* New Haven: Yale University Press.

Huntington, Samuel P., and Jorge I. Domínguez. 1975. "Political Development." In F. I. Greenstein and N. W. Polsby, eds., *Handbook of Political Science. Vol. 3: Macropolitical Theory.* Reading: Addison-Wesley.

Karl, Terry Lynn. 1987. "Petroleum and Political Pacts: The Transition to Democracy in Venezuela." *Latin American Research Review* 22: 63–94.

Kolarska-Bobińska, Lena. 1989. "Poczucie niesprawiedliwości, konfliktu i preferowany ład w gospodarce." In Polacy 88. Warsaw: CPBP.

Lamounier, Bolívar. 1979. "O discurso e o processo." Paper presented at the Conference on the "Prospects for Democracy: Transitions from Authoritarian Rule," Woodrow Wilson Center for International Studies, Washington, D.C., September 25–26.

Lechner, Norbert. 1985. "Pacto social nos processos de democratização: A experiência latinoamericana." *Novos Estudos* 13:29–44.

Lijphart, Arend. 1975. *The Politics of Accommodation: Pluralism and Democracy in the Netherlands,* 2nd ed. Berkeley: University of California Press.

Linz, Juan J. 1985. "Democracy: Presidential or Parliamentary: Does It Make a Difference?" Manuscript.

McCoy, Jennifer. 1987. "State, Labor, and the Democratic Class Compromise in Venezuela." Paper presented at the Meeting of the Southeastern Conference on Latin American Studies, Mérida, Yucatán, April 1–5.

Marsh, Robert M. 1979. "Does Democracy Hinder Economic Development in the Latecomer Developing Nations?" *Comparative Social Research* 2:215–248.

Marx, Karl. 1934. *The Eighteenth Brumaire of Louis Bonaparte.* Moscow: Progress Publishers.

————. 1971. *Writings on the Paris Commune.* Edited by Hal Draper. New York: International Publishers.

Migranyan, A. M. 1988. "Perehod ot totalitarno-avtoritanih regimov k demoktratsii." In E. A. Armbarstumov and J. M. Kliamkin, eds., *Politicheskie Reformy v Stranakh Sozializma.* Moscow: Akademia Nauk SSSR.

Miliband, Ralph. 1975. *Parliamentary Socialism: A Study in the Politics of Labour,* 2nd ed. London: Merlin Press.

Moisés, José Alvaro. 1986. "Sociedade civil, cultura política e democracia: descaminhos da transição política." In Maria de Lourdes M. Covre, ed., *A cidadania que não temos.* São Paulo: Editora Brasiliense.

Moore, Barrington, Jr. 1965. *Social Origins of Dictatorship and Democracy.* Boston: Beacon Press.

Murilo de Carvalho, José. 1987. "Militares e civis: Um debate além da Constituinte." Paper presented at the XI Annual Meeting of ANPOCS, Aguas de São Pedro, São Paulo.

O'Donnell, Guillermo. 1978. "State and Alliances in Argentina, 1956–1976." *Journal of Development Studies* 15:3–33.

————. 1979. "Notas para el estudio de procesos de democratización política a partir del estado burocrático-autoritário." Estudios CEDES 2, no. 5.

O'Donnell, Guillermo, and Philippe C. Schmitter. 1986. *Tentative Conclusions About Uncertain Democracies.* Baltimore and London: The Johns Hopkins University Press.

Pereira, Luis Carlos Bresser. 1978. *O colapso de uma aliança de classes.* São Paulo: Editora Brasiliense.

Pérez-Díaz, Víctor. 1986. "Economic Policies and Social Pacts in Spain during the Transition: The Two Faces of Neo-Corporatism." *European Sociological Review* 2.

Przeworski, Adam. 1966. "Party Systems and Economic Development." Ph.D. dissertation, Northwestern University.

————. 1984. "Ama a Incerteza e Serás Democrático." *Novos Estudos* 9: 36–46.

————. 1985. *Capitalism and Social Democracy.* Cambridge: Cambridge University Press.

————. 1986. "Some Problems in the Study of the Transition to Democracy." In Guillermo O'Donnell, Philippe C. Schmitter and Laurence Whitehead, eds., *Transitions from Authoritarian Rule: Comparative Perspectives.* Baltimore and London: The Johns Hopkins University Press, 1986.

————. 1988. "Capitalism, Democracy, Pacts." Paper presented at the Conference on Micro-Foundations of Democracy, University of Chicago.

————. 1991. *Democracy and the Market: Political and Economic Reforms in Eastern Europe and Latin America.* New York: Cambridge University Press.

Santos, Mario R. dos, ed. 1987. *Concertación político-social y democratización.* Buenos Aires: CLACSO.

Schmitter, Philippe C. 1974. "Still the Century of Corporatism?" *Review of Politics* 36:85–131.

————. 1984. "Pacti e transizioni: Mezzi non-democratici a fini democratici" *Revista Italiana di Scienza Politica* 14:363–382.

Smith, William C. 1987. "The Political Transition in Brazil: From Authoritarian Liberalization and Elite Conciliation to Democratization." In Enrique A. Baloyra, ed., *Comparing New Democracies: Transitions and Consolidations in Mediterranean Europe and the Southern Cone.* Boulder: Westview Press.

Weber, Max. 1968. *Economy and Society.* 3 vols. Edited by G. Roth and C. Wittich. New York.

Wiatr, Jerzy J. 1983. *Spór o treść odnowy.* Warsaw: Książka i Wiedza.

The Military and the Limits to Democratization in South America

Felipe Agüero

Introduction

None of the processes of democratization initiated in South America during the 1980s have to date been reversed by actions of the military. As of this writing, Bolivia and Ecuador are experiencing their third consecutive democratic administrations while Peru prepares for its third consecutive presidential election. Argentina has inaugurated the second civilian president after the "Proceso," shortly after Paraguay held its first post-Stroessner competitive election for president. For Argentina and Peru the transfers of power from one to another civilian democratically elected president were the first to occur in many decades. Brazil and Uruguay have just held elections for their second post-military presidents and Chileans have gone to the polls in the first competitive elections since 1973. The noteworthiness of these remarkable accomplishments is obscured, however, by episodes of military rebellion such as those which haunted Alfonsín's government in Argentina or Febres Cordero's in Ecuador. Indeed, the kidnapping of the Ecuadorean president by military units in 1987, or the striking expressions of military discontent which have been witnessed in Argentina, are stark reminders that military coups remain very real threats to the uncertain democracies of South America.

Nonetheless, current conditions are not especially propitious for coups by the military. Studies on the subject of military intervention have suggested that military decisions to engage in such forceful actions are generally preceded and accompanied by a high level of internal cohesion and the perception of widespread public support.[1] These conditions do not apply well in South America today.

153

The military came out of the authoritarian regimes in public disrepute, of which it has not yet been able to recover fully and, to varying extents, still suffers from the strains of internal divisions.[2] Furthermore, aware of their own inability to prevent serious economic mismanagement in the recent past, the armed forces would not want to see themselves in charge of the disastrous economic situation facing most of these countries today.

Although current conditions may seem unpropitious for military coups, the specter of intervention still manages to exert a perverse influence on the political process. Indeed, the *fear of a coup* is one of the limits which "the military factor" places on the democratization processes in South America. The fear which military attitudes instill among political actors leads these actors to impose restraints on their own strategies and policies, even if the actual likelihood of a coup may not be very high.[3] While self-restraint and moderation may help sustain the practice of democracy, moderation induced by the fear of violent retaliation does not lead to a healthy habituation to the "give and take" practices that normally go along with democracy. Rather, this fear is the expression of an unchecked power capability—armed force—introduced in the democratic game to the advantage of those who control it. This fear imports a "currency"—capacity for organized violence—that is foreign to the democratic exchange and which weakens it when this currency is accepted in the democratic "trade."[4]

The result is doubly undemocratic. On one hand, governments, parties, legislators, and social leaders conceive policies and strategies which already contain elements of appeasement, in anticipation of expected military responses. The formulation and implementation of policies which might otherwise be favored by a majority are thus dealt a deathblow even before inception. On the other hand, fear of a coup stimulates strategies which, aimed at appeasing the military, result in the weakening of civilian institutions which are necessary for the advancement of democratic governance. For instance, Menem's presidential pardon to military officers convicted or awaiting trial for violation of human rights in Argentina weakens the standing of the judiciary and its ability to oversee the observance of these rights. In Peru, control of the countersubversive war granted the military precludes the strengthening of badly needed civil institutions in geographically peripheral areas.

The high level of *autonomy* which the military guaranteed for itself during transitions from authoritarianism is another severe limit to democratization. Entrenched within special domains in which the rules governing the rest of the state and society do not apply, the military claims exclusive sovereignty over the defense sector, and makes sure that civilian democratically elected governments stay clear from it. Under self-defined rules, the military sets its own guidelines, goals and missions, and reproduces its own values in an internal, secluded socialization process. By surrounding itself with clearly delineated boundaries it prevents the government and other representative agencies from applying and monitoring in this area the policies conducted for the state bureaucracy at large.

In this scheme, the ministers of defense, or the service ministers, participate in the government as spokespersons for the armed forces and not as the top officials charged with the implementation of government policy in a particular domain.[5] Government officials and the military hierarchy meet at the top, as would independent sovereigns, to coordinate and exchange mutual claims. The state is thus split into separate realms of authority: one supported by democratic-electoral legitimacy, the other by the legitimacy which the military grants itself from its purportedly special ability to express the "unchanging national essence." Civilian democratic governments are therefore kept from exercising effective authority over a large and important segment of the state, which often includes the powerful military intelligence organizations overdeveloped during the authoritarian period.

From entrenched positions in the state, the military not only resists outside direction and oversight; it also exercises and expands undue influence in nonmilitary spheres. This *expansive entrenchment* of the military within their own states and societies may become a lasting legacy of the previous authoritarian period, and one that could certainly hinder the consolidation of democracy, eventually threatening its very survival.

"Military factors" are certainly not the only ones that hinder democratic consolidation in South America. Although they are the only ones that include the capacity forcefully to act to revert democratization altogether, other factors stemming from political structures on the civilian side—especially from the persistence of old practices that never augured well for the assertion of democracy—play their part as well. These factors are indeed built into the military ones, making the latter partly a result of the former. The purpose of this chapter is to identify and bring forward the factors which account for the military limits and the military's resistance to democratization. Before doing so, we first turn to a description of the legacy of military entrenchment during the postauthoritarian years.

Governments and the Military in the
Postauthoritarian Regimes of South America

The extent to which the military limits democratization is not the same in all countries.[6] For instance, government relations with the military were significantly redefined in Peru and Uruguay, but in Brazil the basic features of civil-military relations that had prevailed during the authoritarian regime remained very much in place throughout the first postmilitary administration. Some of the new democratic governments, such as Alfonsín's in Argentina, made conscious efforts to redefine civil-military relations while others, such as Sarney's in Brazil, attempted no reforms whatsoever. Of all the newly democratized regimes, the Uruguayan is the one that seems closer to attaining patterns of relations that are compatible with democratic government, although it has not yet attained the patterns it exhibited prior to the military period.

In *Uruguay,* democratization started with the military blocking the presidential candidacy of the most popular political leader and establishing special prerogatives for itself during the first year of democratic government in 1985. According to the civil-military transition pact of the *Club Naval,* these special prerogatives — related to control over promotions and the role of the National Security Council — were to be debated by a constituent assembly and eventually incorporated into the Constitution. However, such an assembly never convened and the Act which contained those prerogatives was left without effect in March 1986.

The military had also envisaged important powers for itself in the constitution which it had proposed in 1980. The proposed constitution contemplated military approval of the single candidate that parties had to nominate for the presidential elections that would have taken place in 1981, and of the two candidates who would have been allowed to run in 1986. The constitution also envisaged a military-dominated National Security Council and a military-controlled Council of State with powers to appoint a Constitutional

Tribunal which would serve for a period of ten years. Voters defeated the military proposed constitution in a referendum in 1980.[7]

Still, after 1985 the military managed to claim and obtain important prerogatives such as control over defense intelligence by the Joint Command, previously subordinate to the defense minister. Also, after the first year of democratic government, the post of defense minister was handed over to general Medina, heretofore chief of the army, and military prerogatives on promotions remained high as legislation on the matter was postponed.

But perhaps the most troubling set of events took place around the issue of the responsibility of military officers for human rights abuses. During the transition, the military had made it clear that power devolution would not include submission to trials of the type that at the time were taking place in Argentina. When, nonetheless, military officers were called to appear before the courts, the Defense Minister, General Medina, instructed them not to comply with the summons. Minister Medina's justification to have the military defy judicial authority was the need to safeguard military morale; otherwise, he argued, democracy could not be protected. In order to avoid a "constitutional crisis," President Sanguinetti promptly had Congress pass a law (*Ley de Caducidad*) which precluded legal action against military officers.

Discontented with the military pressures behind the law, various organizations sought to repeal it by pursuing the constitutional right to call a referendum if supported with the signatures of 25 percent of the electorate. After a protracted and bitter campaign, enough signatures were put together. The government called a referendum, and in April 1989, 57 percent of the voters chose not to repeal the law. It is too early to say whether this conclusion of the human rights question will help effectively to bury the past, and whether or not it will strengthen a military that has been absolved in the ballots.[8] With this issue behind for better or worse, however, Uruguay has gone the farthest in actually resuming a more traditional type of civil-military relations.

In *Ecuador* the military conducted a protracted transition to democracy guided by the "Plan for the Juridical Restructuring of the State," which included a plebiscite for a new Constitution held in 1978. Holding the "lead in dictating the terms of the process," the military vetoed the participation of certain candidates and parties in the electoral contest.[9] Before the inauguration of elected president Roldós in 1979, the military made sure that the powers of the president over internal promotions were restricted and that the post of minister of defense be held by an active-duty senior officer in future democratic governments. The military also retained the most seats on the national security council and several on the boards of the largest state firms. Also, the military controlled civil aviation, two commercial airlines, and a new agency for military industries.[10]

Although the country has completed a decade of uninterrupted democratic government, military political activism has not died out. In 1986, senior officers outspokenly criticized President León Febres Cordero, against whom a group rebelled in May that year, although the attempt failed to gain support in the ranks. In a related incident, a special unit kidnapped the president for a day in January 1987. Political activism has also been manifest during electoral periods, in which the military has helped sustain the impression that it can step in to exercise veto, perform arbitrating functions or forcefully to prevent certain outcomes.

A number of factors, such as the persistence of populist-style politics among significant groups, the extremely uncompromising stance of business groups which have called for military action, and the combination of Febres Cordero's intolerance of opposition with his attempts to politicize army promotions, certainly contributed to the reemergence of civil-military clientelism and factionalism. Whether or not the new political style brought about by the more "modern" social democratic party of current president Borja will be able to supersede these constraints remains to be seen.[11]

In *Peru,* democratic institutions were restored in 1980 after twelve years of military rule. A civilian president was elected that year and a new Constitution was inaugurated following approval by a special assembly elected under military auspices in 1978. In 1985, the presidential sash was passed on to another elected civilian for the first time in six decades. Despite deep economic crisis, expanded subversive violence and an unstable political situation during this latter presidential term, overt military intervention did not seem likely.[12] This was not tantamount, however, to full acceptance of civilian control. Quite the contrary, the military inherited high levels of autonomy and influence from the period of military rule.[13]

Much of the structure for military participation developed during the government of the armed forces remained in place after the transfer of power to civilians. This structure—the National Defense

System—involved participation of the Joint Command of the armed forces in state planning and intelligence agencies and in the National Defense Council, which had powers to define national objectives. Also, in periods of constitutional states of emergency, the Joint Command was empowered to assume control over internal security.[14] In 1985, towards the end of the first postmilitary administration, a bill was passed which institutionalized the creation of political-military commands, directly dependent on the Joint Command, and charged them with the control of areas declared to be in states of emergency.[15]

When elected in 1985, president Alan García was committed to withdraw political responsibilities from the military and assert civilian control, following a strict interpretation of the 1980 Constitution.[16] Military participation was reduced and several functions previously assigned to the National Defense Council were devolved to the Council of Ministers. The president asserted his constitutional authority by removing chiefs caught in blatant violation of human rights during countersubversive activities,[17] and especially by trying to reshape the authority structure in the defense sector. The president struggled to create a ministry of defense to substitute for the separate service ministries, and after some resistance, he overcame the open mutiny of the chief of the Air Force and succeeded in inaugurating the new ministry in 1987. Nonetheless, the appointment of the Army chief of staff as the first defense minister signaled both the military's ample autonomy and prerogatives, and the government's recognition of the military's domestic power.[18]

The expansion of *Sendero Luminoso*'s rebellious activities in the highlands and the more recent appearance of the *Movimiento Revolucionario Tupac Amaru,* have increasingly demanded more of the military's attention.[19] While conducting armed repression, the military also maintains that the solution to the struggle is largely political, demanding and expecting leadership from the government, which the military and other sectors find lacking.[20] Criticism of the government, however, does not herald military intervention, because the military is aware of its own inability to provide leadership and of the deleterious effects which a military take over would have by unleashing widespread civil and violent strife.[21] With no clear political leadership, unable adequately to face the subversive threat which it is confronted with, and with no viable alternatives, the military faces the specter of a dangerous situation of anomie.

In *Argentina,* since the return to democracy in 1983, the Alfonsín administration embarked on an unprecedented attempt to subject the interventionist Argentine military to control by civilians. Alfonsín's plan included drastic cuts in military expenditures, the reorganization and civilianization of the central defense structures, and making the military accountable for past crimes.

The government reversed an amnesty law which the military had granted itself and made a case against top military chiefs and former junta members for their responsibility in the killing of nearly nine thousand civilians. After military courts refused to proceed against the generals, the case was taken to civilian courts, which tried and sentenced two former military chiefs and junta members to life terms, another one to seventeen years and two others to shorter terms.[22] Following amendment of the military code, prosecutors were empowered to appeal decisions reached by military judges to civilian courts, taking many more cases before civilian judges. Although the military forced a number of legal concessions, towards the end of Alfonsín's administration some twenty-five upper-level officers still were in line to be tried for their responsibility in the abduction, torture and murder of civilians.

In the area of defense organization, the government created an advisory National Defense Council, composed of civilians only, including representatives from Congress. Also, the top five positions in the ministry of defense were assigned to civilians, and civilians were placed in charge of *Fabricaciones Militares* (the directorate for military industries) and, for the first time ever, of the National Defense College. Innovative program planning and budgeting systems were adopted for central policy making, especially in light of the drastic budgetary reductions which brought spending down to 2.5 percent of the GNP, half the level reached during the military government. Measures were taken also to control military intelligence and to place it under the jurisdiction of a civilian led National Intelligence Agency. Following the forced retirement of fifty generals during the first eighteen months of Alfonsín's administration, military command was reorganized with the creation of a single chairman of the Joint Chiefs in order to facilitate interservice coordination and control by the minister of defense.

After a three-year-long debate, Congress passed a National Defense Law in 1988 which established military subordination to government control and eliminated internal security as an area of permanent military concern. As police and domestic security functions were taken away from the armed forces, the *Gendarmería* and the *Prefectura Naval* were separated from the army and the navy, respectively, and put under the direct authority of the minister of defense. Attempts were also made to redeploy army forces away from the largest cities, and the powerful First Army Corps around Buenos Aires was eliminated, although many of its component sections survived within other army units.[23] Clearly, the government of Alfonsín temporarily held the rare capacity for an Argentine civilian administration to "impose, [if it chose], policies that [were] opposed by the armed forces."[24]

A remarkable feat of president Alfonsín was merely to stay in power and to keep the military from staging a successful coup, especially in light of the unprecedented government policies in the defense sector. Indeed, for the first time in sixty-one years of Argentine history, power was transferred in 1989 from a duly elected civilian to another.[25]

However, many of the reforms in defense organization mentioned above remained very superficial. A combination of military resistance, budgetary constraints and lack of civilian expertise, conspired against effective reform implementation. Progress also was severely undermined by the weighty concessions which the military exacted from the government. Following mutinies by sectors of the army in 1987 and 1988, the government was forced to pass legislation — the "Due Obedience" and the "Punto Final" laws — which immunized large numbers of middle-level officers from criminal and civil responsibility for participating in the killing and torture of civilians. By 1989 the military continued to exert heavy pressure to obtain the release of those generals serving sentences and to extend immunity to officers still pending prosecution. Seeking to avoid the challenge of officers disobeying the summonings of civilian courts, the newly inaugurated president Carlos Saúl Menem announced, amid public protest, the pardons of nearly forty military officers.[26]

Having regained confidence, and reversing a tide initially unfavorable to them, the armed forces, especially the army, persist in denying any wrongdoing in the "dirty war," claiming that the killings were a necessary part in a legitimate strategy. Behind this assertive stance lies a deep resentment which developed among a large number of officers. They feel that legal action against military officers, coupled with the impact of drastic cuts in the defense budget, represent unjust punishment inflicted on the military institution. This resentment is even deeper among middle-level officers who, additionally, feel betrayed by the senior military leadership, whom they claim led them to defeat in the South Atlantic and left them on their own before civilian attacks for their involvement in the "internal war."[27] The state of disarray in the military, and the particular nature of its internal divisions, are certainly not a good foundation for democratic advancement; they may fuel a long term military threat to democracy and to the chances of affirming civilian supremacy in Argentina.[28]

In *Brazil,* progress has been very slight since a civilian president took over in 1985, for the first time in twenty-one years. Of all the South American transitions, the Brazilian is perhaps the least promising with regard to the prospects of civilian supremacy. A few important measures initially were taken by the government without the consent of the military, such as the legalization of independent trade unions and of the small Communist Party, and the reopening of relations with Cuba. This partial removal of what Brazilians called the "authoritarian debris" was reinforced by parts of the 1988 Constitution which replaced the authoritarian Constitution of 1967.[29] The new constitution established severe restrictions on state prerogatives, including drastic limitations on police detention powers, and provided firm guarantees to individual rights. Congress was given special powers to approve declarations of state of defense or state of siege and to order their suspension.

The constitution also redefined the way in which the military is charged with the maintenance of law and order. In the previous 1967 Constitution the military had been charged with the task of maintaining law and order and guaranteeing the normal functioning of the three constitutional powers. Also, the military had been placed under the supreme authority of the president, but only "within the limits of the law." This clause, which, in turn, had been inherited from previous constitutions, made obedience to the president conditional on the military's assessment of what was or was not within the limits of the law.[30] The new constitution eliminated this conditional clause, plainly subordinating the military to the president, and assigned the armed forces with the task of defending law and order, but only on the initiative of any one of the constitutional powers (the executive, the legislative or the judiciary).[31] This apparent improvement maintains, however, the military's concern with internal law and order and does not significantly reduce the autonomy of the armed forces. Indeed, while the military is placed under the authority of the president, other powers are allowed to request its intervention in domestic affairs, giving the military room to lobby and play these powers against each other, enhancing its own bargaining strength.[32]

In practice, the military functions as a separate, fourth power. It lobbied and pressured the constitution-drafting congress with a specialized team of thirty officers, and succeeded in getting its way on several issues, such as the option for presidentialism rather than parliamentarism, the length of Sarney's presidential term, the limitations imposed on agrarian reform, and the maintenance of a domestic role for the armed forces. Also, the military rejected a law which would have reincorporated army officers that had been dismissed during the dictatorship, and has refused, on grounds of "military morale," to admit responsibility for previous human rights abuses, let alone to tolerate judicial investigation. The military develops its own research on the ideological inclinations of inland peasants and has autonomously taken the initiative to defend "law and order" by verbally and forcefully acting against strikes.[33]

Since 1985, the military has had substantial participation in the cabinet with six active duty generals. In fact, five of them were among a total of six ministers who had not been replaced during the entire Sarney administration. The military has strongly rejected any move toward creation of a defense military and has resisted any attempt to reduce its extended presence in public bureaucracy. For instance, it succeeded in transferring the military-controlled secretariat of the recently abolished National Security Council to the new National Defense Council, as an "advisory secretariat," although it had no place in the law that created the new Council. The presence of retired officers in state bureaucracy and public enterprises remains extremely high. And although the military partially relinquished control of the computer sector, it remained in charge of nuclear policy, the weapons industry, and crucial areas of Amazon development. Furthermore, the repressive apparatus remained intact, and the SNI—state intelligence—remained in charge of both foreign and domestic intelligence, and influenced the hiring of public personnel by extensive use of its "dossiers." Not surprisingly, the army minister helped the government shape policies to steer in its favor the race for the first direct democratic presidential elections in two decades.[34]

In sum, in none of these South American countries did the movement toward postauthoritarian regimes lead to the authority patterns in government-military relations that are expected in democracies. In some cases, such as Uruguay, the military remains content with a well delineated institutional autonomy and control of the defense sector, although it also alertly monitors domestic politics. In other cases, such as Brazil, the military additionally establishes institutional forms of tutelage over areas outside the defense sector, and seeks actively to influence the political process itself. The shape of government-military relations in the rest of the countries falls somewhere in between these two cases.[35]

Military Entrenchment: Protective and Expansive

The current South American regimes also differ with respect to the nature of the military's entrenchment in the postauthoritarian political structures. These differences stem from the policy orientations which the military governments developed during the authoritarian period, and from the main sources of opposition to these governments. In those cases where the military conducted anti-oligarchic policies, where the return to democracy was forced by wounded business elites, and where the military perceived the threat of re-clientelization during the return of democracy, the military sought guarantees that were protective in nature. The situation of these military establishments in the postauthoritarian regimes may then appropriately be seen as one of *protective entrenchment*.

For instance, while in control of the government, the Peruvian and the Ecuadorean militaries developed industrialization policies which weakened sectors of the oligarchy. They also opened up new avenues for the participation of previously neglected popular sectors, especially in the case of Peru, and made it harder for business elites directly to influence government policy. Although in both cases the military governments ended up revamping their initially sharp reformist policies,[36] the military alienated the propertied and business elites and earned a deep, long-lasting distrust from them. Indeed, business elites played a leading role in the mounting opposition to these military regimes and in the mobilization for democratic transition.

Given the nature of the opposition and the thrust of the transition movement, the military in Peru and Ecuador attempted to secure the bulk of the transformations which they had brought about by trying closely to steer the transitional opening and the content of the new constitutions.[37] Also, they sought to retain powers for the postauthoritarian period in order to preserve the military institution itself as a guarantee that some of the major reforms would stand.

These militaries also sought to institutionalize its internal autonomy, in search for protection from the return of old elites. They wanted to insulate themselves from the patrimonial, clientelistic, self-serving relations which the elites had conducted with the armed forces in the past, and which had had such divisive effects on the military institutions. Indeed, the military coups of 1962 in Peru—the first truly institutional military coup in South America—and the coup in Ecuador in 1972 could be largely regarded as attempts to break with the old pattern of military-elite relationships, with which the military no longer felt comfortable. Later, the extrication from power was, to a large extent, viewed as necessary by the military in order to halt the weakening of institutional cohesion, which again was making the military vulnerable to the old pattern of relations with the elite.[38]

The search for some kind of "corporate distance" from civilian factionalism was especially critical for the Ecuadorean military, whose corporate identity had developed only recently and which was especially vulnerable to the influx of a patrimonialistic, clientelistic elite. In addition, during the transition and after, the military saw threats to its corporate identity coming from all sides, both from the traditional political factions of the business elite and from the new populist wave represented by *Concentración de Fuerzas Populares*.[39] In Peru, the protective nature of the military's entrenchment during the postauthoritarian period also developed as a reaction to the growing violence and strength of subversive movements.

In the other cases—Argentina, Brazil, Uruguay—the military did not have to fear business elites, who had been overtly favored by the policies of the military governments, often participating in the policy process, and who therefore had no reason for vindictiveness.[40] Also, the military was less vulnerable to the threats of a clientelistic influx from outside, because it had long developed strong corporate boundaries, and in some cases, such as Uruguay, parties were strong enough to sustain a well-mediated representation of interests. Therefore, securing protection from the elites was not the main motive behind military entrenchment in the postauthoritarian period.[41]

More than securing protection, the military in these cases is concerned with attaining a more active tutelary presence from which to influence the political process. The military maintains a profound distrust of parties which is based not as much on the threat which party politics present for the armed forces' institutional cohesion as it is on the disruptive and divisive effects which party politics is seen having on the nation. Politics (i.e., the democratic process) and parties are themselves viewed as part of the national security problem, since they are perceived as critical points of entry for "subversion," "chaos," and "decay."[42] In its self-designated position of trustees of "the national essence," the military secures for itself outpost positions in the state and civil society to guard against the growth of potentially malignant symptoms. In this situation, the position of the military in the postauthoritarian regimes may appropriately be seen as one of *expansive entrenchment.*

Democratization processes appear in all these countries to be unable to proceed any further in curtailing the prerogatives of the military or in trespassing the limits set by military entrenchment, whether protective or expansive. Even slight progress in curtailing these prerogatives has increased the levels of military contestation, and a decrease in the latter has often been achieved at the price of significant concessions.[43] In the sections that follow we explore the factors that stand behind the military limits to democratization.

The Initial Conditions:
Controlled Transitions by Militarized Regimes

In all the South American cases it was the military, rather than a civilian leadership, that made a conscious decision to initiate a process of liberalization and some kind of democratic opening. Of course, this decision often was made in response to or in anticipation of popular protest and pressure, and was the expression of splits within the ruling elite. In some cases (i.e., Peru) the decision to liberalize was more clearly a response to popular protest, whereas in other cases (i.e., Brazil) the initial decision came more as a result of divisions within the regime. These decisions generally envisaged a gradual process of extrication; only in Argentina was a quick decision forced upon the military by the aggravating circumstances of military defeat, which intensified opposition and simultaneously sparked mass protests and fissures in the regime. In all these cases, as Adam Przeworski points out elsewhere in this volume, "decisions to liberalize combine[d] elements from above and from below." While acknowledging this dual origin of liberalization and the rich history of opposition and protest behind it, my emphasis here is on the nature of the elite which, under more or less pressure to do so, took the decision to open up the regime. In the South American cases the elite was military, and the consequence was that, to varying extents, the armed forces exited with great bargaining power and were able to control or significantly influence the transition agenda, setting the conditions for firm subsequent military entrenchment.

In Ecuador, for instance, under pressure from civil opposition and following growing signs of internal fissure, the military decided in 1976 to oust general Rodríguez Lara and replace him with a military triumvirate in order to initiate a return to democracy. The transfer of power to an elected civilian, however, did not take place until 1979, and in the meantime, the military monitored a plebiscite on alternative constitutions, obtained the formalization of autonomy, and shaped the electoral competition by selectively banning candidates and parties. In Peru, a military facing growing opposition and mounting economic difficulties announced the *Plan Tupac Amaru* which would lead to the election of a constitutional convention in 1978 and the subsequent restoration of democracy. Through agreements with APRA—the largest party—the military influenced the assembly's deliberations and set guarantees for itself. In Uruguay, after defeat in the constitutional plebiscite of 1980 the military set out to arrange the transfer of power, the conditions of which were formally agreed to in the *Club Naval,* which also set guarantees for the military. In Brazil, the military held the upper hand in the protracted liberalization process which was initiated by President Geisel in an apparent effort to halt divisions and deformations in the military. The *abertura,* marked by a continuous change in the rules with which the military sought to steer the process in its favor, eventually led to election of a civilian president in 1985 although it did not lead to a substantial break with previous forms of military participation.[44] In Chile, after the government and the opposition agreed on limited constitutional reforms following Pinochet's defeat in the October 1988 plebiscite, the military junta set out to pass legislation which would constrain the future government's policy options in several areas, keep the security and defense establishment protected, and maintain many of its prerogatives untouched.[45] Even in Argentina the military attempted to influence the transition by staying in power for a year after the Malvinas defeat, passing protective legislation for itself.[46]

The controlling position held by the military during the liberalization and transition processes was largely derived from the *position which the military previously occupied in the power structure of the outgoing authoritarian regimes*. In these regimes, the military had participated broadly and more or less directly in the delineation and implementation of government policy. Either regularly established collective military bodies, or a selected group of top military chiefs who kept closely in touch with their services, participated in the delineation, monitoring and assessment of government policy. Also, the military held the power to appoint and dismiss the president or to significantly influence the presidential selection process, and in most cases the military held the power to make the laws and rewrite the constitution. In this sense these authoritarian regimes were *militarized* regimes.[47]

The Argentine military, for instance, imposed in 1976 an Act for the Process of National Reorganization which declared the military junta the supreme organ of the state, holding constituent powers. The junta also appointed and dismissed the president, named members of the Supreme Court, and gave approval for the appointment of ministers. The junta had a legislative advisory committee composed of nine members, three from each armed service. Except for the economic ministries, the military held most of the other cabinet positions, and all the administrative positions in the regions. Most of the presidents remained as commanders of the army, at least for part of their tenure as presidents.[48] Also, state repression — massive killings and torture of opponents — was carried out through the regular structure of the services.[49]

In Uruguay, although only one active-duty military officer held a cabinet position during the years of authoritarian government, real power and control of the government remained tightly with the military.[50] The military developed an articulate system of collegial rule in which the *Juntas de Oficiales Generales* (JOG), formed by all chiefs with the grade of general or admiral, appointed the service branch chiefs and joined the newly created Council of the Nation to select the president, the members of the Council of State (the legislature, where the military were a majority), the Supreme Court and the Electoral Court. The Advisory Committee for Political Affairs, created in 1979 by the JOG, composed by representatives of all the service branches, was charged with engineering and handling a transition from military rule, a job which the service commanders later undertook directly.[51]

The Revolutionary Government of the Armed Forces, established in Peru in 1968, directly involved the military in the attempt to create new organizations for popular mobilization. The second phase, after the ousting of Gen. Velasco by the commanders of the military regions, was headed by former army commander Gen. Morales, who kept closer touch with the generals than had his predecessor. In this second phase, the government's premiership and the war ministry were given to Gen. Fernández Maldonado, the new commander general of the army.[52] Also in Ecuador the military was actively involved in central and provincial government agencies.[53]

In Brazil, despite the guise of legal party activities, elections, and a functioning Congress, the military controlled the government, although the collegial mechanisms of military input were less institutionalized than in the other cases. The presidents were selected by the High Command and then elected by an electoral college where the official party held a majority due to ceaseless manipulation of electoral rules by the government. Although the general-presidents were more autonomous from the armed forces than was the case in Argentina or Uruguay, they nonetheless remained quite responsive to a military amply represented in government by the service ministers, who commanded the forces, and by the chief of the Military Household, the secretary of the National Security Council and the director of the National Information System.[54]

Also in Chile military participation was substantial, despite the personalization of power in the figure of Pinochet. Indeed, government policy became early on almost the exclusive domain of the president, who also retained the post of commander-in-chief of the army, concentrating powers to an extent unknown in the other South American cases, and somewhat reminiscent of Franco's ascent.[55] Pinochet ultimately autonomized his power by having his hold on the presidency ratified in a 1980 plebiscite for a period of nine years. Indeed, this was the only South American authoritarian regime to have a single president during the whole period.[56] However, the personalization of power did not prevent a substantial number of army generals and colonels from sitting in the cabinet, in legislative committees and in governmental committees, such as the Military Household of the presidency, the president's General Staff, and the Presidential Advisory Committee, which had significant input in government policy. The military also headed state enterprises and all the top administrative positions in the regions.[57] Also, the junta, composed of the chief commanders of the three armed services and of the *Carabineros,* held the power to nominate the single presidential candidate presented to the referendum of October 1988, and was to maintain legislative and constituent powers until the inauguration of an almost entirely elected Congress in 1990.[58]

These regimes stand sharply in contrast to other authoritarian regimes which, like the Spanish regime under the last two decades of Franquism, were civilianized.[59] In these latter regimes, while the military is provided with strong representation in the governing institutions, civilians rather than the military are in charge of providing the major policy orientations and decisions. When these regimes undergo a transition to democracy, the military may initially retain the prerogatives it previously held, but finds it harder to upgrade or expand them and even to keep them for long. The formally subordinated position which the military held in the power structure of these regimes precludes direct military influence in the setting of the transition agenda, weakening military attempts to set guarantees for itself for the post-authoritarian period.

Although both the South American (with the exception of Argentina) and the Spanish were pacted transitions in which the elites from the outgoing regime decided to pact reforms with outside groups, they differed critically on the civilian or military character of the elite in control during the transition. This difference is not really captured in the typology of transitions to democracy which Scott Mainwaring proposes elsewhere in this volume, which otherwise is extremely useful in highlighting differences in the extent of elite control. For instance, by pointing to the high level of control exercised by elites from the authoritarian regime, the category of "transition through transaction" subsumes both Brazil and Spain as cases of the same type. However, a focus on the extent to which the dominant elite in the authoritarian regime is military in nature marks significant differences between the Spanish and the Brazilian case, differences which should be underscored when analyzing the limits imposed by the military on the subsequent democratization process.[60]

In Spain, the transition was conducted by civilian elites that had had prominent positions in the Franquist state. These elites set a reform agenda which the military could not influence.[61] Later military reactions to the unfolding of this agenda were successfully overcome, and the road to attaining civilian supremacy was thus facilitated. In the South American countries, to the contrary, the military was at the forefront of the negotiations leading to its retreat, holding the upper hand in the bargaining process with civilians and imposing protective preconditions for itself. The military was in a relatively better position to monitor change and to set or greatly influence the agenda for the transition and to establish sound bases for influence during the postauthoritarian period.[62]

The leverage which the armed forces held in the South American transitions was not enough to ensure that results would fully conform to their wishes. Liberalization and political opening forced the military to live with new actors who, upon entering or reentering the stage, altered the rules of political exchange bringing in new "currencies."[63] In most of these cases the military was surprised and embarrassed by electoral outcomes which it had tried to prevent. For instance, in Ecuador, the military impeded Bucaram from running for president, only to see Jaime Roldós, a relative of his and a member of the same party, elected instead. In Peru, the military reconciled with APRA, seeking support for its transition project, in the expectation that this party would win the presidential elections. But, since APRA suffered electorally from the image of collaboration with the military, Peruvians instead elected Fernando Belaúnde, the president who had been ousted by the military in 1968 and who held a reputation of independence from the military. In Brazil, ceaseless and flagrant manipulation of the rules by the military did not impede the election of Tancredo Neves. In Argentina, protective dealings of the outgoing military with Peronist sectors failed when the majority of Argentines preferred Alfonsín as president.[64] Even in Chile, Pinochet was surprised by his defeat, and the military was faced with the resurgence of political forces crushed in the coup.

Despite these political setbacks, the military managed to assure areas of influence and guarantees for itself that were far superior and more institutionalized than anything that had existed before the authoritarian period. This result is strongly related to the controlling position which the military held during the transition and in the previous authoritarian regimes, and may become a lasting, negative legacy for these emerging democracies.[65]

The Unremitting Perception of Domestic Threats

For a moment there was hope among observers that the military's growing concern with promoting its own modernization and professional enhancement, a concern which accompanied the demise of authoritarian regimes, would help sustain a lasting return to the barracks.[66] The military's renewed interest in professional issues gave the impression, however misleading, that their domestic political concerns would recede.

Military interest in force modernization stemmed from the realization that the sources of regional conflict remained firmly in place. The short war between Ecuador and Peru in 1981, the high level of tension in the relations between Chile, Peru and Bolivia in the late 1970s and the warlike atmosphere on the southern borders of Argentina and Chile in the same period, testified to the resurgence of regional conflict and rivalries. Militarization in Central America also increased feelings of uneasiness in the militaries of Colombia and Venezuela, which harbored old rivalries and border disputes. The reawakening of old conflicts took place simultaneously with a significant upgrading of the means of combat available to the military, as a result of new opportunities for the diversification of arms imports as well as for the expansion and greater sophistication of local arms industries.[67] The military operated in the 1980s within a more threatening regional environment, to which it had no doubt contributed, partly by unearthing old regional disputes and by pushing for the introduction of increasingly sophisticated weapons systems.[68] Nonetheless, the Malvinas war showed that extraregional powers could engage military forces rather easily, with little or no concern for prerogatives claimed by "regional powers," highlighting the relative technological and organizational backwardness of the South American militaries. In this context, the military sought to give greater attention to the modernization of its forces.

Military interest in stressing increased professionalization was also spawned by the divisive effects which the burdens of government had had on the armed forces.[69] The military thus found renewed virtues in professionalism as a means of halting internal divisions and of recovering public prestige. Toward the end of authoritarian rule the military's public discourse emphasized modernization and professionalization leading many to hope that, by concentrating on its own specific functions, the military would be leaving the political stage for good.

These hopes, however, soon proved to stand on rather weak foundations. The military's greater concern with modernization proved to be neither a sharp break with recent practices nor a distraction from domestic political roles. Although the political role of the military in government had obscured the visibility of modernization efforts, these had not been completely abandoned during the authoritarian period. Sectors in the army, and even more so the navy and air force, had always remained attentive to professional modernization including space research, missile technology, submarine development and other areas.[70] However, greater attention to these projects in the 1980s did not mean that the military would give up domestic concerns and roles.

The "return to military professionalism" initially associated with the end of authoritarian regimes had quite a different meaning for the military than it had for other groups. Most of the elites pursuing democratization hoped that the military would return to a position subordinate to civilian government and concentrate on external threats to national security.[71] For the military, however, the "return to" professionalism only involved a more focused emphasis on the appropriate ways to deploy the armed forces in the institutional context of elected civilian governments, in order to deal with a broad, self-defined security mission which encompasses both external and internal roles. The resulting situation of "expansive entrenchment," in practice combines the old professionalism of external security with the "new professionalism of internal security" which Stepan argued had superseded the former in the 1970s.[72] In this new "politicized professionalism," the military sees itself legitimately concerned not only with *defense* against external and internal threats but also with the active *promotion* of the country's ability to achieve its national objectives.[73]

Although the armed forces did concern themselves more with external defense as they bequeathed government functions, the security doctrines developed in the 1960s and 1970s, which led to "military role expansion," remained basically unchanged. In fact, the military is still oriented by doctrines which see major security threats in what is perceived as the multifaceted action of Communist-inspired subversion. This anticommunist emphasis is likely to weaken as a result of the dramatic crumbling of communist governments in Eastern Europe during 1989, and of the ongoing changes in the Soviet Union, but this will not be automatic nor will it occur overnight. Besides, the blurring of the "Soviet connection" will not affect the military's concern with subversion, unions and strike activities, mass mobilizations and party politics.[74] The military continues to regard the monitoring of domestic social, economic and political spheres, in which subversion "lurks," as part of its own professional incumbency. Thus, more professionalism encouraged by democratizing elites leads the military not to exclusive concern with external defense but to improved performance of its external and internal self-assigned roles.[75]

In Uruguay, for instance, even after the plebiscite of April 1989, military publications harped on the continuing threat which Marxists and other sectors on the left pose for the armed forces and the nation.[76] In Argentina, post-Malvinas military pressure for rearming the forces with a view to the needs of external defense is combined with a strong justification of the repression conducted during the "Proceso" and of a continuing role for the armed forces as custodians of internal order against subversion.[77] In Brazil, the military combines concern with the technological requirements of modern external defense and power projection, with a close monitoring of labor and peasant unrest, of projects in the Amazon area and electoral developments. In all these cases, where a diversity of roles is admitted within the concept of professionalism, the military perceives democracy itself as creating vulnerabilities for national security. Deeply rooted role-beliefs and recalcitrant security doctrines in the military stand, therefore, as a major hurdle for democratic advancement by civilian governments.[78]

An Inauspicious International Environment

When contrasting the international military environment of different democratization processes, much more propitious opportunities for placating the armed forces were found, for instance, in Southern Europe in the 1970s and 1980s than exist in South America today.[79] In the Southern European transitions to democracy, doctrines on security and professionalism which prevailed among the military did not stand as roadblocks to democratic advancement. Although the military there also had *internal* security concerns, these were not wrapped in the assertive and expansive roles assigned the military in the national security doctrines distinctive of the South American militaries.

In Portugal and Spain, the prospects of integration in Europe helped further democratization. A network of European institutions played an active role in encouraging these countries to inaugurate democratic political systems. For Spain in particular, democratization offered the added incentive of joining a well established and functioning military alliance which could help in the overall drive for modernization. The nature and structure of NATO, based on unequivocal political civilian leadership by member governments, helped civilian leaders in Spain assert their leadership over the armed forces. By positioning itself as a central, inescapable link between the benefits of the new international connection and the military, the Spanish government was further empowered to assert domestic control and lead the modernization of the military.[80]

In contrast to the well functioning North Atlantic Treaty Organization, the Inter-American Treaty of Reciprocal Assistance has remained moribund for nearly two decades. It has, therefore, been unable to provide the kind of opportunities for the strengthening of civilian leadership which NATO provided during the South European transitions. The Interamerican alliance was unable to maintain the sense of a common regional purpose which NATO gave its members and which also existed initially among the South American militaries in the context of "hemispheric security." Changing U.S. strategic priorities ended up reducing the alliance's importance, redefining the role of each country's armed forces, and giving rise to manifest differences between the U.S. and Latin American positions on regional issues. One of the results was a loosening of hemispheric cohesion which, as noted above, opened the way to a reawakening of the potential for regional conflict.[81]

Nonetheless, interamerican military institutions were influential in the 1950–1970 period by reinforcing military security doctrines which were clearly pitted against democratization. The Latin American military became the preferred institutional carrier in the region for the U.S. global policies of containment. By training thousands in U.S. or inter-American schools and camps, entire generations of Latin American officers internalized the emphasis on domestic security roles against a well identified common enemy, and received encouragement for active participation in what was called the challenge of security and development. These security conceptions, embodied in the creation and evolution of the hemispheric security system, persisted well after the ethos and institutions of the system had ceased to work. A living legacy of the "hemispheric security" views, in the current context of greater South American military autonomy, is found in the active inter-American military network in which the armed forces set out independently to determine long-range goals with almost no civilian input or control.[82]

Overall U.S. influence on the South American militaries has waned significantly over the past two decades. Partly as a result of shifting U.S. policies, the South American militaries became more autonomous and self-sufficient in most areas, including training, education, and arms procurement, rendering U.S. leverage over them lower than had been in the 1950s and 1960s. Regardless of their actual level of influence, policies and orientations developed by the U.S. and its military create situations which do not lead to opportunities favorable for democratization.[83] For instance, new doctrinal emphases on "low intensity conflict," following assessment of Central American armed movements, do not differ much from traditional counterinsurgency doctrines which led to military role expansion in the recent past.[84] The salience which the "drug war" has acquired internationally and domestically over recent years has also prompted renewed interest in internal military roles which do not bode well for attempts to depoliticize military professionalism.[85] These new emphases add to the unbalanced approach to democratic institution-building which for decades has underscored support to the militaries via "civic action" and other policies still at the core of U.S. security doctrine toward the region. Certainly, this international scenario is not one that encourages overt resistance by the military to political democratization; but it neither is one that excites military support for democratization or the chances of promoting civilian control.

Civilian Structures and Policies

The return of civilian elected governments unearthed weak civilian structures, this time compounded by the limitations imposed by an institutionally more assertive military. Weak institutions complicate governance, and weak parties make it harder to sustain policies and reforms through the bureaucratic and clientelistic interstices of the administration and the legislature. Poor government performance discredits civilian democratizers before the public, especially where the public's perception of the military's previous performance in government is positive, and weakens the civilian government's ascendancy over the military. Brazil has especially suffered from poor government performance in the context of weak parties, whereas other countries such as Uruguay have fared much better.

Policy orientations and leadership failures have added to the complications stemming from structural legacies. For instance, civilian elites have been unable to produce or sustain the high levels of coalescence which the magnitude of the military challenges and the civilian institutional weaknesses called for. Civilian coalescence has been lacking not only regarding the major economic and social challenges of the postauthoritarian period, but also in regard to the specific policies toward the military. By failing to display a united front, civilians have shown no common understanding of the obstacles which the military present for the prospects of democratic consolidation. A critical deterrent against the military, which would increase the costs of military domestic assertiveness, is thus given away, opening up civilian fissures for utilization by the military.[86] In this way, not only is resistance in the armed forces not discouraged; lack of unity among civilians also fails to provide critical reassurance about the prospects for long-term stability in military policies, which would help reduce uncertainty and make officers feel less threatened by democratic politics.[87]

Still more distressing is the unwillingness on the part of some civilian political groups to renounce the use of violent force as a means of pursuing their goals, an unwillingness which lurks behind the obstacles to civilian coalescence. In cases, such as Peru, where armed groups openly seek violent seizure of power, there is an obvious challenge to the military's claim to the monopoly of state armed force; this challenge in turn supports the military's continuing vigilance in internal affairs. However, other groups participating in state structures and running in elections maintain an ambiguous discourse which fails to renounce armed groups or armed strategies against "dominant structures." Such ambiguity, as can be found in sectors in the left in Peru and Chile, certainly lends no credence to a purported commitment to democratic procedures and can not strengthen attempts to reduce the enduring domestic involvement of the military. The complacence with which sectors on the right witness military political pressures and conditionings on democratic processes has similar effects.[88] Successful cases of democratization and civilian control exhibited no such ambiguities or complacencies. In Spain, for instance, the left gave remarkable proofs of democratic commitment and the right never resorted to military influence when the electoral or constitutional tide did not favor her preferred options. All major parties united in rejecting nationalist violence or terrorism from leftist or right-wing organizations.[89]

Finally, civilian political elites have been sluggish in crafting their own empowerment to deal authoritatively with military and defense affairs.[90] Deliberate efforts to develop expertise among civilian officials in government agencies concerned with defense and security have been slow to take off or have not taken off at all. In most cases, objective impediments exist as civilians find it hard to trespass military trenches in the state. As we noted earlier, only in Argentina have postmilitary governments been able to appoint civilians in the defense ministry. However, mostly concerned with the compelling need of defusing and weakening the military's political power, adjusting it to the new economic and political realities, civilians there have as yet failed to instill, under their own direction, a new sense of purpose in the security establishment.[91] Legislatures in these countries have been unable actively to monitor military affairs and to develop an appropriate support staff, perhaps frustrated by the meager oversight capacities given the legislatures on military matters. This sluggishness on the part of civilians reflects the difficulties of hurriedly developing expertise in a field neglected for so long by civilian political elites; it also reflects the lack of an adequate understanding of the long term approach which a military policy demands.

In addition, the staying power of the military's legal or de facto domestic prerogatives instills a feeling of pragmatic realism among many elites. This pragmatic attitude leads to a search for ways of institutionalizing civil-military coexistence under norms which are neither fully democratic nor authoritarian, but which purportedly have the advantage of better expressing the existing power relations. In support of this view it has been argued, for instance, that the large size of the military establishment, coupled with the absence of external threats, create a situation of "structural unemployment" for the military which can only be solved by employing the military in selected domestic areas.[92] This argument is similar in its conclusions to that which has for long supported an active participation of the military in "development tasks." Both arguments, however, give in to the military's claim to rightfully expanded domestic roles, and abdicate the need to define new military roles in line with the kind of "democratic professionalism" which the consolidation of democracy would require.

Conclusion

With differences across countries, the military presents solid barriers to democratic advancement in the postauthoritarian period in South America. The armed forces have cemented a situation of autonomy for themselves which prevents elected civilian officials from duly exercising full authority over military affairs. From this situation the military actively monitors the political process and institutions and remains professionally concerned with internal security. The resulting institutional and de facto framework of civil-military relations blurs the otherwise democratic character of the postauthoritarian regimes.

The ability of the military to stand in the way of democratization stems from a number of factors. First is the lasting impact which the initial conditions of the transition have had during the subsequent process of democratization under civilian elected regimes. The military occupied the leading positions in the outgoing authoritarian regimes, which enabled it to secure institutional guarantees and a large domestic role. Elected civilian officials were better positioned to resist military pressures and to assert their supremacy in other cases where the previous authoritarian regime, such as the Franquist regime in Spain, was largely civilianized.

Second, is the continuing vitality of doctrines which assign the military a vigilant role in all domestic areas with a view to defense against internal subversion. The persistence of these views has practically redefined the notion of military professionalism in ways that severely block any commitment to democracy. In successful cases of democratization in Southern Europe the military was not empowered with a comparable doctrine. Third, the relative unavailability of international opportunities which could strengthen democratization efforts and empower elected civilian officials vis-à-vis the military. The military international context seems, on the contrary, to affirm those internal trends which prevent military support to democratization.

Finally, failures in civilian policy orientations and leadership add to resurrected flaws in civilian institutions. Low levels of civilian political coalescence, ambiguous positions by various leftist and rightist groups on the uses of violence, and inability of civilians to provide leadership on defense and military matters, all contribute to a persistent resistance by the military to further political democratization.

Advancement of democratization requires the reversal of recalcitrant legacies of authoritarianism and of firmly held military perceptions about the nature and sources of major security threats. It also requires a special ability by civilians to overcome deeply rooted leadership flaws, especially in a structural context which will not suddenly become propitious for unconditionally committing the military to democratization. Finally, it will take commitment, resolution and expertise on the part of civilian leaders, coupled with the development of innovative concepts in the field of defense and security, to make it possible to enhance the ability of political elites to subdue the military obstacles to the consolidation of democracy.

NOTES

I am grateful to Paulette Higgins, Scott Mainwaring, Guillermo O'Donnell and David Pion-Berlin for helpful comments on earlier drafts. I also wish to thank the Helen Kellogg Institute of International Studies at the University of Notre Dame, where most of this paper was written while I was a fellow during the Fall of 1989.

1. Some of the best studies are: John Samuel Fitch, *The Military Coup d'Etat as a Political Process: Ecuador 1948–1966* (Baltimore: The Johns Hopkins University Press, 1977); Alfred Stepan, *The Military in Politics: Changing Patterns in Brazil* (Princeton: Princeton University Press, 1971); and Guillermo O'Donnell, "Modernization and Military Coups: Theory, Comparisons, and the Argentine Case," in *Armies and Politics in Latin America,* edited by Abraham F. Lowenthal and J. Samuel Fitch (New York: Holmes and Meier, 1986). See also Abraham F. Lowenthal, "Armies and Politics in Latin America: Introduction to the First Edition,"

and J. Samuel Fitch, "Armies and Politics in Latin America: 1975–1985," in *Armies and Politics;* Arturo Valenzuela, "A Note on the Military and Social Science Theory," *Third World Quarterly* 7, no. 1 (January 1985); and Martin C. Needler, "Military Motivations in the Seizure of Power," *Latin American Research Review* 10, no. 3 (1975).

2. The image of the military, however, did not deteriorate as much in those cases, such as Ecuador and Brazil, in which the military regime was comparatively perceived as successful. Anita Isaacs, "The Obstacles to Democratic Consolidation in Ecuador," paper prepared for the Latin American Studies Association XV International Congress, San Juan, Puerto Rico, September 21–23, 1989.

3. This fear and its utilization by actors' "playing coup poker" is especially relevant in the liberalization and transition periods, but it continues to influence actors' behavior during the democratic period. For its role in transitions, see Guillermo O'Donnell and Philippe C. Schmitter, *Transitions From Authoritarian Rule: Tentative Conclusions About Uncertain Democracies* (Baltimore: The Johns Hopkins University Press, 1986).

4. For an analysis of Latin American politics in terms of "power contenders" and "power capabilities" see "The Latin American Political System," chapter 4 in Charles Anderson, *Politics and Economic Change in Latin America* (Princeton: Princeton University Press, 1967). For an analysis of the different "currencies" which actors bring to bear in the Latin American political game see Eldon Kenworthy, "Coalitions in the Political Development of Latin America," in Sven Groennings, E. W. Kelley and Michael Leiserson, eds., *The Study of Coalition Behavior: Theoretical Perspectives from Four Continents* (New York: Holt, Reinhart and Winston, 1970).

5. As of this writing, all the defense or armed services ministers of the new South American democracies, with the exception of Argentina, Chile, and Uruguay, were military officers.

6. For an insightful review of recent trends see J. Samuel Fitch, "The Armed Forces and Democracy in Latin America," paper prepared for the Inter-American Dialogue, Working Group on Armed Forces and Democracy, Lima, August 16–17, 1987; and "Toward a Democratic Model of Civil-Military Relations for Latin America," paper presented to the International Political Science Association, Washington, D.C., August 31, 1988. See also chapter 5, "Preserving Democracy: The Military Challenge," in *The Americas in 1988: A Time for Choices,* a report of the Inter-American Dialogue jointly with the Aspen Institute for Humanistic Studies (Boston: University Press of America, 1988). Alfred Stepan, *Rethinking Military Politics* (Princeton: Princeton University Press, 1988) reviews the post-transition state of military contestation and prerogatives in Argentina, Brazil and Uruguay. See also, Alain Rouquié, *The Military and the State in Latin*

America (Berkeley: University of California Press, 1987), and Jan Knippers Black, *Sentinels of Empire: The United States and Latin American Militarism* (New York: Greenwood Press, 1986).

7. See Howard Handelman, "Politics and Plebiscites: The Case of Uruguay," *Working Paper* no. 39, Latin American Program, The Wilson Center, Washington, D.C., and "Prelude to Elections: The Military's Legitimacy Crisis and the 1980 Constitutional Plebiscite in Uruguay," in *Elections and Democratization in Latin America 1980–1985,* edited by Paul W. Drake and Eduardo Silva (San Diego: Center for Iberian and Latin American Studies, University of California, San Diego, 1986). Also, see Charles G. Gillespie, "Uruguay's Transition From Collegial Military-Technocratic Rule," in *Transitions From Authoritarian Rule: Latin America,* edited by Guillermo O'Donnell, Philippe C. Schmitter and Laurence Whitehead (Baltimore: The Johns Hopkins University Press, 1986).

8. The military and the government expected a 70 percent vote for retaining the amnesty law; the results were only 57 to 43 percent, with the majority coming mostly from the rural interior. In Montevideo, 55 percent of the voters favored a repeal of the amnesty law. Although amnestied, the military could hardly see its position strengthened from these tallies (*Southern Cone Report,* 25 May 1989). See also Germán Rama, "Verde o Amarillo? Plebiscito sobre amnistía a los militares en Uruguay," *Cono Sur* (Santiago) 8, no. 4 (1989); Guillermo Waksman, "Uruguay: Consagración de la democracia tutelada," *Nueva Sociedad* no. 102 (julio–agosto 1989); and Cynthia Brown and Robert K. Goldman, "Torture, Memory and Justice," *The Nation,* March 27, 1989. For a more general account of civil-military relations during redemocratization in Uruguay, see María del Huerto Amarillo, "La estrategia 'democrática' de la Seguridad Nacional," *Fuerzas Armadas y Sociedad* (Defensa y Desarme en América Latina y el Caribe) 3, no. 1–2 (enero–julio 1988); and Juan Rial, *Las Fuerzas Armadas: Soldados-políticos garantes de la democracia?* (Montevideo: CIESU-CLADE-Ediciones de la Banda Oriental, 1986).

9. See Catherine M. Conaghan, *Restructuring Domination: Industrialists and the State in Ecuador* (Pittsburgh: University of Pittsburgh Press, 1988), pp. 122–123 and 86–87, and "Party Politics and Democratization in Ecuador," in *Authoritarians and Democrats: Regime Transition in Latin America,* edited by James M. Malloy and Mitchell A. Seligson (Pittsburgh: University of Pittsburgh Press, 1987), p. 147. See also, Osvaldo Hurtado, *Political Power in Ecuador* (Albuquerque: University of New Mexico, 1980).

10. An excellent analysis of the changing context of civil-military relations during the democratization process in Ecuador and Peru is found in Fernando Bustamante, "Los militares y la creación de un nuevo orden democrático en Perú y Ecuador," paper presented at the XIV International

Congress of the Latin American Studies Association, New Orleans, March 1987. See also, by the same author, "El rol de los términos de la democratización post-militarista en la evolución democrática de los países andinos de América del Sur," *Documento de Trabajo* no. 328, FLACSO, Santiago de Chile, 1987, and "The Armed Forces of Colombia and Ecuador in Comparative Perspective," in Augusto Varas, ed., *Democracy Under Siege: New Military Power in Latin America,* (New York: Greenwood Press, 1989).

11. See Conaghan, *Restructuring Domination,* p. 126, and "Ecuador Swings Toward Social Democracy," *Current History* 88, no. 536 (March 1989).

12. Cynthia McClintock, "The Prospects for Democratic Consolidation in a 'Least Likely' Case: Peru," *Comparative Politics* (January 1989).

13. However, while the constituent assembly was in session prior to the transfer of power, members of the assembly rejected various requests by the military to delete transitory clauses in the Constitution which limited military power in civilian spheres. See Julio Cotler, "Military Interventions and 'Transfer of Power to Civilians' in Peru," in O'Donnell et al., *Transitions from Authoritarian Rule: Latin America.*

14. Days before stepping down from government in 1980, the military passed a Mobilization Law which guaranteed the continued involvement of the armed forces in matters related to national defense or domestic security. See Victor Villanueva, "Peru's 'New' Military Professionalism: The Failure of the Technocratic Approach," in Stephen M. Gorman, ed., *Post-Revolutionary Peru: The Politics of Transformation* (Boulder: Westview Press, 1982).

15. See, by Marcial Rubio Correa, "The Perception of the Subversive Threat in Peru," in Louis W. Goodman, Johanna S. R. Mendelson and Juan Rial, eds., *The Military and Democracy: The Future of Civil Military Relations in Latin America* (Lexington, Mass.: Lexington Books, 1990), and "The Armed Forces in Peruvian Politics," in Varas, ed., *Democracy Under Siege.* Also Luis A. Abugattas, "Populism and After: The Peruvian Experience," in Malloy and Seligson, *Authoritarians and Democrats.*

16. The Constitution sought to raise the cost of coup-making by declaring the people's right of insurgency against a usurper government (art. 82) and by denying state guarantees to public debt contracted under unconstitutional governments (art. 141). The Constitution also mandates the armed forces not to deliberate, and takes away their role of guarantors of the Constitution. Jurisdiction of military courts over civilians was severely limited (arts. 282 and 235), and the president was made the supreme chief of the armed forces and the police (art. 273). For a contrast of these norms against interpretations by military chiefs, see Luis Pásara, "La 'Libanización' en democracia," in Luis Pásara and Jorge Parodi, *Democracia, sociedad y gobierno en el Perú* (Lima: CEDYS, 1988). See also Mar-

cial Rubio and Enrique Bernales, *Perú: Constitución y sociedad política* (Lima: Desco, 1981).

17. Unrestrained military control of areas declared in state of emergency has led to a deplorable human rights situation. See reports by Amnesty International, and "Peru: Blanket Killings Are Policy Once More," *Latin American Weekly Report,* 31 August 1989, p. 9.

18. The second minister of defense, appointed in May 1989, also was an active-duty army general. For background discussion on the creation of the ministry see Marcial Rubio, *Ministerio de Defensa: Antecedentes y retos* (Lima: APEP-Friedrich Ebert, 1987). Other relevant works are Sandra Woy-Hazelton and William A. Hazelton, "Sustaining Democracy in Peru: Dealing with Parliamentary and Revolutionary Changes," in George A. Lopez and Michael Stohl eds., *Liberalization and Redemocratization in Latin America* (New York, Westport and London: Greenwood Press, 1987); Henry Pease García, "Perú: Construir la democracia desde la precariedad," *Revista Mexicana de Sociología* 50, no. 2 (April–June 1988), and Carlos A. Astiz, "A Postmortem of the Institutional Military Regime in Peru," in Constantine P. Danopoulos, ed., *The Decline of Military Regimes: The Civilian Influence* (Boulder and London: Westview Press, 1988).

19. At this writing, one third of Peru's territory was under state of emergency. See *The New York Times,* 26 October 1989, p. 6.

20. In contrast, the Venezuelan countersubversive struggle of the 1960s was staged under strong presidential leadership, helping to affirm democratic government. The military countersubversive campaigns did not substitute for emerging civil institutions. See Felipe Agüero, "The Military and Democracy in Venezuela," in Goodman et al., *The Military and Democracy.* For different military views on the war against *Sendero* see Philip Mauceri, *Militares: Insurgencia y democratización en el Perú 1980–1988* (Lima: Instituto de Estudios Peruanos, 1989).

21. See Cynthia McClintock, "Prospects for Democratic Consolidation."

22. Members of the last junta were acquitted from human rights cases but were later tried and sentenced by military courts for their responsibility in the outbreak, conduct and conclusion of the war over the Malvinas. For an account of the transition see Aldo Vacs, "Authoritarian Breakdown and Redemocratization in Argentina," in Malloy and Seligson, *Authoritarians and Democrats.*

23. For military reforms in Argentina, see *Civil-Military Relations: The Argentine Experience,* National Democratic Institute for International Affairs, The Report of an International Conference, Santo Domingo, December 16–18, 1988; Andrés Fontana, "La política militar del gobierno constitucional argentino," in José Nun and Juan Carlos Portantiero, eds., *Ensayos sobre la transición democrática en la Argentina,* (Buenos Aires:

Puntosur Editores, 1987); Carlos J. Moneta, "Fuerzas Armadas y Gobierno Constitucional Después de Malvinas: Hacia una Nueva Relación Civil-Militar," in C. J. Moneta et al., *La Reforma Militar* (Buenos Aires: Editorial Legasa, 1985); Gerardo R. Gargiulo, "Gasto militar y política de defensa," *Desarrollo Económico* 28, no. 109 (April–June 1988); Robert A. Potash, "Alfonsín and the Argentine Military," paper prepared for the Latin American Studies Association XV International Congress, Miami, December 4–6, 1989; Deborah L. Norden, "The Conceptual Game of Civil-Military Relations," paper presented in the XVII Latin American Congress of Sociology, Montevideo, December 1988.

24. J. Samuel Fitch, "Toward a Democratic Model."

25. Juan Domingo Perón succeeded himself in the presidency in 1951, having been duly elected both times. The year 1989 was the first time since the introduction of universal suffrage in which rival parties alternated in power. See *Latin America Weekly Report,* 25 May 1989, and Gary W. Wynia, "Campaigning for President in Argentina," *Current History* no. 536 (March 1989).

26. The pardons ended trials of officers for human rights abuses and were extended also to those accused of participation the 1987 and 1988 rebellions. President Menem, while receiving one of the rebel leaders in his presidential residence, announced that in the near future he would also pardon the former junta members serving prison terms. *New York Times,* 9–10 October 1989.

27. See Ernesto López, *El último levantamiento* (Buenos Aires: Editorial Legasa, 1988).

28. See Isidoro Cheresky, "Argentina: A Blackmailed Democracy," *Telos* 75 (Spring 1988).

29. See Jorge Orlando Melo, "La Constitución brasileña: liberalismo, democracia y participación," *Análisis Político* (Bogotá) No. 6 (January–April 1989).

30. See Alfred Stepan, *The Military in Politics: Changing Patterns in Brazil* (Princeton: Princeton University Press, 1971), p. 75; Roberto A. R. de Aguiar, *Os militares e a Constituinte* (São Paulo: Editora Alfa-Omega, 1986) and Felipe Agüero, "La Constitución y las Fuerzas Armadas en Algunos Países de América del Sur y España," *Revista de Ciencia Política* (Santiago), Vol. 8, Nos. 1–2, 1986.

31. ". . . under the authority of the President of the Republic, [the Armed Forces] are assigned with the defense of the Fatherland, the guarantee of the constitutional powers and, on the initiative of any one of these powers, of law and order" (my translation). Article 142 in Title V (On the Defense of the State and of Democratic Institutions) of the 1988 Constitution of the Federal Republic of Brazil.

32. This view is maintained by Eliézer Rizzo de Oliveira, "O papel

das Forças Armadas na nova Constituição e no Futuro da Democracia no Brasil," *Vozes* 82, no. 2, (July–December 1988).

33. The SNI chief, a general and cabinet member, reflects the broad powers which the military holds by acting as a liaison between the president and influential groups outside the government, and even between these groups themselves. For the Brazilian case see Walder de Góes, "Military and Political Transition," in Julian M. Chacel, Pamela S. Falk, and David V. Fleischer, eds., *Brazil's Economic and Political Future* (Boulder: Westview Press, 1988), and "Militares e Política, Uma Estratégia Para a Democracia," in Fabio Wanderley Reis and Guillermo O'Donnell, eds., *A democracia no Brasil: dilemas e perspectivas* (São Paulo: Vértice, 1988); Alfred Stepan, *Rethinking Military Politics;* Eliézer Rizzo de Oliveira "Constituinte, Forças Armadas e Autonomia Militar," in Oliveira et al., *As Forças Armadas no Brasil* (Rio de Janeiro: Espaço e Tempo, 1987), and "O Aparelho Militar: Papel Tutelar na Nova República," in João Quartim de Moraes et al., *A Tutela Militar* (São Paulo: Vértice, Editora Revista dos Tribunais, 1987); Alexandre Barros, "The Brazilian Military in the Late 1980s and Early 1990s: Is the Risk of Intervention Gone?" in Goodman et al., *The Military and Democracy;* Paul Zagorski, "The Brazilian Military Under the 'New Republic'," *Review of Latin American Studies* 1, no. 2 (1988); Daniel Zirker, "Civilian-Military Mediation in 'Post-Authoritarian' Brazil," paper prepared for the Annual Meeting of the Midwest Political Science Association, Chicago, April 13–15, 1989; Benicio Viero Schmidt, "Transición y crisis de gobernabilidad en Brasil," *Revista Mexicana de Sociología* 2 (April–June 1988); Thomas E. Skidmore, *The Politics of Military Rule in Brazil 1964–1985* (New York and Oxford: Oxford University Press, 1988); Frances Hagopian and Scott Mainwaring, "Democracy in Brazil: Problems and Prospects," *World Policy Journal* (Summer 1987); William C. Smith, "The Travail of Brazilian Democracy in the 'New Republic'," *Journal of Interamerican Studies and World Affairs* 28, no. 4 (Winter 1986–1987), and Edmundo Campos Coelho, "Back to the Barracks: the Brazilian Military's Style," in Danopoulous, ed., *The Decline of Military Regimes.*

34. Peter Flynn, "Brazil and Inflation: A Threat to Democracy," *Third World Quarterly* no. 3 (July 1989).

35. In Bolivia, since democratization resumed in 1982, military factions remain watchful of the ability of changing governing coalitions to keep popular mobilization at bay. See Raúl Barrios, "The Armed Forces and Democratization in Bolivia, 1982–1986," in Varas, ed., *Democracy Under Siege;* James M. Malloy, "Democracy, Economic Crisis and The Problem of Governance: The Case of Bolivia," paper prepared for the Latin American Studies Association XV International Congress, San Juan, Puerto Rico, September 21–23, 1989; James M. Malloy and Eduardo A. Gamarra,

"The Transition to Democracy in Bolivia," in Malloy and Seligson, eds., *Authoritarians and Democrats;* Claude E. Welch, Jr., *No Farewell To Arms? Military Disengagement From Politics in Africa and Latin America* (Boulder and London: Westview Press, 1987); Laurence Whitehead, "Bolivia's Failed Democratization, 1977–1980," in Guillermo O'Donnell, Phillipe C. Schmitter and Laurence Whitehead, eds., *Transitions From Authoritarian Rule: Latin America* (Baltimore: The Johns Hopkins University Press, 1986), and Eduardo A. Gamarra, "Bolivia: Disengagement and Democratization," in Constantine P. Danopoulos, ed., *Military Disengagement From Politics* (London and New York: Routledge, 1988).

36. In Peru by replacing general Velasco Alvarado with general Morales Bermúdez in the presidency, following the coup of 1975; in Ecuador by replacing president general Rodríguez Lara with the triumvirate led by Admiral Poveda in 1976.

37. In Ecuador, the military sponsored a plebiscite on the constitution in 1978, getting its way; in Peru, also in 1978, the military called for the election of a constitutional convention in which the military struck a deal with APRA, a historic adversary but which held similar policy orientations. APRA held a plurality in the convention and its old leader Víctor Raúl Haya de la Torre presided the Assembly. For Peru, see Carol Graham, "APRA (1968–1978) from Opposition to Government: The Elusive Search for National Integration in Peru," (Ph.D. dissertation, Oxford University, 1989).

38. For a discussion of the "institutionalist" perspective among Peruvian officers, see Mauceri, *Militares.*

39. The military banned the leader of *Concentración de Fuerzas Populares,* Assad Bucaram, from running in the first postmilitary presidential elections, and has later played with coup rumors every time this party has had a good electoral chance. On the other hand, the fear of patrimonialistic behavior on the part of the business political factions were strongly confirmed during the presidency of former business leader León Febres Cordero, whose "imperial presidency" was largely responsible for the reawakening of the military's political activism. See Catherine M. Conaghan, *Restructuring Domination,* p. 131; Fernando Bustamante, "Los militares y la creación de un nuevo orden democrático en Perú y Ecuador," and Osvaldo Hurtado, "Changing Latin American Attitudes: Prerequisite to Institutionalizing Democracy," in Robert Pastor, ed., *Democracy in the Americas: Stopping the Pendulum* (New York and London: Holmes & Meier, 1989).

40. See Guillermo O'Donnell,. *Modernization and Bureaucratic-Authoritarianism: Studies in South American Politics* (Berkeley: Institute of International Studies, University of California, 1973); *Bureaucratic Authoritarianism: Argentina 1966–1973 in Comparative Perspective* (Berke-

ley and Los Angeles: University of California Press, 1988), and Robert R. Kaufman, "Liberalization and Democratization in South America: Perspectives from the 1970s," in Guillermo O'Donnell, Philippe C. Schmitter and Laurence Whitehead, eds., *Transitions From Authoritarian Rule: Comparative Perspectives* (Baltimore and London: The Johns Hopkins University Press, 1986).

41. However, as a result of the extremely repressive policies which these militaries conducted against working class organizations and parties during the authoritarian regime, the military has sought protective guarantees against eventual legal action for human rights violations.

42. Within the armed forces of Peru and Ecuador, distrust for parties is based on the clientelistic threat but mostly on the view that parties fail to perform their proper functions. In this view, the problems of national security are intimately connected with the problems of national integration, social progress and development. Solutions to these problems — it is held — are principally political, and therefore, parties and political institutions ought to play the central role. The main criticism of parties is precisely that they fail to perform this function.

43. Military contestation and military prerogatives are analyzed in Stepan, *Rethinking Military Politics*.

44. Excellent analyses are Luciano Martins, "The 'Liberalization' of Authoritarian Rule in Brazil," in O'Donnell et al., *Transitions From Authoritarian Rule: Latin America* and, with a specific focus on the military, Alfred Stepan, *Rethinking Military Politics*. For elements of continuity in the Brazilian transition see the chapter by Frances Hagopian in this volume.

45. In reaction to the incipient program of the opposition on defense, the military emphatically specified critical areas that should remain out of the government's sphere of action. See *La Época* (Santiago) 24 August 1989, p. 13, and "Chile: Pinochet Issues an Ultimatum," *Latin American Weekly Report,* 7 September 1989.

46. Ultimately the military had little success but, by staying in power passing obstructive legislation for the successor government, it made the latter's task more difficult and raised the stakes in the civil-military confrontations which followed. The differences with the Greek transition, with which the Argentine transition is often compared, are striking in this regard. Following similar international embarrassment and collapse, the military in Greece exited instantly and a new civilian government was inaugurated almost overnight, finding the road to democratization "cleaner" than was the case in Argentina. On Greece see Harry J. Psomiades, "Greece: From the Colonels' Rule to Democracy," in John Herz, ed., *From Dictatorship to Democracy* (Westport: Greenwood Press, 1982), and Nikiforos Diamandouros, "Regime Change and the Prospects for Democracy in

Greece: 1974–1983," in O'Donnell, et al., *Transitions from Authoritarian Rule: Southern Europe* (Baltimore: The Johns Hopkins University Press, 1986). On Argentina see David Pion-Berlin, "The Fall of Military Rule in Argentina, 1976–1983," *Journal of Interamerican Studies and World Affairs* 27, no. 2 (Summer 1985); Aldo Vacs, "Authoritarian Breakdown," and Andrés Fontana, *Fuerzas Armadas, partidos políticos y transición a la democracia en Argentina* (Buenos Aires: CEDES, 1984), and "De la crisis de Malvinas a la subordinación condicionada: conflictos intramilitares y transición política en Argentina," *Working Paper* no. 74, Kellogg Institute, August 1986.

47. Obviously, as O'Donnell's concept of bureaucratic authoritarianism highlights, civilian technocrats played critical roles in these regimes, especially in the economic sector, along with former party leaders of the right and businessmen, particularly in the cases of Argentina, Chile, Brazil and Uruguay. In Peru, civilian technocrats also played critical, albeit different roles. The notion of a *militarized regime* points, however, to the centrality of the military in governing roles such as passing laws, making crucial appointments in the administration, and defining broad orientations for the government, all of which require the military to develop the appropriate structures that are necessary to be involved and well informed. Functionally this is quite different from the role of the military in *civilianized authoritarian regimes,* where the military can afford to remain somewhat more aloof.

48. The *Proceso,* as this period (1976–1983) was called, differed from the first part of the previous dictatorship (1966–1973), in that its first leader, president Onganía, retired from active duty, obtained greater independence from the military to govern and appointed civilians to all cabinet positions. He, nonetheless, succumbed to military pressure and was replaced by General Levingston and, later, by General Lanusse. During the *Proceso,* on the contrary, the top chiefs were from the start accountable to their respective council of generals or admirals. See Daniel García Delgado and Marcelo Stiletano, "La participación de los militares en los nuevos autoritarismos: la Argentina del 'Proceso' (1976–1983)," *Opciones* no. 14 (May–August 1988); O'Donnell, *Bureaucratic Authoritarianism;* and Peter G. Snow, "Military Government in Argentina," in Robert Wesson, ed., *New Military Politics in Latin America* (New York: Praeger, 1982).

49. Along with paramilitary death squads, "each service branch, military district, police district and police station had its own 'operative' group." See Paul G. Buchanan, "The Varied Faces of Domination: State Terror, Economic Policy, and Social Rupture during the Argentine 'Proceso', 1976–81," *American Journal of Political Science* 31, no. 2 (May 1987).

50. The minister of the interior was a military officer while, quite uncharacteristically, the defense portfolio remained in the hands of a ci-

vilian. Whereas the cabinets in Uruguay's authoritarian government were almost entirely civilian, Peru, at the other extreme, had an all-military cabinet under the presidency of Gen. Velasco Alvarado (1968–1975). Following the coup that put general Morales Bermúdez in the presidency, only two civilians were appointed as ministers of economy and foreign affairs. The other South American cases stand somewhere in between. Starting out with high levels of cabinet participation, especially in the Chilean and Argentine authoritarian regimes, the military ended up with about one third of the total number of government ministers. For these latter cases see Carlos Huneeus and Jorge Olave, "La participación de los militares en los nuevos autoritarismos: Chile en una perspectiva comparada," *Opciones* (Santiago) no. 11 (May–August 1987), and Daniel García Delgado and Marcelo Stiletano, "La participación."

51. See Juan Rial, *Fuerzas Armadas.*

52. See Julio Cotler, "Military Interventions," and the articles by Peter S. Cleaves and Henry Pease García, "State Autonomy and Military Policy Making"; by Lisa L. North, "Ideological Orientations of Peru's Military Rulers," and by Luis Pásara, "When the Military Dreams," in Cynthia McClintock and Abraham F. Lowenthal, *The Peruvian Experiment Reconsidered* (Princeton: Princeton University Press, 1983).

53. According to Hurtado, "the entire upper echelon of the military, and in some instances even certain other officers' groups, participate in all fundamental policy decisions carried out by the regime." Also, "all cabinet positions and public institutions headed by nonmilitary ministers or directors had as undersecretaries or subdirectors ranking officers in the military establishment." *Political Power in Ecuador,* p. 259 and p. 355.

54. All these agencies expressed the various forms of military participation which Alfred Stepan described as military-as-government, military-as-institution, and the information community. See Stepan, *Rethinking Military Politics,* as well as Maria Helena Moreira Alves, *State and Opposition in Military Brazil* (Austin: University of Texas Press, 1985). Also, see Ronald Schneider, "The Brazilian Military in Politics," in Wesson, *New Military Politics;* and Robert Wesson and David Fleischer, *Brazil in Transition* (New York: Praeger, 1983).

55. The personalization of power around Pinochet was combined, however, with high levels of military participation, and this is a critical difference with Franquism. Although the military under Pinochet did not have an institutionalized presence in different state organs as did the military in Franquist Spain, in Chile the military was closer to government decision making and, above all, the junta, as the supreme institutional expression of the armed forces, maintained control of legislation until the end.

56. With the exception of Stroessner in Paraguay. But even his long lasting reign was ended by a military coup in 1989. For a recent study on

Paraguay see Diego Abente, "Stronismo, Post-Stronismo and the Prospects for Democratization in Paraguay," *Working Paper* Kellogg Institute, no. 119, March 1989.

57. All the president's advisory committees were integrated in 1983 under the new post of Minister Secretary General of the Presidency. See Carlos Huneeus and Jorge Olave, "La participación" and Carlos Huneeus, "El Ejército y la política en el Chile de Pinochet: su magnitud y alcances," *Opciones* no. 14 (May–August 1988). See also Genaro Arriagada, *Pinochet: The Politics of Power* (Boston: Unwin and Hyman, 1988); Augusto Varas, *Los militares en el poder: régimen y gobierno militar en Chile 1973–1986* (Santiago: FLACSO and Pehuén Editores, 1987); Karen L. Remmer, "Neopatrimonialism: The Politics of Military Rule in Chile, 1973–1987," *Comparative Politics,* January 1989; and Felipe Agüero, "La autonomía de las Fuerzas Armadas" in Jaime Gazmuri, ed., *Chile en el umbral de los noventa* (Santiago: Editorial Planeta Chilena, 1988).

58. After a new constitution was promulgated in 1980, the junta retained the power to initiate constitutional reforms, but these would have to be approved in referendum. Regarding the appointment of the president, the junta designated its own president — Pinochet — officially to the post of President of the Republic and Supreme Chief of the Nation in 1974. The referendum of 1980 on the constitution prolonged Pinochet's mandate until 1990. For the presidential plebiscite that the Constitution prescribed for 1989, the junta had to nominate a single candidate. Pinochet, the junta's nominee, was defeated in the referendum of October, 1988. According to the Constitution, competitive elections were held in December 1989 and a new government was installed in March, 1990.

59. See Juan Linz, "An Authoritarian Regime: Spain," in Erik Allardt and Stein Rokkan, eds., *Mass Politics* (New York: The Free Press, 1970); Raymond Carr and Juan Pablo Fusi, *Spain: Dictatorship to Democracy* (London: Allen and Unwin, 1983); Stanley Payne, *The Franco Regime 1936–1975* (Madison: The University of Wisconsin Press, 1987); José Antonio Olmeda, *Las fuerzas armadas en el estado franquista* (Madrid: Ediciones El Arquero, 1988), and "The Armed Forces in the Francoist Political System," in Rafael Bañón and Thomas M. Barker, eds., *Armed Forces and Society in Spain: Past and Present* (New York: Columbia University Press, 1988).

60. Alfred Stepan, who focused on the specific nature of the actors leading the transition, already pointed to the inadequacy of grouping Spain and Brazil together. See his "Paths Toward Redemocratization," in O'Donnell et al., *Transition from Authoritarian Rule: Comparative Perspective,* pp. 74–75. Also Guillermo O'Donnell's chapter in this volume points to several other important differences between the Brazilian and Spanish transitions. For a comparison of Brazil and Spain, see Donald Share and Scott

Mainwaring, "Transitions Through Transaction: Democratization in Brazil and Spain," in Wayne Selcher, ed., *Political Liberalization in Brazil* (Boulder: Westview Press, 1986). Also, the category of "transition through regime defeat," under which the cases of Argentina, Greece and Portugal are often placed together, fails to account for critical differences in the nature of the elite actually in control *during* the transition. These differences influenced the post-transition processes which unfolded in quite distinct ways in these countries.

61. Juan Linz has observed that if the armed forces in Spain had been able to expand their prerogatives during the transition, they most certainly would have made the negotiation of the autonomy statutes for the historic regions, an issue critically sensitive for the military, much more difficult if not entirely impossible. Juan J. Linz, "Some Comparative Thoughts on the Transition to Democracy in Portugal and Spain," in Jorge Braga de Macedo and Simon Serfaty, eds., *Portugal Since the Revolution: Economic and Political Perspectives* (Boulder: Westview Press, 1981), p. 32.

62. I have compared the initial conditions of Southern European and South American transitions in my "The Military in the Processes of Political Democratization in South America and Southern Europe: Outcomes and Initial Conditions," paper presented to the XV International Congress of the Latin American Studies Association, Miami, December 4–6, 1989. I have analyzed the Spanish case in "Democracia en España y Supremacía Civil," *Revista Española de Investigaciones Sociológicas* no. 44 (1988), and in "Militärwesen in Spanien nach dem Ende der Franco-Zeit," in Walther L. Bernecker and Josef Oehrlein, eds., *Spanien Heute* (Frankfurt: Vervuert, 1990). See also Fernando Rodrigo, "El papel de las Fuerzas Armadas españolas durante la transición política: algunas hipótesis básicas," *Revista Internacional de Sociología* 43, no. 2 (abril–junio 1985); José María Comas, "The Central Organization of Defense in Spain," in *Central Organizations of Defense,* edited by Martin Edmonds (Boulder: Westview Press, 1985); Stanley Payne, "Modernization of the Armed Forces," in *The Politics of Democratic Spain,* edited by Stanley Payne (Chicago: Council on Foreign Relations, 1986), and Rafael Bañón, "The Spanish Armed Forces During the Period of Political Transition, 1975–1985," in Bañón and Baker, eds., *Armed Forces and Society in Spain: Past and Present.*

63. For instance, Pinochet said: "I should have held my grip tight until the very end. Freedom of the press was granted much too soon . . . they [the press] were authorized to speak with the politicians, who should not have spoken. That is the problem." Quoted in *El País* (Madrid), 12 August 1989, p. 3. (My translation).

64. After the Malvinas debacle and unable to reach a compromise with the Multipartidaria, a front expressing all the opposition parties, the military attempted to strike deals with parts of the Peronist party and the

labor movement, in the belief that the Peronists would win the presidential elections. Vacs, "Authoritarian Breakdown," pp. 30–31.

65. Other important dimensions which affect the power of the military during and after the transition include the extent and depth of cleavages within the military and the extent of policy success of the authoritarian regime. Some of the consequences of policy success are analyzed in Guillermo O'Donnell's chapter in this volume.

66. This hope emerged especially with the Brazilian case in mind. See Stanley E. Hilton, "The Brazilian Military: Changing Strategic Perceptions and the Question of Mission," *Armed Forces and Society* 13, no. 3 (Spring 1987); Alexandre de S. C. Barros, "Back to the Barracks: An Option for the Brazilian Military?" *Third World Quarterly* 7, no. 1 (January 1985); Alfred Stepan and Michael J. Fitzpatrick, "Civil-Military Relations and Democracy: the Role of the Military in the Polity," paper prepared for the project, "The Role of Political Parties in the Return to Democracy in the Southern Cone," sponsored by the Latin American Program of the Woodrow Wilson International Center for Scholars and the World Peace Foundation, 1985.

67. See the yearbooks published by the Stockholm International Peace Research Institute during the 1980s, *SIPRI Yearbook: World Armaments and Disarmament* (published in London by Taylor and Francis until 1986, and from 1987 onwards in Oxford by Oxford University Press).

68. See *Arms Production in the Third World,* edited by Michael Brzoska and Thomas Ohlson (London: Taylor and Francis, 1986); Michael Morris and Victor Millan, eds., *Controlling Latin American Conflicts* (Boulder: Westview Press, 1983); Augusto Varas, *Militarization and the International Arms Race in Latin America* (Boulder: Westview Press, 1985); Jack Child, *Geopolitics and Conflict in South America* (New York: Praeger, 1985); Philip Kelly and Jack Child, eds., *Geopolitics of the Southern Cone and Antarctica* (Boulder: Lynne Rienner, 1988).

69. Alfred Stepan, for instance, introduced the distinctions "military-as-government" and "military-as-institution" to account for the divisions that emerge during military authoritarian rule (see note 54 above).

70. This was true especially for the relatively more advanced militaries of Brazil and Argentina. In other countries, military modernization was more restricted to acquisitions of modern weaponry. See Stanley Hilton, "The Brazilian Military"; Scott D. Tollefson, "Brazil, the United States and the Missile Technology Control Regime," paper presented at the XV International Congress of the Latin American Studies Association, Miami, 4–6 December 1989; Keith E. Wixler, "Argentina's Geopolitics and her Revolutionary Diesel-Electric Submarines," *Naval War College Review* 42, no. 1 (Winter 1989). However, none of these militaries pursued organizational changes aimed at enhancing their ability for joint

planning and operations in any serious way as part of the modernization effort.

71. In Peru, however, the quick rise of Sendero Luminoso's threat along with the inauguration of democracy in 1980 prevented this hope from emerging.

72. Alfred Stepan, "The New Professionalism of Internal Warfare and Military Role Expansion," in Stepan, ed., *Authoritarian Brazil* (New Haven: Yale University Press, 1973).

73. The term "politicized professionalism" is used by J. Samuel Fitch. For a thorough and broader discussion of military professionalization and professionalism, both conceptually and empirically, see the excellent review in his "Military Professionalism, National Security and Democracy: Lessons From the Latin American Experience," paper prepared for the Latin American Studies Association XV International Congress, Miami, December 4–6, 1989.

74. A connection which had long ceased to exist, for instance, for the militaries concerned with popular rebellion in Peru or with union activities and electoral mobilization of the left in Brazil.

75. As Alexandre Barros argues in the case of Brazil, the "process of military professionalization is intertwined with the process of politicization of the military. Virtually any senior military officer is likely to have been through some civilian or quasi-civilian assignment during his career. In addition, the contents of military education stress the role of the military in functions that are not strictly military. Thus, because the military has been involved in politics and in administration for such a long time, professionalization almost necessarily involves some sort of civilian appointment. In the Brazilian case, then, professionalization, in and of itself, does not diminish the degree of military interventionism." Alexandre Barros, "The Brazilian Military in the Late 1980s and Early 1990s," pp. 181–182.

76. See the editorial of *El Soldado* no. 122 (May–June 1989), and Carina Perelli, *Someter o convencer: el discurso militar* (Montevideo: Ediciones de la Banda Oriental, 1987).

77. Even the massive civil reaction against the crimes committed by the armed forces is viewed by the military as one more expression of Marxist subversion. See Deborah L. Norden, "Democratic Consolidation and Military Professionalism in Argentina," paper presented to the Latin American Studies Association XV International Congress, Miami, December 4–6, 1989. See also, by David Pion-Berlin, "The National Security Doctrine, Military Threat Perception, and the 'Dirty War' in Argentina," *Comparative Political Studies* 21, no. 3 (October 1988), and "Latin American National Security Doctrines: Hard- and Softline Themes," *Armed Forces and Society* 15, no. 3 (Spring 1989).

78. In most cases, "politicized professionalism" is more prevalent in the land army than in the navy and the air force, which are much more absorbed in technological modernization and the challenges of external defense.

79. Although changing policies of U.S. administrations toward authoritarian governments have influenced the prospects for democratization and the expectations of local militaries, I focus here on more permanent aspects of the international military context and, more specifically, of the inter-American military context. For more general analyses of international variables surrounding the transitions, see Laurence Whitehead, "International Aspects of Democratization," in *Transitions From Authoritarian Rule: Comparative Perspectives,* and Alfred Tovias, "The International Context of Democratic Transition," in Geoffrey Pridham, ed., *The New Mediterranean Democracies: Regime Transition in Spain, Greece and Portugal* (London: Frank Cass, 1984). For changing elements in U.S. policies see, by Lars Schoultz, *Human Rights and United States Policy toward Latin America* (Princeton: Princeton University Press, 1981), and *National Security and United States Policy Toward Latin America* (Princeton: Princeton University Press, 1987). For a case study see Heraldo Muñoz and Carlos Portales, *Elusive Friendship: A Survey of U.S.-Chilean Relations* (Boulder: Lynne Rienner, 1989).

80. This has been the most clear positive impact of entering NATO for the establishment of civil-military relations consistent with political democratization. For general accounts see Federico G. Gil and Joseph S. Tulchin, eds., *Spain's Entry into NATO* (Boulder and London: Lynne Rienner Publishers, 1988), and John Chipman, ed., *NATO's Southern Allies* (London and New York: Routledge, 1988). More general statements about the connections between NATO and democratization are less clear, as countries have been NATO members while sustaining repressive dictatorships, such as Greece, Portugal and Turkey.

81. See Heraldo Muñoz, "The Rise and Decline of the Inter-American System: A Latin American View," in Richard Bloomfield and Gregory F. Treverton, eds., *Alternative to Intervention: A New U.S.-Latin American Security Relationship* (Boulder and London: Lynne Rienner Publishers, 1990); Jack Child, *Unequal Alliance: The Inter-American Military System 1938–1978* (Boulder: Westview Press, 1980); Gregory F. Treverton, "Interstate Conflict in Latin America," in *The United States and Latin America in the 1980s,* edited by Kevin J. Middlebrook and Carlos Rico (Pittsburgh: University of Pittsburgh Press, 1986), and Jack Child, "Interstate Conflict in Latin America in the 1980s," in Jennie K. Lincoln and Elizabeth G. Ferris, eds., *The Dynamics of Latin American Foreign Policies: Challenges for the 1980s* (Boulder: Westview Press, 1984).

82. For instance, participants in the XVII Conference of American

Armies, held in Mar del Plata in 1987, agreed to exchange information on "subversive activities," which were seen as including ideological subversion promoted by the "international communist movement" as well as drug trafficking. See J. Samuel Fitch, "Inter-American Military Relations: Past, Present and Future," unpublished paper, University of Colorado and Carlos J. Moneta, "El papel de la cooperación intermilitar en la autonomia y la democratización de América Latina," *Defensa y Sociedad* no. 3 (diciembre 1988). Also, Martin Edwin Andersen, "The Military Obstacle to Latin Democracy," *Foreign Policy* no. 73 (Winter 1988–1989).

83. This view is certainly less optimistic than General Fred F. Woerner's, former chief of the U.S. Southern Command, who argued that accompanying the trend towards democratization there "has been a decisive turnaround in U.S. policy. We no longer see an incompatibility between our ideals and our strategic interests." Quoted in "The United States Southern Command: Shield of Democracy in Latin America" (public relations release, U.S. Southern Command, n.d.).

84. See Lidia Bermúdez, *Guerra de baja intensidad: Reagan contra Centroamérica* (México: Siglo XXI, 1986); Loren B. Thompson, *Low Intensity Conflict: The Pattern of Warfare in the Modern World* (Lexington: Lexington Books, 1989), and Fernando Bustamante, "Los intereses estratégicos de los Estados Unidos y América Latina en los años 80," Documento de Trabajo no. 398, FLACSO, Santiago de Chile, March 1989. See also the articles in *Military Review,* May–June 1986.

85. Louis W. Goodman and Johanna S. R. Mendelson, "The Threat of New Missions: Latin American Militaries and the Drug War," in Goodman et al., *The Military and Democracy.*

86. President Menem's and Peronist sectors' willingness to fraternize with some of the officers who rebelled during the Alfonsín administration is a dramatic example. Short term benefits for politicians and parties blur the longer term gains which would very likely obtain for democratic consolidation if the major civilian parties persevered in the support of policies which were initially supported by a broad consensus.

87. For instance, significant variations in military expenditures in a short period of time make little sense unless they are either forced by a recessionary period, or supported by a long-term policy rationale. Neither of these factors were initially behind the variations experienced in the postmilitary period in Peru, where sharp increases by Belaúnde's administration in the early 1980s were followed by sharp cuts. Variations of this kind indicate no shared view among civilian leaders about the direction for military policies.

88. This complacent attitude is especially visible among Brazilian elites, and also in Chile, both cases in which military regimes were comparatively successful. For Argentina, see Atilio A. Borón, "Authoritarian

Ideological Traditions and Transition Towards Democracy in Argentina," *Papers on Latin America* no. 8, The Institute of Latin American and Iberian Studies, Columbia University; Edward L. Gibson, "Democracy and The New Electoral Right in Argentina," *Papers on Latin America* no. 12, The Institute of Latin American and Iberian Studies, Columbia University; and Carlos Altamirano, "Realmente hay una nueva derecha en Argentina?" *Nueva Sociedad* no. 102 (Julio–Agosto 1989). For an interesting discussion see Laurence Whitehead, "The Consolidation of Fragile Democracies: A Discussion with Illustrations," in Pastor, ed., *Democracy in the Americas.* For attitudes from the Left see Luis Pásara, "Perú: La izquierda legal en la precariedad democrática," CEDYS, Lima, August 1989, and Augusto Varas, ed., *El Partido Comunista en Chile* (Santiago: FLACSO, 1988).

89. See Juan Linz and Alfred Stepan, "Political Crafting of Democratic Consolidation or Destruction: European and South American Comparisons," in Pastor, ed., *Democracy in the Americas.* In Venezuela, which also is a good example, political handling of armed opposition played a critical role in democratization and civilian control. See my "The Military and Democracy in Venezuela," in Goodman et al., *The Military and Democracy.*

90. See Alfred Stepan, *Rethinking Military Politics,* and Juan Linz and Alfred Stepan, "Political Crafting." Some important works with innovative thinking in this area can be found in Carlos J. Moneta, "Fuerzas Armadas y gobierno constitucional después de Malvinas: hacia una nueva Relación civil-militar"; Augusto Varas, "Civil-Military Relations in a Democratic Framework," in Goodman et al., *The Military and Democracy;* Augusto Varas, ed., *Hacia el Siglo XXI: La proyección estratégica de Chile* (Santiago: FLACSO, 1989), and Centro de Estudios del Desarrollo, *Fuerzas Armadas, Estado y Sociedad: el papel de las Fuerzas Armadas en la futura democracia chilena* (Santiago: Hachette/CED, 1989).

91. Morris Janowitz rightly argued that "the task of civilian leadership includes not only the political direction of the military, but the prevention of the growth of frustration in the profession, of felt injustice, and inflexibility under the weight of its responsibilities." Morris Janowitz, *The Professional Soldier* (New York: The Free Press, 1971), p. lviii.

92. In my view, three important misrepresentations are made in this argument. The first one is the assumption that there are no real security concerns in South America that can really justify the maintenance of armed forces. Admittedly, the nature of the security problems for South American countries should be a matter of debate, from which conclusions should be drawn about the best type of armed forces (probably much smaller and efficient) to maintain; but it would be hard to sustain that there are no security problems. The second misrepresentation is that the situation of "structural unemployment" of the armed forces can only be disproved by

the occurrence of frequent warfare. This view fails to understand the deterrent character of armed force. The third misrepresentation is that domestic employment of the military is the only solution to a situation in which warfare is very infrequent and unlikely. Why this is a better solution than the reduction of the armed forces to a size commensurate to the perceived security threats is not clear. The logic of the argument I criticize would lead the United States, for instance, to give domestic uses to its military rather than to reduce the forces as has been proposed following the evident decrease of the Soviet and Warsaw Pact threat during 1989. For criticism of the argument as well as a presentation of the debate in the Brazilian context see Walder de Góes, "Militares e Política, Uma Estratégia para a Democracia." Alexandre Barros has referred to the institutional unemployment of the military in Brazil following protracted authoritarian rule, as a factor which politicians should especially consider in order to define a new, legitimate function for the military to perform. See his "The Brazilian Military in the Late 1980s and Early 1990s" and Alexandre de S. C. Barros and Edmundo C. Coelho, "Military Intervention and Withdrawal in South America," *International Political Science Review* 2, no. 3 (1981).

Capitalists, Technocrats, and Politicians: Economic Policy Making and Democracy in the Central Andes

Catherine M. Conaghan

Introduction

For domestic capitalists in the central Andes, the return to democracy meant the chance to create or resuscitate their instruments of influence over economic policy making. Indeed, much of the impulse for democratization in Ecuador, Bolivia, and Peru came from business leaders and organizations tired of the uncertainties generated by military policy makers and frustrated by their lack of access to them. The business community's anxieties about influence were deeply felt and continued unabated even when military regimes enacted policies that were highly favorable to the private sector. Even though the military governments of the 1970s rescued the domestic bourgeoisie from certain economic and political problems, many groups within the private sector never perceived public policy under the military as the "bail-out" program it was. Their lack of representation in policy making nagged at them in varying degrees and was a core element in dominant class critiques of the military regimes. In all three countries, business interest groups played leading roles in promoting the transition to civilian rule.

To what extent have business elites been successful in reasserting their direct influence over economic policy making in the new democratic governments? This essay argues that domestic capitalists, despite some important political gains, remain highly frustrated by a continuing lack of access to decision-making processes. On the surface, the business community appears to have enormous advantages at its disposal, sufficient to assure it a "privileged position" in the policy process of democratic regimes.[1] Among its advantages are: (1) the professionalization of business groups and the development of a more sophisticated business lobby; (2) the reestablishment of some corporatist mechanisms to ensure business access to state entities; (3) the integration of high-ranking individuals from the private sector into government "economic teams"; and (4) the strengthening of political parties on the center-right and their attempts to alter the ideological climate of policy making by injecting antistatism into public discourse.

But despite these developments, business leaders continue to be alarmed by the tendency of democratic governments to "seal off" economic policy making from interest group politics. Technocrats and politicians, like their predecessors in the previous military regimes, gravitate toward an exclusionary style of policy making—i.e., decision-making practices that are not consultative in reference to either domestic capitalists or labor. There are both structural and conjunctural factors at work that undermine the capacity of business organizations to shape economic policy and that reinforce the lack of responsiveness of state managers. First, the problems posed by the management of the international debt and the severity of the current economic crisis permits and legitimizes the decisions of state managers to bypass consultations with local actors. The extreme centralization of power in the executive branch reduces the ability of opposition groups to veto those decisions through other branches of the government. Moreover, presidents and their economic teams can look to a powerful set of external allies in international financial circles when they act to implement economic stabilization programs and neoliberal economic models.[2] Second, these external alliances allow state managers to resist attempts by local business organizations to penetrate the decision-making process and alter the externally approved model adopted by the economic team. Third, divisions and internal differentiations inside domestic capital fragment interests and undermine class unity vis-à-vis the new politics of stabilization and neoliberalism. While nearly all segments of the business community are ideological defenders of market principles, that consensus about abstract values does not translate into consensus about policy, since many groups within domestic capital are highly dependent upon state subsidies and protection. Given this divergence of interests among domestic capitalists and the lack of consensus about how to deal with the economic crisis at hand, state managers opt to ignore the "fuzzy" policy cues from business interest groups and strive to implement coherent economic models.

Before examining the relationship of domestic capitalists to these new political regimes, it is essential to understand how a representation crisis emerged during the preceding military period and set the domestic bourgeoisie on a search for an alternative to military authoritarianism.

Business and the Military in the 1970s

The common theme that runs through many of the analyses of the military regimes in place by the 1970s is that they were responses to the ongoing "hegemonic crisis" of dominant classes in these political systems.[3] By the 1970s, the traditional bases of oligarchical power in these economies had eroded. While some prominent families experienced difficulties in adjusting to economic changes, many others moved to diversify their investments and alter their positions in the accumulation process. The intersectoral character of dominant class economic interests was, of course, not a development unique to the 1950s and 1960s. Historical studies of the oligarchy in Peru, Bolivia, and Ecuador indicate that many of these economic elites traditionally had maintained diversified portfolios.[4] What was new was the widening scope of investment opportunities. The "economic groups" (investors linked through kinship and friendship networks) moved their capital into manufacturing and agro-industry as well as maintaining their old ties to commercial, real estate, and traditional exporting activities.[5] The capacity of groups to move into new economic sectors was facilitated by their control over banking and financial institutions. Linkages between domestic economic groups and foreign capital allowed for a penetration of foreign capital through joint-venture arrangements, transfer of technology agreements, and the local financial network.

Yet, even as the recomposition of dominant class economic interests was underway, the unilateral capacity of oligarchic elites to control the political process had broken down in the face of populism and more radical popular movements. In Bolivia, the 1952 Revolution put an end to the remaining political power of the tin barons and large landowners. Likewise in Peru and Ecuador, the emergence of new populist parties such as *Acción Popular* (AP) and the *Concentración de Fuerzas Populares* (CFP) along with the development of centrist reform and leftist parties eroded the ability of rightist electoral cliques to dominate elections. From the perspective of the dominant classes in all three countries, it was all too apparent that the state was slipping from their grasp as political power shifted to groups capable of using the state for redistributive ends. Evidence of the threat to privilege was everywhere. In Bolivia, the radical thrust of the military governments of Generals Ovando and Torres (1969–1971) and the appearance of the *Asamblea Popular* masterminded by the *Central Obrera Boliviana* (COB) sent shock waves through the private sector. Class conflict reverberated throughout pre–1968 Peru in form of strikes, guerrilla activity, and peasant movements. Even in relatively quiescent Ecuador, a prospective victory by the CFP's Assad Bucaram in the 1972 presidential election raised dominant class fears of populist distribution of the new revenues generated by petroleum sector.

In the context of this loss of control over the political system by previously dominant groups, the military intervened and took up the tasks of political management. But the ideological and programmatic solutions provided by the military regimes differed widely, as did the tenor of their relationships with the private sector. Nonetheless, they all shared a commitment to expanding the role of the state in the economy, bringing about major adjustments in state-society relations.

On the left side of the spectrum, the military government of General Juan Velasco Alvarado (1968–1975) committed itself to undertaking basic structural reforms. Agrarian reform, workers' management, and controlled mass mobilization to support the reforms were key elements of government policy. Through the creation of a public enterprise sector, the state took up responsibility for developing basic industries (steel, electricity), managing strategic export sectors (mining, oil, fishmeal), and restructuring the financial system. While some economic groups were displaced by state takeovers, most private investment in the profitable sectors of the economy was not affected. Generous economic incentives to promote private investment in industries were provided by the 1970 General Law of Industries. Capital accumulation in the private sector was further subsidized by the pricing policies of state enterprises that provided basic inputs.[6]

The government of General Guillermo Rodríguez Lara (1972–76) in Ecuador used some of the same reformist rhetoric as that of Velasco Alvarado, but displayed less of a substantive bite. The attempt at social change was limited; a conservative agrarian reform was enacted and social spending increased but workers' management schemes and the promotion of popular organization were conspicuously absent. The role of the state in the economy expanded as in Peru, but with less emphasis on public enterprises. Some were created, most notably the government oil company, CEPE. More important in the Ecuadorean case was the emphasis on state participation in firms through minority stockholding under the auspices of the National Finance Corporation and the extension of credit to targeted sectors through such entities as the Export Promotion Fund.[7]

In complete contrast to the Peruvian and Ecuadorean governments of the period was the Banzer administration in Bolivia (1971–78) which mimicked some of the characteristics of the bureaucratic-authoritarian regimes of the Southern Cone. The regime of General Hugo Banzer undertook policies of wage compression, political repression, and an opening to foreign capital. Riding on the economic boom created by oil export, Banzer increased the size of the state bureaucracy and underwrote the expansion of agribusiness in the region of Santa Cruz through the generous provision of credit through state development banks.[8]

While these three military governments did not share much in the way of ideological principles, the historical record points to one important similarity. The Velasco Alvarado, Rodríguez Lara, and Banzer governments all engaged in an aggressive expansion in the size of the state. The buoyancy of the international commodities market, the availability of international credit, and deficit spending provided the financial fuel for the expansion. Employment in the public sector swelled as did the number of state entities. Along with this quantitative expansion, there was a qualitative shift that thrust the state more directly into the management of the economy. The creation of public enterprises and new efforts at government direction and regulation of market behavior were evidence of the increased state presence. The shift was especially marked in Peru and Ecuador where there had been only a skeletal structure of state enterprise and a weak tradition of regulation. For Bolivia, Banzer's policies were not so much a departure; the proliferation of public enterprises under Banzer was a continuation of the state-oriented economic model implanted during the first MNR governments of the 1950s.

Business Reaction in Peru and Ecuador

How did business react to these hyperactive states of the 1970s? The comparative literature on the political behavior of business elites provides us with an important rule of thumb on the subject; one should always expect businessmen to voice an aversion to state intervention as a matter of principle.[9] Even when businessmen benefit from state interventions (as they frequently do), any overall expansion in state power creates at least some latent anxiety in the business community since that state power could be turned and wielded against them. The actual tenor of business-state relations is determined by how much that potential threat is translated into real incursions on the autonomy of the private sector; and this, of course, is closely related to the extent to which their interests are represented in policy-making processes.

The anxiety within business circles concerning the growth of state power in Peru, Bolivia, and Ecuador was aggravated by the fact that privileged groups had lost their old sway over policy-making institutions. In Peru and Bolivia military personnel replaced civilians in key policy-making posts, while in Ecuador career civil servants took over slots in the military government's economic teams that were previously the province of business leaders. In all three countries, occasional consultations between business groups and military leaders took place. But no formal institutional linkages were created to ensure a steady exchange between the two sets of actors or to replace the other channels of access (i.e., parties, the legislature) suspended by the military governments.

In Ecuador and Peru, heightened state power translated into what businessmen perceived as *real* incursions on the rights of capital. For Peruvian capitalists, the most devastating blow came in the form of the Industrial Community law; it created profit-sharing schemes originally framed to lead eventually to workers' participation in management. In Ecuador, efforts by the Superintendency of Companies to force the public sale of stocks of certain types of firms was interpreted as the first step toward more radical Peruvian-style reforms. In both countries, business opposition to reform reflected two types of concerns. Business dissatisfaction with the policy direction of these regimes was based on the belief that the reforms would have deleterious effects (both immediate and future) on capital. In other words, there were objections to the *content* of policy. But, in addition, there was a more generalized discontent having to do with the possible procedural and ideological precedents being established by the self-aggrandizing state. In short, there was a problem of *style* in addition to substance. For a variety of reasons (which will be left aside for now), this more general fear about precedents appeared in its clearest form in Ecuador where business interest groups across sectors successfully mobilized in the defense of the rights of capital.[10]

A comparison of business reaction to the agrarian reform measures in Ecuador and Peru reveals differences in the perceptions and strategies of dominant class actors across these two settings. In Peru, there was no consensus in the private sector on agrarian reform issues; the confiscatory agrarian reform was actually endorsed by the industrialists' interest group, the National Society of Industries (SNI). According to several prominent industrialists, the SNI adopted this position out of fear and with the hope that an acceptance of agrarian reform would stave off reforms in other sectors.[11] In Ecuador, business interest groups representing industry, commerce, and agriculture closed ranks and lobbied heavily in favor of "agrarian reform based on the respect for agricultural property." Ecuadorean business groups were unwilling to legitimate any threats to private property, even when sectoral interests were not directly affected.

The net effect of these reformist military governments in Peru and Ecuador was that they created the conditions for a renaissance of formal organizations of the bourgeoisie—a process that deepened once civilian rule was reestablished. This process included the creation of new organizations to represent both sectoral and general interests and the modernization and institutional development of already existing interest groups. The enforced absence of political parties from policy making under the military regimes made corporate organizations even more important.

In Peru, the associational life of economic elites was altered in the search to develop means to influence policy making under the military. The legal dissolution and the confiscation of the property of the National Agrarian Society (SNA) galvanized the private sector. The originally meek position of the SNI was dropped in favor of an aggressive stance adopted by its president, Raymundo Duhuarte, who relished confrontations with General Velasco. In an effort to bolster the legitimacy of the SNI as an organization that represented the private sector in its entirety, Duhuarte embarked on a campaign to increase membership in the SNI that brought hundreds of new members onto its rolls.[12] The press became the vehicle used by the SNI in its campaign against the Velasco reforms; official communiqués from the SNI appeared in Lima dailies demanding everything from a scrapping of the industrial community's reforms to a return to elections. Duhuarte's shift toward direct opposition was supported by other prominent figures of the SNI including Alfredo Ferrand and the Lanata brothers who believed in the need to unite the private sector to hold the line against further reform. Ernesto Lanata and Alfredo Ferrand spearheaded the first failed attempt at creating a single peak association to represent the entire private sector. This effort brought to life briefly an organization in 1978, the Private Entreprenuers Union (UEP).[13]

In contrast to the SNI, a more accommodationist strategy was adopted by a new organization, the Association of Exporters (ADEX). Originally created in 1969 as the *Comité de Exportadores* within the SNI, ADEX was founded as a separate organization in 1973 to represent the interest of industrial and other firms engaged in export activities. According to one of its founders, Alejandro Tabini, political motivations were a critical consideration in the formation of the organization. According to Tabini, exporters needed an organization to act as an "interlocutor" with the government, so as to have input into the policy-making process as the state moved to nationalize strategic sectors of the economy.[14] The SNI was unable to take on this role because it did not represent a complete array of export-oriented firms outside the industrial sector and because of the confrontational style adopted under Duhuarte's direction. This confrontational style had earned the SNI a "derecognition" from the Velasco government by the end of 1972. Forcing the SNI to remove *"Nacional"* from its title, the military government declared that the organization did not represent the industrial sector after having refused to incorporate labor representatives from the industrial communities onto its board of directors.

Although the renamed SI continued to function, the withdrawal of its corporate status clearly meant that businessmen interested in maintaining some institutional dialogue with the government would have to look elsewhere. ADEX became the new link. Because ADEX represented firms involved in export markets, the organization reflected the interests of the modern and dynamic sectors of the bourgeoisie. Duhuarte's campaign to expand SI membership brought an influx of members, but largely from the ranks of small businessmen and artisans.

In assessing the associational experiences of the top strata of the Peruvian bourgeoisie, it is important to keep in mind that even with the appearance of ADEX, large industrialists did not desert the ranks of the SI. Rather, both ADEX and the SI formed part of the organizational arsenal that business used in its struggle to limit the scope of Velasco's national revolution.[15] At the same time, the top strata of the bourgeoisie continued to utilize the remaining formal and informal channels of access to policy makers. The Business Administration Institute (IPAE) continued to hold its annual conferences (*Conferencia Anual de Ejecutivos*) that put the military in touch with business leaders. Some consultative commissions within the ministries continued to function and provided prominent business leaders with another point of entry. Links between certain firms and the military were maintained by appointments of officers to boards of directors.[16] In short, while relationships between business and the state were rocky under the Velasco administration, there was never a complete cessation of interchange between the military policymakers and groups within the private sector. But, as Francisco Durand points out, the access enjoyed by groups within the private sector (including ADEX) was limited and conditional.[17]

In Ecuador, the Rodríguez Lara regime undertook no concerted attack on the representative institutions of the bourgeoisie in the style of Velasco Alvarado's attacks on the SNA and the SNI in Peru. Nonetheless, there were bitter conflicts between the major business associations (most notably the regional Chambers of Industry, Agriculture, and Commerce of Quito and Guayaquil) over specific policies, as well as constant complaints from these organizations over their lack of input into policy making. As in the case of Peru, the press became the major forum used by these organizations to hound, cajole, and embarrass the regime. But in contrast to the Peruvians, the Ecuadorean business groups demonstrated a high level of solidarity among themselves, often pronouncing collectively on issues in joint statements to the press. The increasing cooperation across organizations was reflected in the creation of a national federation in 1972 that brought the two powerful regional Chambers of Industry together for the first time. At the same time, new specialized producers' associations were being formed. The growing importance of nontraditional export activities and the Andean Pact market was reflected in the foundation of FEDEXPOR, an organization sponsored by several of Ecuador's largest consumer goods producers. These organizations also developed technical staffs charging with formulating policy papers to be used in lobbying the government.

As in Peru, business organizations in Ecuador were also subject to a suspension of their traditional avenues of influence in the policy process during the reformist phase of military rule. This took the form of a derogation of the voting rights that Chamber representatives exercised on some of the boards of government institutions. The more irregular types of contacts between business leaders and the military continued. The Chambers sent delegates to seminars at the Army's *Instituto de Altos Estudios Nacionales,* and a high-level "summit" conference with private sector leaders and the Rodríguez Lara cabinet was staged at the beach resort of Salinas in 1974.

This distancing of dominant class organizations from state power imposed by military reformists in Peru and Ecuador had significant effects on the class consciousness of the bourgeoisie. For the first time, important groups of the private sector were marginalized from policy making, forced to stand outside the inner circles of power. While it may be impossible to assess the net psychological impact of this experience in any definitive way, the emotions expressed in interviews and in the public pronouncements of business interest group leaders suggest that the experience was a highly traumatic one—and that it was instrumental in motivating business leaders to look for new strategies to reestablish their influence.[18]

Business under Banzer

Bolivia under Banzer does not fit neatly into the pattern of business-government hostilities just described in the other two countries. The Banzer regime had no reformist aspirations and did nothing to alter the state-centric capitalist model established in 1952 by the populist Nationalist Revolutionary Movement (MNR). Many of the analyses of the Banzer period identify the private sector as one of Banzer's key allies and as the major beneficiary of Banzer's economic policies.[19] Nonetheless, a simple functionalist reading of the Banzer period that reduces the state to a tool of the bourgeoisie misses the complex and contradictory relationships between the state and business during this period. Banzer's continuation of state-centric capitalism combined with his personalist style of governing created a logic that eventually alienated segments of the private sector from the regime. This led the bourgeoisie to a search for an alternative political formula; the search gained urgency in the 1978–82 interim that featured a dizzying array of ad hoc military and civilian governments which ended in the nadir of the García Meza administration (1980–81).

With the economic boom provided by oil export in the 1970s, Banzer expanded the size of the already large Bolivian state. Public sector growth under Banzer was staggering. From 1970 to 1974, the number of employees on the government payroll went from 66,000 to 141,000. At least twenty new public enterprises were created to swell the size of the state bureaucracy to more than 200 separate entities. In the 1970–75 period, public sector investment accounted for 75 percent of the total investment in the Bolivian economy.[20]

Banzer used this expansion to establish a political base for his regime among the urban middle classes who were highly dependent on state employment. But Banzer was no political institution-builder. Patronage flowed not through institutional channels (e.g. parties), but through highly personalized patron-client networks. In short, it was a political style that rendered irrelevant "modern" organizations aggregating group interests. Malloy and Gamarra have characterized the system as neopatrimonial and argued that political decay was the net result.[21]

This neopatrimonialism extended to Banzer's relationships with the dominant classes and their organizations. Banzer incorporated several top private mine-owners into his cabinet, most notably Carlos Iturralde, Carlos Calvo, and Mario Mercado. Yet, this incorporation of dominant class interests was highly individualized and revolved around the close personal relationships that developed between Banzer and his devotees. They became (as they themselves acknowledge) *banzeristas*. Business associations like the Association of Medium Miners (AMM) and the Bolivian Business Confederation (CEPB) remained marginalized as institutions from the policy-making process. Fernando Henrique Cardoso's notion of "bureaucratic rings" may be useful here in capturing the complexity of this phenomenon. As Cardoso notes, individuals with ties to specific economic interests may be integrated into the state bureaucracy and this permits the "inclusion of private sector interests" inside the state. But as Cardoso points out, these rings "are not a form of class organization, and the state can radically disarticulate the pressures on it from civil society by removing the key figures in the state apparatus around whom the ring is centered."[22]

The most important example of the incomplete character of the influence exercised by key fractions of the dominant class under Banzer is illustrated in the conduct of tax policy. With prices rising on the international market, Banzer enacted a tax on the mining sector to capture a portion of the windfall profits. The measure was adopted with the approval of ministers Calvo, Mercado, and Iturralde — all of whom had important investments in mining companies. Although originally enacted as a temporary measure, the tax was kept in place for seven years, long after the price boom was over. This turned privately owned mining into one of the most heavily taxed activities of its kind in the world.[23] And despite the presence of important mining investors inside the government and the constant appeals from the AMM, the Banzer government maintained the tax. In interviews, business leaders of the mining sector were quick to point to the failure of mine-owners in Banzer's cabinet to act as effective sectoral representatives.[24]

The individual incorporation of prominent members of the private sector did not translate into a reliable avenue of corporate representation; and dominant class leaders in Bolivia clearly perceived this to be the case. This is not to argue that the policies of the Banzer government were, in any broad sense, unfavorable to the private sector or even the mining sector per se. Banzer's tough labor policies and his anti-nationalization stance created the "stabie investment climate" sought by mine owners. The point is that, even given Banzer's pro-business stance, access and influence for private sector groups was not stable or predictable. Rather, it ebbed and flowed with the peculiar logic of a neopatrimonial regime in which personal ties predominated over institutionalized relations.

Domestic capitalists in the Central Andes closed the decade with an extremely mixed scorecard of economic gains and political losses. While all three of the military regimes discussed above were interested in underwriting the growth of certain pockets (both regional and sectoral) of local capital, policies of preferential treatment often engendered dissatisfaction among businessmen "left out" of the economic model. Moreover, preferential policies via tax incentives and credit were not sufficient to defuse private sector resistance to those policies that businessmen perceived as instances of overregulation by the state. In all three cases, the forces in civil society seemed progressively overshadowed by a larger and more demanding state — a state out of the direct control of the privileged classes. It was within this context that dominant class organizations turned their attentions toward democracy as a means to reopen the state to interest group politics.

Business and the Transition

The relative weight of business organizations in structuring the mechanics of the transition differed and reflected the distancing that had taken place between these organizations and the military. In Ecuador and Peru, business organizations were secondary to political parties which were designated by the military as the intermediaries of the transition. In Ecuador, the Chambers of Production (i.e., the Chambers of Industry, Agriculture and Commerce) were consulted by the interim military government of Admiral Poveda Burbano during the public "dialogues" held with groups and parties in 1976 to discuss different legal options for the transition. But the Chambers' complaints about inadequate representation on the three civilian commissions charged with drafting constitutional and electoral law fell on deaf ears, as did their objections to one of the constitutional options which extended the franchise to illiterates, eliminated functional representatives in the legislature, and provided for a "communitarian" sector of the economy.[25] Outraged by the design of the constitutional plebiscite of 1978, the Chamber of Industry of Guayaquil sponsored a protest "null vote" campaign. It was unsuccessful and the transition proceeded along the lines dictated by the military.

In Peru, the transition via constituent assembly transferred the bulk of the responsibility to the professional political class of party leaders, leaving business interest groups without any formal role in the determination of constitutional structure.[26] But business organizations were not completely frustrated in their search for representation. While the succeeding military governments in Ecuador and Peru maintained a high degree of control over the mechanics of the transition, they were ready to let business have more influence macroeconomic policy making.[27] Both the Poveda Burbano government in Ecuador (1976–79) and the Morales Bermúdez administration in Peru (1975–80) embarked on more orthodox lines of economic and social policy and adopted a conciliatory stance toward the private sector.

The commitment to transition, the pro-business stance of the interim military regimes, and good conditions in the international market lulled business organizations in Peru and Ecuador into temporary quiescence. As the transition unfolded, parties became the focus of dominant class attention while business groups pulled back to await the election results.

In Bolivia, the private sector took a more directive role in designing the mechanics of the transition process. The CEPB, the peak association that grouped together all sectoral and regional business associations, became one of the key organizational architects of the transition. The CEPB, along with other important groups in civil society (especially the Catholic Church and trade unions), were able to assume leadership roles in the transition because of the extreme state of disarray within the Armed Forces. Rivalries inside the military coupled with erosion of professionalism under the corrupt regime of General García Meza left the Armed Forces unable to devise a coherent political formula to halt the dizzying governmental instability of the post-Banzer period. By 1982, the Bolivian business elite faced a qualitatively different dilemma from that of their Peruvian or Ecuadorean counterparts. For the Bolivian bourgeoisie, the question was not so much one of how to alter a regime type, but how to stave off the complete disintegration of political order.

Inside the CEPB, the search for a political alternative began with a small informal group of prominent business leaders, known as the "consulting group"; they met for luncheon brainstorming sessions and advised the president of the CEPB. The participants in the consulting groups represented the most important financial and industrial firms in the private sector. The group was, in effect, the cream of the Bolivian private sector and included its most sophisticated and savvy ideologues. Within the group, a consensus emerged that the reestablishment of democracy was the route to saving political order. A member of the group described the calculations that led to the consensus.

> We always looked at the military as an important force to save us from the extreme leftist groups in this country. And the less prestige they have, the less we could count on them . . . And we knew that this meant that the longer they [the military] stayed, the bigger the chances that the extreme left would have in getting in the country with a coup. And when that happened we thought it would be very hard to remove them. They would take measures like Nicaragua and it would be hard for us to

take them out. So we could not allow the prestige of the military to suffer, so we started a campaign to go into a true democratic process . . . We decided to come out with a document, *¡Democracia Ya!* And this was the first document that came out openly for such a position.[28]

The proposal contained in *¡Democracia Ya!* was to return to civilian rule by recalling the 1980 Congress, which had been elected but never installed due to the García Meza coup.[29] According to electoral law, the Congress could then designate the new executive since none of the three 1980 presidential candidates had won a majority. Given the constellation of forces in Congress, it was clear that the reconstitution of the 1980 Congress would bring the *Unión Democrática y Popular* (UDP) alliance to power and Hernán Siles to the presidency. The COB and political parties endorsed the proposal.

The CEPB's sponsorship of this plan to bring what would certainly be a left of center government to power revealed much about the character of the political crisis; the desperation of the private sector for a rationalization of politics coupled with a recognition that a rightist alternative was not possible, given the exhaustion of the military and the looming power of the COB. Members of the "consulting group" realized that their support for the installation of the Siles government was a calculated risk — but one that had to be taken in the absence of any other viable alternative. But rather than alleviating the decay of political authority, the Siles government put in bold relief the extent to which the state had lost its capacity to order Bolivian society. Yet the torturous course of the Siles government had political payoffs for the Bolivian bourgeoisie. In the attempt to cope with what the private sector conceived as catastrophic economic management by Siles, the CEPB grew and its leaders moved to develop a new political project that revolved around neoliberalism and Banzer's political party, the *Acción Democrática Nacionalista* (ADN). As in the cases of Velasco Alvarado in Peru and Rodríguez Lara in Ecuador, the adverse political climate of the Siles period proved to be a catalyst for heightened dominant class consciousness and organization.

Lobbying in the 1980s

With the installation of elected civilian governments, business organizations were poised and ready to reenter the standard play of interest group politics. Certainly, they appeared well prepared to engage in the pressure politics of a pluralist system. The suspension of party politics under the military regimes made business organizations into more than just a refuge for economic interests. Military rule brought an unprecedented politicization of these organizations.[30] At the same time, economic changes during the period (e.g., the growth of nontraditional exports, and the increasing importance of finance capital) altered the composition of dominant class economic interests. The end result of this combination of politicization and economic change was a modernization and maturation of bourgeois organization that spread across corporate bodies and extended to right wing parties in the 1980s.

One dimension of this modernization of bourgeois organization was the increasingly technocratic character of business associations. Leaders of business organization made important efforts to develop technical expertise inside their organizations for the purpose of engaging in more effective lobbying in macroeconomic policy making. To deal effectively with technocrats inside the state apparatus, business organizations developed their own technical corps *and* imported expertise from abroad. At the same time, there were internal efforts to extend this new technical sophistication to group members.

The best example of this phenomenon in the case of Peru can be seen in the behavior SNI and ADEX. In 1980, the Institute of Economic and Social Studies (IESS) was created as a special agency inside the SNI by its president, Ernesto Lanata Piaggo. The idea behind its creation was to build a professional staff of economic experts capable of formulating technocratic critiques of government policy affecting industry.[31]

In addition to creating their own in-house technical staff, the SNI also mobilized professional economists by contracting studies and organizing conferences. According to Lanata, the SNI "bought" an alternative econometric model from the *Economic Intelligence Review* of New York city to counter the IMF model that was adopted by President Belaúnde's Minister of Finance, Manuel Ulloa, and used to justify the draconian reduction of industrial protection in the early 1980s.[32] The new technocratic thrust in the SNI was matched with efforts to educate the SNI membership on aspects of economic policy and political issues. The publications of the IESS provide basic economic data as well as stake out the position of the private sector on political questions.[33] According to Lanata, the purpose of the publications was to create a common knowledge and a "national consciousness" among industrialists.

Like the SNI, ADEX also engages in this mobilization of professional economists and technocratic lobbying. In their battles with the Belaúnde regime over the reduction of export incentives, ADEX contracted a study by Boston University economists Daniel Schydlowsky and Shane Hunt to defend their position.[34] ADEX's educational efforts within its membership included the creation of its own junior college in 1982, the Advanced Technological Institute of Foreign Trade.

In Bolivia, the technocratic bent of private sector associations took a fascinating turn that spilled over into parties. Some of the key figures of the consulting group of the CEPB (who were also ADN members) came together in early 1985 for the purposes of drafting economic policy for Hugo Banzer. Under pressures from parties and the CEPB, the Siles government had agreed to speed up the timetable for presidential election. It was finally rescheduled for July 1985. Banzer, along with Víctor Paz Estenssoro, was an early frontrunner. The prospect of a new Banzer government led to some intensive soul-searching among *banzerista* businessmen, many of whom had worked in the Banzer military government. Since some of the members of the group were ex-Harvard students, Harvard was chosen as the site for forging a consensus on an economic model for what they believed would be the upcoming Banzer government. Under the auspices of the Kennedy School, Banzer and this elite group of *banzeristas* met with U.S. economists in a seminar on the Bolivian economy.[35] The most influential economist in these meetings was Jeffrey Sachs. Sachs later came to Bolivia at the invitation of the ADN to put the "finishing touches" on the model right before the July election. The program was neoliberal in inspiration, prescribing salary austerity, budgetary reductions, the opening of the Bolivian economy, and a drastic overhaul of public sector enterprises.

Although Banzer won the popular vote by a narrow margin, he did not assume the presidency. The Bolivian constitution mandates the selection of the president by Congress in the event that no candidate polls a majority. Intense deal making in Congress resulted in the election of the MNR candidate, Víctor Paz Estenssoro, as president. Yet the Paz victory did not kill the idea of implanting a neoliberal economic model. Disappointed with the work of his in-house MNR economic team, Paz undertook frantic efforts in August 1985 to devise an economic program. For this purpose, he set up an emergency economic team that included two "independent" members of the Harvard group.[36] After 17 days of round-the-clock sessions, the team emerged with an austerity plan that paralleled the ADN Harvard program. The measures were issued as an executive decree (D.S. 21060). Paz even hired Jeffrey Sachs to act as an advisor on its implementation. Frustrated by their marginalization from policy making and upset by Paz's appropriation of neoliberalism, the in-house MNR team created its own research institute, the Foundation for National Development, to formulate an alternative economic program.

The adoption of this technocratic approach by business organizations has had an important impact on the nature of politico-economic discourse — the language of interests is forsaken for the language of economic models. As ideological constructs, economic models provide an appealing consistency and coherence. While the advocacy of a coherent economic model by business organizations may indeed bolster their lobbying capabilities and enhance their positions in the eyes of state technocrats, it also sets the stage for internal conflicts in business organizations, especially for heterogeneous peak associations. Given the heterogeneity of private sector interests, they are not easily accommodated within the framework of a single coherent economic model, especially a neoliberal one that forsakes subsidies and removes protection for certain sectors. As such, the advocacy of a neoliberal model can aggravate the strains inside organizations charged with representing the interests of the private sector in its entirety. This took place in Bolivia where discord in the private sector over Paz's neoliberal economic model was reflected in internal conflicts in the CEPB. Fernando Romero, a member of the economic team that designed D. S. 21060, resigned as President of the CEPB in wake of criticism from industrialists who were angered by the provisions for dismantling protectionism.

Attempts to create umbrella business organizations in Peru and Ecuador attest to the difficulties of aggregating private sector interests and reaching a consensus on the economic policies the groups should favor. In 1981, an Ecuadorean Council of the Chambers and Associations of Production was created but never functioned. The organization never got beyond the declaration of general principles — i.e., that the state should respect private property and provide for private sector input into policy making.[37] In Peru, the National Confederation of Private Business Institutions (CONFIEP) was founded in 1984, as the successor to the failed UEP.[38] It remains to be seen, however, whether CONFIEP can arrive at any real internal consensus on economic policy and assume a permanent role as the principal representative of the private sector.

In assessing the development of the associational practices of capitalists in the democratic period, it is important not to lose sight of the difficulties posed by the heterogeneity of capital in the process of interest representation. Certainly, this heterogeneity of interests is nothing new. In all three countries, economic policy has always been a battleground for different fractions of capital — e.g. exporters vs. importers, importers vs. import-substituting industrialists, etc. In Bolivia and Ecuador, these clashes coincide with tensions between regional groups of capitalists (La Paz v. Santa Cruz, Quito v. Guayaquil). But, considering the economic changes these countries underwent in the 1970s, there is reason to believe that the structure of cleavages in the private sector in these countries (and the rest of Latin America) is becoming even more complex. The growing importance of finance capital imposes yet another cleavage, opening a breach between groups of capitalists engaged in production and highly dependent upon the state and those more "predatory" financial/speculative groups of the bourgeoisie.[39] These competing economic interests undermine class unity in reference to economic models and bifurcate capitalists into statists and antistatists. This divide (material and ideological) is more profound than the kinds of sectoral conflicts that these classes have previously experienced, since it involves a fundamental clash as to whether the state should act to promote accumulation or deaccumulation.[40]

Complicating the process of interest representation is the domination of these economies by diversified economic groups whose interests may span both "productive" and "predatory" activities.[41] The importance of these economic groups raises the extremely complex question (one that cannot be adequately treated in this essay) of whether the formal interest group structure accurately expresses the interests of capitalists — or whether it misleads us by reflecting a highly fragmentary and static picture of those interests. In other words, the objective and subjective interests of capitalists in these economies may be more fluid and flexible than the formal interest group structure suggests. Thus, while the ability of business organizations to act as effective lobbyists in the policy process is enhanced by the technocratization of their organizations, these organizations may be increasingly wracked by rationality problems as bourgeois interests themselves become more contradictory. The controversies that took place inside the Bolivian CEPB over D.S. 21060 are illustrative of the problems involved in forging a consensus within a bourgeoisie on a single economic model.

Exclusionary Policy Making

So far, the discussion has focused on the technocratization of business organizations and the implications of the discourse of economic models for organization. These phenomena, of course, are not confined to the ranks of the bourgeoisie. Policymakers on the economic teams of these democratic governments are themselves *technocrats* who speak the language of models; and business organizations undertook their own technocratization as a defensive reaction against the growing presence of this technocratic corps within the state. The constitutions of all three countries centralize power in the executive branch, and legislatures are assigned limited powers in regard to economic policy making. As such, decisions on macroeconomic questions are concentrated in the office of the President, and by extension, his economic team in the cabinet.

The predominance of the technocratic corps inside the cabinet has important implications not just for the *content* of economic policy, but also for the *style* of decision making that is evolving. What is striking in interviews with members of economic teams is their belief that economic policy making should be "sealed off" from pluralist politics. Economic team members described the ideal circumstances for policy making as being a situation in which: (1) there is a very small number of participants in the deliberations; and (2) no public scrutiny of the formulation process. In short, groups in society (business, labor, and parties) are regarded not as actors to be consulted or negotiated with in the formulation of economic policy, but as potential disrupters of rational and coherent policy making. One economic team member in Ecuador described the closed character of the process:

> We four (the economic ministers and the President) *exclusively* ran economic policy. The cabinet and ministries were consulted only on very specific problems. They were informed only after

we made decisions. So there were no debates within the cabinet on economic policy. Unfortunately, Latin American culture is such that secrets are not well kept. We could not subject economic policies to great debates because this would have weakened our ability for implementation.[42]

The decision-making process surrounding D.S. 21060 in Bolivia provides an excellent example of this secretive approach to policy formulation. Under the supervision of President Paz, the decree was hammered out by a group of six advisors that included two businessmen, two economists, and two MNR politicians. Other than outside consultations about certain technical questions, the economic team did not solicit input from any organizations or groups. Prior to the public announcement of the measures, Paz sought the approval of the cabinet in a dramatic 24-hour-long meeting. To ensure the secrecy of the matters under discussion, Paz locked the cabinet members in a meeting room and disconnected the phones.[43] All this was to guarantee that the measures would take the public by surprise and make organized protest against them more difficult. The COB's resistance to the measures was met with Paz's declaration of a state of siege and the imprisonment or exile of key labor leaders. By his tough actions, Paz demonstrated his commitment to keeping intact the neoliberal model by making it into a non-negotiable item — one off limits to the pulls and pushes of pressure politics, even if that implied suspending civil liberties.

Business organizations, like labor, find themselves increasingly marginalized from the economic decision making process that is consciously crafted by state technocrats and presidents to be exclusionary. This marginalization appears to be particularly acute during "crisis" situations that involve the imposition of austerity measures, as the governments of Osvaldo Hurtado (1981–84) in Ecuador and Víctor Paz Estenssoro (1985–89) in Bolivia demonstrate. But this exclusion is not based simply on a lack of access to economic team members by business leaders. The physical isolation of economic teams from societal groups during "crises" is both a reality and a metaphor of a deeper estrangement. Once a team adopts an economic model, a mental curtain seems to drop over the team members, making them relatively impervious to the demands of groups that threaten the model's coherence.

Leaders of business organizations in all three countries pointed to what one informant characterized as the problem of "access without receptivity" in democratic governments. While democracy opens up the political sphere to outright lobbying by business organizations, this access does not necessarily translate into the policy outputs demanded by these organizations. The case of Peru during the Belaúnde government (1980–85) is the best example of how an economic team can be accessible to business groups, but at the same time remain impermeable and disdainful of interest group jockeying.

The design of Belaúnde's economic program was put in the hands of the government's Minister of the Economy and Prime Minister, Manuel Ulloa. Experienced in international banking, Ulloa was a monetarist and surrounded himself with young technocrats of the same peruasion. Ulloa's economic program, with its inspiration in monetarism, was designed to accomplish two things: (1) reduce domestic inflation by "burning up" monetary reserves through a liberalization of the economy; and (2) ensure a continued flow of international credit to the government to finance Belaúnde's pet projects of public construction. The flow of foreign credit was facilitated by the adoption of a neoliberal model, the preferred prescription of the International Monetary Fund (IMF). With this commitment to neoliberalism firmly guiding the economic team, the SNI failed in its repeated lobbying efforts to modify the antiprotectionist measures. These efforts included frequent formal meetings between the economic team and SNI leaders and informal personal contacts among individuals.[44]

The consensus within the economic team and their commitment to orthodoxy left industrialists without allies inside the institutional machinery governing economic policy. The ability of the Ulloa economic team (and later that of Carlos Rodríguez Pastor) to withstand the pressures emanating from civil society, however, was more than just a product of their inflexibility. Ulloa's economic team had powerful allies in their conflict with domestic capitalists — President Belaúnde, the IMF, and the World Bank. According to business leaders, Ulloa enjoyed the complete personal confidence of Belaúnde. It was this confidence and Belaúnde's dependence on Ulloa's skills in securing international credit that made Belaúnde himself resistant to the claims of the SNI and ADEX. Furthermore, Belaúnde's lame duck status reduced the personal political costs of the implementation of the program. With no possibility of a second consecutive term, Belaúnde could afford to ignore the claims of domestic businessmen and ally with the IMF.

Belaúnde's record suggests that the personal priorities of presidents can have an important effect on influence of business organizations in the policy process. Like Belaúnde, Víctor Paz Estenssoro could not run for a second successive term under Bolivia's current constitution; and given his advanced age, it was unlikely that he would ever return to the presidency. Freed from immediate electoral calculations, both Belaúnde and Paz appeared to have played out a "personal-historical" project through their economic policies. Belaúnde saw his legacy as that of being Peru's great architect and builder — and he was willing to support an economic model that could provide him with the international credit that he needed for his public works campaign.[45] In Bolivia, Paz came to see his historical mission as that of dismantling the overdeveloped and nearly feudal state enterprise sector (especially the state mining firm, COMIBOL) that was a product of the MNR Revolution of 1952 which he led. And the neoliberal economic model embodied in D.S. 21060 became his weapon. In the words of one of his economic ministers, Paz came to see himself as "Louis XIV fighting the Duke of COMIBOL." Recognizing his central role in Bolivian history, Paz argued to his advisors that he was the only politician *capable* of changing the Bolivian economic model.[46] With their sights on their own historical records rather than the next elections or the fate of their parties, Belaúnde and Paz were unwilling to respond to what appeared to them to be the more selfish and short-term demands of domestic interest groups. Instead, they opted to join forces with external allies in the international financial community to implement the neoliberal programs that coincided with their personal priorities.

The Marginalization of Parties

This coincidence of a presidential personal-historical project with a neoliberal economic model backed by powerful external actors proved to be a strong combination in Peru and Bolivia — one that drew an impermeable mental curtain around the administration's decision makers. Business leaders tried to use parties to change the course of policy, but to no avail. Pressures from their respective parties to alter the economic programs went largely ignored by Belaúnde, Paz, and their economic teams. A high ranking leader of Belaúnde's Acción Popular (AP) described the cool relations between the party and Prime Minister Manuel Ulloa:

Ulloa never took into account the opinions of people from his party—not from me, not from Alva, and not from the other party leaders. . . . There were meetings of AP leaders interested in trying to change economic policy where they tried to show Ulloa what his errors were. We got together every week and invited Ulloa because he was also a senator from the party—and many times he didn't come to the meetings. But the few times he did come, we told him very clearly that his economic policy was mistaken . . . and he just persisted in his policy.[47]

For Peruvian business organizations, the marginalization of AP party leaders from decision making turned the party into an ineffective vehicle for the representation of business interests. AP Senator Javier Alva attempted to mount a technical lobbying effort on behalf of SI and ADEX, but failed. In 1981, while he was president of the Senate, Alva organized a study group charged with preparing a comprehensive technical critique and a list of alternatives to Ulloa's policies. The group included AP leaders, economists, and representatives of the SNI and ADEX. The result was a document entitled "Informe sobre la situación económica" which recommended restrictions on the opening of the economy to imports, a halt in the spending of monetary reserves, and the lowering of interest rates. Alva presented the study to Belaúnde. But Belaúnde stood fast in his total support for Ulloa.[48]

The economic decision-making process of the government of Osvaldo Hurtado in Ecuador was marked by some of the same stylistic qualities and external alliance structures just described, although it differed in content from the neoliberal modes of Belaúnde and Paz. In anticipation of the renegotiation of Ecuador's debt with the IMF, Hurtado took standard stabilization measures in 1982–83 (devaluation, reduction of government spending, gas price increases). But these measures were not accompanied by the brusque opening of the market to imports or retreat from state intervention in economic management. In their theoretical approach to policy, Hurtado and his team were not wedded to any particular school of economics. In contrast to the Ulloa team in Peru that was dominated by technocrats with experience in international finance, the Hurtado team was more broadly representative of the interests at play in the Ecuadorean private sector. The Minister of Finance, Pedro Pinto, was a long-time industrial leader and owned a large textile firm. José Correa, the head of the Monetary Board, came to his post with experience in banking and diplomatic circles. Abelardo Pachano, director of the Banco Central, was a trained economist. Hurtado himself was a well-known intellectual and university professor of political sociology. In practice, this eclectic team formulated policies that were highly favorable to the private sector and did not impose clear costs on particular groups of domestic capitalists, as did the neoliberal model. Despite these favorable policies, however, the Hurtado administration was subject to severe criticism by business organizations and this criticism was, in part, related to the consciously constructed insularity of the administration. Hurtado firmly believed that economic decisions, especially in the context of the debt crisis, had to be closed to the pressures emanating from groups and parties. Moreover, Hurtado's undisguised disdain for the traditionally "privileged position" of the business chambers in economic decision making was such that he set out to make the executive branch as independent as possible. According to Hurtado, his was the first administration in the history of Ecuador in which "the Chambers couldn't pick up the phone and give the president orders."[49] Thus, even though the economic team was generating pro-business policies, the leaders of business organizations found themselves effectively shut out of deliberations on the economy.

Parties, including Hurtado's own Popular Democracy (DP), suffered the same fate as business organizations. Hurtado did not open up economic policy to internal debates or discussions within the party. From Hurtado's perspective the marginalization of the DP was justified for a number of reasons: (1) there was no technocratic stratum within the party capable of engaging in serious economic deliberations; (2) since Hurtado had not been elected to the presidency (he succeeded upon the death of Jaime Roldós) and the DP held only nine seats in Congress, Hurtado needed to design policies that would create broader bases of support and not be identified with a tiny minority party; and (3) the lack of direct participation by other party leaders, especially in the stabilization plans, might transfer the political costs to Hurtado himself and mitigate the electoral effects of the austerity program. The net result was, as in the cases of the Belaúnde and Paz governments, the freezing out of the government party as a channel into the administration.

On the whole, an exclusionary approach to participation in economic decision making emerged in the Central Andean governments of the 1980s. This exclusionary style marginalized business organizations, trade unions, and political parties from direct participation, and even sometimes included the suspension of informal consultations. The notable exception was the government of Hernán Siles in Bolivia (1982–85). Coming to power with an extremely heterogeneous coalition, Siles adopted a policy-making style that was highly consultative in relation to his coalition parties of the UDP and the labor organization, the COB. According to one of his top economic advisors, Siles strongly believed that he could not act without a consensus on economic policy that included the COB.[50]

Siles' opening of the decision-making process went so far as to include the offer of co-government (*cogobierno*) to the COB, i.e., the institutional integration of the COB into the cabinet. Such an arrangement had taken place once before, during the radical phase of the MNR government of 1952. The COB refused the offer, but Siles' legitimation of the COB as the key institutional consultant enhanced the COB's capacity effectively to initiate changes in policy as well as exercise a veto. The analogous organization of business, the CEPB, never came close to the official status afforded the COB to oversee economic policy. This uneven opening of the policy process to social actors produced predictable results. The COB used its power to force salary hikes, and left-wing ministers attempted a partial assault on the private sector, especially financial groups.[51] While the policies did not produce the results expected by these ministers, the private sector was alarmed by what it saw as the surrendering of economic policy making to the extreme left. The CEPB responded by a high profile attack on the Siles administration, using the media as a forum. Once this confrontational triangle was in place—COB, CEPB, and the Siles administration—the social and political stalemate became so profound that the government was incapable of implementing any economic policy and staggered from the announcement of one economic package to the next.[52]

Notwithstanding the differing partisan origins of the democratic regimes of the region, the attempt by technocrats and presidents to exclude business from the formulation of economic policy was visible in all three polities in the 1980s. The results of this exclusion varied. Sometimes exclusion brought immediate economic costs for fractions of capital left out of the deliberations, while in other cases the costs of nonparticipation were more political and even psychological. In the cases of the Belaúnde and Paz governments, the adoption of neoliberal economic models threatened the position of domestic industrialists. In the case of the Siles government, the private sector was able to successfully maneuver through hyperinflation and government's ill-designed plan to "de-dollarize" the economy through speculation. Nonetheless, the Siles government's toleration of the militant COB created high levels of uncertainty about the future for local capitalists. In the case of the Roldós-Hurtado administrations, business organizations were uneasy about the lack of representation more than the content of economic policy itself. The question of representation continues to haunt the private sector in all three countries — and it is these past experiences of exclusion (both in the military and democratic periods) that motivate the calls for *concertación* and a renewed interest in parties.

Corporatism and Electioneering

That the new democratic regimes of the 1980s opted to maintain and resurrect certain traditional forms of corporatist representation adds even more irony to the bourgeoisie's difficulties in penetrating and influencing economic policy making. The old-fashioned incorporation of representatives of business organizations into entities within the executive branch was continued in Peru and Ecuador.[53] In Peru, the integration of business leaders takes place largely through the system of consultative commissions. Typically, these commissions are created to deal with specific problem areas and are constituted by representatives from the relevant ministries and business organizations. The trade and tariff commissions are examples of such arrangements. In Ecuador, business groups are assigned seats on the boards of directors of such organisms as the Monetary Board, the Social Security Institute, and the Industrial Development Center. There is also some formal business representation in Bolivia in entities ranging from the Social Security Institute to state banks.

From the perspective of the bourgeoisie, the persistence of such arrangements can be as frustrating as they are useful. While this quasi corporatism does provide some institutionalized entrée into the executive branch for these groups, the power of business organizations inside these entities is limited by their minority status; ministerial representatives typically outnumber business representatives. Moreover, apart from the power problems that business representatives experience inside the entity, there is the larger problem of the lack of influence that these commissions/boards have on the policy process within the executive branch. A number of Peruvian business leaders characterized commissions as mechanisms that are used by the executive to "bury" a problem—a commission is created, members are appointed, and the commission never meets. Or, if it does meet, its recommendations are ignored.[54]

In short, the persistence of these quasi-corporatist arrangements has not effectively staved off the shift toward the centralization of macroeconomic decision making by economic teams nor does it substantially erode the isolation and autonomy of these teams. What these arrangements do allow for when they function, however, is for some fragmented and highly specific input into some decisions by business organizations while effectively "roping off" macroeconomic policy for the economic team. Notwithstanding the limitations on representation and influence that are part of these relations, the maintenance of the trappings of corporatism carries with it an important ideological effect—i.e., the arrangements legitimate corporatist formulas of representation and keep such options open to actors in their search to gain control over the state. As such, the creation of corporatist structures that would endow business organizations with *real* power is a key theme in the discourse of these organizations and a vital part of their conceptual picture of how business-state relations should be structured under democracy.

Demands for corporatism have been voiced most persistently in Peru. The notion of *concertación* surfaces frequently in the rhetoric of business leaders and in the official publications of their organizations.[55] The business community's enthusiasm for *concertación* is understandable in light of the trauma provoked by the Velasco reforms and fears of replaying of reformist policies. Both memories of the past and anxieties about the future are at play in the search by Peruvian capitalists for stable and institutionalized relationships to the state. The formation of CONFIEP in 1984 was part of this business push for the development of institutionalized decision making involving the private and public sector. To achieve such an arrangement, private sector leaders realized that it was essential to create a single organization that would act as the primary negotiator vis-à-vis the state. One of the important peculiarities in the Peruvian discussion of *concertación* is the emphasis it places on the development of agreements (*políticas concertadas*) between the state and business. This contrasts with the Western European notion of concertation which includes labor as a party in macroeconomic decision making along with business and the state. Labor is sometimes, but by no means frequently included by business leaders in their discussions of *políticas concertadas*. For some of Peru's top ranking business leaders, the essence of *concertación* lies in the tough process of first forging a consensus within the private sector on policies and then reaching an agreement with the state.[56] The lack of consideration of labor's role may be indicative of the exclusionary spin that business has attached to the notion of *concertación*. Survey results point to similar exclusionary beliefs in the case of Ecuador. In a 1979–80 survey administered to 43 top executives of the largest industrial firms, 56 percent identified the private sector and the state as the groups that should make economic policy; only 26 percent included labor as a legitimate participant in the process.[57]

Party and electoral politics present another obvious route that business interest groups look to in order to influence policy making; but it is also a route with its own frustrations and offers little of the predictability that business organizations seek. There are two dimensions to the uncertainty inherent in electoral politics. The first one stems from the impermanence of electoral outcomes. If parties sympathetic to business concerns cannot win elections with some regularity over time, they are a useless tool to their constituency.

In all three countries, the long-term electoral appeal and organizational strength of right-wing parties remains an open question. While the electoral prospects of these parties did not appear bright in the early 1980s, the economic crisis seems to have worked in their favor and revived their appeal. Capitalizing on popular frustrations with the economic situation, right-wing parties were able to project themselves as the alternative to unsuccessful economic management by the center-left and populists. This resuscitated the right, particularly in presidential elections.

Peru offers an example of the dramatic reversal of the electoral standing of the right. In interviews conducted in Peru in 1986, businessmen were extremely pessimistic about the electoral future of the right, specifically of the staunchly pro-business Popular Christian Party (PPC). Extremely poor showings in the 1980 and 1985 elections led businessmen to believe that the party that most accurately reflected their ideological position was doomed to defeat. This negative perception of the PPC led many businessmen to cultivate ties with other parties (particularly APRA) to ensure at least some measure of access to policy makers.[58] But the deepening of the economic crisis under President Alan García and the policy battles between business and the García administration revived political organization on the right. The Democratic Front, composed of the PPC, AP and the Freedom Movement (*Movimiento Libertad*), was created to contest the 1990 presidential election with novelist Mario Vargas Llosa as its candidate.

In a similar fashion, the economic crisis proved to be a critical factor in the revival of the right in Ecuador's 1984 presidential election. The right, traditionally fragmented across several small parties, united in the National Reconstruction Front (FRN) to endorse the presidential candidacy of Social Christian candidate León Febres Cordero. Febres Cordero, a top businessman and Congressman, grabbed the public's attention by spearheading the opposition to the economic stabilization program undertaken by the government of Osvaldo Hurtado. By presenting himself as a "protest" candidate, Febres Cordero went on to narrowly defeat his social democratic opponent, Rodrigo Borja.

In Bolivia, the rightist ADN led by ex-general Hugo Banzer has turned in solid electoral performances in 1985 and 1989. Banzer won the popular vote in 1985 and narrowly lost to Gonzalo Sánchez de Lozada, the MNR candidate and intellectual architect of Paz's neoliberal program, in 1989. But Bolivian electoral laws thwarted Banzer's polling victory (and Sánchez de Lozada's) by throwing the races into Congress for a final selection. Nevertheless, the ADN's electoral strength has allowed it to play a central role in the formation of the political pacts that elect the president and lay the basis for the incoming government. The ADN collaborated with the Paz Estenssoro government and has continued its collaborative stance with his successor, Jaime Paz Zamora, of the social democratic MIR.

While businessmen have found this rightist electoral revival heartening, these electoral victories are transitory at best and cannot guarantee a stable policy environment. This brings us to the second dimension of uncertainty that comes with electoral politics — accountability. Once in power, elected officials are often able to assume some autonomy and shed their immediate class attachments. Business leaders are quick to point out that the occupation of ministerial positions by fellow capitalists does not necessarily guarantee sympathy or access. Politicians in capitalist democracies have to respond to accumulation, legitimation, and electoral imperatives that structurally limit their capacity to respond to business demands, even when they may be personally sympathetic to them.[59] The quest for political survival among politicians has its own rationale that may lead them away from interests of the original coalition that supported them. This dynamic unfolded dramatically in Ecuador during the Febres Cordero administration (1984–88). As León Febres Cordero's problems with the military and the economy mounted, he reversed his neoliberal monetary policies and increased public spending — alienating a significant segment of his business supporters.[60]

As much as business elites in all three countries play the card of electoral politics through financial contributions to parties and candidates, it is a game with rewards that are partial and transitory — where the "fit" between business expectations and actual party performance leaves the private sector disgruntled with its partisan allies.

Political Efficacy, Uncertainty, and Democracy

Reflections on the problems of consolidating democratic regimes by Adam Przeworski, Albert Hirschman, and others have focused on the dilemmas posed by the uncertainties inherent in democratic systems.[61] Simply put, the argument is that democracies require political actors who are "good losers." Political players in a democracy must agree to abide by the formal and legal rules even when they incur losses in the electoral and policy making arenas. As such, democracies are demanding systems; they are built around the presence of actors who are tolerant of uncertainties and prospective losses. This toleration is bred by the fluidity of democratic politics — the fact that there are multiple points of access and influence and that losses can be reversed, either through the legislature, the courts, elections, or in the next round of bureaucratic politics. From this perspective, thinking about democracy in Latin America leads us into the shadowy realm of gauging actors' perceptions — of self and others — along with their calculations of the future. This is a difficult task especially since such perceptions may shift dramatically with the conjuncture at hand.

Do the phenomena described in this essay point to the development in these countries of self-confident and tolerant capitalist classes who have concluded (along with Lenin) that democracy is the "best possible political shell" for Latin American capitalism?[62] Or is it simply the chronicle of pragmatic adjustments in the face of a temporary disillusionment with military rule that will break down as policy frustrations mount? In trying to answer these difficult questions, it is useful to think about how the patterns of business-government relations described in these three cases affect the sense of political efficacy of business groups and their constituents. There are two dimensions to political efficacy: *internal efficacy* has to do with how actors perceive their own capacities to affect the political process, while *external efficacy* relates to an actor's perceptions of the responsiveness of government to citizen demands.[63]

On one level, it appears that the private sectors in these countries are now well equipped to successfully engage in the give-and-take of pluralist politics. The growth of the organizational capacity of local capitalists is impressive. The new sophistication is reflected in the proliferation of specialized producers' associations, the movements to create inclusive peak associations, and the professionalization of existing organizations. Through these organizations, capitalists make use of all the traditional instruments available in a democracy to influence public policy. Business groups engage in "technical" lobbying of state managers in the executive branch; they mobilize opinion through the press. As individuals, businessmen maintain ties to parties through campaign contributions and often participate directly as candidates. Furthermore, at least a partial representation of business interests takes place through the quasi-corporatist consultative mechanisms inside the executive branch. All the pieces seem to be in place to ensure what Lindblom called the "privileged position" of business in capitalist democracies.[64]

While democracies are supposed to be "permeable" states, it is the constant and sometimes drastic shifts in levels of permeability across elected governments and within any one government that worry businessmen and lead them to regard the policy process as erratic and irrational. The inclusiveness or exclusiveness of governments in regard to business participation in economic decision making is the product of factors in the internal and external environments. The partisan character of the government sets the tone for public-private sector relations. But perhaps even more critical in determining the levels of permeability are the procedural and stylistic approaches adopted by state managers. State managers can consciously structure business organizations out of decision making or opt to let them in.

What was striking in the Central Andean countries throughout the 1980s was the efforts by presidents and economic teams to fashion an exclusionary approach to macroeconomic policy making—one that strove to keep labor and business interest groups out of the deliberations. This exclusionary approach to economic policy making is not confined to Latin America, nor is it particularly unusual. The advanced capitalist democracies of Europe and North America have also developed institutional mechanisms and technocratic policy-making styles that reduce interest group politicking on certain types of economic decisions such as monetary policy.

Let me suggest, however, that the political meaning and implications of exclusionary policy making in the Latin American setting differ significantly from that of advanced capitalist democracies. In advanced capitalist democracies, the movement toward technocratic decision making developed in the postwar period; it occurred within a context of economic growth and in a situation in which a Keynesian "class compromise" was struck. Capitalists were assured of the ideological hegemony of capitalism in their respective countries—and shared in the general consensus on Keynesian policies.[65] Moreover, exclusionary policy making did not extend uniformly into all policy spheres. In a number of countries, elaborate corporatist arrangements allowed domestic capitalists to bargain in certain policy areas.[66]

The context of exclusionary policy making in the Andes is quite different—and as such carries a different meaning for domestic capitalists. It is important to recall the past political trajectory of economic elites in these countries. These economic elites hold an extraordinarily "privileged position" in these highly stratified and unequal societies; and as such, they lay a special claim to the state as another arena of that privilege. Domestic capitalists, both as individuals and in their organizations, are well schooled in nondemocratic political behavior. Thus, exclusion may feed alienation and provoke a slide into outright coup-mongering (e.g., actively lobbying the military to take over, engaging in disruptive economic actions that invite military intervention to restore "order," etc.). Such behavior took place in Ecuador during business' battles with the Hurtado administration; business organizations also engaged in provocative actions during the Siles government in Bolivia.

Second, because of the extreme volatility of these economies, domestic capitalists may possess less of a marginal propensity to

accept short-term losses stemming from what they perceive as unfavorable macroeconomic policies. The economic debility of these
groups may create a further incentive to engage in coup-mongering.
This feeds an atmosphere of "omnipresent fear" in these polities;
political democracy appears fragile to all actors and political strategies are deeply affected by the seeming tenuousness of the situation.[67]

The current debt crisis and the imperatives that the crisis creates for state managers (i.e., responding to demands from international creditors) prompts state managers to opt for even more
exclusionary modes of decision making. The ethos of "crisis management" legitimates the insulation and autonomy of economic
teams from the pressures of domestic lobbyists. This exclusionary
mode is highly suited to the formulation and implementation of neoliberal economic models which impose costs on fractions of domestic capital, particularly in import-substituting industries. Yet, the political cost of coherence and consistency in the implementation of
economic models is that the models clarify exactly who the winners
and losers are. The more state managers strive toward coherence in
the management of economic affairs, the more they risk alienating
important groups. Peter Hall describes the benefits of deliberate non-
coordinated policy making:

> A state faced with multiple tasks and well-defined conflicts of
> interest among the social classes it governs, or the groups within
> these, may find it necessary to maintain a degree of deliberate
> malintegration among its various policy-making arms so that
> each can mobilize consent among its particular constituencies
> by pursuing policies which, even if never fully implemented,
> appear to address the needs of these groups. In many cases the
> pursuit of incompatible policies renders all of them ineffective,
> but this strategy prevents any one group from claiming that
> the state has come down on the side of its opponents.[68]

Thus, deliberate malintegration and rampant pluralism in economic policy making rather than orthodox coherence and insulation may be a way to enhance the sense of external efficacy among
business leaders and reduce feelings of uncertainty in the private
sector. In a strange way, wheeling and dealing incrementalism might
be the best guarantee of dominant class loyalty to democracy — but,
given the international pressures on state managers and the magnitude of the economic problems they face, just "muddling through"
may be a fast fading option.

The development of internal efficacy remains problematic. In an objective sense, the growth of bourgeois organization certainly can be seen as contributing to a heightened class capacity to intervene in the policy process. But the subjective interpretations by capitalists of their capacity as political actors do not reflect an image of self-confidence and security. One of the striking themes that emerged in my interviews with leaders of business associations was the recurrent references to the lack of internal unity within the private sector and their weakness vis-à-vis other groups in society. It is important to keep in mind that the flourishing of bourgeois organization over the last fifteen years has been *defensive* and *reactive* in nature. Similar to the patterns of business interest group formation elsewhere, these organizations have been founded and are active in response to the threats posed by the state and labor movements.[69] As such, businessmen perceive themselves as being on the defensive in these societies. Especially in Peru and Bolivia, these feelings of insecurity are reinforced by traumatic political memories of popular class militancy and state directed reforms; the *Asamblea Popular* in Bolivia and the Velasco Alvarado regime in Peru are central experiences in attempting to understand the mentality of these dominant classes. A prominent Bolivian businessman offered a dark assessment of the character and political capacity of his own class:

> I do not think the interests between the parasitic and productive sectors of the bourgeoisie can be made compatible . . . I think all of us will be screwed and I'm scared . . . This is not a solid bourgeoisie . . . We are still very primitive . . . We know we are weak and we don't give a damn. Everybody's just interested in the next deal they can make—the next fast buck. The majority of the private sector is a fast-buck private sector. It's not a creative private sector and they've got a tremendous complex about their weakness . . . You're distorting your whole study if you think the private sector is powerful. I think the other sectors are going to beat us.[70]

Looking for signs of a self-confident and democratic Andean bourgeoisie is a disappointing exercise. The history of the return to civilian rule is, in part, a story of elites who "backed into" democracy as a retreat from reform and a preemption of the left.[71] But this ambivalence toward democracy on the part of business elites is not unique. The comparative history of business elites reveals a long record of antidemocratic attitudes and behavior; an examination of U.S. history provides a sobering reminder of the antidemocratic postures adopted by capitalist elites.[72]

The comparative historical record draws our attention to an important point as we speculate on the future of Latin American democracy. Democratic development in its early stages does not hinge on the distribution of an abstract commitment to democracy inside the business community or even the society at large. The prospects for the consolidation of democracy initially depends on how the relationships among key groups — the military, the bourgeoisie, state bureaucrats, and labor — coalesce during specific conjunctures. As Barrington Moore and others have shown, democracy is a product of class alliances and pragmatic choices.[73] In the same vein, Przeworski argues that stability of European democracy in the postwar period was rooted in a Keynesian "class compromise" among the state, capital, and labor. Labor dropped its radical challenge of capitalism in exchange for political representation and state intervention that smoothed out fluctuations in the business cycle. In short, stable democracy was part of a larger social transaction among social classes that was mediated by parties, interest groups and the state bureaucracy.[74]

What is clear is that, at least in the Central Andes, domestic capitalists remain skeptical about the ability of politicians and technocrats to engineer a stable investment climate and policy predictability. Nor do domestic capitalists seem predisposed toward a historic "class compromise" that would be responsive to labor demands for material improvements in exchange for a "gentlemen's agreement" on capitalism and democracy. All this is not to say that these civilian regimes are on an inevitable road to collapse; a simple lack of alternatives to the current regimes may keep actors inside the bounds of play for some time to come. At this point, however, anxiety and ambivalence still define the bourgeoisie's relationship to political democracy.

NOTES

The original version of this essay was written in 1986. I thank Frances Hagopian, Scott Mainwaring, Guillermo O'Donnell, Ernest Bartell and Caroline Domingo for their helpful comments. The interviews referred to were conducted as part of a joint research project being undertaken with James M. Malloy of the University of Pittsburgh. This essay draws on fifty-four formal interviews with business interest group leaders, party elites and economic policy makers that took place in Lima, La Paz, and Quito from January through March 1986. To ensure the anonymity of the informants, the material taken from interviews is cited only by date and location.

1. The argument that business holds a "privileged position" in advanced capitalist democracy is made by Charles Lindblom, *Politics and Markets: The World Political-Economic Systems* (New York: Basic Books, 1977): 170–188.

2. The term "neoliberal" is used to denote economic policies that combine orthodox stabilization measures with a long-term commitment to restructuring the economy by reducing the role of the state and subjecting economic activity to market forces. This is the definition developed by Alejandro Foxley in *Latin American Experiments in Neoconservative Economics* (Berkeley: University of California Press, 1983): 15–17. Foxley, however, preferred to use "neoconservative" rather than the Spanish "neoliberal" for his English-speaking readers. For more discussion of the policies see Joseph Ramos, *Neoconservative Economics in the Southern Cone of Latin America* (Baltimore: Johns Hopkins University Press, 1986). For an analysis of the origins of the neoliberal experiments in the Central Andes see Catherine M. Conaghan, James M. Malloy, and Luis A. Abugattas, "Business and the 'Boys': The Politics of Neoliberalism in the Central Andes," *Latin American Research Review* 25, no. 2 (1990): 3–30.

3. For such interpretations of the Peruvian case, see for example: Aníbal Quijano, *Nationalism and Capitalism in Peru: A Study in Neo-Imperialism* (New York: Monthly Review Press, 1971); Henry Pease García, *El ocaso del poder oligárquico: Lucha política en la escena oficial 1965–75* (Lima: DESCO, 1977); E. V. K. Fitzgerald, *The Political Economy of Peru 1956–1978: Economic Development and the Restructuring of Capital* (Cambridge: Cambridge University Press, 1979). For an interpretation of the Bolivian case, see James Dunkerley, *Rebellion in the Veins: Political Struggle in Bolivia, 1952–82* (London: Verso, 1984).

4. Important works on the traditional Peruvian oligarchy include Francois Bourricaud, *Power and Society in Contemporary Peru* (New York: Praeger, 1970), and Dennis Gilbert, The Oligarchy and the Old Regime in Peru," Latin American Dissertation Series no. 69. (Ithaca: Cornell University, 1971). Also on Peruvian economic groups sée Germán Reaño and Enríque Vásquez, "Dinámica empresarial de un grupo económico en el Peru: El caso Romero (1890–1985)," *Apuntes* 19 (segundo semestre 1986): 109–117; Alfonso Quiroz, "Financial Leadership and the Formation of Peruvian Elite Groups, 1884–1930," *Journal of Latin American Studies* 20, no. 1 (May 1988): 49–81.

5. For a discussion of the literature on economic groups see Nathaniel H. Leff, "Industrial Organization and Entrepreneurship in the Developing Countries: The Economic Groups," *Economic Development and Cultural Change* 26, no. 4 (July 1978): 661–675.

6. There is a large literature on the Velasco period. Some of the important treatments of the period include: Alfred Stepan, *The State and Society: Peru in Comparative Perspective* (Princeton: Princeton University Press, 1978); Abraham Lowenthal, ed., *The Peruvian Experiment: Continuity and Change under Military Rule* (Princeton: Princeton University Press, 1975); Abraham Lowenthal and Cynthia McClintock, ed., *The Peruvian Experiment Reconsidered* (Princeton: Princeton University Press, 1983); David Booth and Bernardo Sorj, *Military Reformism and Social Classes: The Peruvian Experiment 1968–80* (New York: St. Martin's Press, 1983); George Philip, *The Rise and Fall of the Peruvian Military Radicals 1968–76* (London: Athlone Press, 1978); Carlos Franco, ed., *El Perú de Velasco* (Lima: Centro de Estudios para el Desarrollo y la Participación, 1986).

7. On the Rodríguez Lara period in Ecuador, see Nelson Argones, *El juego del poder: De Rodríguez Lara a Febres Cordero* (Quito: Corporación Editora Nacional, 1985); Instituto de Investigaciones Económicas y Políticas, *El capitalismo ecuatoriano contemporáneo: Su funcionamiento* (Guayaquil: Universidad de Guayaquil, n.d.); Augusto Varas and Fernando Bustamante, *Fuerzas armadas y política en Ecuador* (Quito: Ediciones Latinoamérica, 1978).

8. Jerry R. Ladman, ed., *Modern-Day Bolivia: Legacy of the Revolution and Prospects for the Future* (Tempe: Center for Latin American Studies, Arizona State University Press, 1982).

9. For a discussion of this ideological aversion in the U.S. case, see David Vogel, "Why Businessmen Distrust Their State: The Political Consciousness of American Corporate Executives," *British Journal of Political Science* 8, no. 1 (January 1978): 169–173. Readers should note that my use of the gender-specific term "businessmen" reflects the continuing domination of this sphere by males.

10. This period is discussed at length by the author in *Restructuring Domination: Industrialists and the State in Ecuador* (Pittsburgh: University of Pittsburgh Press, 1988).

11. Interview, 30 January 1986, Lima; Interview, 22 January 1986, Lima.

12. Interview, 22 January 1986, Lima.

13. Interview, 30 January 1986, Lima; Interview, 15 January 1986, Lima.

14. See the interview with ADEX founder Alejandro Tabini, "Cómo y por qué nació ADEX?" *Perú Exporta,* no. 99 (June–July 1986): 4–7.

15. Anthony Ferner, "Industrialists and the Developmental Model" in Booth and Sorj, eds., *Military Reformism,* 55–56. Ferner's complete work on the subject is *La burguesía industrial en el desarrollo peruano* (Lima: Editorial Esan, 1982).

16. Interview, 23 January 1986, Lima.

17. Francisco Durand, *Los industriales, el liberalismo y la democracia* (Lima: Fundación Friedrich Ebert/DESCO, 1984), p. 8. Also see Durand's *La década frustrada: Los industriales y el poder 1970–1980* (Lima: DESCO, 1982).

18. Interview, 4 February 1986, Lima; Interview, 22 January 1986, Lima.

19. See the previously cited work by Dunkerley. Also see Christopher Mitchell, *The Legacy of Populism in Bolivia: From the MNR to Military Rule* (New York: Praeger, 1971): 121–132; Jerry Ladman, "The Political Economy of the 'Economic Miracle' of the Banzer Regime," in *Modern-Day Bolivia,* 321–344.

20. L. Enrique García-Rodríguez, "Structural Change and Development Policy in Bolivia," in *Modern-Day Bolivia,* p. 176.

21. For further discussion of the Banzer period see James M. Malloy and Eduardo A. Gamarra, *Revolution and Reaction: Bolivia 1964–85* (New Brunswick: Transaction, 1988).

22. Cardoso cited in Anthony Ferner, "Industrialists," in Booth and Sorj, eds., *Military Reformism,* p. 56.

23. Malcolm Gillis et al., *Taxation and Mining: Nonfuel Minerals in Bolivia and Other Countries* (Cambridge, Mass.: Ballinger, 1978).

24. Interview, 20 February 1986, La Paz; Interview, 19 February 1986, La Paz.

25. The positions taken by business organizations and political parties during the "dialogues" can be found in Luis Orleans Calle Vargas, *La constitución de 1978 y el proceso de reestructuración jurídica del estado 1976–78* (Guayaquil: Universidad de Guayaquil, 1978). For Chamber pronouncements on the mechanics of the return see "Informe del Sr. Presidente de la Federación Nacional de Cámaras de Industrias del Ecuador, Ing. León Febres Cordero, ante la Junta General realizada en Quito, el 15 de diciembre de 1976," *Revista de la Cámara de Industrias de Guayaquil* 9, no. 31 (1976); "El Plan de reestructuración jurídica del estado y el destino nacional," *Boletín Informativo* (Cámara de Industrias de Guayaquil) 4, no. 46 (September 1977); "Informe anual presentado por el Presidente de la Cámara de Industrias de Guayaquil," *Revista de la Cámara de Industrias de Guayaquil* 9, no. 38 (1978); "Informe anual de labores del Presidente de la Cámara de Industriales de Pichincha, Ing. Gonzalo Vorbeck, 1977–78," *Carta Industrial,* no. 31 (January–February 1978); "Reflexión política," *Carta Industrial,* no. 34 (September 1978).

26. For a review of the events of the Peruvian transition see Sandra L. Woy-Hazelton, "The Return of Partisan Politics in Peru," in *Post-Revolutionary Peru: The Politics of Transformation,* ed. Stephen M. Gorman (Boulder, Colo.: Westview, 1982): 33–72.

27. For a discussion of different types of transition processes see Eduardo Viola and Scott Mainwaring, "Transitions to Democracy: Brazil and Argentina in the 1980s," *Journal of International Affairs* 38 (Winter 1985): 193–218.

28. Interview, 20 February 1986, La Paz.

29. *¡Democracia Ya!* along with other important CEPB documents from the period can be found in Confederación de Empresarios Privados de Bolivia, *Pensamiento y acción de la empresa privada 1982–85* (La Paz: CEPB, 1986).

30. For more discussion concerning the politicization of the Chambers of Production in Ecuador see Jorge Hidobro, "Acción política de las clases sociales y las políticas agraria e industrial: Ecuador 1972–79" (paper, Center for Latin American Studies, University of Pittsburgh, August 1981).

31. For Lanata's discussion of the creation of IESS see, "El IESS: Un lustro al servicio de la empresa industrial privada," *Industria Peruana,* no. 610 (August 1985): 18–23.

32. Interview, 15 January 1986, Lima.

33. A major project of the IESS was a comprehensive study and critique of the Peruvian economy; SNI leaders saw the study as a means to educate members and create a common viewpoint among industrialists on economic matters. The study was published as *Proyecto Perú: Hacia un proyecto nacional de desarrollo a mediano y largo plazo,* Volumes I and II (Lima: Instituto de Estudios Económicos y Sociales, Sociedad Nacional de Industrias, 1986).

34. The 1981 issues of ADEX's magazine, *Perú Exporta,* contains a series of articles by Daniel Schydlowsky that summarize his position. For Schydlowsky's evaluation of Peruvian economic policies see "The Tragedy of Lost Opportunity in Peru," in *Latin American Political Economy: Financial Crisis and Change,* ed. Jonathan Hartlyn and Samuel A. Morley (Boulder, Colo.: Westview, 1986).

35. Interview, 17 February 1986, La Paz.

36. Interview, 22 February 1986, La Paz.

37. See "Declaración del Consejo de Cámaras y Asociaciones de la Producción," *Informe Final,* Convención Nacional de Industriales, Quito, 1981.

38. For background on CONFIEP see "Discurso del Ing. Julio Piccini Martín, Presidente saliente del CONFIEP" and "Discurso del Dr. Miguel Vega Alvear, al asumir la Presidencia de la CONFIEP," in *Industria Peruana,* no. 613 (November 1985): 10–16.

39. This distinction between productive and predatory fractions of the bourgeoisie is made by Guillermo O'Donnell. See his "Lineas temáticas del Proyecto 'Consolidación'" (Mimeo, Kellogg Institute, University of Notre Dame, 1986). A similar distinction between capitalists managing "fixed assets" and those manipulating "liquid assets" is made by Jeff Frieden in his study of comparative debt policies, "Classes, Sectors, and the Foreign Debt in Latin America," *Comparative Politics* 21, no. 1 (October 1988): 1–20.

40. For a discussion of how the state promoted deaccumulation through the implementation of a neoliberal model in Chile see Carlos Fortín, "The Political Economy of Repressive Monetarism: the State and Capital Accumulation in Post–1973 Chile," in *The State and Capital Accumulation in Latin America, Volume I: Brazil, Chile, Mexico,* ed. Christian Anglade and Carlos Fortin (Pittsburgh: University of Pittsburgh Press, 1985): 139–209.

41. For a discussion of the operation of economic groups in Bolivia see Susan Eckstein and Frances Hagopian, "The Limits of Industrialization in the Less Developed World: Bolivia," *Economic Development and Cultural Change* 32, no. 1 (October 1983): 63–95. On economic groups in Ecuador see Guillermo Navarro, *La concentración de capitales en el Ecuador* (Quito: Ediciones Solitierra, 1976). On Peru see Carlos Malpica, *Los dueños del Perú,* 2nd ed. (Lima: Editorial Ensayos Sociales, 1989).

42. Interview, 19 March 1986, Quito.

43. Interview, 22 February 1986, La Paz.

44. Interview, 27 January 1986, Lima; Interview, 4 February 1986, Lima.

45. Belaúnde's interests in the development of public works and infrastructure were a priority in his first administration (1963–68). For a description of policy making in that period see Pedro Pablo Kuczynski, *Peruvian Democracy under Economic Stress: An Account of the Belaúnde Administration, 1963–68* (Princeton: Princeton University Press, 1977).

46. Interview, 22 February 1986, Lima.

47. Interview, 12 February 1986, Lima.

48. Interview, 4 February 1986, Lima.

49. Interview, 10 December 1984, Quito. For further discussion of the Hurtado style and his problematic relationships with business organizations see Howard Handelman, "Elite Interest Groups under Military and Democratic Regimes: Ecuador 1972–84," paper delivered at the Latin American Studies Association meeting, Albuquerque, New Mexico, April 17–20, 1986.

50. Interview, 24 February 1986, La Paz.

51. For a discussion of the measures and effects involved in *desdolarización* see Kenneth P. Jameson, "Dollarization and Dedollarization in

Bolivia" (Paper, Department of Economics, University of Notre Dame, 1986).

52. For further analysis of the Siles period see Robert Laserna, comp., *Crisis, democracia y conflicto social* (Cochabamba: CERES, 1985).

53. Ecuador has an especially well-developed tradition of corporatism. Constitutional law prior to 1978 provided for functional representation in the legislature from the Chambers of Commerce, Agriculture and Industry.

54. Interview, 4 February 1986, Lima.

55. See, for example, the 1985–86 issues of ADEX's *Perú Exporta* and *Industria Peruana,* published by the Sociedad de Industrias.

56. Interview, 27 January 1986, Lima. For a discussion of definitions of corporatism and concertation in the European setting see Gerhard Lembruch, "Concertation and the Structure of Corporatist Networks," in *Order and Conflict in Contemporary Capitalism,* ed. John Goldthorpe (Oxford: Clarendon Press, 1984): 60–80.

57. *Restructuring Domination,* 67.

58. Interview, 28 January 1986, Lima.

59. For a discussion of the autonomy of state managers that emerges out of conflicting demands see Theda Skocpol, "Political Response to Capitalist Crisis: Neo-Marxist Theories and the Case of the New Deal," *Politics and Society,* no. 2 (1981): 155–201; Kenneth Finegold and Theda Skocpol, "State, Party and Industry: From Business Recovery to the Wagner Act in America's New Deal," in *Statemaking and Social Movements,* ed. Charles Bright and Susan Harding (Ann Arbor: University of Michigan Press, 1984): 159–172. Work on this topic has been greatly influenced by the now classic piece by Fred Block, "The Ruling Class Does Not Rule: Notes on the Marxist Theory of the State," *Socialist Revolution* 33 (May–June 1977): 6–28. For further discussion of the debates on the autonomy of politicians see Eric Nordlinger, *On the Autonomy of the Democratic State* (Cambridge: Harvard University Press, 1981).

60. For a discussion of how Febres Cordero's drive for political survival as president led to an eventual abandonment of the neoliberal economic model, see Catherine M. Conaghan, "Dreams of Orthodoxy, Tales of Heterodoxy: León Febres Cordero and Economic Policymaking in Ecuador, 1984–1988" paper presented at the XV International Congress of the Latin American Studies Association, Miami, December 4–6, 1989.

61. Adam Przeworski, "Some Problems in the Study of Transition to Democracy," in *Transitions from Authoritarian Rule: Comparative Perspectives,* eds. Guillermo O'Donnell, Philippe Schmitter, and Laurence Whitehead (Baltimore: The Johns Hopkins University Press, 1986). Also see his discussion of the democratic state and class compromise in *Capi-

talism and Social Democracy (Cambridge: Cambridge University Press, 1985). See Albert Hirschman's commentary, "On Democracy in Latin America," *New York Review of Books* 6, April 10, 1986: 41–42. The idea that security and tolerance among elites are central to democracy is also found in the work of Robert Dahl, *Polyarchy: Participation and Opposition* (New Haven, Conn.: Yale University Press, 1971).

62. Bob Jessop, "Capitalism and Democracy: The Best Possible Political Shell?" in *States and Societies,* ed. David Held (New York: New York University Press, 1983): 272–289.

63. For a discussion of how the notion of political efficacy is used in the literature on public opinion see Paul Abramson, *Political Attitudes in America: Formation and Change* (San Francisco: W.H. Freeman, 1983): 135–145.

64. Lindblom, *Politics and Markets,* 170–188.

65. For a discussion of European political development in the postwar period Charles S. Maier, *In Search of Stability: Explorations in Historical Political Economy* (Cambridge: Cambridge University Press, 1987): 153–184. For further discussion of the spread of Keynesian policies see Peter Hall, ed., *The Political Power of Economic Ideas: Keynesianism Across Nations* (Princeton: Princeton University Press, 1989).

66. For a discussion of the development of corporatist arrangements in Europe see Peter J. Katzenstein, *Corporatism and Change: Austria, Switzerland, and the Politics of Industry* (Ithaca: Cornell University Press, 1984). Also see Goldthorpe, *Order and Conflict.*

67. For further consideration of how the fear of coup affects the unfolding of political transition and thereafter see Guillermo O'Donnell and Philippe Schmitter, *Transitions from Authoritarian Rule: Tentative Conclusions about Uncertain Democracy* (Baltimore: Johns Hopkins University Press, 1986), 23–27.

68. Quoted in David Held and Joel Krieger, "Accumulation, Legitimation and the State: The Ideas of Claus Offe and Jürgen Habermas," in *States and Societies,* ed. David Held (New York: New York University Press, 1983), p. 491.

69. The formation of business interest groups in response to the growing power of the state and labor is a common phenomenon. For a discussion of how this occurred in the U. S., see Burdett Loomis and Allan Cigler, "Introduction: The Changing Nature," in *Interest Group Politics,* ed. Allan Cigler and Burdett A. Loomis (Washington: Congressional Quarterly Press, 1983): 1–30.

70. Interview, 17 February 1986, La Paz.

71. Goran Therborn has argued that this pattern also operated in the formation of democracies in Western Europe see "The Rule of Capital and the Rise of Democracy," in *States and Societies,* 261–289. Also see

Dankwart Rustow, "Transitions to Democracy," *Comparative Politics* 2, no. 3 (April 1970): 337–363.

72. For discussions of antidemocratic attitudes of U. S. businessmen see the previously cited work by Vogel. Also see Edward Kirkland, *Dream and Thought in the Business Community* (Chicago: Quadrangle Books, 1956); James Prothro, *Dollar Decade: Business Ideas in the 1920s* (Baton Rouge: Louisiana State University Press, 1954); Robert McCloskey, *American Conservatism in the Age of Enterprise 1865–1910* (New York: Harper & Row, 1951); Francis X. Sutton et al., *The American Business Creed* (New York: Schocken Books, 1956).

73. The classic argument on the relationship between the structure of class relations and democratization is Barrington Moore Jr., *Social Origins of Dictatorship and Democracy* (Boston: Beacon Press, 1966).

74. See the previously cited work by Przeworski, *Capitalism,* 205–211.

The Compromised Consolidation:
The Political Class
in the Brazilian Transition

Frances Hagopian

Much of the early literature on democratization in Latin America appropriately focused on the problems of transition from military rule.[1] While militaries in the region either clung stubbornly to power or frequently retreated from promised liberalizations, when and how far military governors would allow their regimes to open, and if they would renege on their promises to submit power to civilians, were intensely debated questions. Once civilian government was restored, scholarly attention fixed on the issues most salient for breaking the cycle of military intervention and consolidating democracy: how to keep the military in their barracks, and how to provide guarantees to those segments of civilian society who had customarily knocked at the barracks door that a democratic regime would not harm their interests. With the future of civilian regimes in doubt, relatively less attention was paid to their emerging forms. Without taking consolidation for granted (the essays in this volume attest to the difficulty of that task) it does seem apt — at a time when many Latin American countries are engaging in "second round" elections which will transfer power from civilian presidents to elected successors — to shift the focus of our discussion about democratization to the political institutions and processes of the new civilian regimes.

One of the most challenging and least studied problems bearing on the political organization of new democracies is the question of how, after a protracted period of authoritarian rule, the political realm is redefined during periods of transition and consolidation. How and why are old political parties resurrected and new ones formed? What systems of political representation reemerge and which are discarded? How stable and secure are democratic institutions, and can these inspire the loyalty of the political activists upon whom Dahl (1971) placed so much hope to perform the role of democracy's faithful legions?

I approach this problem from the premise that the legacies of premilitary and military regimes weigh heavily on post-transition political systems, and that the extent to which each of these shapes the democratic political terrain is determined by the nature of the process of transition from authoritarian rule. More significant than the more familiar debates about whether or not democratization came about "from above" or "from below" is whether the transition to democracy is opposed or abetted by once-loyal authoritarian forces. Popular struggles to bring about democracy can significantly constrain the activities of elites in future democratic regimes, but rarely serve to design institutions. Therefore we speak of two broad types of transitions: those which take place without or in opposition to military regime supporters and other antidemocratic actors which may predate military rule, and those which take place with their active participation. We expect the former type to have occurred in countries with strong premilitary democratic institutions and traditions where authoritarian leaders more often sought to crush all political activity than to court civilian supporters among the political class, and the latter in those countries which lacked such traditions of pluralist, fully participatory democracy, and where the political class found it easy to collaborate with dictators to preserve their positions in the state.

In the first set of countries, where transitions are launched only with great difficulty and incumbent authoritarian elites refuse to compromise with the proponents of democracy, the democratic camp is forced to resolve differences within its ranks and to unite to overthrow military rule. In these cases, the old regime forfeits influence in the new, and there is a clear break between authoritarian and democratic government. The democratic regimes which result from such transitions may bear the strong imprint of reinvented premilitary institutions, parties, and procedures, preferably strengthened to weather economic crises and political polarization. In the second set of countries where, on the other hand, prescient elements of the "old regime" jump on the democratic bandwagon, and transitions occur more easily with their participation, the old regime merges with the new. There is broader space for the participation of those actors with dubious commitments to democracy. The new regimes produced by this type of transition draw from more than one source for their institutional design and leaders: they may be a hybrid of traditional and nontraditional democratic forms with varying doses of military authoritarianism.

This paper is centrally concerned with the second type of transition, and accordingly focuses on the transition to democracy in what is perhaps its archetypal case in Latin America — Brazil. Brazil's military regime is distinctive among South American dictatorships in that elections and functioning state and national legislatures required the participation of the political class. And it goes without saying that the New Republic had an authoritarian birth.[2] The old regime's leaders agreed to a political opening before it was demanded from below; as Stepan (1988:32–33) has convincingly argued, no opposition activity can account for the regime's initial decision to liberalize. Important social actors such as industrialists, labor, and the Catholic Church did protest regime policies and hasten the military's departure from politics, but the pace and scope of the transition to civilian rule were dictated by incumbent elites, up to and including the indirect election of the civilian president.[3]

But while many works have stressed the elite origins of the democratization in Brazil, differing only in the *degree* of control they credit regime elites with being able to maintain throughout the process of democratization, few have systematically examined the participation of the elite in the latter stages of the transition. Those which have distinguished within the elite differentiate only "state elites" (the "technobureaucracy") and "societal elites" (the bourgeoisie) and, when they invoke "regime elite," they do so broadly and loosely, most often equating "regime elites" with military elites. Missing from these works is an explicit treatment of *political* elites who hedged regime and opposition camps — especially those who embraced the 1964 "Revolution" and participated in the authoritarian regime, but once democratization gained momentum, advocated a controlled liberalization. Despite these elites' having navigated the transition and presided over the birth of the new regime, there has been insufficient attention paid to the participation of the political class, and this group has not been disaggregated in a conceptually useful fashion.[4]

The "political class" in Brazil is obviously an eclectic group. At a simple level, it includes defenders and opponents of authoritarianism, neatly identifiable by membership in the proregime ARENA (National Renovating Alliance) party and the opposition MDB (Brazilian Democratic Movement). Within both camps, and across this divide, another line can be drawn demarcating political elites who can be considered "traditional" in the Brazilian context, and those who cannot. "Traditional" political elites are normally related to one another and to previous political generations, and they exercise domination through highly personalized, clientelistic networks. Because there was a great deal of continuity in Brazil between traditional elites who practiced a form of closed, antidemocratic politics before the coup d'état of 1964 and the politicians who backed the military, practically there is a great deal of overlap between "authoritarian" and "traditional" political elites.

This article examines the role in the transition to democracy in Brazil of those traditional politicians who supported the authoritarian regime and their counterparts who rose to prominence through traditional politics without and perhaps in opposition to military rule, as well as those opportunistic newcomers who hoped to climb politically by collaborating with military rulers. It is concerned with the effects of their incorporation by the new regime on political organization and the institutions of the New Republic in Brazil, and attempts to assess the extent to which they were able to influence the reconstruction of politics after two decades of military rule. Its specific focus is on a class of elite political actors whose role and power in the authoritarian regime was considerable if largely unacknowledged. I refer to the traditional political elite of the state of Minas Gerais — ardent supporters, indeed perpetrators, of the 1964 coup d'état. Even if Minas politics today can no more be equated with a single national pattern than it could in the 1945–1964 era,[5] this state's politics are not inconsequential in national politics, and the Minas oligarchy is not one among equals. This state's elite has consistently been able to impose its preferences nationally; its actions sparked every major regime change in Brazil in this century. It helped launch the 1930 "Revolution"; its 1943 *Manifesto dos Mineiros* hastened the end of the *Estado Novo;* it led the movement to depose President Goulart in 1964; and once again, in 1984, the *mineiro* elite was one of Brazil's first regional elites to plot its escape from the sinking authoritarian coalition — it proposed the realignment of forces which made the transition possible and placed it under traditional political elite control. Tancredo Neves, the victor in the 1985 presidential election and heralded "founding father" of the New Republic, was a native son. Political elites in Brazil have traditionally been organized on a state by state basis. By tracing the role of a regional elite within national political negotiations, we gain a unique perspective on local, state, and national politics.

I divide the Brazilian transition to democracy into separate periods of transition and consolidation. The transition from authoritarian rule began in 1974, but here, I consider the years from 1974 to 1982 to be authoritarian per se, and I speak of the period of freer elections and intense negotiation (1982–85) as the period of the transition to democracy. The period of consolidation, or the foundational period of the new or "transitional democracy"[6] began with the assumption of the presidency by José Sarney in March 1985,[7] and accelerated with the direct presidential election of 1989. Brazilian democracy is well on its way to being consolidated; one civilian president has handed power to a directly elected successor, and the "New Republic" is now six years old.

The central argument of this paper is that the support for democratic transition of traditional political elites facilitated and made possible the transition, but also put the new democracy at a considerable disadvantage; it was the most significant contributing factor to what O'Donnell elsewhere in this volume calls the "paradox of success."[8] Old regime political elites figured prominently in state and national politics during the transition. Invited to help construct a new civilian regime by opponents of the authoritarian order seeking to accelerate the demise of the military regime, these elites used their importance to the democratic camp — which stemmed both from their weight in the electoral college and their proximity to the military — as bargaining tools with which to recapture state-level executive positions (lost in the 1982 elections) that carried with them control over political patronage. In migrating from the decaying Democratic Social Party (PDS) to the Party of the Brazilian Democratic Movement (PMDB), they appropriated and transformed the new party of government. The persistent influence of traditional political elites over primary political institutions, in turn, blocks the passage to what O'Donnell (1985b) has called the extension of democracy — a stage of democratization marked by "increased transparency" in policy deliberation and in interest representation.[9] In other words, it limits the representation of popular interests, an essential ingredient in a democracy. In Brazil, the most appropriate po-

litical strategy to consolidate civilian rule—building the broadest
possible coalition for keeping the military in its barracks—may conflict with that best suited to achieve the transition from a consolidated to an extended democracy. The future extension of political
democracy, in short, may have been compromised by efforts to consolidate a democratic regime.

The argument developed here implies that once the new regime
elevates old politicians by inviting their cooperation, those politicians carry with them, in proportion to their strength, features of
the old regime they represent—whether premilitary or military, conservative and/or traditional. And their influence is felt regardless
of whether or not there has been a change in the electorate.[10] In
Uruguay, two nineteenth-century parties, the *Colorados* and the
Blancos, survived yet one more "modernizing impulse" to be resurrected, and the two leading candidates in the most recent presidential election were both descendants of the political families that
dominated politics in this century. In Brazil, the high-level participation of political elites of both the oligarchical and military systems in the new democratic regime resulted in important continuities
from the military regime to the civilian regime in its first five years,
and in the contamination of democratic political forms by traditional, antidemocratic practices, most notably an extreme version
of political clientelism. While many "realistic," consolidated democracies in the world today exhibit one or more of what I label "antidemocratic practices," in Brazil, democracy is dominated by these.
Most significantly, clientelism there does not complement other forms
of representation; it crowds them out.

The principal question which this essay raises but cannot yet
answer convincingly is of what consequence it is for *future* Brazilian democracy that the executive branch and political parties have
been dominated by traditional elites during the period of regime transition. What it hopes to show is that the current democratic regime
suffers from birth defects which seriously impair its functioning. But
this is a story whose conclusion has yet to be written.

The Political Elite in Twentieth-Century Brazil

Brazilian politics has long been dominated by regional political elites who shaped political institutions and arrangements for their
self-aggrandizement. They conspired in Republican clubs to overthrow the emperor a century ago, and once victorious, they fashioned

a federal republic to maximize their power and autonomy. These elites governed their states as closed oligarchies, and though forced to adapt in the decades after 1930 to a stronger central government and a more open political system, they exhibited a remarkable degree of resiliency, and their members played prominent roles in national and state politics. They were largely responsible for the fact that on the eve of the 1964 coup, politics in most of rural Brazil, and even in many cities, was organized much as it was at the turn of the century.

At least three pillars of oligarchical domination buttressed the rule of the political elite, in Minas Gerais headed by members of many of the state's most "traditional families," during this century: the exercise of political clientelism; the oligarchical control of a dominant political party closely linked to a centralized state executive; and restrictions on political competition. Whether in a nominally authoritarian or democratic regime, the distribution of state resources according to political criteria allowed traditional elites to enforce loyalty to themselves and to the regime, and control of a dominant party allowed the traditional elite to control elite recruitment, enforce unity and discipline in policy and succession questions, and marshall popular, electoral support for the candidacies of its members, however restricted the franchise. At least until the mid-1950s, effective limits on political competition engendered a monopoly of power which preserved traditional political elite tenure in the state and the patterns of political organization it orchestrated.

In the decade leading up to the coup, the old system came under attack, especially in the countryside, as rural workers began to form peasant leagues and rural unions. The populist government failed to seize the initiative in this process, but by making the attempt, incurred the wrath of traditional, especially agrarian, elites.[11] Politically, it appeared in many parts of Brazil that the system was becoming truly competitive, and oligarchical victories could no longer be assured.[12] The coup of 1964, whatever else it was designed to accomplish, was staged at least in part in order to apply the brakes to rapid change.[13]

After the fact, the military attempted to implement its own economic and political projects. It was reasonably successful first at economic stabilization and then at producing high growth rates (although the benefits were not distributed widely). But its ambition to rationalize administration and excise the blight of corruption and clientelism from the political system ran aground. Despite military ambitions and short-term success to the contrary, the bureaucratic-authoritarian regime did not ultimately revamp the way politics was practiced in Brazil. It undermined its own objectives by departing from standard authoritarian practices and boldly holding elections throughout the dictatorship. Once it had cancelled the political rights and electoral mandates of its most dangerous opponents, transferred budgetary and other important decision-making authority from the elected legislative to the nonelected, national executive branch, and reorganized the party system into a progovernment party (all but guaranteed hegemony) and a legal opposition, it assumed it had little to fear from presenting its record to the electorate for ratification.[14] When it discovered in 1974 that its electoral majorities were in obvious jeopardy, it resurrected its former allies, the traditional political elite, to marshall electoral support for the regime at the polls, and it infused clientelistic networks with new cash reserves (Ames, 1987; Hagopian, 1986; Cammack, 1982). Because only the traditional political elite could secure the electoral victories needed to legitimize military rule and prevent the radicalization of the polity and the development of class- or interest-based politics, the military could not rule indefinitely without the active complicity of the regional oligarchies and the toleration of traditional political practices. Unlike the Uruguayan regime, which banned 15,000 politicians from engaging in political activity for 15 years (Gillespie, 1986:177), and the Chilean regime, which declared parties and the congress in recess and sent even Christian Democratic party leaders into exile, the Brazilian bureaucratic-authoritarian regime relied on traditional politicians to govern.

Traditional regional elites throughout the course of the military regime used political parties, albeit extremely weak in relation to the powerful national executive, as oligarchical vehicles to uphold their power. But in the second decade of bureaucratic-authoritarianism, they especially dispensed state patronage and channeled regime support through ARENA, the "semi-official" political party. Even during an authoritarian regime that excluded the vast majority of the population from participation in political life and economic gain, administering state patronage allowed the regional oligarchies to remain electorally competitive. They achieved electoral victories in not only small cities and rural areas where they might be expected to poll well, but also in many mid-sized cities which had significant, rapid urban and industrial growth where they might not. Bureaucratic-authoritarianism, and the political centralization and monopoly of power which were its defining features, established an immutable political alignment from national executive to local city councillor which effectively rendered political opposition quixotic. Benefitting from authoritarianism, the traditional political elite may have been stronger in the second decade of military rule than it was on the eve of the 1964 coup.

During the transition to democracy, the three sources of traditional dominance — patronage, oligarchical party, and restricted political competition — came under attack, creating the potential for new leadership and new forms of political organization in Brazil. For the first time, the promise of democratization was real. In 1945, a previous transition from authoritarian rule which broadened participation and political competition — the political system for the next two decades permitted at times a frenzied scramble for individual and group votes — nonetheless failed to produce lasting democratic institutions. Popular access to the state in the postwar period was restricted by elite-organized clientelist and corporatist networks, and the dominant parties of the postwar era — organized by outgoing dictator Getúlio Vargas and in opposition to him — primarily served to keep the traditional elite in place. The current transition began differently in two important respects. Unlike the first postwar contest, state elections in 1982 evicted many traditional political elites from office, depriving them, at least momentarily, of an important power base in the state. And second, the success of the opposition party organized by regime foes, the PMDB, enhanced the prospects that democracy's adherents might shape the political and party systems. Thus, when the new regime lifted the ban on real political competition, it removed the obstacles to political participation and autonomous local politics and laid a new basis for competitive interest representation to supplant state clientelism. These developments auspicious for democratization, however, were soon reversed by negotiation and compromise with the traditional political elite.

From Authoritarian Regime to Civilian Rule: Traditional Elites in Minas and the Transition to Democracy, 1982–1985

State Politics, 1982–1984

The outcome of the November 1982 elections did not bode well for the traditional political elite. In these elections in which state governors were elected directly for the first time in 17 years, the PMDB won nine governorships (of a possible 22) and legislative majorities in the most developed states including São Paulo, Rio de Janeiro, Paraná, and Minas Gerais. The PDS failed to achieve an outright majority in the federal Chamber of Deputies, and the government was forced to enter into coalition with the Brazilian Labor Party (PTB) of Ivete Vargas. In Minas Gerais, Tancredo Neves was elected governor as the party's standardbearer with 45.8 percent of the vote;[15] Itamar Franco was reelected senator; the party elected 27 federal deputies to the 26 of its rival, the PDS; and it captured a slim majority in the state Legislature Assembly (40 to 37), with a single representative to both houses elected by the Workers' Party (PT) (Table 1). While the PDS won control of many more city halls and city councils than the PMDB—the PDS elected 461 mayors to 247 for the PMDB, and 4662 city councillors to 2788 for the PMDB— the PMDB won the local elections in the most important and largest cities in the state, including those in the metropolitan region of Belo Horizonte, the state capital, and 10 of 16 mid-sized "dike cities" into which the government had pumped considerable sums of money precisely in order to preserve control in the 1982 elections.[16] In Barbacena, a bastion of the traditional Minas oligarchy (Murilo de Carvalho, 1966), voters for the first time elected candidates from outside the political machines of the two families who dominated local politics—the Bias Fortes and the Bonifácio de Andradas. In that city, the PMDB won the races for mayor and vice-mayor, a majority of city council seats (8 to 7 for the PDS). Most significantly, 41.6 percent of the vote in the state deputy election to a PMDB candidate whose vote total surpassed that of the candidates of the two families *combined.*

Most observers interpreted the 1982 PMDB vote as a rejection of the authoritarian regime, a logical inference given the place the party's predecessor, the MDB, occupied in the political system as the party of protest (Cardoso and Lamounier, 1978; Lamounier, 1980). In its 1982 victory, however, the PMDB in Minas Gerais had only partially and temporarily defeated the traditional political elite. Tancredo Neves's victory was produced by a sporadic coalition of opposition and traditional elite forces. His candidacy attracted the first wave of defections in what was to be a progressive detachment on the part of the oligarchy from the government coalition.

The traditional political elite in Minas Gerais was initially di-

Table 1

Minas Gerais: Party Electoral Strength, 1982–1988

Party*	1982				1986	1988**
	Chamber Deputies # Seats	State Assembly # Seats	Mayors # Elected	City Councillors # Elected	Chamber Deputies # Seats	Mayors # Elected
PDS	26	37	461	4662	3	36
PDT	-	-	-	-	1	13
PT	1	1	-	16	3	7
PTB	-	-	-	-	1	27
PMDB	27	40	247	2788	35	307
PFL					10	176
PDC						116
PL						17
PSDB						7
PMB						6
PSC						5
PJ						4
PSB						2
TOTAL	54	78	708***	7466	53	723

* PL = Liberal Party; PSDB = Brazilian Social Democratic Party; PMB = Brazilian Municipalist Party; PJ = Youth Party (renamed to Party of National Reconstruction); PSB = Brazilian Socialist Party.

** 1988 City Councillor elections not available.

*** Fourteen mayors from the state capital and "national security" areas were named by the state governor, not directly elected.

Source: TRE-MG.

vided over how to approach the 1982 gubernatorial elections, the most important political contest since the coup. While most preferred to side with the apparent safe option, the eventual PDS nominee, some staked their hopes for maintaining power in a liberalizing political environment on the new "Popular Party" (PP). The PP, a primarily Minas- and Rio-based party (its leading officers — Tancredo Neves and former Minas governor Magalhães Pinto — were *mineiros*) formed soon after the party reform of 1979 opened the door to a multiparty system.[17] For those abandoning the government party who had been staunch regime allies, such as Magalhães Pinto, the PP provided an opportunity to jump from a sinking ship and land on secure ground. For those moving from the MDB, such as Tancredo Neves, the PP offered the possibility of putting together a winning coalition which strict reliance on traditional MDB constituencies might not have afforded and which the military would find nonthreatening. The PP in Minas Gerais was extremely successful at attracting traditional oligarchs anxious to shed the baggage of the government's economic failures (Brazil was in a deep recession in 1981–82), and an agricultural policy unpopular with rural elites, without what for many in 1980 was anathema — sharing a party slate with the PMDB. Their adherence gave the PP an impressive statewide network of local organizations.

This segment of the traditional political elite was forced to rethink its decision to contest elections on a third-party label soon after a government riposte of an opposition offensive rendered this strategy nonviable. The decision to form the PP had been taken under electoral rules which permitted ticket splitting and electoral alliances among parties. It was reasonable under such conditions to expect that Neves, the strongest of the opposition candidates, would receive the gubernatorial nomination of more than one party. Because the PP was relatively new and not well established in every electoral district, Neves's hopes for winning the gubernatorial contest rested on capturing the votes of PMDB and PDS constituents who in other races planned to support their own party candidates. In late 1981, the military government abruptly changed the rules of the electoral game.

Electoral "reform" was set in motion earlier that year when Congress voted to abolish the *sublegenda* over the wishes of the government. The *sublegenda,* or "sub-ticket," was an electoral device which permitted up to three candidates of the same party to contest the same elected position (in Brazil, these were employed for the races decided by plurality vote), and the office was awarded to the candidate who polled the most votes of the *party* whose tickets received the highest combined vote total. By allowing each internal party faction to run its own candidate, this arrangement permitted the military to retain within the ranks of its supporters traditional rivals on the state and local levels, and thereby to maximize the progovernment vote. With the coming gubernatorial elections, party discipline among the government majority could not be maintained because PDS politicians had crosscutting interests in the *sublegenda*. PDS congressmen from the Northeast wished to retain it, while PDS representatives from the South, where this system benefitted the PMDB, did not. These PDS defectors, together with the opposition, defeated the *sublegenda*. In the fall of 1981, military intelligence discovered that without the *sublegenda,* the government was in danger of losing the governors' races in more states than the military cared to tolerate. Accordingly, that November, it issued a decree known as the "November package" which, among other provisions, banned electoral coalitions and prohibited ticket splitting. A reverse coattails effect was expected to obtain in the elections: the military anticipated that voters preferences in *local* races (determined by particularistic criteria and relatively immune from antiregime sentiment) would swing votes in the state races.[18] The reform intended to make successful opposition by new and especially small opposition parties more difficult. It also appeared to doom Neves's gubernatorial candidacy. Without the possibility of jointly nominating candidates, each party was forced instead to nominate its own candidates for every office, including that of governor. Moreover, the new legislation, by forcing electors to vote for a single party slate from governor to city councillor, meant that they could only vote for Neves at the cost of abandoning their own party's candidates altogether.

Neves responded to the "November package" by dissolving the PP and instructing its members to join or rejoin the PMDB. The merger of the two parties in Minas Gerais and nationally was presided over by men loyal to Neves who placed his many supporters in a strong position in the new party.[19] From this organizational base Neves plucked the party's gubernatorial nomination from Itamar Franco, the PMDB's other senator, in large part because the veteran Neves, a masterful politician, was accurately perceived as the most electable candidate of the opposition.

Within the government party, intraelite rivalries which had been artificially contained for 18 years were rekindled by the defeat of the *sublegenda* and the emergence of Tancredo Neves's candidacy. Had the *sublegenda* been utilized, competing oligarchical factions which coalesced along pre–1965 partisan lines could have been accommodated: one *sublegenda* would have been occupied by a former member of the PSD (the Social Democratic party); one by a member of the UDN (National Democratic Union) camp; and one by either a technocrat or a member of the defunct PR (Republican party).[20] When the *sublegenda* was abandoned, however, the government could nominate only one candidate, thereby inevitably exacerbating intraparty tensions. The choice, if left as by custom to the incumbent governor, most likely would have been an ex-UDNer.[21] The nomination of an ex-UDNer, however, would surely have precipitated a reaction from the embittered ex-PSD wing of the PDS who felt it was "their turn"; every governor of the post-coup period had been an ex-UDN member with the single exception of Ozanam Coelho who, as Aureliano Chaves' lieutenant governor, became the state's chief executive for eight months when Chaves had to resign to "run" for vice-president. The patience of the PSD group with its traditional enemies was about to lapse with redemocratization.

In every scenario but one—if a member of the ex-PSD were to be the party's standardbearer, a development the ex-UDN faction would surely not allow—the government was left in a no-win situation: any move to counter Neves's nomination would set in motion the *mineiro* oligarchs' disengagement from the regime. When in an effort to stop UDN-PSD feuding, the *Planalto*[22] intervened in the gubernatorial succession in Minas—nominating Eliseu Resende, an engineer-technocrat, as the PDS's candidate—it is hardly surprising that the government's attempted compromise failed. Many oligarchs not satisfied with President João Figueiredo's gesture flocked to Neves's camp; in Tancredo Neves they now had an alternative to the UDN and the MDB—one of their own. In the North of Minas, the sons and grandsons of regional cattle barons threw their support behind Neves, partly to manifest their discontent with the PDS's candidate, and partly to protest recent agricultural policies which they guessed would not change under a technocrat. The support the traditional political bosses delivered to the PMDB in the cities and towns of the interior, when combined with that mobilized by the left among a genuinely discontented populace, accounted for the narrow opposition victory.[23]

If some traditional elites exercised sound political judgment in supporting Neves, the leading political representatives of the oligarchy, including many federal deputies, did not. Although the new administration did not threaten elite interests in the policy realm, those who had stayed with the PDS, like kingmakers Bias Fortes and Bonifácio de Andrada, lost something important in the 1982 elections: the control over state patronage in the cities and towns that gave them their greatest vote totals. In Minas Gerais for at least four governors' administrations, the "political command" (*comando político*) of a municipality, which entailed the right to appoint virtually every public officeholder, had been awarded openly to the deputy from the state's majority party who had received the most votes in that *município*. When the PDS lost its majority, the "political command" in many cities passed to PMDB deputies, even where old elites polled better. This blow to the personal patronage machines of old elites was compounded by their loss as a class of the power to make high-level federal and state appointments in Minas. Such losses, if not recuperated, would cost future voters and spell certain doom for the medium- and long-term survival of the traditional political elite. The opportunity to recover the machinery of state patronage and secure its statewide dominance presented itself when the old elite had something to trade: its support for the governor in the electoral college which would convene to elect the next president.

The Negotiated Transition and the Role of the Minas Oligarchy

In preparing the terrain for the transfer of power to civilians, the military had aspired to retain considerable control over the new government by guaranteeing a civilian president acceptable to itself. It intended to accomplish this by the "indirect" election of the first civilian president in January 1985; this election was to take place in an electoral college of national, state, and local politicians in which the military enjoyed a secure majority.[24]

The opposition camp had for some time debated how to approach the "indirect" election for president. With a government victory presumed to be a foregone conclusion, many advocated boycotting the electoral college rather than legitimize an electoral farce. This group galvanized public opinion in favor of direct popular elections which took shape in early 1984 in a Campaign for Direct Elections, a highly visible campaign abetted by the media whose public demonstrations in Brazil's major cities drew millions of protesters. The Campaign's central demand was for congress to pass an amendment providing for direct popular elections for president later that year. Others in the opposition advocated focusing efforts upon the electoral college. The most notable proponent of this position was Tancredo Neves. Never believing the congress would approve the amendment for direct elections nor that the military would permit them (he called the demonstrations "lyric"), Neves lent nominal support to the Campaign while never losing sight of his candidacy within the electoral college.[25]

Once the amendment was defeated and it became clear that an electoral college would choose Figueiredo's successor, Tancredo Neves became the opposition's candidate for president. In a blatant display of the politics of *"café com leite,"* the governors of Minas Gerais and São Paulo, Neves and Franco Montoro, took the decision which the rest of the party had little choice but to ratify.[26] The opposition was disposed to participate in the electoral college because of the opportunity Neves's candidacy presented for a partisan realignment. Since PDS electors were the clear majority in the electoral college, any opposition candidate needed the backing of former military supporters among the political elite to win. Of all PMDB politicians, Neves, rooted in the oligarchy, stood the best chance of attracting votes from the government forces. His task was facilitated by the politically suicidal decision on the part of President Figueiredo to permit the government party to nominate Paulo Maluf — the governor of São Paulo who had more than a few enemies in high places — as the party's standard bearer.[27] Many PDS deputies, disgruntled with Maluf for personal reasons and genuinely apprehensive for their own political futures of electing a president so unpopular within the electorate, defected. Understanding the stakes and recognizing the opportunity that uniting with the PMDB offered for preserving their positions in the state, many political elites scrambled to line up behind Neves to secure a place in the new order. A motley coalition of PMDB "radicals," PDS deserters later to become the Liberal Front (*Frente Liberal*), and dissident PDS governors of the northeast states coalesced rapidly in the months of June–September 1984 to ensure Tancredo Neves's victory.

To secure the support of the old regime's elite, Tancredo Neves was prepared to accept considerable constraints on his campaign and to bargain away political spoils which were won in the hard-fought 1982 elections. In exchange for the agreement to back the candidate of the PMDB in the electoral college, the Liberal Front of the PDS was assured that he would neither run as a representative of the "opposition" nor criticize the "Revolution" or the [incumbent] Figueiredo government; that the vice-presidential nominee would come from the ranks of the Liberal Front, or, if prohibited by electoral law, be *someone who supported the "movement of April, 1964"* [the coup]; and that there would be *an equitable distribution of administrative posts* (*Istoé,* 1984a:24, emphasis added). For Figueiredo's vice-president and fellow *mineiro* Aureliano Chaves, Neves even put in writing that all those who backed him would be repaid with posts in his government (*Veja,* 1985a:36). This promise was extracted as a condition for not only the vice-president's support (and with it the votes of the hedging members of the Minas PDS delegation) but also for that of ex-president Gen. Ernesto Geisel, which was critical if a preemptive coup were to be avoided.[28]

While a political settlement of this magnitude could be sealed in principle relatively easily on the national level—it was a fairly simple matter to promise federal cabinet posts to a handful of influential figures—in order to secure the votes of the deputies and other delegates in the electoral college, agreements had to be hammered out and implemented in the states. Careful, detailed, and explicit bargaining was conducted on a state-by-state basis between the two parties wherever such an accord was struck. The success of these state-level negotiations hinged on the mutually satisfactory division of state patronage between two uneasy allies. At stake was the distribution of 15,000 federal jobs. In many states, regional presidents of the PMDB and the FL drew up agreements stipulating explicitly which federal and state posts would be assigned to each party's pork barrel (*Veja,* 1985b:20). Federal Deputy Oscar Alves of Paraná reported that Neves promised the Liberal Front in Paraná a number of federal posts in equal proportion to the number of *"frentista"* votes in the electoral college. Since Front members had cast 25 percent of Neves' votes in the Paraná delegation, Alves calculated they were owed one-fourth of these posts in the state (*Veja,* 1985b:26–27). Israel Pinheiro, one of the FL's founders and most enthusiastic backers of the "Democratic Alliance," used the same rationale as a basis for proposing that the FL in Minas Gerais merited a one-third participation in state government (*Estado de Minas,* 1984b:3).

In Minas Gerais, dissident PDS deputies drove their own hard bargain—the *"Acordo de Minas,"* or "Minas Agreement." The embryonic core of the new Liberal Front in the state agreed to support Neves, to "put a *mineiro* in the presidency," in exchange for the return of the power of patronage they lost in the 1982 elections. According to the terms of the accord, the new governor, Hélio Garcia,[29] agreed to accept at least two members of the Liberal Front into the cabinet; the "political command" of a municipality would be handed back to the deputy who won a majority of the votes in that municipality, irrespective of party; and Liberal Front federal deputies would regain another prime source of state patronage—the right to make appointments to 72 second- and third-echelon federal posts in the state (e.g., regional directors of the National Housing Bank and the Brazilian Coffee Institute).[30] The accord was understandably opposed by those who stood most to lose from the agreement: local, recently victorious, PMDB politicians, especially young mayors who had made an electoral breakthrough in 1982. Yet, local resistance to the state-imposed agreement was offered in vain.

The terms of the agreement represented a unilateral victory for the traditional political elite. On each count, the traditional elite was able to impose its preferences. Hélio Garcia reversed his public position that he would not accept members of the Liberal Front into his cabinet (*Estado de Minas,* 1984a); he had agreed only to review the firings in the interior of those primary school directors, regional school administrators, and police chiefs who were PDS ward bosses (*cabos eleitorais*) associated with the FL. The FL member whom he selected to head the department of Public Security, moreover, was Bias Fortes, a stalwart of the Minas oligarchy. Secondly, the manner in which the issue of the *comando político* was resolved was an outright victory for the ex-PDS elite: the PMDB had wanted "proportionality" to save at least some patronage resources. Finally, the agreement called for direct elections for mayor to be held in the state's thirteen *estâncias hidrominerais* in November 1985, at the same time that the mayor of Belo Horizonte was to be elected directly for the first time since 1965. The *hidroestâncias,* or spas, are resort or tourist cities with fountains and natural mineral water springs which allegedly possess healing properties. In these cities, along with those designated "national security areas," mayors were appointed rather than directly elected.[31] As long as these posts were appointed by the governor and approved in the state legislature, the majority party was assured control over them. By having the schedule moved up, the PDS-FL dissidents hoped to recover by direct elections at least some of what they had lost for the first time in 1982.

The defection of 17 members of the Minas PDS delegation set in motion a major realignment of political forces. In Brazil, once it is apparent that an "out" can win, the "ins" scramble to be sure to back the winning side.[32] The *"Acordo de Minas"* had the immediate effect of cementing Tancredo Neves's election as president in January 1985 in an electoral college composed of mostly old elites from the authoritarian regime. The major consequences of the pact were more enduring. Members of the traditional political elite who endorsed the *"Acordo de Minas"* retook the leading positions in state politics. Nationally, the agreement compromised the foundations of democratic politics in Brazil.

From Transitional Democracy to Democratic Regime: The Political Class in the First Five Years

Because of the high degree of territorial integration of Brazilian politics, developments at one level of the political system inevitably reverberate throughout the system. Just as a realignment of forces in state politics during the transition to democracy triggered a major shift in national politics, once the regime had changed, the exercise of power at higher levels shaped the political landscape at lower levels of the political system.

Agreements negotiated at both the state and national levels smuggled into the new democracy, at least during the phase of consolidation, antidemocratic political practices inherited from both the military regime and its civilian predecessors. These practices are most evident in the reproduction of clientelism at each level of the political system and in the dramatic weakness of political parties. They were carried in, and reinforced by: (1) the persistent domination of traditional political elites in federal, state, and local executive positions which afford access to state patronage resources; (2) control of the PMDB, the new party of government, and the ability to design the new party and electoral systems; and (3) ultimately, through their representation in the Congress which doubled as a Constitutional Convention (the *Constituinte*), a position from which to influence heavily future constitutional arrangements.

Cabinets and Clientelism

Traditional elite support for Neves's gubernatorial candidacy secured continuity in elite tenure in the cabinet of the state of Minas Gerais, the base for patronage in Minas politics. To thank the state's agrarian elite for its support, Neves named Arnaldo Rosa Prata, president of such powerful agrarian societies as the Brazilian Association of "Zebu" Cattle Raisers and the Rural Society of the Minas *Triângulo,* and former ARENA mayor of the important *Triângulo* city of Uberaba (1970–1972), as his secretary of Agriculture. The original cabinet included only four secretaries who rose in politics through the ranks of the MDB. After the traditional politician Renato Azeredo died and more portfolios were added, two other former members of the MDB were appointed to the cabinet, though both had temporarily abandoned the MDB for the PP.[33] Seven others traced their political origins, and a portion of their power, to pre-1964 parties dominated by traditional elites—the PSD, UDN, and PR (Table 2);[34] two of the seven originally joined ARENA in 1965. At least four of the 13 politicians in the cabinet were members of the traditional political elite.[35]

Neves also did not depart from the patterns of the allocation of state cabinet posts ingrained under the military. He left much of the economic decision-making machinery to the secretaries and undersecretaries of economic departments in previous state governments who, for all intents and purposes, had masterminded economic policy in Minas during the authoritarian era. The key posts of Finance and Planning remained in technocratic hands; moreover, Luiz Rogério de Castro Leite (secretary of Finance), Ronaldo Costa Couto (secretary of Planning), and Márcio Garcia Vilela (president of the state bank, the BEMGE), had all worked for ARENA and PDS governments.

With an eye on the Planalto, and shrewdly cognizant of the surest path to this goal, Neves not only did not dismantle the clientelistic system which had long pervaded the politics of his Minas Gerais, he hardly even redirected it. PMDB mayors in the interior who had risen through the ranks of the opposition without the benefit of family connections received few state benefits from the governor who had helped to elect them; rather, Neves used the spoils of the governor's office to coopt, by and large successfully, PDS deputies. With the exception of the vote in November 1983 to create the new

Table 2

Partisan Origins of State Cabinet Politicians, Minas Gerais, 1982–1987

	Party Background					
	(0)	(1)	(2a)	(2b)	(3)	N/D
Tancredo Neves	3	3	4	3		
Hélio Garcia (I)*	6	3	4	5	1	
Hélio Garcia (II)*	2	1	1	2		

Key:

(0) Nonaligned

(1) PTB, MDB/PMDB only

(2a) MDB/PMDB w/PP

(2b) PSD, UDN, PR + MDB or PMDB

(3) PSD, UDN, PR + ARENA/PP, PDS, PFL

* Hélio Garcia's cabinets have been divided into two periods: 1984 to mid–1986; and mid–1986 to March, 1987. After mid–1986, technocrats are overrepresented in the cabinet due to the vagaries of Brazilian election law—all officeholders must resign their posts six months before an election in order to be eligible to run for elective office.

Source: *Minas Gerais*, 1983–1987.

ministries of Transportation, Sports, Recreation and Tourism, Culture, and Special Affairs, in which the entire PDS delegation (37
deputies) voted against the governor, there is little indication of traditional political elite opposition to Neves, and indeed, less as time
passed. Indeed, the more significant opposition came from the "Bloco
da Virada" faction of the PMDB. Neves routinely used PDS politicians to isolate the left of his own party who opposed his projects.

Neves's successor, Hélio Garcia, did not substantially alter these
recruitment patterns. More secretaries were "authentic PMDBers"
(nine in Garcia's first two years in office), but more (five) had also
belonged to ARENA. Politicians in general and traditional elites
in particular gained ground in Hélio Garcia's cabinet. His secretary
of planning, Luiz Alberto Rodriguez, was a politician—the third
leading vote-getter of all candidates for state deputy representing
the PMDB in 1982. And the return to the cabinet of Chrispim Jacques
Bias Fortes as part of the *Acordo de Minas* restored the post of public security, which had been in the hands of the military since 1970
(and a civilian judge in Neves's brief term), to the traditional political elite. This post had been a traditional source of the most overt
form of clientelism: control of the state's police forces.

National agreements also placed remnants of the traditional
elite and ARENA politicians in the presidential cabinet. For their
crucial support of his national candidacy, Tancredo Neves awarded
four posts to PFL defectors, including the largest budget ministry
of Mines and Energy to fellow *mineiro* Aureliano Chaves, and the
ministry of Communications to Antônio Carlos Magalhães, the PDS
governor of Bahia whose vitriolic opposition to Paulo Maluf helped
elect Neves president. Not only did Sarney swear in the cabinet which
Neves nominated, but as former president of the PDS, he drew even
more from the ranks of those politicians who supported the military than did the traditional politician Neves. As time went on, even
after the "Democratic Alliance" formally collapsed in 1987, the cabinet was increasingly dominated by uniformed military officers and
members of the ex-PDS (*Veja,* 1988a:34–35).[36]

The ample participation of traditional, promilitary and conservative elites in state and federal cabinets during the transition and
consolidation periods had profound consequences in two areas: policy and political practice. Cabinet positions provide a powerful foot-
hold from which to influence policy. But more subtly, they afford
traditional elites the resource base from which to mount their cli-

entelistic operations. Even during the period of consolidation, when state executives and federal and state legislators were chosen according to democratic procedure, they behaved precisely as they had during the military and premilitary governments. In a self-reinforcing circle, clientelism in turn helped to maintain traditional elite dominance in state and local politics in Minas Gerais after the transition.

The Party System

In Brazil, political parties have been long prevented from representing nonelite interests by the traditional political elite. They have been used for decades as patronage machines, private weapons in intraoligarchical disputes.[37] There were exceptions to this rule, parties which had nonelite constituents in the postwar era, but even the populist PTB doled out patronage through the labor ministry and built vertical channels of interest representation which restricted mass access to the state. The party created by the military in 1965 to support its rule, ARENA, carried on this tradition, even affording for its UDN members more uniform access to state resources than they had previously enjoyed in many states in the pre–1964 period. The MDB, marginalized from power, rarely engaged in clientelism — probably more due to circumstance than to conviction. Outside of Rio de Janeiro, where Governor Chagas Freitas headed his own political machine (Diniz, 1982), the MDB had no resources to distribute. Instead, its identity was based on a clear, ideological opposition to the regime. For voters who could not identify party positions on issues (Lamounier, 1980:39–41, 78), the 1965–79 party system offered a plebiscitary choice: regime versus opposition. The MDB came to represent excluded classes and issues, above all in the races most devoid of potential clientelistic gain, the senatorial contests. During the transition, the regime/opposition dichotomy faded, and to the extent it resurfaced during the consolidation period when economic policy went awry, just who represented the "ins" and "outs" was no longer discernible.

Among the most crucial consequences of the negotiated, elite-led transition from authoritarian rule was the manner in which this elite redefined the party system. In 1985, it created a new party, the party of the Liberal Front (PFL), which successfully contested some state elections, elected 133 federal deputies (10 in Minas Gerais) in the 1986 election in which the PMDB ran an especially strong race, and participated in the federal cabinet until 1987. Even in 1988, it elected 176 mayors in Minas Gerais (Table 1). More significant for the period of transition, previous supporters of the military regime muscled their way into, and transformed, the new party of government, the PMDB. This occurred at the state, national, and local levels, and had important implications for the blurring of the party's identity in government and its transformation from a "catch-all" to a "traditional, clientelistic" party.[38]

The faction of the PMDB loyal to Neves emerged from the party's 1983 elections in the state in undisputed control of the party commissions. The so-called *"Constituinte"* slate won all but 16 seats on the *diretório* (of 71), and all but 16 delegates and 16 alternates to the national convention (of 58 for each). In exchange for these few seats, the "radical" group, "Direct Elections" (*Eleições Diretas*), had to cede pivotal posts on the Executive Commission, including that of president, to conservative and traditional politicians imposed by the governor who had only recently joined the party and whom many in the PMDB found distasteful.

A few months later, national PMDB president Ulysses Guimarães was brought to the bargaining table to negotiate the terms of the surrender of the national party to Tancredo Neves's loyalists as well. The command of the national PMDB was negotiated in November 1983, prior to its ratification in the party's national convention that December. The *Unidade* (Unity) group loyal to Tancredo Neves emerged from the negotiations ahead of the *Travessia* group led by party president Ulysses Guimarães. Guimarães ceded half the posts on the Executive Commission and 43 percent of those on the national directory to the *Unidade* group. His own *Travessia* received 35 percent (the remaining 17 percent were allocated to a third *Propartido* faction composed of independents and first time members of congress). The complexion of the Executive Commission, too, changed. "Radical" Francisco ("Chico") Pinto was pushed out of his position of first vice-president by "moderate" senator Pedro Simon. In return for retaining the presidency, Guimarães allowed Neves to name the party's secretary-general, the post which controls the party's organization. Neves's choice, Affonso Camargo, the "bionic" (appointed) senator from Paraná who had only recently joined the PMDB via the PP and ARENA, precipitated strong reaction from party regulars, including threats from the *Travessia* rank and file to organize resistance, cancel the convention, and resign from the party. The threats were to no avail. By all accounts, Neves by this time was in extraofficial command of the party.

In Minas Gerais, a PMDB governor in the statehouse swelled the party with new recruits, and this process accelerated most dramatically after the PMDB gained the presidency in March 1985. Individual party membership more than doubled between 1982 and the end of 1984, while that of its old rival, the PDS, rose by only 44 percent (Table 3). Between March and June, 1985, party membership jumped from less than 200,000 to nearly 300,000, while that of the PDS began to decline.

Once the party attracted much of the state oligarchy and established itself as more than a transient party of government, moreover, local elites and party bosses flocked to its ranks. Anxious to join the "ins" and not be excluded from state resources, at least 200 mayors and local party *diretórios* (governing bodies) changed partisan affiliation virtually overnight in mid–1985 from the PDS to the PMDB.[39] These mayors and party bosses for the most part shared little or nothing ideologically with the party's veteran national leaders. The mayors were part of a cohort elected in 1982 that carried on Minas Gerais's political tradition. In a survey of 387 (of 708) mayors elected in Minas Gerais in 1982 conducted by the state Planning department (SEPLAN, 1983), nearly 60 percent had "political tradition in the family," meaning that fathers, grandfathers, uncles and/or brothers had participated in politics in an elected capacity. Thirty percent had been active in politics for more than 20 years, and another 25 percent from 12 to 20 years. Only one-fifth had entered politics within the preceding four years. Two-thirds had previously occupied political posts. Hand in hand with their "political tradition," approximately 30 percent identified themselves as *fazendeiros* by profession; nearly 60 percent were from families of *fazendeiros*.

The ready and efficient mass conversion of this traditional, rural political elite was possible because of the extreme ideological and programmatic weakness of parties in the state. In the same 1983 survey of the mayors elected in Minas Gerais in 1982, 58.9 percent of the mayors sampled attributed their victories to "personal attributes"; 28.9 percent to "political tradition"; and only 8.3 percent to party program (3.9 percent not available) (SEPLAN, 1983:43).

The migration of the old elite into the PMDB was not confined

Table 3

Minas Gerais: Individual Party Membership, 1982–1989*

Party	1982	1983	1984	1985 (M)	1985 (J)	1985 (D)	1989 (M)
PDS	163,501	163,007	221,298	235,272	231,847	228,572	165,132
PDT	11,796	13,656	22,692	27,103	28,468	30,788	51,707
PT	22,641	23,872	34,883	36,348	36,907	38,447	66,082
PTB	12,256	12,390	21,406	24,276	26,575	28,216	67,871
PMDB	91,530	105,125	190,939	199,097	297,413	319,657	419,879
PFL						5,775	104,329
PDC							70,973
PL							48,791
PMB							21,344
PJ (PRN)							17,162
PSDB							15,346
PSC							14,527
PSB							12,460
Others**							10,764

(M) = March; (J) = June; (D) = December.

* "Individual Party Membership" signifies those who are "affiliated" (*filiados*) with the parties, not those who are "members" (a term reserved for members of the local and state *diretórios*).

** PCB, PCdoB, PH, PS, and 8 parties each with less than 1,000 members.

Source: TRE-MG.

to the municipalities of Minas Gerais (though perhaps the process is most dramatically illustrated there). In other states, politicians who had supported the military regime were quick to change their partisan affiliation. One-third of all ARENA congressmen had, by 1987, joined the PMDB (Fleischer, 1987:4). Forty-four percent entered the PFL, and only 15 percent remained with the PDS.

The infusion of state and federal deputies as well as local *coronéis* into the PMDB fanned the party's electoral fortunes, which reached their zenith when in the 1986 elections the PMDB won a majority in the Congress and Constituent Assembly, and 22 of 23 state governorships. While this victory was undoubtedly purchased by the Sarney administration with the loose monetary policy and real wage increases of the Cruzado Plan, it was also abetted by the entrance into the party of the bosses of the interior and their state patrons.

This same mass conversion which made the impressive PMDB victory in the 1986 elections possible, however, also diluted that victory. Of the 35 members of the Minas PMDB delegation to the Chamber of Deputies elected in 1986, five had belonged to ARENA or the PDS, and three had begun their careers in the PSD or UDN (Figure 1). Seven who began in the MDB had detoured through the PP before rejoining the PMDB. Only 57 percent could be considered "historical" PMDBers. In national terms, one-fourth of PMDB representatives to the Constituent Assembly (deputies and senators) elected in 1986 were once members of ARENA; slightly under half (47.3 percent) had been members of the (P)MDB. Fleischer's (1987:2) research shows that in 1987 "the largest delegation in the Constituent Assembly [was] not [the 1986] PMDB, but in 1979 terms, it [was] ARENA." Two hundred seventeen members of the Assembly were members of ARENA prior to 1980, as opposed to 212 who identified themselves with the PMDB. Thus, Fleischer (1987:5) notes, the "real" PMDB was represented by only 40 percent of the Congress, not the 53.3 percent it appeared to have by formal affiliation. These data led him to remark wryly that in Brazil, politicians "change their party affiliations like star players change the shirts of their soccer teams" (Fleischer, 1987:2). The murky political origins of party representatives clouded the meaning of the sizeable PMDB majorities. While most of the opponents of the military dictatorship remained members of the PMDB until 1988,[40] the traditional elite presence in the party disallowed the interpretation of party electoral victories

Figure 1

Party Migrations

Partisan Trajectories of Minas Deputies, 1987

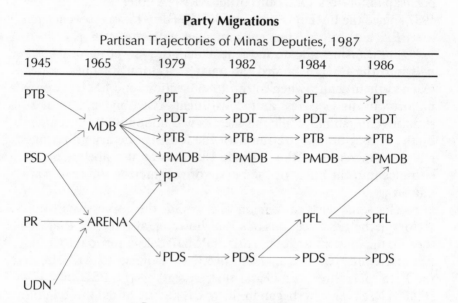

| 1945 | 1965 | 1979 | 1982 | 1984 | 1986 |

PMDB Trajectories (35)

MDB-PMDB (9)
PTB-MDB-PMDB (2)
PMDB only (8)
MDB-PP-PMDB (3)
PSD, PR, UDN-MDB-(PP)-PMDB (7)
(UDN)-ARENA-(PP, PDS)-(PFL)-PMDB (6)

PT Trajectory (3)

PT only (3)

PTB Trajectory (1)

PTB only (1)

PFL Trajectories (10)

PSD-ARENA-PDS-PFL (5)
ARENA-PDS (3)
PFL only (2)

PDS Trajectories (3)

UDN-ARENA-PDS (2)
ARENA-PDS (1)

PDT Trajectory (1)

PDT only (1)

as a popular rejection of the old order, the future replacement of its elite, or the overhaul of its institutions and political practices.[41] Traditional and conservative forces were much stronger in the New Republic than vote totals for the PDS and PFL implied.

The realignment of political elites which took place during the transition to democracy in Brazil had several adverse effects on democratization. In democratic societies in which political parties realign, however infrequently, over salient, crosscutting issues, the process of realignment broadens the possibilities for democratic representation by providing electors with the opportunity to express their preferences along a new axis of conflict in society. In Brazil, where realignment was precipitated instead by oligarchical factionalism—the PFL differed initially from its parent, the PDS, only in its preference for Tancredo Neves over Paulo Maluf—when the oligarchy opted for realignment, its old divisions were fitted into the current party system, and the PMDB—which had sheltered opponents to authoritarianism and those who had suffered from it—now opened its ranks to those who had supported and profited from the military regime. In so doing, it actually *diminished* its potential to represent a broader segment of interests.

Second, the realignment precipitated by the large-scale migration of traditional and authoritarian political elites into the PMDB also weakened party identity both because it shifted the balance of conservative and progressive forces within the PMDB and because it inevitably diluted the party's already weak programmatic message. Given the eclectic character of the new PMDB, party discipline could not be maintained, making it difficult for the party to stake out *any* coherent policy positions. While most parties are not as ideologically coherent as textbooks would lead us to believe are the highly disciplined parties found in parliamentary systems, the ideological heterogeneity of the PMDB congressional delegation was easily greater than that characteristic of multiclass, catch-all political parties.

A third consequence of realignment was that it undermined the ability of the party to carry out in government the programs it advocated while in opposition, principally because the party's new leaders and federal representatives did not even endorse the party platform. Traditional political elites inside the party were in a position to veto any policy positions which they perceived to be not in their own interest or in the interest of their constituents. In such circumstances it is not surprising that votes on key policies and constitutional issues, as we shall see below, but across partisan lines which were left with little substantive meaning.

Democratic Constitution, Weak Democracy

Two cleavages persist as features of Brazilian politics: traditional vs. nontraditional and progressive/democratic vs. conservative/authoritarian. The ideological axis is superimposed above but does not perfectly overlap with that one along which traditional and nontraditional political forces are distributed. During the constitutional debates, ideological position was more salient; ideological position, in turn, was defined more by the traditional/nontraditional cleavage than by blurred partisan divisions. Political "traditionalism" stopped certain constitutionally governed policies, moderated others, and built an inherent conservatism into constitutionally defined institutions.

The democratic Constitution ratified in 1988 is strong on civil and social rights: Article 5 grants equal rights for women, prohibits torture and censorship, and guarantees freedom from searches, of assembly, and the writ of habeas corpus. In all, it contains 77 sections. In the realm of social rights, the Brazilian constitution grants a 120-day maternity leave, an 8-hour-day/44-hour work week; and 30 days' notice for firings and layoffs. Article 9 of the Constitution grants labor the right to strike.

The Constitution also consciously guards against authoritarian encroachments on democratic political rights. It strengthens Congress — emasculated by the military regime — by granting it the right to review the national budget and the public debt, including any agreements about the foreign debt. By abolishing the two main instruments of military government — decree-laws and the *decurso de prazo,* the fixed term within which congress could vote on executive-initiated legislation before its automatic enactment into law — it dismantled much of the authoritarian apparatus of the document it replaced. Article 15 bears the imprint of a nation seeking to prevent future military abuses of political rights: it prohibits *"cassações."*

The original document was even more liberal than the final product. The draft version of the constitution which emerged from committee provided for an agrarian reform, but Article 185 of the final version exempts "productive property" from expropriation. And while its principal institutions are truly democratic, their design is also consistent with what might be termed "oligarchical democracy." The potential of presidentialism, the five year presidential term, and federalism to advance democratization in Brazil is ambiguous at best.

Whether Brazil should have maintained the presidential system of government or moved to a parliamentary system, and the more general question of the autonomy and prerogatives of the powerful Brazilian executive and its relationship to the legislature, were the objects of the most intense battles of the constitutional convention — and arguably the most consequential for the future of Brazilian democracy. The Brazilian presidential system has historically engendered a strong executive, weakened political parties, and been conducive to federal patronage. The traditional political way of life depended on the maintenance of presidentialism: it is hard to imagine that state clientelism could be operated as efficiently in a parliamentary as in a presidential system. Parliamentarism would also have distanced the executive from subtle and direct forms of control by the military. Most Brazilians agreed that parliamentarism represented an excellent opportunity to make the system less accountable to the military and more so to its citizens, and perhaps the best chance to strengthen political parties and the legislature.[42] At one early point, given the support of the mass public and of prominent politicians, the adoption of some form of parliamentarism seemed almost inevitable. Yet, by a sizeable margin, the Constituent Assembly retained the presidential system.

Hand in hand with the issue of presidentialism was the question of the length of the presidential term, which Congress voted to extend to five years at the behest of the incumbent president. There is of course nothing inherently undemocratic about a five-year term, but in Brazil the sole rationale for the five-year term was a thinly disguised effort on the part of the sitting president to remain in office for an additional year. On ideological grounds, the measure's only supporters were the military and others who wished to postpone the transfer of executive power from incumbent president Sarney to any candidate whom authoritarian forces could potentially not control.

Finally, the 1988 Constitution reinvigorates federalism by restoring some power and resources of subnational governments. The shortfall of resources for state government budgets had been a constant complaint of the finance departments of Brazilian states during the military dictatorship. In reversing the trend toward fiscal centralization which was the hallmark of the bureaucratic-authoritarian regime, this new federalism enhances local control over government spending, but it also strengthens regional political oligarchies by restoring to them the resources with which to grease their political machines.

The moderation of these and other policies and procedures in the final document can be attributed to the activism of traditional and conservative politicians in the Constituent Assembly. In late 1987, these politicians formed a group which cut across partisan lines and traditional rivalries called the *Centrão* (literally, the "Center") to contest what they saw to be excessively liberal articles in the draft text of the Constitution. Some 280 members of the PDS, PFL, and PMDB felt equally comfortable signing their adherence to the group whose greatest early victory was to change the procedure by which the constitutional convention would ratify the constitution from a single vote to a separate vote on each article, section, and amendment. In practice, this procedure gave the parliamentarians the opportunity to defeat certain measures and it made the adoption of others more likely.

The voting records of the Minas delegation to the Constitutional Convention on labor issues, agrarian reform, presidentialism, and the five-year presidential term illustrate particularly well the role the traditional elements of the political class played in moderating the Constitution on agrarian reform and bringing about an institutional configuration whose propitiousness for democracy is dubious. The deputies who either began their careers in the MDB, that is, in opposition to military rule, or who had joined the PMDB as their first and only party, voted more frequently in favor of labor (their "rankings" on these issues were 5.44 and 5.61 respectively) than those who had begun their careers in an "oligarchical" party (2.33) or who had served the military government in ARENA (2.95) (Table 4). Somewhat surprisingly, even those who had followed Tancredo Neves and Magalhães Pinto into the PP voted more consistently for measures granting labor rights (5.04) than those who had begun their careers in the PTB (2.38). The voting record of the Minas delegates was less favorable to labor than that of any Northeast state save Sergipe, and not surprisingly, lower than Rio Grande do Sul, São Paulo, and Rio de Janeiro (Table 5). The average "labor ranking" of the state's PMDB deputies was 4.47 of a possible 10 (as compared with 2.03 of the PFL and 9.67 for the Workers' Party, or

Table 4

Voting Records: Minas Gerais PMDB Deputies, Constituent Assembly*

	PMDB							PFL	PT
	"Authentic"			"Migrants"			Total		
	1A	1B	1C	2A	2B	3			
Labor Ranking**	5.44	2.38	5.61	5.04	2.33	2.95	4.47	2.03	9.67
Agrarian Reform									
Yes:	7	0	4	3	1	3	18	1	3
No:	2	2	3	3	2	2	14	9	0
Abs:	-	-	2	1	-	-	3	0	-
Presidentialism:									
Yes:	3	2	5	5	2	4	21	9	2
No:	7	0	4	2	1	0	14	1	0
Abs:	-	-	-	-	-	-	-	-	1
Five Year Term									
Yes:	6	2	6	4	3	5	26	10	0
No:	3	0	3	3	0	0	9	0	3
Abs:	-	-	-	-	-	-	-	0	-

* The labor rankings, and votes on agrarian reform and the five year term include the votes of the alternate Israel Pinheiro who replaced Deputy Luiz Leal while the latter served in the state cabinet. Leal returned to the Assembly for the vote on presidentialism to cast a conviction vote against the measure.

** Labor Ranking: The union group DIAP (Departamento Intersindical de Assessoria Parlamentar) "ranked" deputies by scoring yes votes in the first and second rounds of voting in the constitutional convention on job tenure, the 40 hour work week, the six hour shift, the right to strike, vacation pay, (30 day) notice for firings, and job security for union leadership as either a .5, 1, or 1.5 and no votes, abstentions, and unexcused absences as 0. The maximum score a deputy could receive was 10.

1A = MDB-PMDB;   2A = MDB-PP-PMDB
1B = PTB-MDB-PMDB;   2B = PSD, PR, UDN-MDB-(PP)-PMDB
1C = PMDB only;   3 = (UDN)-ARENA-(PP, PDS)-(PFL)-PMDB

Source: Calculated from DIAP, 1988: 261–318.

Table 5

Voting Records, PMDB Deputies, Constituent Assembly

State	N=	Labor Ranking	Agrarian Reform (Yes)	5 Year Term (No)	Partisan Origins*		
					Group 1	Group 2	Group 3
North							
Amazonas	2	4.63	2	1	2	-	-
Northeast							
Alagoas	3	8.5	3	3	2	0	1
Pernambuco	14	7.5	11	9	11	-	3
Piauí	2	7.13	1	1	1	-	1
Paraíba	7	7.0	5	2	2	1	4
Bahia	23	6.06	14	16	13	4	6
Rio Grande do Norte	4	5.81	3	0	2	1	1
Ceará	12	5.66	8	2	6	-	5
Maranhão	7	4.93	5	1	4	1	2
Sergipe	4	2.69	1	0	3	-	1
Southeast							
São Paulo	28	5.63	16	13	22	3	3
Rio de Janeiro	12	5.0	7	6	7	2	2
Minas Gerais	35	4.47	18	9	20	10	5
South							
Rio Grande do Sul	17	6.6	14	9	15	1	1

* Partisan Origins:
Group 1 = PTB-MDB-PMDB. For the purposes of this table, left of PMDB
        parties (PDT, PSB, PCB) were also included in Group 1.
Group 2 = PSD, PR, UDN (PDC, PRP) + MDB - (PP) - PMDB; MDB-PP-PMDB
Group 3 = (UDN) ARENA (PP, PDS, PFL) PMDB

Source: Calculated from DIAP, 1988

PT) (Table 4). Eighteen members of the delegation voted in favor of agrarian reform, while fourteen voted no and three were absent for the vote. The percentage of the Minas delegation opposing agrarian reform (50 percent) was higher than that of any northeast Brazilian state. Half of those *mineiros* opposing agrarian reform were recent converts to the party label. Seven of nine whose only partisan affiliations had been the MDB and the PMDB voted in favor of the reform. All votes but one from the Minas delegation opposing presidentialism were cast by deputies whose partisan roots lay in the MDB, PP, and/or PMDB. On the issue of a five-year mandate for President Sarney, 26 PMDB deputies from Minas voted for the five-year mandate, while only nine voted against. All nine deputies had begun their political careers in the ranks of the opposition, and seven subsequently defected from the PMDB to join the Brazilian Social Democratic party (PSDB). The traditional elites who remained in the PFL raised conservative vote totals: only one PFL deputy (of ten) broke ranks to vote in favor of agrarian reform, and all ten voted to give the sitting PMDB president a five-year term.

The machinery of clientelism was set in motion to assure a victory for the presidential system. The governor of Minas Gerais, Newton Cardoso, by his own admission swung 10 votes from his state's delegation to presidentialism in exchange for a "torrent of appropriations" for the state from Sarney (*Veja,* 1988b:50). The Housing Minister, Prisco Vianna (an ex-PDS leader), selectively committed nine billion cruzados worth of resources from his department to win votes. If the vote on presidentialism was influenced by offers of patronage, the issue of the extension of the presidential term to five years was settled virtually entirely by political opportunism. Given the potential rewards for a yes vote, the five year term was immensely popular in all regions, and in most parties. Most Northeast congressmen in particular voted with the president; in Sarney's native Maranhão, only one deputy voted against the five-year term.

The strengthening of Congress notwithstanding, the defeat of parliamentarism undoubtedly limits the potential for the Brazilian legislature to be an equal partner in government with the executive branch, and for political parties to play a role in policy formation and implementation. Presidentialism constitutionally reinforces the strength of Brazil's executive, its insulation from popular pressures, and the weakness of political parties.

Toward Consolidation: What Next for Brazilian Democracy?

In Brazil, where much of the political class supported military rule, constructing a coalition sufficiently broad to bring about a transition to civilian rule required the participation of the political elite of the old order.[43] The political transactions which accompanied the transition from authoritarian rule in Brazil allowed these protagonists of the *ancien régime* to assume a commanding position at the helm of the central institutions of political life in the new, and traditional politics to survive at least the initial stages of civilian government. In Minas Gerais, members of the traditional political elite were returned their primary political resources — their positions in the state and access to political patronage. They also entered the "democratic" era in the leadership of nearly all potential parties of government. What began as a realignment of promilitary and antimilitary forces within one state's borders had ripple effects in other states and precipitated a national regime change.

Had old regime elites not reached an accommodation with proponents of the New Republic in 1984, the short- and long-term results for Brazilian democracy would in all probability have been different. Immediately, a PDS president would have been selected in the electoral college, and the nature of the regime would have been ambiguous. With the succession to civilian rule rigged by the military, the new executive would have enjoyed no more, indeed less, legitimacy than Sarney. Yet, in the longer run, political coalitions might have aligned along new axes, parties might have developed stronger identities, and local PMDB victories might have disrupted clientelistic networks. Instead, because the traditional political elite played a leading role in the transition, the PMDB was transformed from a party poised to represent popular classes into an oligarchical vehicle, traditional clientelistic networks were revitalized, and public and constitutional policy were bartered for personal political gain. The ability of this elite to control the transition from authoritarian rule in Brazil and appropriate all major political parties except the PT does not augur well for democracy's extension. Ultimately, even if traditional political elites who dominate executive cabinets and political parties are subject to ratification under democratic rules, they have won a decisive round in the struggle for the political future of Brazil. The rise of the Workers' Party in São Paulo notwithstanding, outside greater São Paulo political change has been slower to arrive, and traditional political domination endures.

The first casualty of the elite-managed transition to democracy was what it did *not* accomplish; the democratizing potential of the regime change was by and large squandered. First was lost the opportunity to separate the traditional political elite from the principal source of its modern power: clientelism. In the latter stages of the military regime, political competition had given opponents of the oligarchy in the PMDB an opening through which to attack the foundations of elite power. The opposition was able to overcome the advantage with which their adversaries had begun — the spoils of the pork barrel — due to the coincidence, at least in Minas Gerais, of the unpopularity of the military regime and the winning coalition constructed by Tancredo Neves. With a PMDB governor, politics in principle might have been reorganized. Clientelism could have been weakened, or more modestly perhaps, redirected to support a new alignment of political forces. However genuine the possibilities were for democratization in Minas Gerais, they were forfeited almost before the euphoria over the electoral results had subsided. The governor made plain his intent to govern *with,* not against, the Minas oligarchy. His practices reinforced the power of local bosses, permitting them, and not their ideological and political rivals, to inherit the votes of the symbolic opposition to military rule.

Second, the immediate transformation of the party system in the transition to democracy was limited to the redefinition of party labels. In the 1970s, the PMDB raised hopes that it might articulate the interests of classes previously excluded from politics. But in the birth and rebirth of political parties accompanying the transition, the traditional political elite gained control of the PMDB, making it unlikely that it could become an agent of democratization. Ideological and substantive disputes do exist in Brazil today — the vitality of both the *Centrão* and the Workers' Party attest to that — but the parties most apt to process demands and contest substantive and ideological issues during the period of democratic consolidation were robbed of the opportunity to do so during the partisan realignment which accompanied the birth of the New Republic.

Third, a conservative bias has been built into Brazil's democratic institutions. Presidentialism and federalism, which though not antidemocratic in theory were in practice exploited in the past by antidemocratic forces, were strengthened in the new Constitution. Elements of the old regime may now survive within and because of them, which in turn will make needed democratizing changes harder to effect. With the defeat of parliamentarism was lost the last best opportunity to undermine clientelism and excessive executive power, and to give real strength to parties and the legislature.

In addition to what it failed to do, the exaggerated role of the traditional political elite in the "faulted" transition[44] hindered the process of democratization for what it *did* accomplish: it carried over many traditional and antidemocratic political practices and institutions into the new political regime.

The "New Republic" in Brazil differs in significant ways from its predecessor. Arbitrary military abuses of human rights have been curbed, political rights restored to political "undesirables," censorship lifted, illiterates enfranchised,[45] and direct elections resumed for state and national executive posts. Many of these advances have been constitutionally guaranteed. The right to strike and other social legislation will protect the interests of labor to a degree unprecedented in Brazilian history. The right to political expression is real. The loosening of the electorate from the grip of old party bosses and the opportunity to vote for real alternatives was made manifest in the huge protest vote which nearly elected the former metalworker Luis Inácio da Silva to the presidency on the ticket of the Workers' Party in December 1989. Perhaps for the first time ever, the electorate was able to register a groundswell of discontent with one of the world's most egregiously unequal distributions of wealth and income.

These important differences notwithstanding, there are also major continuities. The new order carries over from the old not only its personnel but many political procedures and practices as well. The military retains the constitutional prerogative to guarantee "law and order." National cabinet posts are still awarded to satisfy politically determined state quotas and to bolster adherents in the states. State governors retain formidable power, and in most places, are forging new political machines—made richer by the Constitution's support of federalism—on the unshaken foundations of the old. Public posts are still filled by top bosses to maximize political returns. Party candidates are still approached by their convention and general electors who solicit home roof repairs and lunches for their families as payment for their votes. Minas governor Hélio Garcia, when asked in 1986 what the country's political and administrative picture would have looked like had Eliseu Resende defeated Tancredo Neves for governor of Minas, and Mário Andreazza wrested the PDS presidential nomination from Paulo Maluf in 1984 and been elected president in the electoral college—in other words, if the "democratization" had not advanced nearly as far or as fast as it had—replied: "It would look very much as it does now" (*Istoé*, 1986:20).

Subsequent events have confirmed Garcia's bold judgment. Fernando Collor de Mello was elected president on a party label which virtually did not exist prior to the campaign—the PRN (Party of National Reconstruction). In the 1990 elections, traditional politicians returned in force to capture a series of important gubernatorial races. In Brazil today, political parties, local governments, the executive-legislative relationship, electoral codes, and modes of interest association and representation, even if not formally "authoritarian," are not like corresponding institutions and arrangements in a democratic polity. They are well suited to restricting mass political participation and the arena of decision making. Party positions on issues are sacrificed systematically to the particularistic calculations of a closed elite—an oligarchy. While strong executives, weak parties, and pervasive clientelism do not in and of themselves undermine democracy, Brazilian democracy is flawed by each of these to an extreme paralleled by few countries. When these three are combined as they are in Brazil, moreover, their perverse effects on democracy are multiplied.

The question remains open of whether or not patterns of politics established now may become semipermanent features of the political landscape. On the one hand, it is possible that in moments of transition and convulsion there may arise unique opportunities to discard the constraints of the organizational forms inherited from previous regimes, and that political arrangements, once in place, condition future political behavior and possibilities. On the other hand, it is not apparent why a system whose antidemocratic practices are not constitutionally bound cannot change. Clientelism is not a political right, and there are no structural obstacles to the formation of new, ideological parties. The prosperity of the PT serves as an eloquent example of this possibility.

Comparative evidence suggests that democratization is often slowed or stopped in regimes spawned by political pacts negotiated with traditional and authoritarian elites. The Pact of Punto Fijo secured democracy in Venezuela, but in Colombia, nearly three decades of formal and effective consociational rule by traditional and conservative political elites have slowed the process of extending democracy to a glacial pace. Perhaps the most nebulous yet instructive case is Italy. At a moment of transition in Italy in 1876, Agostino de Pretis, the newly elected prime minister, invited opposition deputies from the *Destra* party to shift their votes to the government majority in exchange for personal benefits, access to state patronage, and the right to rule locally. The deputies, finding themselves newly marginalized from power and state spoils (the *Destra* had controlled the Parliament since Italian unification 16 years earlier), agreed. Unfettered in their conversion by ideological or programmatic constraints—the parties represented only loosely knit coalitions of elite factions—they "transformed" themselves from the opposition into a stable part of the governing majority. For decades, southern deputies voted with any government, regardless of program or ideology, which supported its practice of clientelism. As Chubb (1982:21) explains its consequences:

> *Trasformismo* successfully eliminated any effective opposition from the Italian Parliament. . . . The organization of politics around personality and patronage rather than ideas and practical programs not only absorbed and neutralized the opposition but ultimately emptied the very concept of "party" of any meaning beyond that of a loose congeries of personal clienteles.

To date, Brazil closely resembles the southern Italian pattern. If change is not impossible, many old practices have been written onto the system—some reinforced structurally, others not, and both types serve as major impediments to an "extension of democracy" at all levels of the political system. At first, Tancredo Neves pursued a strategy of *trasformismo* with much the same effects which became apparent in Italy: immediate success for the government majority, the cooptation of opposition, and a long-term blow to political parties as vehicles of nonelite interest representation at precisely the moment they were most needed and held their greatest potential to advance democratization. The early indications are that this regime born of political compromise is as devoid of democratic representation as the southern Italian system which *trasformismo* wrought.

In appropriating parties that have direct access to the state, the oligarchy can perpetuate state clientelism as the principle which orders politics itself. Local political bosses of the interior who rode the wave of partisan conversion to emerge with their political health intact in 1988, the cogs in the traditional patronage machines, will serve the oligarchy from within whatever governing party they form or appropriate in the perpetual reconstruction of clientelistic networks. The migrations of the traditional political elite to any party of the *situação* has contributed mightily to the instability of the party system and the volatility of the electorate.

At the heart of our question is what relative significance formal political rules, the most obvious distinguishing features of political regimes, should be accorded vis-à-vis political practice? We should expect the efficacy of formal political rules to rise as extrapolitical forms of domination erode. In the Old Republic (1889–1930), democratic rules were easily bent by extrapolitical sources of local domination: land dependence and private armies. Political elites of the Old Republic routinely engaged in electoral fraud, physical intimidation, and subversion of the judicial process (Reis, 1980). Economic change in the past four decades and the professionalization of the military and police forces under a bureaucratic-authoritarian regime has rendered traditional political elites more subject to the formal political rules of a modern state than ever before.

But if rules matter more, their full potential to root out antidemocratic forms of political organization and foster democratic practices in their place may be realized only over the course of time. In the short to medium term, antidemocratic political practices, now ingrained in national political culture, may reproduce themselves. Even if constitutions provide for institutional change, in the absence of cataclysmic political events it is in practice hard to change the rules of the game. If democratization takes place in Brazil, it would appear that it will do so only in the long run. It may take some time for open political competition to create choice and encourage local opposition to form in the cities and the countryside, and eventually, for challengers to unseat incumbent groups in the states, and even in the federal government. But even so, the formal rules of democratic competition guarantee that what the political class in Brazil has long resisted may yet come to pass: the transformation and democratization of politics.

NOTES

Research for this paper was made possible by a Seed Money Grant from the Kellogg Institute and a Travel Grant from the Monadnock Fund of Harvard University. The author gratefully acknowledges the valuable comments received from Suzanne Berger, Houchang Chehabi, Caroline Domingo, Jorge Domínguez, Samuel Huntington, Guillermo O'Donnell, Silvia Raw, J. Samuel Valenzuela, Jennifer Widner, and especially Scott Mainwaring on earlier versions of this work.

1. For example, O'Donnell and Schmitter (1986).

2. The "New Republic" (*A Nova República*), a phrase coined by Tancredo Neves in his presidential campaign, has been widely used to describe the post–1985 civilian regime.

3. Diniz (1985) has disputed the view that regime elites were entirely successful in implementing their project for democratization. She argues that the process of democratization departed from elite plans due to popular protest and pressure. She also rejects, however, the alternate view that attributes too much strength to popular forces.

4. There are those who have sounded such a call, and highlighted the importance of this dimension in studies of democratization, but few have systematically conducted such studies. O'Donnell (1985a:11–13) recognized the capacity of an incumbent elite of an authoritarian regime to control a transition to democracy as a critical variable in explaining the success and direction of democratization. O'Donnell and Schmitter (1986) identified a "political moment" during the transition from authoritarian rule as a time for politicians and political parties to be "heroic." Viola and Mainwaring (1984) pointed out in general terms that the ability of the elite to control the "transition from above" in Brazil kept significant features of the authoritarian regime alive during the transition. Werneck Viana (1985:31–33) postulated that the power retained by the forces of the old regime would, to a large extent, determine the outcome of the most important issues facing Brazil in its transition to democracy—agrarian reform and strike laws—and also define the center in the party and political systems.

5. Lima (1981) has argued convincingly that in the 1945–1964 period, there was no single pattern of national politics, merely an amalgamation of many state patterns.

6. A term used by Kaufman and Stallings (1989) and Haggard and Kaufman (1989) to connote a young, formally democratic regime which has yet to be consolidated to the point that it can be sufficiently secure of its tenure and thus shortens its time horizon in the conduct of economic policy.

7. José Sarney, the newly elected vice-president, was sworn in as president after the death of the president-elect, Tancredo Neves.

8. O'Donnell identifies other favorable factors — relative economic success and low levels of repression of the preceding bureaucratic-authoritarian regime chief among them — which paradoxically may contribute to a slow death for democracy.

9. In O'Donnell's scheme, political democracy is considered consolidated when civilian rule has been established and the procedural minima for democracy identified by Dahl are present. These minima are: the freedom to form and join organizations; the freedom of expression; the right to vote; eligibility for public office; the right of political leaders to compete for support; alternative sources of information; and free and fair elections. They embody those institutional guarantees required for the opportunity to formulate preferences, to engage in individual and collective action to bring those preferences to the attention of fellow citizens and government, and to have preferences weighted equally in the conduct of government (Dahl, 1971:3). A "consolidated democracy" largely resembles the Schumpeterian model. O'Donnell sees the consolidation of the procedural minima as a precondition for the extension of political democracy. But he also (1985b:52) acknowledges that consolidation does *not necessarily* enhance the prospect for democracy's extension.

There is a third stage, "socialization," or "socioeconomic democratization." Socioeconomic democratization extends the principle of citizenship to various public and private organizations and makes advances in distributional equity. O'Donnell, I think correctly, doubts that an advance of socioeconomic democratization is possible at the same time that civilian rule is being consolidated. Of course, conceptualizing "socialization" as a third stage of democratization runs counter to a tradition in the social sciences which posits socioeconomic democratization to be a *prerequisite* of political democracy.

10. Remmer (1985:269–270) argues that authoritarian rule tends to promote political change and that the cases of redemocratization in Latin America in the postwar period entail major shifts in party strength, electoral realignments, and the rise of new partisan alternatives. Based on the length of the authoritarian episode, the relatively low levels of repression, and the instability of the precoup party system, she expects major discontinuities in Brazil from its pre-1964 democratic regime. Based on surveys, Lamounier (1989:63) makes a similar case that a massive realignment of the electorate took place in Brazil during authoritarian rule — between 1970 and 1974.

11. This somewhat obvious point has been lost in much of the literature on the breakdown of democracy. The forgotten contribution of the militance of the sugar workers of Pernambuco and the reaction of Northeast agrarian elites to the coup is carefully treated in Pereira (1991). In confessing twenty years after the fact to the plot to overthrow Goulart's government, José Monteiro de Castro, the secretary of Public Security of

Minas Gerais in 1964, identified landowners as the "most ardent revolu-
tionaries" (*Istoé*, 1984b:92–94).

12. Schmitter (1973) makes this point, though he characterizes the
system as "semi-competitive." Soares (1973) argues forcefully based on the
rising vote totals of the PTB that the oligarchical system was breaking apart
electorally. By 1962, the PTB had in many parts of Brazil, but not Minas
Gerais, surpassed the UDN.

13. The competing explanations of the coup of 1964 — macroeconomic crisis, the mobilization of urban masses, presidential ineptitude, and
the polarization of political parties, among others — are well known. Here
I will only direct the interested reader to Stepan (1978), O'Donnell (1973),
Wallerstein (1980), and the essays in Collier (1979).

14. Lamounier (1989) argues that a pluralist tradition was behind
military ambivalence.

15. Tancredo Neves changed his partisan affiliation three times in
his political career. He started out in the old PSD ("Social Democratic"
party). As a cabinet minister in Goulart's government, he was part of a
minority in the PSD that did not accept the military incursion into politics
and thus, in 1965, when the military offered politicians an exclusive choice
of membership in either a pro- or an antigovernment party (both of their
creation), he opted for the opposition MDB. He remained with the MDB
until its dissolution by the party reform law in 1979, when he co-founded
the new "moderate" PP (Popular Party), and rejoined the PMDB in 1982.

16. These cities received urban development funds under the federal
and state "Intermediary Cities" Programs, backed by the World Bank and
the Inter-American Development Bank, respectively. They were called "dike
cities" because their envisioned role was to contain migratory flows headed
for metropolitan capital regions.

17. Party leaders were selected to submerge pre–1964 party divisions.
With Tancredo Neves (national president) from the old PSD and Hélio
Garcia (state president) and Magalhães Pinto (honorary national president)
representing the old UDN, PP ranks would not be restricted to members
of only one of the extinct parties.

A refuge for the traditional political elite, the PP was a welcome
development of the architect of party reform, retired General Golbery de
Couto e Silva, who understood well the value of dividing the opposition.
As a last resort, if the military had to accept defeat, better to concede to
members of the traditional political elite than to the popular classes.

18. It turned out that the true electoral effect may have been in the
opposite direction; Tancredo Neves's candidacy appears to have benefitted
politicians in local races running on the PMDB ticket.

19. Hélio Garcia, who oversaw the state merger, had been a member
of ARENA until 1969, when, as a federal deputy, he became disgusted

with the closing of Congress. He did not run again in 1970. "Out of politics," he was appointed by Minas governor Aureliano Chaves as president of the state savings institution, the *Caixa Econômica,* a post which he held from 1975 to 1978. In 1979, he returned to politics under the PP banner. He was elected lieutenant governor in 1982, and jointly served as mayor of Belo Horizonte. Thus, the governor in 1984 had never been a member of the MDB. Affonso Camargo, the "bionic" senator from Paraná who presided over the national merger, was also from the PP via ARENA.

20. The PSD was formed by Vargas and the UDN in opposition to the former dictator in 1945. The primary cleavage separating these parties throughout the postwar era and beyond continued to be pro-Vargas/anti-Vargas. The PR, headed in the state by Artur Bernardes, was more important in Minas Gerais in this period than in any other state in Brazil.

21. Indeed, Francelino Pereira openly favored Maurício Campos, a member of the former UDN faction who at the time was mayor of Belo Horizonte.

22. The *Planalto* is literally the presidential palace. In common parlance in Brazil, it is used to signify the president and his advisors.

23. The left's role in the campaign was important if understated. Neves accepted the support of the left, but made no deliberate effort to mobilize it. In fact, he preferred that its potential lay dormant. Taking for granted a PMDB victory in Belo Horizonte, he had no campaign planned for the state capital. Soon it became clear, however, that the campaign in the interior would be difficult: the PMDB had *diretórios* in only 303 cities (*Estado de Minas,* 1983). To win, the party needed to carry Belo Horizonte and the 50 largest cities by a wide margin. The burden for delivering the urban vote fell to the left.

24. The electoral college was composed of all senators, federal deputies, and 132 state delegates (a total of 680). After the 1982 elections, the partisan representation in the college stood as follows: PDS: 359; PMDB: 269; PDT: 30; PTB: 14; PT: 8 (Wesson and Fleischer, 1983:119).

25. According to one member of the Executive Commission of the state PMDB, the idea of the campaign was discussed only once: a subcommittee of three was appointed to study the idea, and two members, upon being named, departed immediately for personal vacations. Minas Gerais was virtually the last state, and Belo Horizonte the last major city, to organize public demonstrations for direct elections. (Interview with Roberto Martins, Belo Horizonte, August 16, 1985.)

26. "Café com leite," or "café au lait," refers to an alliance between the states of Minas and São Paulo during the Old Republic. Coined for the coffee-producing São Paulo and the dairy-producing Minas Gerais, this term refers to the collaboration each state's delegation lent the other in the national Congress.

27. Why Figueiredo behaved so passively has been the subject of much speculation. One theory is that he, himself, wished to stay on as president for another four-year term (*Veja,* 1985a:24–27).

28. The fear of a coup attempt was not irrational. Security forces had attempted in 1981 to sabotage the political opening by planting a bomb (which exploded prematurely in the lap of a saboteur) at the Riocentro complex in Rio de Janeiro during a public gathering on May Day. Between August and November 1984, once it became apparent Neves had the votes to triumph in the electoral college, the PMDB steeled itself for a coup. Expecting a coup to originate in Brasília under the command of General Newton Cruz, it even planned in detail a resistance. *Veja* (1985a:40–45) provides a full account of the events of these months.

29. Tancredo Neves, according to Brazilian law, had to resign his post as governor in order to run for president. Thus Hélio Garcia became governor in July 1984. Much of the negotiating for the *"Acordo"* with Aureliano Chaves (representing the FL) fell to Garcia.

30. How the prerogatives to make these appointments were parcelled out to the dissident deputies illustrates the persistence of traditional politics. Reportedly, when deputies could not agree amongst themselves on how to divide the spoils (different posts, of course, had different real and relative value), Israel Pinheiro provided the solution. Recalling how such disputes were resolved during the *Estado Novo,* he suggested that they employ the method he learned from Benedito Valadares (Vargas's interventor and later governor of Minas Gerais): the names of each post be put on separate pieces of paper, and the deputies pull these scraps of paper from a hat. Later, they could be traded amongst deputies seeking to strengthen their positions in different parts of the state (*Veja,* 1985b:26–27).

31. There is no satisfactory explanation for why the *hidroestâncias* were treated in this way.

32. At the popular level, this has been called the "Flamengo effect," so named for the popular soccer club of Rio de Janeiro whose success has spawned a new generation of loyal supporters.

33. Luiz Otávio Valadares, Sílvio de Abreu Junior, Maurício de Padua Souza, and Ronan Tito were appointed to head the Departments of Administration, Interior and Justice, Public Works, and Labor and Social Action. Abreu, Carlos Cotta who succeeded Renato Azeredo in the department of Government and Political Coordination, and Leopoldo Bessone who headed the new department of Tourism and Sports, all detoured through the PP before rejoining the PMDB (*Minas Gerais,* 1983). At least once in Neves's short term in office two of this group were threatened with dismissal (*Diário do Comercio,* 1983:3).

34. David Fleischer (1981:109), author of the most detailed studies of elected political representatives in Minas, estimates that 91.4 percent

of the state's federal deputies from 1946 to 1975 had relatives in politics. More ex-members of the precoup oligarchical parties, the PSD (97.1 percent), UDN (100 percent) and PR (100 percent), and ARENA deputies (87.5 percent) had these connections than did the federal representatives of the labor and opposition parties (PTB, 71.4 percent; MDB, 63.6 percent).

35. Traditional political elite is here defined as either a member of the "27 governing families of Minas Gerais" (Rebelo Horta, 1956) (operationally, the "oligarchy") or as a politician with older relatives in politics at the state level. Data are from Hagopian (forthcoming).

36. Among the secretaries in Sarney's cabinet in 1988 who either belonged to the PDS or to ARENA or who supported the military coup of 1964 were: Prisco Viana (Housing and Urban Development), Borges da Silveira (Health), Aluízio Alves (Administration), Aureliano Chaves (Mines and Energy), Antônio Carlos Magalhães (Communications), Hugo Napoleão (Education), and Paulo Brossard (Justice), though Brossard later earned democratic credentials.

37. The quintessential clientelistic party was the PSD. The supreme party of the "ins," the PSD conducted itself in such a way to perpetuate its government role. Hippólito (1985:124–127), who studied extensively the PSD, identified as essential attributes for securing control of state-level politics within the PSD: (1) to be a top vote-getter; (2) to have public resources to distribute; (3) to be able to liaise with local leaders; and (4) to be able to control the state's representatives in congress. Each was geared toward the entirely instrumental goal of achieving and maintaining power. Indeed, Hippólito describes a party leadership which was obsessed with retaining power, even in relation to party leaders in other times and places. She coins the PSD the "Michelian party par excellence."

38. Cardoso (1985:3) identified three types of parties: the catch-all, typified by the PMDB; the ideological, of which the Workers' Party (PT) was the best example; and the traditional clientelistic, which accurately described both the PDS and the PFL. He admonished that the PMDB had to avoid evolving into what ARENA had been. Three years later, in an interview explaining why he had left the PMDB, he criticized the party for becoming just that, a machine to dispense government patronage (*Veja*, 1988c:5–6).

39. *Senhor* (1986:43) reports: "The number of mayors who have sought refuge in the PMDB is about four or five per month. Two hundred mayors have submitted to [Governor Hélio] Garcia's charisma." A PMDB vice-president suggested that the time in which these 200 mayors converted to the PMDB during the Brazilian winter (June–August) months of 1985 was shorter, and furthermore that they were accompanied by entire PDS *diretórios* (Interview, Belo Horizonte, August 16, 1985).

40. In early 1988, some of the most prominent leaders of the PMDB

in São Paulo — Fernando Henrique Cardoso, former head of the government in congress, Franco Montoro, former state governor, and Mário Covas, PMDB senator and the party's leading vote getter in the 1986 congressional elections — bolted from the party to form a new party, the Brazilian Social Democratic party (PSDB), whose main aims are to fight for parliamentarism and to "reform the state." They are popularly known as the *"tucanos"* (toucans).

41. Guimarães (1985:41) aptly argued that PMDB victories in the 1985 mayoral races did not signal an advance of progressive and leftist forces in Brazil. He saw two (or more) PMDBs in places, and "in the majority of cities, the more conservative PMDB won."

42. Most, but not all. Parliamentarism was opposed by Leonel Brizola and his supporters in the PDT, who in hoping for a victory in the 1989 presidential race, did not wish the powers of the office to be diluted. Parliamentarism, Brizola remembered, was used by the oligarchy in 1961 to weaken the hand of his brother-in-law, João Goulart.

43. Guimarães (1985:38-39) has pointed out that a coalition formed to hasten the dissolution of the old regime aims to be as broad as possible, and thus encumbers itself as a governing coalition.

44. The term "faulted transition" is borrowed and adapted from Dahrendorf's (1969:49ff) description of Germany as a "faulted society."

45. Silvia Raw has pointed out that the enfranchisement of illiterates, while a positive step toward democratization, creates the danger that clientelistic practices might be reinforced. Traditionally, landowners manipulated the votes of their illiterate rural workers; the *disenfranchisement* of illiterates was an urban, liberal demand after 1930.

REFERENCES

Ames, Barry. 1987. *Political Survival: Politicians and Public Policy in Latin America.* Berkeley: University of California Press.

Cammack, Paul. 1982. "Clientelism and Military Government in Brazil," pp. 53-75 in Christopher Clapham, ed., *Private Patronage and Public Power.* New York: St. Martin's Press.

Cardoso, Fernando Henrique and Bolivar Lamounier. 1978. *Os partidos e as eleições no Brasil,* 2nd edition. Rio de Janeiro: Paz e Terra.

Cardoso, Fernando Henrique. 1985. "Opinião: O PMDB," *Folha de São Paulo.* February 19:3.

Chubb, Judith. 1982. *Patronage, Power and Poverty in Southern Italy: A Tale of Two Cities.* New York: Cambridge University Press.

Collier, David, ed. 1979. *The New Authoritarianism in Latin America.*
    Princeton: Princeton University Press.
Dahl, Robert A. 1971. *Polyarchy: Participation and Opposition.* New
    Haven: Yale University Press.
Dahrendorf, Ralf. 1969. *Society and Democracy in Germany.* Garden City,
    New York: Anchor Books.
DIAP (Departamento Intersindical de Assessoria Parlamentar). 1988. *Quem
    foi quem na Constituinte nas questões de interesse dos trabalhadores.*
    São Paulo: OBORÉ/Cortez.
Diário do Comercio. 1983. August 4:3.
Diniz, Eli. 1982. *Voto e máquina política: Patronagem e clientelismo no
    Rio de Janeiro.* Rio de Janeiro: Paz e Terra.
————. 1985. "A transição política no Brasil: uma reavaliação da dinâmica
    da abertura." *Dados* 28 (3): 329–346.
Estado de Minas. 1983. "PMDB elegerá Freire presidente e Kumaira para
    secretária-geral." November 17.
————. 1984a. September 4.
————. 1984b. September 7.
Fleischer, David V. 1981. "As origens socio-econômicas e regionais das
    lideranças partidárias em Minas," pp. 96–115 in David V. Fleischer,
    ed., *Os partidos políticos no Brasil,* Volume II. Brasília: Editora Uni-
    versidade de Brasília.
Fleischer, David V. 1987. "O Congresso-Constituinte de 1987: um perfil
    sócio-econômico e político." Unpublished paper, Universidade de
    Brasília.
Gillespie, Charles G. 1986. "Uruguay's Transition from Collegial Military-
    Technocratic Rule," pp. 173–195 in Guillermo O'Donnell, Philippe C.
    Schmitter, and Laurence Whitehead, eds., *Transitions from Authori-
    tarian Rule,* Vol. 2, *Latin America.* Baltimore: Johns Hopkins Uni-
    versity Press.
Guimarães, César. 1985. "Avanço à esquerda, inclinação à direita," pp. 37–
    42 in "As eleições municipais de 85 e a conjuntura política." *Cader-
    nos de Conjuntura,* no. 3, Rio de Janeiro: Instituto Universitário de
    Pesquisas do Rio de Janeiro (IUPERJ).
Haggard, Stephan and Robert R. Kaufman. 1989. "Economic Adjustment
    in New Democracies," pp. 57–77 in Joan Nelson, ed., *Fragile Coali-
    tions: The Politics of Economic Adjustment.* New Brunswick: Trans-
    action Books for the Overseas Development Council.
Hagopian, Frances. Forthcoming. *Traditional Politics and Regime Change
    in Brazil.* New York: Cambridge University Press.
Hippólito, Lúcia. 1985. *De raposas e reformistas: o PSD e a experiência
    democrática brasileira (1945–64).* Rio de Janeiro: Paz e Terra.
Istoé. 1984a. "Em estado de graça." July 18:22–24.

————. 1984b. Interview with José Monteiro de Castro. July 25:92–94.

————. 1986. "Em pé de guerra." February 26:20–21.

Kaufman, Robert and Barbara Stallings. 1989. "Debt and Democracy in the 1980s: The Latin American Experience," pp. 201–223 in Barbara Stallings and Robert Kaufman, eds., *Debt and Democracy in Latin America.* Boulder: Westview Press.

Lamounier, Bolivar. 1980. "O Voto em São Paulo, 1970–1978," pp. 15–80 in Bolivar Lamounier, ed., *Voto de desconfiança: Eleições e mudança política no Brasil, 1970–1979.* São Paulo: Vozes/CEBRAP.

Lamounier, Bolivar. 1989. *"Authoritarian Brazil* Revisited: The Impact of Elections on the *Abertura,"* pp. 43–79 in Alfred Stepan, ed., *Democratizing Brazil: Problems of Transition and Consolidation.* New York: Oxford University Press.

Lima Jr., Olavo Brasil de. 1981. "O sistema partidário brasileiro, 1945–1962," pp. 24–45 in David V. Fleischer, ed., *Os Partidos Políticos no Brasil,* Volume I. Brasília: Editora Universidade de Brasília.

Minas Gerais. 1983. "Os novos secretários do Governo de Minas," Part I, Diário do Executivo, March 16:8–16.

Murilo de Carvalho, José. 1966. "Barbacena, a família, a política, e uma hipótese," *Revista Brasileira de Estudos Políticos* 20 (January): 153–193.

O'Donnell, Guillermo. 1973. *Modernization and Bureaucratic-Authoritarianism: Studies in South American Politics.* Berkeley: Institute of International Studies, University of California.

————. 1985a. "Projecto: Dilemas de la consolidación democratica en América Latina," unpublished proposal, CLADE.

————. 1985b. "Notes for the Study of Democratic Consolidation in Latin America." Kellogg Institute, University of Notre Dame.

O'Donnell, Guillermo and Philippe C. Schmitter. 1986. *Transitions from Authoritarian Rule,* Part IV, *Tentative Conclusions about Uncertain Democracies.* Baltimore: Johns Hopkins University Press.

Pereira, Anthony W. 1991. "Regime Change without Democratization: Sugar Workers' Union in Pernambuco, Northeast Brazil, 1961–89." Ph.D. dissertation, Department of Government, Harvard University.

Rebelo Horta, Cid. 1956. "Familias Governmentais de Minas Gerais," pp. 45–91 in Universidade de Minas Gerais, *Segundo Seminário de Estudos Mineiros.* Belo Horizonte (October 22–27).

Reis, Elisa P. 1980. "The Agrarian Roots of Authoritarian Modernization in Brazil, 1880–1930." Ph.D. dissertation, Department of Political Science, Massachusetts Institute of Technology.

Remmer, Karen. 1985. "Redemocratization and the Impact of Authoritarian Rule in Latin America," *Comparative Politics* 17, no. 3 (April): 253–275.

Schmitter, Philippe C. 1973. "The 'Portugalization' of Brazil?" pp. 179–232 in Alfred Stepan, ed., *Authoritarian Brazil: Origins, Prospects, and Future*. New Haven: Yale University Press.

Secretaria de Estado de Planejamento e Coordenação Geral (SEPLAN-MG). 1983. *O prefeito mineiro (1982-1988)* (Jack Siqueira, Coordinator), Belo Horizonte.

Senhor. 1986. "Minas, depois de Tancredo," special section, February 25: 40–69.

Soares, Gláucio. 1973. *Sociedade e Política no Brasil.* São Paulo: DIFEL.

Stepan, Alfred. 1978. "Political Leadership and Regime Breakdown: Brazil," pp. 110–137 in Juan Linz and Alfred Stepan, eds., *The Breakdown of Democratic Regimes, Latin America*. Baltimore: Johns Hopkins University Press.

————. 1988. *Rethinking Military Politics: Brazil and the Southern Cone*. Princeton: Princeton University Press.

Tribunal Regional Eleitoral de Minas Gerais (TRE-MG), Division of Statistics, file data.

Veja. 1985a. "Os segredos da vitória da oposição." January 16:20–55.

————. 1985b. "Tenebrosas transações." July 17:20–27.

————. 1988a. "O ministério com cara de PDS." August 3:34–35.

————. 1988b. "O óbvio no placar." March 30:44–51.

————. 1988c. "Sarney parece Figueiredo" (interview with Fernando Henrique Cardoso). June 29:5–8.

Viola, Eduardo, and Scott Mainwaring. 1984. "Transitions to Democracy: Brazil and Argentina in the 1980s," Working Paper no. 21, Kellogg Institute, University of Notre Dame.

Wallerstein, Michael. 1980. "The Collapse of Democracy in Brazil: Its Economic Determinants." *Latin American Research Review* XV, no. 3:3–40.

Werneck Vianna, Luiz. 1985. "A ofensiva do antigo regime e a conjuntura pós-eleitoral," pp. 31–36 in "As eleições municipais de 85 e a conjuntura política," *Cadernos de Conjuntura* no. 3, Rio de Janeiro: Instituto Universitário de Pesquisas do Rio de Janeiro (IUPERJ).

Wesson, Robert, and David V. Fleischer. 1983. *Brazil in Transition*. New York: Praeger.

Transitions to Democracy and Democratic Consolidation: Theoretical and Comparative Issues

Scott Mainwaring

In the 1980s, an extensive literature emerged on transitions to democracy and prospects for democracy in Latin America. This literature has responded to two fundamental developments in the region. First, the current analyses have emerged in the context of the withering of many authoritarian regimes and their replacement by democratic governments. Never before in Latin American history have so many democratic governments survived for so long as in the last decade.[1] The sheer number of transitions and the predominance of democratic governments have stimulated academic debates about transitions.

The second development is the increased intellectual interest in and commitment to democracy. Intellectuals have expressed more interest in writing about and supporting democracy than ever before. In previous democratic periods, many intellectuals remained indifferent or even hostile to liberal democracy. After suffering horrendous persecutions, witnessing the deaths of friends and colleagues, and experiencing the palpable reduction of forms of sociability during the past wave of authoritarian rule, intellectuals became convinced of the desirability of democracy. This change is especially marked in South America but has even exercised some influence in the generally inauspicious climate of Central American nations embroiled in civil wars.[2] Along with the renewed normative commitment to democracy has come greater interest in studying democratic transitions and processes. In terms of quantity and often of quality as well, the new literature on these subjects represents a leap over what was produced in earlier decades in Latin America.

A relatively new subject notwithstanding the much older academic concern with democracy, the study of transitions became a veritable growth industry for several years. Along with colleagues engaged in research on Southern Europe, Latin Americans and Latin Americanists have been the leaders in this new field of research. Perhaps because it is a more established theme in the social sciences, no comparable innovations have yet appeared in the burgeoning literature on democratic consolidation. Nevertheless, the literature on this subject has enhanced our understanding not only of current problems in Latin America, but also of democracy in general.

Considering the abundance and quality of this literature, a review of some of the major themes, debates, and disagreements has been overdue. This chapter takes on that task, addressing some key comparative and theoretical issues in the literature on transitions to democracy and democratic consolidation. I begin with the problem of how transition and democracy should be defined.

Key Definitions: Transition and Democracy

The controversy in the literature begins with the very notion of transition. O'Donnell and Schmitter (1986) offer a useful definition in their excellent succinct work. "The 'transition' is the interval between one political regime and another. . . . Transitions are delimited, on the one side, by the launching of the process of dissolution of an authoritarian regime and, on the other, by the installation of some form of democracy, the return to some form of authoritarian rule, or the emergence of a revolutionary alternative" (p. 6). They add that "the *terminus ad quo* of our inquiry [is located] at the moment that authoritarian rulers announce their intention to extend significantly the sphere of protected individual and group rights — and are believed. . . . The advent of political democracy is the preferred *terminus ad quem*" (pp. 10, 11).

As O'Donnell and Schmitter use the term, it is clearly conceptualized and delimited. This is not always the case. Nun and Portantiero (1987) opt for a less bounded usage whose meaning is elusive. Writing nearly four years after the inauguration of a democratic government in Argentina, they still referred to "the transition to democracy" in the title of their book. But in 1987 democracy already existed in Argentina; the problem was ensuring its consolidation. These are different issues and involve different dynamics.

There are more fruitful ways of conceptualizing the current moment than speaking of a "transition to democracy." O'Donnell's contribution to this volume gets at the difference between the current moment and the period of demise of authoritarianism by speaking of two transitions: a transition to democracy, and then a transition to a consolidated democracy. The first transition involves defeating authoritarianism and establishing democracy, while the second involves consolidating democracy. In a similar vein, in his contribution in this volume, Przeworski distinguishes between two different aspects of democratization: the extrication from authoritarian rule and the constitution of a democratic regime. Alternatively, we could distinguish between establishing a democratic government and consolidating a democratic regime (Hagopian and Mainwaring 1987). Regime, of course, is a broader concept than government and refers to the rules (formal or not) that govern the interactions of the major actors in the political system. The notion of regime involves institutionalization, i.e., the idea that such rules are widely understood and accepted, and that actors pattern their behavior accordingly.

The distinction between two transitions is especially important in Latin American countries where democracy is surviving not so much because of its own achievements as because of the seeming exhaustion of alternatives. Aware that they contributed mightily to the current crises and that they have no new answers, the militaries are reluctant to intervene again. Conaghan (1985) coined the term "democracy by attrition" to describe the transition in Ecuador, and some years later this felicitous phrase describes the reality in several other countries as well.

Debates about the concept of democracy are old indeed, and it would be impossible to provide a detailed overview here. The key point here is a notable shift in how this term has been employed by social scientists working on Latin America. In the 1960s and 1970s, many analysts derogated "bourgeois democracy" and insisted that political systems with marked social and economic inequalities were not truly democratic. The wisdom of defining democracy in procedural terms (i.e. according to the rules governing politics) rather than substantive terms (i.e., by some outcomes of politics) was lost to many. The problems of such outcome-oriented conceptions of democracy were vast, ranging from making the concept impossible to operationalize to reflecting an ambivalence about liberal democracy.

In the past decade, the pendulum has swung the other way,

and procedural definitions now dominate the scholarly debate. To a considerable extent, Schumpeter's definition (1950:269), focusing on electoral competition among political elites and parties, has prevailed: "The democratic method is that institutional arrangement for arriving at political decisions in which individuals acquire the power to decide by means of a competitive struggle for the people's vote."[3] Most subsequent procedural definitions modified Schumpeter's analysis by insisting on nearly universal suffrage, a criterion that Schumpeter neglected.[4] By adding this dimension of participation to Schumpeter's emphasis on competition, we arrive at Dahl's (1971) influential scheme for conceptualizing polyarchy.

If analysts in the past often erred in proposing a substantive definition of democracy, in the recent discussion the opposite problem has emerged: a subminimal procedural definition that equates democracy with the holding of elections (Karl 1986b). Seligson (1987a:3), for example, argued that "Throughout the region, there have emerged formal, constitutional democracies, replete with comparatively honest and open elections, active party competition, and a relatively uncensored press. By mid-decade, only Chile and Paraguay seemed impervious to the trend." In addition to neglecting cases such as Cuba and Haiti that did not meet his own criteria, Seligson conflated the holding of competitive elections with the existence of democracy. Schumpeter's minimalist definition of democracy insisted on the possibility of alternation in power, a condition that Mexico and Nicaragua did not meet as of 1987. Serious limits on civil liberties made the inclusion of El Salvador, Guatemala, Honduras, and Peru dubious. Finally, at the time when Seligson was writing, Brazil had not held democratic elections for president since 1960, and the extent of military intrusion in politics made it an ambiguous case.

A democracy must meet three basic procedural criteria: (1) Competitive elections must be the route to forming governments. There must be competitive popular elections for the legislature and there usually are for the president as well in a presidential regime. Fraud and coercion may not determine the outcome of democratic elections. Elections must offer the possibility of alternation in power even if, as has occurred in Japan, no actual alternation occurs. (2) There must be broad adult citizenship. In recent decades, this has meant nearly universal citizenship. Almost all countries have some exclusions—criminals, the insane, military personnel, and the illiterate are often among them. The illiterate, however, may be so numerous that their exclusion undermines the notion of generalized adult suffrage. It is impossible to establish an exact threshold at which exclusions mean that a regime is no longer democratic, in part because the tolerance for exclusions has diminished over time. (3) Democracies must protect minority rights and must ensure respect for basic civil liberties: freedom of the press, freedom of speech, the right to habeas corpus, etc. This dimension is important because a regime can hold competitive elections with broad participation, yet in the absence of guarantees of civil liberties, it is not fully democratic. Contemporary El Salvador illustrates the point (Karl 1986b).

Although this is a liberal, procedural, and minimalist definition of democracy, it is a more demanding definition than that proposed by Seligson. Even if we stick to a procedural definition, deciding what governments should be classified as democratic is not always easy. This problem is particularly acute at a time when several major Latin American nations with elected civilian governments have mixed or controversial records on at least one of the three defining criteria of democracy.

Liberalization and Democratization

O'Donnell and Schmitter (1986) correctly insisted on the distinction between liberalization and democratization. This distinction calls attention to the value of democracy as opposed to changes within authoritarian rule, and to the fundamental difference between the two. Political liberalization refers to an easing of repression and extension of civil liberties *within* an authoritarian regime, whereas a transition to democracy implies a change *of* regimes. Democratization has been used in different ways, but as used here it refers to a movement *toward* democracy, that is, toward a different political regime. In recent transitions, this movement has occurred through an expansion of political contestation (competition); in most early cases of democratization, it occurred primarily through an expansion of participation in polities that already had some competition.

Liberalization does not always lead to a democratic transition. Liberalization is sometimes aborted and leads to renewed repression. Even successful transitions to democracy are usually characterized by vicissitudes: threats by the hardliners to lead a coup, efforts by the softliners to use the threats of the hardliners to bolster their own situation, real if temporary reverses in the process of liberalization, and authoritarian crackdowns. There are no recent cases, if there are any at all, in which the instauration of a democratic government came about easily.

What accounts for the beginning of political liberalization? Most authors who have addressed this issue have focused on elite processes, especially those within the authoritarian regime. Kaufman (1986), O'Donnell and Schmitter (1986), Chalmers and Robinson (1982), and Przeworski (1986) argue that liberalization begins with schisms within the authoritarian coalition. Stepan (1988) focuses specifically on schisms within the military. In some cases, the schisms that precede liberalization begin because of the failures of authoritarian regimes. In others, they arise because of a paradox of success: major successes convince authoritarian elites that they have little to lose by opening the political system, and a good deal to gain—international and domestic legitimacy, as well as the defusion of tensions in the armed forces.

The current emphasis on splits within authoritarian coalitions as a starting point in processes of political liberalization was a useful corrective to those who naively—sometimes with tragic consequences—hoped that mass mobilization would overthrow authoritarian regimes backed by powerful modern militaries. Yet exclusive attention to internal tensions can lead to neglecting the impact of opposition actors in general, including mass mobilization. Many transitions involve complex interactions between regime and opposition forces from an early stage (Smith 1987:183–187).

Internal schisms are necessary if an authoritarian regime is to liberalize; it is difficult to imagine a regime change in the face of a cohesive authoritarian coalition committed to remaining in power. However, liberalization can be affected by actors outside the authoritarian coalition from an early stage. Even though authoritarian elites may seem to hold all the cards, this appearance can be deceiving. Often their actions take into account calculations of how the opposition will react, and some government leaders may attempt to coopt moderate opposition groups. Strategic interaction is contextual; some actors within an authoritarian coalition may begin to support liberalization primarily in response to actors outside the coalition (see Adam Przeworski's chapter in this volume).

Moreover, it is not even necessary that major actors within the authoritarian coalition support liberalization for the wheels of regime change to begin moving. It is tempting to think that liberalization always begins because some actors in the authoritarian coalition want it to, but there is also another possibility. Schisms that have little to do with democracy or liberalization may emerge within the authoritarian coalition. For example, nationalistic actors can oppose the open-market orientation of governmental policy, but without dissenting from the idea of maintaining authoritarian rule. Even in the absence of any liberalizing advocates within the authoritarian coalition, this scenario can make possible increasing mobilization against the authoritarian regime, thereby intensifying the internal schisms. In this case, the emergence of a proliberalization faction within the authoritarian coalition is not so much a prerequisite for liberalization as a response to the erosion of the regime. The Argentine case of 1969–1973 suggests that this scenario is more than a hypothetical possibility (O'Donnell 1982). This case indicates that, contrary to some arguments (Chalmers and Robinson 1982), authoritarian regime leaders may not freely choose to liberalize, but may do so under pressure in order to minimize their losses.

Although liberalization usually begins with a split within the authoritarian elite, democratization is not a product of these elites (Bresser Pereira 1984; Moisés 1986; Smith 1987). The authoritarian elites who initiate liberalization want it limited to some form of political regime in which they retain power. Some may envisage a political regime that allows for competition for the main electoral positions, but they do so with the illusion that they will be able to win such positions. There are few true democrats among those who initiated liberalization schemes, even if these leaders are often less authoritarian, or at least less disposed to resort to massive repression, than their predecessors.

Miscalculations committed by leaders of authoritarian regimes figure in some transitions. Many authoritarian rulers take the imposed silence that hovers over society as a sign of support or at least acquiescence. They consequently are willing to liberalize or even hold elections, expecting that they will be able to retain power. But the political opening allows for new expressions of protest and opposition, often ultimately leading to a process of regime change rather than one of mere liberalization.

Even if liberalization begins with a decision by some members of the authoritarian coalition, that decision sends signals to other actors that changes in the political system are possible. Many actors get involved in and influence the political process. All recent transitions have been marked by constant interplay between regime and opposition forces once the regime signals its intention to liberalize. In no recent transitions has an authoritarian government been so thoroughly defeated that it was incapable of asserting influence over the transition. Even in a case like Argentina in 1982, in which the government suffered an embarrassing external defeat, the military was able to protect some of its interests. This fact was obscured at the time by the stunning magnitude of the military's failures, but subsequently it has been all too apparent as the armed forces have reasserted themselves in the political scenario. Conversely, even the authoritarian regimes that exercise most influence and control over transitions engage in constant negotiations with and maneuvers to outdo the opposition.

Opening the political system subjects regime leaders to conundrums they had not faced during the apex of authoritarianism. As Stepan (1988) shows, military leaders may establish alliances with civilian elites to help them offset the threat of a coup by the hardliners. But establishing such an alliance also has a cost: the civilian elites assume more responsibility and gain greater influence. One of the early steps in most liberalization processes, allowing greater space for expressions of dissent, can lead to massive repudiation of authoritarian rule. Opposition actors of various stripes and colors reenter the political stage, demanding the end of authoritarian rule. This is the resurrection of civil society of which O'Donnell and Schmitter write. The process contains no inevitable outcomes, but once a certain momentum is gained, it is difficult for authoritarian regimes to contain it. Transition processes can have a snowball effect in which the satisfaction of one demand, far from dampening further demands, does the opposite.

In addition to the dynamic between the authoritarian coalition and the opposition, divisions within the authoritarian elite and within the opposition are crucial in transitions. One could not get very far with a simple model of regime and opposition forces. As noted above, divisions within the regime itself usually lead to the beginning of liberalization. Some forces within the regime almost invariably try to block liberalization, but others seek alliances within the opposition as a means of overcoming these attempted vetoes. Some actors within the opposition may oppose negotiation with the government and opt for a "maximalist" strategy; when this is the case, the probability of a successful transition diminishes (O'Donnell 1979a). This was one of the major problems blocking a transition in Chile until 1988 (Cortázar 1987).

O'Donnell's scheme (1979a) for conceptualizing differentiations within the regime and the opposition is an enduring contribution. O'Donnell categorized the regime supporters into hardliners and softliners, the latter being more willing to negotiate with the opposition and to entertain possibilities of promoting liberalization. The opposition comprises the opportunistic opposition, generally former regime supporters who have no serious commitment to democracy but who hope to gain something by their tentative and late opposition to authoritarian rule; the moderate opposition; and the maximalists, who are unwilling to negotiate anything with the authoritarian government and who are generally not committed to political democracy.

Many authoritarian governments eventually convoke elections as a means of bringing the process to an end, still hoping that they will be able to remain in power or at least score electoral victories that vindicate their rule and give them a cornerstone in a nascent democracy. Most often, these hopes are frustrated. When they subject their legitimacy to the electoral arena, authoritarian rulers depend on political parties. By the time open competitive elections have been set, most authoritarian regimes have limited support in society. In nations where parties have been important political actors, they cannot easily create new spaces in the party system. With few exceptions (most notably Brazil and Paraguay), authoritarian elites have railed against parties in an effort to convince the nation of the desirability of authoritarian rule, a fact that makes it more difficult to win the support of extant parties. Authoritarian leaders may have vast advantages in distributing patronage and in controlling and in gaining access to publicity, but they rarely succeed in structuring a viable political party in countries with a prior history of democracy and parties. Chile has proved to be an exception.

Elites, Masses, and Democracy

In the past two decades, political scientists have focused mostly on the role of political elites in sustaining democracies. The transitions literature has furthered the analysis of democracy as a product of elite interactions. Rustow's seminal article (1970) argued that democracy "is acquired by a process of conscious decision at least on the part of the top political leadership. . . . A small circle of leaders is likely to play a disproportionate role" (356). Many recent works on transitions have continued this emphasis.

Huntington (1984) wrote that "democratic regimes that last have seldom, if ever, been instituted by mass popular action. Almost always, democracy has come as much from the top down as from the bottom up; it is as likely to be the product of oligarchy as of protest against oligarchy" (212). Despite its careful wording, this passage misses a key feature of many transitions to democracy: that they involve a dynamic interaction between elites and masses. Huntington is right that enduring democracies are not created by mass action alone, but mass action has contributed to enduring democracies (Therborn 1977; Stephens 1987).

Transitions usually begin with splits within authoritarian regimes, but over time more and more actors become involved. Exclusive focus on elite actors will not do for this reason; the efforts of popular sectors to redefine the political scene are also important. In virtually all recent transitions, a panoply of popular organizations struggled against authoritarian governments and on behalf of establishing democracy. Labor unions, peasant groups, neighborhood associations, and Church groups played prominent parts in the struggles that ended authoritarian rule. Without some initial cracks in the authoritarian coalitions, their impact was limited, but once such cracks appeared, they bolstered the efforts to oust autocratic governments.

Equally apposite, the *linkages* between elites and masses are crucial in transition periods. As liberalization proceeds, governments and oppositions alike attempt to win popular sympathies in efforts to bolster their bargaining power. Countering their past implacable hostility to popular groups, governments establish policies designed to win popular support and to mollify some popular organizations. Opposition groups often attempt to organize popular sectors and to win the support of extant popular organizations in their battles against dictators. Once elections are convoked, competing parties jockey to secure popular favor.

The tendency to understate the impact of common people and see politics as an exclusive elite affair has carried over to discussions of the new democracies in Latin America. Granted, most of these feckless democracies have failed to implement policies that safeguard popular interests. However, their failures do not imply that democratic politics is exclusively an elite affair, or even that the masses are absent in the current political scenarios in these countries.

Some analysts have overstated the extent to which "the people" are not interested in, or do not participate in, democratic politics. In a variety of ways, common people do participate in movements, institutions, and practices that either are controlled or simply do not exist under authoritarian governments. Democratic politics allows for more spaces of popular participation than many authors in the current literature suggest. Because relatively few citizens are well informed and because the decision-making process in democracies is largely restricted to elites, it can appear that democratic politics is almost exclusively an elite affair. However, elites must constantly vie for popular sympathies if they are to build successful political careers. Democratic politics is a system of interactions and accountability between rulers and ruled. One need not romanticize how effective accountability is to perceive that the position of the rulers depends on their ability to appeal to the majority (Dahl 1956: 124–151; Dahl 1961; Sartori 1987:86–130). This accountability of elites to the masses through elections is one of the characteristic features of democracy.

As Reis (1988) has argued, the nature and beliefs of the electorate affect what kinds of parties are viable. This is one of the many ways in which the beliefs of the masses affect the functioning of democracy. Citizen predilections are not infinitely protean, even though they are shaped by elite institutions. Of course, the interaction is mutual: the nature of political parties shapes the characteristics of the electorate, just as the electorate's predilections shape the parties.

Legitimacy and Democracy

Earlier I noted that declining legitimacy can help induce authoritarian governments to leave office. However, the explanatory value of the notion of legitimacy has been questioned by Adam Przeworski (1985:133–170; 1986). Przeworski juxtaposes two explanations of regime change from authoritarianism to democracy:

(1) The regime loses its legitimacy, and since no regime can last without legitimacy, it disintegrates.
(2) Conflicts within the ruling bloc cannot be reconciled, and some ruling factions decide to appeal to outside groups for support.

Przeworski prefers the second alternative. But the dichotomy between (1) and (2), between an erosion of legitimacy and the emergence of conflicts within the ruling bloc, may not be as sharp as Przeworski suggests. The way conflicts within the ruling bloc emerge and are handled ultimately cannot be divorced from the question of legitimacy. When a regime enjoys legitimacy, the problems that governments inevitably face are less likely to unleash unresolvable conflicts within the ruling bloc.

As Linz (1973) has observed, one of the fundamental dilemmas for contemporary authoritarian regimes in the west is that they lack legitimizing formulae. The defeat of the fascist countries in World War II led to an eclipse of ideologies and organizational models that could create long-term legitimacy for authoritarian regimes, at least in the West. This backdrop helps explain why Western authoritarian regimes have difficulty in sustaining themselves in power over a long period of time. If they enjoyed legitimacy, authoritarian regimes would be better able to face problems without internal schisms and defections.

My argument here supposes a point that Przeworski disputes: that legitimacy cannot be reduced to self-interest or to some other explanation. Before defending this viewpoint, I concede that regime stability cannot always be explained on the basis of legitimacy. As Przeworski notes, at least three other factors could explain regime stability:

(1) People are intimidated and coerced into obeying.
(2) People follow the rules out of self-interest.
(3) It does not occur to people that a different kind of regime could exist, so they passively assent.

In contrast to Przeworski, however, I believe that none of these three factors, or even all of them, can adequately explain regime stability. Following Weber (1978:31–38, 212–271), I believe that stability based solely on coercion, self-interest, or apathy/resignation is dubious in modern polities. Effective coercion requires cohesion within the repressive apparatus itself, and this cohesion is almost certain to erode if the legitimacy of authoritarian rule crumbles, for such crumbling inevitably reverberates within the coercive apparatus.

The self-interest explanation of obedience need not postulate that actors attempt to undermine a regime simply because their interests are not realized. The cost of attempting to subvert a regime when no other actors are doing so could explain why actors accept the outcomes when their interests are thwarted. Rational actors would join a conspiracy against democracy or an effort to mobilize against authoritarianism only if there were a reasonable chance of success. Otherwise, the costs of action would drastically outweigh the costs of acquiescence. But without the notion of legitimacy it is impossible to understand why the costs of attempting to undermine democracy are so high in consolidated democracies; because actors believe in the system, they are willing to make concessions to abide by the rules of the game. Similarly, when authoritarian regimes enjoy considerable support, it is more difficult to mobilize against them.

Where self-interest is the rationale for obedience, the stability of the political system rests heavily on payoffs, especially of a material nature. Przeworski is quick to recognize this fact (1985:133–169). Yet all political systems have periods when payoffs are low, and such periods do not necessarily undermine democratic institutions. The difference between consolidated democracies and democracies that falter is not the ability of the former to avert recessions so much as the acceptance by major political actors of low payoffs when recessions come. The cost of antidemocratic action is high only because other actors do not approve of it, regardless of their own objective situation.

Legitimacy is every bit as much the root of democratic stability as objective payoffs, and it is less dependent on economic payoffs than Przeworski or Lipset (1959) indicate.[5] As many Latin American cases evince, where elites and popular organizations subscribe to democracy primarily out of self-interest, democratic stability is precarious. Democracy's fundamental claim to legitimacy is not a substantive one (greater efficiency, equity, or growth), but rather a procedural one: guarantees of human rights, protection of minorities, government accountability, and the opportunity to get rid of rulers who lose their popular support. For this reason, democratic regimes can retain legitimacy even when they do not perform well economically (Linz and Stepan 1989). This observation is especially germane today in Latin America, where the new normative commitment to democracy and the fact that most of the military governments mishandled the economy have somewhat insulated democratic regimes from relying on economic performance to build legitimacy.

Finally, it is true that many people passively assent to a given mode of domination. But no political regime in the contemporary world can exist simply because of the inertia of the population. This is particularly the case of democracy, where the rulers need periodic electoral consecration to retain their positions of power. Moreover, where people passively assent because they cannot conceive of a different kind of regime, this very fact expresses a form of legitimacy.[6]

Przeworksi's critique of the notion of legitimacy supposes that the analysis of politics can be analyzed on the basis of (1) actors' preferences; (2) the distribution of resources; and (3) the rules that govern interaction. In his view, concepts such as legitimacy, identity, or political culture do not enrich analysis. With Pizzorno (1985), I would insist on the ongoing importance of such concepts. Actors bring baggage to the situations and contexts in which they fight for their interests. Depending on their identities, different actors in similar objective situations can respond in radically different ways (Sahlins 1976). Conversely, actors with very different objective situations can respond in similar ways if they have similar identities. Actors' preferences are not only bound by a set of preferences and objective conditions, but also mediated by subjective determinations, including their understanding of legitimacy.

The notion of legitimacy is easily plagued by a tautology: we can infer a problem of legitimacy ex post facto and then attribute a regime crisis to eroding legitimacy. But the concept is still useful heuristically, for it underscores the importance of how actors perceive the political regime and the relative autonomy of such perceptions vis-à-vis regime performance.

In brief, the theme of legitimacy remains fundamental to understanding democratic politics. Legitimacy does not need to be universal in the beginning stages if democracy is to succeed, but if a commitment to democracy does not emerge over time, democracy is in trouble. Where common citizens are not committed to democracy, they will be open to "disloyal opposition" leaders and groups, and such actors are often lethal. This is not to deny the problems in operationalizing the concept of legitimacy, but some concepts have heuristic value even though they cannot be neatly operationalized. Nor is this to reduce all explanations of regime change to arguments about legitimacy. Przeworski is right that a crisis of legitimacy is not sufficient to explain regime changes, though it may be necessary.

Three caveats are in order. First, legitimacy among the masses is more important in democratic regimes than in authoritarian ones.

Przeworski is right that some authoritarian regimes never enjoyed broad popular legitimacy, hence that decreasing support does not adequately explain regime changes from authoritarianism to democracy. If the military is the main pillar behind an authoritarian regime, as long as it remains united, the regime can withstand low levels of legitimacy in society. Second, in all political regimes, the legitimacy of actors who participate actively in politics is more important than the legitimacy of passive citizens (Dahl 1971; Lamounier 1979a; Linz 1978:21). This observation is especially relevant for authoritarian regimes. Finally, the notion of legitimacy should not be idealized. It does not imply that citizens actively participate in government or that they support a particular government. Rather, it suggests a broad acceptance of a political regime, above and beyond any particular government and set of substantive issues. Linz's statement (1978:18) is useful: "A legitimate government is one considered to be the least evil of the forms of government. Ultimately, democratic legitimacy is based on the belief that for that particular country at that particular historical juncture no other type of regime could assure a more successful pursuit of collective goals."

Democracy and Democrats

Recent democratic theory has focused mostly on behavior and less on values. In conjunction with the recent emphasis on elites and institutions, this shift has meant that elite behavior has been the primary focus of attention; even elite values are often seen as secondary. Theorists have consequently downplayed the importance of a normative commitment to democracy on the part of political elites.

Rustow (1970) synthesized this orientation. "Democracy, like any collective human action, is likely to stem from a large variety of mixed motives. . . . In so far as it is a genuine compromise it will seem second best to all major parties involved. . . . What matters at the decision stage is not what values the leaders hold dear in the abstract, but what concrete steps they are willing to take" (357). In other words, what matters is not that political elites have a normative commitment to democracy, but that they be willing to accept it as a compromise. Huntington (1984) and Karl (1986c) likewise argue that democracy has been an unintended consequence, and that political elites viewed democracy as a means of realizing other objectives.

This dismissal of the importance of a normative commitment

to democracy is questionable. Certainly there are cases where democracy emerged in part as an accident. In the United States, for example, the Founding Fathers foresaw neither the broad participation that emerged in the first half of the nineteenth century, nor a competitive party system. Even so, political elites were committed to the notion of free government; they simply did not foresee or intend the mechanisms that would make modern mass democracy possible. Moreover, conditions in the early democratizing nations are not the same as those in later cases. In Latin America, democracy has worked only where political elites saw it as a best solution, not as an instrumental means of securing some of their interests. Contrary to the argument that democracy has generally been an unintended consequence, it has rather resulted from the purposeful efforts of people who have devoted much of their lives to the democratic cause (Levine 1988).

Many of the particulars of a democracy may represent a second-best compromise, but in Latin America democracy has not succeeded unless political elites were committed to it as a first choice of regime type. Indeed, many particulars necessarily represent a second-best choice for a wide range of actors, for compromise about particulars is the stuff democracy is made of. Negotiations about electoral systems, labor legislation, responsibilities of the various branches of government, etc., may require that all sides compromise. But compromise on these issues does not imply that democracy itself is viewed as a second-best solution.

I am not suggesting that all political actors must be committed to democracy if it is to thrive. In many cases, the actors who supported authoritarian rule remain equivocal at best about democracy as a form of government. For these actors, democracy itself may be a second-best solution, a means of institutionalizing ways of resolving conflict so that they can cut their losses. In the early phases of a new democracy, it is more feasible to induce these actors to abide by the democratic rules out of self-interest, by creating a high cost for antisystem action, than to transform their values. Some powerful actors, including business elites, may have instrumental attitudes towards democracy even in well established democracies. On the other hand, as I argued earlier, democracy without legitimacy tends to be unstable, for all political systems experience periods when payoffs are low. This means that over the medium term, it is important to induce most actors to believe in democratic rules.

Moreover, while most new democracies can withstand some antisystem actors, if the political elites who are running the government and who led the main opposition parties are ambivalent about democracy, prospects for democracy are dim (Dahl 1971). Conversely, a firm commitment to democracy on the part of the political elite can help overcome adverse conditions in constructing democracy (Lijphart 1977). Arguably the outstanding distinctive feature that explains why the oldest democracies in Latin America are found in Costa Rica, Venezuela, and Colombia is the commitment of political elites to establishing and maintaining a polyarchy (Hartlyn 1988; Levine 1973; Peeler 1985). In all three countries, after periods of bitter fighting, political elites realized that for survival they needed to compromise and construct an institutional system that placed preserving democracy above immediate partisan objectives. They have continuously reaffirmed this commitment to preserving democracy, arguably even at the expense of neglecting important problems. This elite commitment and the resulting institutional arrangements made democracy possible despite formidable obstacles. Inequalities are not noticeably less pronounced in these countries than in the rest of Latin America (though Costa Rica is among the least inegalitarian nations of Latin America), nor were standards of living vastly higher than the Latin American average when democracy was inaugurated. Political elites wanted to construct a stable democracy and devised institutions that made possible their goal.

Although commitment to democracy is especially critical for the political elite, common people and especially leaders of popular groups may also care more about preserving democracy than some of the literature suggests. Caring about this issue, of course, may not always lead to an effective ability to contribute to democratic consolidation. But a society in which there is limited support for democracy does not bode very well for this form of government. Conversely, where popular leaders are committed to democracy and enjoy broad legitimacy in their organizations and movements, prospects for democracy are better.

Vivid analyses of political elites and actors who were not committed to democracy explain part of the appeal of the contributions by Cavarozzi (1983; 1986), O'Donnell (1982), Ollier (1986), and Viola (1982) on Argentina, and by Malloy and Gamarra (1987) on Bolivia. To the extent that groups and parties fought for democracy, it was primarily for instrumental reasons, i.e., to further objectives that had nothing to do with democracy. Democracy does not work under these conditions, for no political regime can satisfy a majority of the actors all the time.

While commitment of political elites and parties to democracy is a necessary condition if democracy is to thrive in the medium term, it is not a sufficient condition for stable democracy. Political elites must create institutions that represent interests in society and exercise moderating power over those interests. Societal polarization makes this process more difficult; moderation does not depend exclusively on the will and skill of political elites. Nevertheless, commitment to democracy helps make possible the creation of effective democratic institutions, and it also generates a legitimacy that can help new democracies withstand less-than-excellent policy performances.

Even though the methodological problems in studying legitimacy are greater than those in examining behavior, this does not mean that we can neglect the former. The way people, classes, institutions, movements, and state agencies act cannot be inferred from their "objective" circumstances. Notions of what constitutes legitimate political authority and self-interest vary somewhat independently of class and other "objective" factors, and in turn affect the identities of political actors. Political action is contextual and strategic, but it also reflects the ideologies, values, and perceptions of actors.

These abstract arguments about the importance of a normative commitment to democracy are relevant in analyzing contemporary South America. One of the few auspicious factors in the current situation has to do with a greater commitment to democracy than ever before in South American history. Politicians, intellectuals, Church leaders, and leaders of social movements are more interested in preserving democracy than they ever have been (Coutinho 1980; Lamounier 1979b; O'Donnell 1986; Packenham 1986; Weffort 1984). Economic conditions are dismal, and if they were determining factors, few of the new democracies would have survived this long.

Ideology, values, and expectations affect how citizens evaluate public policy performance. Given exaggerated expectations and demands, a high growth rate coupled with reformist initiatives may not suffice; consider the reactions to Frei in Chile (1964–70) and Illia in Argentina (1963–66). The ascendency of bureaucratic-authoritarian regimes coincided with a prolonged period of rapid growth in Latin

America, though as Hirschman (1987) notes, only recently have some
of the achievements of the 1960–75 period been recognized. Economic problems recurred despite rapid growth, but this is nothing
specific to Latin America, nor do these problems adequately explain
the demise of democracy (Hirschman 1979; Serra 1979). On the other
hand, most of South America is currently experiencing what Whitehead (1985) aptly called a revolution of falling expectations. Democracy can withstand economic performances far worse than those that
generated widespread discontent two decades ago. Indeed, democracy in Southern Europe was consolidated in the context of struggling economies.

This is one of the great – and tragic – paradoxes in Latin America as we begin the last decade of the twentieth century: the period
of most dismal economic results the region has experienced this century has also been the most democratic decade ever. Horrendous
inflation rates, economies that are moving backwards, socially regressive policies, and greater misery have accompanied the dawning
of democracy in most countries. With the exception of Chile and
Uruguay, democratic governments have not only failed to amelio-
rate these problems, they have actually exacerbated them. This is
not to suggest that democracy will thrive if public policy performance continues to be as dismal as it has been in most countries.
It is rather to underscore the importance of subjective evaluations
and ideologies as an intermediating factor between policy performance and public response to that performance, in general, and of
the new commitment to democracy, in particular.

Democracy and Uncertainty

One of the interesting issues in the literature is the connection
between democracy and uncertainty. Przeworski's excellent contributions have argued that uncertainty is a salient characteristic of
democracy.

> The process of establishing a democracy is a process of institu-
> tionalizing uncertainty, of subjecting all interests to uncertainty.
> In an authoritarian regime, some groups, typically the armed
> forces, have the capacity of intervening whenever the result of
> a conflict is contrary to their program or their interests. . . . In
> a democracy, no group is able to intervene when outcomes of
> conflicts violate their self-perceived interests. Democracy means

that all groups must subject their interests to uncertainty. (1986: 58; see also 1988)

To argue that uncertainty is a distinctive feature of democracy, Przeworski needs to establish not only that the outcomes of conflicts in democracy must be uncertain but also that the outcomes of conflicts in democracy must be, in general, *more* uncertain than in other political regimes. The sentences quoted above evince his awareness of this dual exigency, but Przeworski fails to muster sufficient support to sustain this second point. He overstates the uncertainty of democratic regimes and overdraws the contrast to authoritarian regimes.

Przeworski bases his argument about uncertainty on the fact that democracies allow for alternation in power, and that new governments may change decisions of previous ones. Consequently, "It is within the nature of democracy that no one's interests can be guaranteed: in principle, workers endowed with universal franchise can even vote to nationalize the privately owned means of production, to dissolve the armed forces, and so on" (1986:59). However, even if workers did vote to nationalize the means of production, this fact in itself would have no legal effect (though it might have profound political repercussions) in democratic regimes, because it is not generally workers who make this kind of decision, but rather executives and legislatures functioning in well-defined (and sometimes even seemingly stultified) institutional and legal structures. Workers help elect those who decide, but modern mass democracy is representative democracy, not direct democracy.

Uncertainty in representative democracies is limited by a complex set of individual and institutional guarantees. Democracy necessarily (definitionally) involves protection of minority rights, which means that government decisions must observe some limits. When these limits are infringed upon, we no longer have democracy (Sartori 1987:21-38). The range of possible outcomes is therefore not unlimited or completely uncertain; rather, respect for minority rights can entail complex constitutional and political engineering that has major consequences in structuring political life and in limiting the range of possible outcomes. The mechanisms found in consociational democracies to ensure the rights of minority groups are the most evident example (Lijphart 1977). These mechanisms exist precisely to ensure a high level of certainty on key issues.

Almost all democracies have written constitutions (Israel, the

United Kingdom, and New Zealand are exceptions), and constitutions deliberately reduce uncertainty to promote mutual security. In most democracies, changing constitutions is a difficult matter that requires more than a temporary majority. It often requires not one but several majorities (for example, both chambers of a bicameral national legislature and ratification by state assemblies). Moreover, constitutional changes often require qualified majorities, i.e., a specified percentage greater than an absolute majority. In brief, it takes more than a temporary majority to change some rules of the game. The difficulty of changing constitutions in consolidated democracies helps explain why major constitutional change does not occur with great frequency.

Of course, some rules are easier to change than those that are found in constitutions. Even so, it often takes more than one simple majority. Moreover, uncertainty in consolidated democracies is reduced by the fact that a majority of professional politicians have generally done well with the current rules. Constitutions have a significant impact on the logic of actors in consolidated democracies: actors structure their behavior according to the rules of the game, and over time they form their political identities in relation to those rules. In short, formalization of the rules of the game, the difficulties of changing some of the most important rules once they have been established, and the tendency of the strongest parties to stick to rules that have done them well mean that it takes more than a majority to overturn some past decisions, that powerful actors usually have a stake in avoiding such changes, and that uncertainty is not so ubiquitous as Przeworski indicates.

Przeworski's argument on uncertainty focuses strictly on substantive matters, and individual rights, protection of minorities, and other constitutional arrangements pertain to procedural questions. But a radical separation between substantive and procedural issues does not obtain in practice. Procedural formats shape what substantive outcomes are possible, hence limiting uncertainty and enhancing security. For example, allowing minority groups to have veto power over certain legislative matters is a procedural issue, but it has powerful substantive implications that limit uncertainty for the minority group.

There is another quite different sense in which policy agendas and therefore uncertainty are limited in democratic politics. As recent experiences in the new democracies of Latin America show, two actors have veto power over crucial items on the agenda. Perhaps most important, the new democracies face limits in terms of military strategy. They cannot abolish the militaries or drastically attack the military institution, even if that is what the majority (of elected representatives, of the people, or both) wants. Such efforts would lead to a military attack on the democracy, and there is little doubt as to which side would win.

Capitalists also retain some veto power because in the absence of certain broad guarantees, they can sabotage democracy. At a minimum, these guarantees include the preservation of the capitalist system and the continuing opportunity to make profit. Where such guarantees do not exist, capitalists can undermine the economy by withdrawing investment, engaging in massive speculation and capital flight, etc. As Przeworski writes elsewhere (1985:138), "Capitalism is a form of social organization in which the entire society is dependent upon actions of capitalists." This fact enhances capitalists' political power (Przeworski 1988).

Where capitalists act to undermine democracy, its prospects are dim. This is true not so much because capitalists have enormous power of persuasion as because of their capacity to disrupt the economy. Well established democracies can withstand lengthy economic recessions, but new democracies are less likely to be able to do so when recessions are coupled with speculative behavior, high rates of inflation, and the panoply of other problems that beset most Latin American nations.

Przeworski can counter that where an actor holds veto power, we are not really dealing with a democratic government, or at least not a democratic regime. Where an actor's veto power is extensive, this argument is correct. But my claim here is that in all new democracies, the military and capitalists can torpedo some decisions. They can not eliminate uncertainty of outcomes, but they can limit it.

Przeworski is right that some groups can avoid undesirable outcomes in authoritarian regimes, but this point, too, can be overstated. As Stepan's works show, even military governments do things that the military-as-institution does not like. The military-as-institution may act against a particular measure, but it does not always win.

Capitalists and conservative middle-class actors often support coups in the name of order, stability, and certainty. But the certainty of authoritarian rule proves more elusive than they imagine in the praetorian pre-coup moments. Military governments often prove far less reliable than civilian groups had imagined — which, as Kaufman suggests, is one of the reasons the initial coup coalition eventually begins to disintegrate. This is so not only because policy outcomes sometimes are very different from what their formulators hoped would be the case, but also because the highly closed nature of the decision making process can produce erratic results. Decision making in authoritarian regimes is less institutionalized and hence in an important sense more uncertain than in democratic regimes. This lower degree of institutionalization of the decision making process frequently has a spillover effect on outcomes, which are often more erratic and every bit as uncertain as in democratic regimes. As Conaghan suggests in her chapter in this volume, this is one of the reasons why capitalists in several Latin American countries supported a return to democracy.

Authoritarian regimes sometimes manipulate this element of uncertainty and unpredictability to instill fear and produce demobilization. Przeworski emphasizes the institutionalized character of democratic regimes, but he suggests a radical gulf between a high degree of regularity in procedures and a low degree of certainty in outcomes. Yet the gulf between procedure and outcome is not that great; in many authoritarian regimes, the lack of institutionalization of procedures can result in greater, not less, uncertainty in outcomes for most actors.

Although Przeworski's argument about uncertainty has some questionable implications, it is correct in one meaningful sense. The highest ranking leaders of an authoritarian regime generally face fewer obstacles in decreeing policies than their counterparts of a democratic government. This situation engenders greater certainty of one kind (i.e., the ability of the highest leaders to ensure that they will be able to implement their policies), but it creates uncertainty of other kinds (e.g., arbitrary decision making). Moreover, if we analyze the implementation side of policies, the differences between authoritarian and democratic governments in establishing certainty are less dramatic.

On first impression, Przeworski's emphasis on uncertainty is reproduced by O'Donnell and Schmitter (1986). O'Donnell and Schmitter reiterate throughout the "extraordinary uncertainty of the transition, with its numerous surprises and difficult dilemmas" (p. 3). Later, however, they explicitly disagree (p. 67) with Przeworski's emphasis on uncertainty as a central distinguishing characteristic of democracy.[7] To characterize the transition period as one of considerable uncertainty is different from arguing that uncertainty is a central feature of democratic regimes, for in the former case the very nature of the regime is undergoing redefinition, while in the latter it is well institutionalized. During democratic transitions, the basic rules of the political game are in constant flux; often actors do not know what the rules are. For this reason, it is more appropriate to characterize transition periods than stable democracies as being marked by uncertainty.

Different Modes of Democratic Transitions

To what extent do transitions follow a modal pattern, as opposed to several different patterns? Important common points can be found in most contemporary transitions, but transitions differ markedly in other ways. At the same time, it is unappealing to focus only on the peculiarities of each individual case. Rather, I would call for a multiple strategy of awareness of general dynamics and problems, as well as empirical analysis of concrete cases. But there is a bridge between the most general reflections and the most specific ones: comparative analysis. Without neglecting general tendencies and country level specificities, it is essential to put country studies in comparative perspective and, conversely, to differentiate among kinds of transitions in more general reflections. Both tasks require thinking about the main modes of contemporary transitions.[8] Despite some helpful efforts, this problem has not been wholly resolved. In this section, I first look at how this issue has been addressed in the literature, then present a skeletal outline of a classification of transitions that I have found useful.

O'Donnell and Schmitter do not explicitly address this question at length, but their analysis generally differentiates between kinds of transitions. They correctly argue that the dynamics of transitions are very different in cases of "successful" as opposed to "unsuccessful" authoritarian regimes. Elsewhere, O'Donnell (1989) has extended this analysis in fruitful ways. At times, however, they make general affirmations that appropriately characterize some transitions but that do not apply to others. For example, the assertion that "political democracies are usually brought down by conspiracies involving few actors" is debatable. In Chile in 1973 and Brazil in 1964, mass mobilizations against democratic governments did occur.

O'Donnell and Schmitter also argue that a cycle of mobilization accompanies transitions. In early phases, the opposition is quiescent because of the massive costs of opposing authoritarian rule. But over time, liberalization enables the opposition to mobilize, and a "resurrection of civil society" takes place. Finally, after the transition follows a process of demobilization with a return to democratic normalcy. Again, however, this cycle depends on the kind of transition and on specific cases. In Argentina, in 1982–83 there was no massive mobilization following the military's bellicose adventure. Mobilization increased notably after elections were already announced, hence, after a transition was all but certain. O'Donnell and Schmitter state that "the popular upsurge during the transition is by no means a constant" (p. 54), but some of the time they write as if it were. The "enormous backlog of anger and conflict [that] accumulates during these authoritarian regimes" (p. 53) cannot be generalized. There was no such widespread collective anger toward the Franco regime (McDonough et al. 1981; López-Pintor 1987). On the other hand, not all transitions are followed by demobilization, as Argentina between 1973 and 1976 convincingly showed (Viola 1982).

Baloyra's (1987b) model of transitions is less attuned to differences among cases. He argues that regime transition is begun by the deterioration of the authoritarian government, wrongly assuming that deterioration is always a condition for initiating the process of extrication. In fact, some authoritarian regimes begin a process of liberalization at a moment of strength rather than from a position of weakness. The authoritarian regimes in Brazil, Spain, and possibly Ecuador are examples. Baloyra argues that "a collapse of the incumbent government followed by a marked discontinuity in the nature of the regime" is a necessary condition for regime transition (p. 10). This obscures crucial differences in processes of democratic transition, as well as flying in the face of empirical evidence. Among the recent transitions in Latin America, only in Argentina can we speak of regime breakdown. The other authoritarian regimes suffered internal erosion (varying in magnitude from one case to the next), but none of them collapsed.

Baloyra's typology distinguished among four patterns of democratic transitions: early-internal, delayed-external, delayed-internal, and late-external. In addition to being somewhat cumbersome, these terms are neither self-explanatory nor well explained. Baloyra says that the first two patterns are difficult to distinguish (p. 17), which means that regime transitions as radically different as those in Spain and Argentina (1982–83) are grouped close to one another. He groups into the same category transitions that differ in fundamental regards, such as those in Ecuador and Portugal; the former transition was initiated by the authoritarian regime, and the latter only after a collapse of the authoritarian regime.

Morlino's typology (1987) gets us no farther. He proposes comparing democratic transitions on the basis of nine variables, ranging from the duration of the transition to the level of continuity in administrative and judiciary positions between the authoritarian and democratic periods. The problem is that even if we measure these dimensions in a simplified polar model (high vs. low) with two possible rankings, we would still get 512 feasible kinds of transitions. To be useful, a typology must be more parsimonious.

Stepan's "Paths toward Redemocratization" (1986) is an ambitious attempt to conceptualize the major modes of redemocratization. Notwithstanding the chapter's comparative breadth and interesting arguments, it does not wholly succeed. The problems begin with the notion of redemocratization, which is used excessively loosely. The word redemocratization can obscure a key difference in current political processes in Latin America: some countries really are undergoing a process of redemocratization, while others are for the first time having a reasonably sustained experience of polyarchy. Uruguay and Chile have democratic institutions that are far more solid than those of any other country that has recently undergone a transition, and this difference stems largely from the fact that they are Latin America's outstanding examples of redemocratization (Gillespie 1986; González 1988).

Stepan establishes eight (or ten, depending on how we count) paths toward redemocratization. In the first three, war and conquest play a decisive part: 1) internal restoration after external reconquest; 2) internal reformulation; 3) externally monitored installation. In the second broad category, authoritarian elites themselves initiate the move toward democratization. Stepan subdivides this category into three, but still considers it as only one path. Why these subdivisions are not considered distinct paths, as is the case with the subdivisions of redemocratization through war and conquest or through society-led transitions, is not apparent. One of the three categories, redemocratization initiated by military as government, is apparently a null set. The final four paths are all led by opposition forces: transitions caused by social upheavals, party-pact induced transitions, an organized violent revolt coordinated by democratic parties, and a Marxist-led revolution. Two of these four paths (the first and last) are null sets, and the penultimate has only one historic case — Costa Rica. Stepan indicates that most empirical cases fit into more than one path of democratization.

This panoply of paths to democracy usefully draws attention to the variety of ways in which democracies can be instituted. Nevertheless, the fact that there are so many null sets helps point to a problem: we are not consistently dealing with paths to democratization or kinds of transitions, but rather in some cases with a categorization of what forces lead different transitions. The reason why few transitions fit well into the categories is that most transitions have an interactive character. They are based on negotiations, dialogues, bluffing, and power plays among different regime and opposition forces, rather than led by a particular actor from beginning to end. This point is generally missing from Stepan's typology, though his excellent book (1988) on the military in processes of democratization in Brazil and the Southern Cone insists on it. He shows how intrastate conflicts have induced military leaders to seek support in civil society as a means of furthering their own project.

Share (1987) develops a fourfold typology of transitions to democracy, derived by focusing on two dimensions. "First, is the democratic transition brought about with the participation or consent of leaders of the authoritarian regime, or does it transpire without such participation or consent?" (529). The former transitions are termed consensual; the latter, nonconsensual. Second, "does the transition to democracy occur gradually, transcending a single generation of political leaders, or is it a relatively rapid phenomenon?" (530). These two dimensions produce the following two-by-two matrix:

Figure 1

Democratization Led by or against Authoritarian Regime

		By Regime Leaders	**Against Regime**
Pace of Democratization	Gradual	Incremental democratization	Transition through revolutionary struggle
	Rapid	Transition through transaction	Transition through rupture

Following Dahl (1971), Share notes that incremental consensual democratization — the pattern followed by the early democratic nations — is increasingly implausible in the contemporary world. Among other reasons, this is because in later processes of democratization, demands for mass participation emerge simultaneously with greater competition in the political system. There are no cases of a gradual transition against the leaders of an authoritarian or oligarchic regime, so the category of "transition through protracted revolutionary struggle" is a null set. This means that only two remaining categories describe contemporary transitions: transition through rupture and transition through transaction. At this point, Share's typology comes close to distinctions made by O'Donnell 1989 (transition by collapse versus transition by transaction); Linz 1981 (ruptura by golpe versus reforma pactada); and Martins 1986 (continuous versus discontinuous transitions).

I do not radically disagree with Share's typology or these other distinctions, and indeed think they are on the right track. But where Stepan's typology may be insufficiently parsimonious, Share's is excessively parsimonious. Few of the current transitions in Latin America can be described as cases of transition through transaction *or* transition through rupture. The Brazilian case most closely approximates the model of transition through transaction, but the regime erosion between 1982–85 led it to deviate from the paradigmatic Spanish case. The Argentine transitions of 1971–73 and 1982–83 both approximate the category of transitions through rupture, but the recent transitions in Peru, Uruguay, Ecuador, and the Dominican Republic do not fit either category well. The transitions in Peru and Uruguay were negotiated, and the outgoing authoritarian regimes were able to impose some basic rules over the transitions. This excludes them from the category of transitions through regime defeat. Yet neither of these military governments influenced or controlled the transition process as strongly as the Spanish or Brazilian regimes, nor were they capable of organizing a political party that could compete in democratic elections. For these reasons, it would be misleading to classify the transitions in Peru or Uruguay in the same category as the Spanish or Brazilian transitions. Share is aware of this and seems to group the Peruvian and Uruguayan transitions in the category of "ruptures," but this is equally inappropriate. Moreover, doing so would imply that almost every single contemporary transition would be lumped together, while three of the four ideal types would have few, if any, contemporary empirical references. This situation calls attention to the need for an intermediate category between transitions through transaction and transitions through rupture.

In comparing recent transitions in Latin America and Southern Europe, I have worked with a threefold typology (see Mainwaring and Viola 1985; Mainwaring and Share 1986). A transition through regime defeat takes place when a major defeat of an authoritarian regime, such as those suffered by Argentina in 1982–83, Portugal in 1975, and Greece in 1974, leads to the collapse of authoritarianism and the inauguration of a democratic government.[9] Just as democratic governments face serious crises, respond inadequately to challenges, and sometimes break down, so do authoritarian governments. The processes by which they break down are varied, and such breakdowns may lead to a different form of authoritarian regime rather than a democracy. In some cases, however, regime elites hold elections and leave office as one of the ways of dealing with breakdown. Here the authoritarian leaders have little choice; they must relinquish office, given severe internal schisms and delegitimation.

At the other end of the spectrum, in a transition through transaction, the authoritarian government initiates the process of liberalization and remains a decisive actor throughout the transition. It chooses to promote measures that eventually lead to democratization. This does not imply that the opposition plays an insignificant role in the process or that the government controls the entire process. In the middle is transition through extrication; an authoritarian government is weakened, but not as thoroughly as in a transition by defeat. It is able to negotiate crucial features of the transition, though in a position of less strength than in cases of transition through transaction.

Figure 2 outlines these three possibilities.

This classification indicates differential positions of power in the negotiations and interactions between regime and opposition, underscoring decisive differences in how much authoritarian regimes influence the transition process. The threefold categorization developed out of my conviction that twofold typologies did not do justice to the intermediary category of transitions through extrication. As noted above, neither the category of transition through transaction, nor that of transition through rupture, captures the reality of most recent transitions in Latin America. Of course, one could object that

Figure 2

**Paths from Liberalization to Democratization:
A Classification of Contemporary Transitions to Democracy**

I. Transition through Transaction: The authoritarian regime chooses to continue opening the political system because:

    A. The costs of staying in power increase and/or the costs of liberalizing decrease

        1. The costs of staying in power increase because of:
            a) a succession crisis
            b) declining military cohesion
            c) declining legitimacy

        2. The costs of democratizing decrease because of:
            a) elimination of perceived threat
            b) stability of socioeconomic order

    B. The initial idea was to intervene in a crisis situation and restore democracy after a short interlude

II. Transition through Extrication: The authoritarian regime is weakened, but remains strong enough to dictate important terms of the transition

III. Transition through Regime Defeat: The authoritarian regime collapses

all transitions are different and that ideal types never do justice to reality. But this kind of objection leads to vacuous empiricism, for it denies all possibility of categorization. Alternatively, one could claim that three categories are still too few — but at a certain point, the inevitable tradeoff between parsimony and completeness tips in the other direction.

Transitions through transaction are especially noteworthy because of the element of choice by government leaders. It seems paradoxical that an authoritarian government would pursue policies that could lead to its own extinction, but some regime leaders may perceive benefits in doing so (Mainwaring and Share 1986; Stepan 1988). The conscious choice of a government to promote democratization can be understood in terms of the costs and benefits of authoritarian rule. As Dahl (1971:15) put it, "The more the costs of suppression exceed the costs of toleration, the greater the chance for a competitive regime." Or to state it differently, the perceived costs of staying in power increase and/or the perceived costs of undertaking democratization decrease.

The perceived costs of staying in power might increase for three principal reasons (Mainwaring and Share 1986). A succession crisis can unleash grave difficulties for an authoritarian regime. Succession rules are clearly spelled out in democratic regimes, but this is usually not the case in authoritarian regimes. This fact makes succession a more difficult problem for authoritarian regimes to face. In addition, most authoritarian regimes are "top-heavy" in the decision making process; the president and a few close associates make most of the weighty decisions. The histories of many authoritarian regimes are integrally connected to a single personality, who often is the only person who can maintain the authoritarian coalition intact. This may be because of his/her particular political skills, or because no one else has the trust of the major actors who support the authoritarian coalition, or both. Leadership succession tends to be most complicated in cases where a single person has ruled for a long time and enjoys charismatic legitimacy among some actors. But almost without exception, succession poses serious problems for authoritarian regimes. It is not rare for authoritarian regimes to collapse when a ruler dies or appears likely to die in the immediate future. Alternatively, the difficulties created by succession may lead new incumbents to decide that remaining in power is likely to be too costly.

Military regimes generally face tensions that can lead them to withdraw from office. In particular, there is invariably tension between the military as government and the military as institution. The military as institution strives to remain above politics and to keep intact the professionalism and unity of the armed forces. The military as government, conversely, involves the military in politics, albeit to varying degrees. Political differences within the military as government or between it and the military as institution can cause troublesome divisions within the armed forces. Military leaders may opt for leaving office as a means of reducing these divisions.

Finally, declining legitimacy increases the costs of staying in power. In the post–World War II era, Western authoritarian regimes have lacked a stable legitimizing formula. It is common for authoritarian regimes to justify their actions in the name of furthering some democratic cause. This justification may be plausible to some sectors of the nation, and it may help win legitimacy for a limited period of time. But appealing to safeguarding democracy is a two-edged sword for authoritarian governments, for their very appeals eventually call attention to the hiatus between their discourse and their practice.

Most authoritarian governments initially seek a kind of "negative legitimacy": they are against chaos, corruption, eroding moral values, inflation, and communism. In praetorian moments, such appeals can have considerable success, for most citizens value political stability. Yet negative legitimacy formulae are almost inherently unstable in the contemporary Western world. If a government "restores order," the problems that legitimated military intervention no longer exist. If it fails to restore order, its inability to deal with the "threats" to the nation can suggest that it is no more effective than the civilian government that preceded it. Garretón (1986) termed this initial phase a "reactive" period and noted the unstable bases of such appeals.

The costs of democratization for an authoritarian regime can decrease for two main reasons. First and most important, if the regime has defeated the "subversive" threat that challenged the dominant order, reestablishing a more open political system seems less threatening. In many South American cases, the military wiped out guerrilla organizations, thereby eliminating the biggest "enemy." In most cases, the left that survived began to eschew violent revolution as an ideal, so the prospect of revolutionary upheaval became dim. Second, if in addition the military has managed some economic successes, the prospect of economic chaos seems remote, especially if the economy has done well over a period of time.

A special case of regimes that initiate political liberalization deserves separate mention. Sometimes coups have responded to an immediate sense of threat, and military leaders actively plan to return power to civilians within a delimited period of time. This is the "moderating pattern" of which Stepan (1971) wrote; it has been common in Brazil. These military governments never seriously entertain the possibility of staying in power for a long time.

Many authoritarian rulers perceive compelling advantages in relinquishing power and may hope that they can reproduce the Spanish or Brazilian path. In most cases, this hope is an illusion because this kind of transition requires conditions that few authoritarian regimes meet (Mainwaring and Share 1986; Share 1987). In particular, in order to effect a transition through transaction, an authoritarian regime must have a high level of support in society. Ironically, however, when authoritarian governments have considerable support they generally resist making changes. Most authoritarian governments undertake changes only in response to crises, when controlling the major contours of a transition is extremely difficult given conspicuous defections from the regime and a bolstering of the opposition.

Socioeconomic Conditions, Political Factors, and Democracy

Social scientists have long debated the conditions that facilitate democracy. Here I address only one facet of this debate: the relative importance of socioeconomic ("structural") conditions and of political factors in the strict sense. Arguably the most important dividing line in contemporary work on democracy is between those who see it primarily as a result of propitious economic, social, or cultural conditions, and those who see it primarily as a result of political institutions, processes, and leadership.

In the 1950s and 1960s, the dominant trend in political science was to emphasize the socioeconomic, structural, or cultural requisites of democracy. These approaches have subsequently been criticized (for example, Barry 1978:47–98), and in the past two decades, political science has generally emphasized the autonomy of political factors more than it did in the 1950s and 1960s. Among Latin Americanists, this change toward greater focus on political variables came about somewhat later. In the second half of the 1960s and first half of the 1970s, the dependency and the bureaucratic-authoritarian paradigms were prominent; both saw politics primarily as derivative, i.e., they saw politics as primarily determined by the socioeconomic system and by international variables. Both paradigms have been widely criticized, in part *because* they tended to see politics as derivative.

Increasingly, social scientists who study Latin America have emphasized the autonomy of political factors. Democracy has been seen more as a product of political elites and arrangements, electoral and party systems, than of a level of modernization, a mode of interaction with the international system, or a form of social structure. Only the naive would argue that these latter factors are insignificant, but the emphasis has shifted somewhat. González (1988), Lamounier (1979b), Levine (1973), Linz (1973), Santos (1986), A. Valenzuela (1985), and A. Valenzuela and J.S. Valenzuela (1983), among others, have contributed to this redefinition of the field. There has been a revival of institutionalism in the study of Latin American politics,[10] just as there has been in political science in general (March and Olsen 1984).

Where does the present literature on democratic transitions fit in? The dominant trend is toward greater emphasis on the autonomy of politics with respect to social structure and class. Several authors in the O'Donnell, Schmitter, and Whitehead volume were leading contributors to the earlier dependency and bureaucratic-authoritarian paradigms: Fernando Henrique Cardoso, Julio Cotler, Luciano Martins, O'Donnell himself. All of them have reformulated their understanding of democracy somewhat over the years and emphasize the automony of politics more than they did in years past.

Among recent works that have underscored socioeconomic factors that make democracy possible, those of Karl (1986a) and Seligson (1987a and 1987b) are representative. Karl's well-crafted piece seeks to establish a balance between socioeconomic and political factors, but it probably overstates the extent to which Venezuelan democracy was dependent on petroleum revenue. Mexico benefitted from enormous oil wealth in the 1970s, but did not evolve into a democratic polity. Only later, with the economy in shambles, did real political competition emerge. Argentina has long met some basic structural conditions generally conducive to democracy, but has not managed to create a stable democracy. Finally, Venezuelan democracy withstood a severe and protracted economic crisis in the 1980s. Karl is not oblivious to these facts but assigns greater weight to oil's importance than I would. Several works by Levine (1973, 1978, 1989) provide an alternative explanation of democracy in Venezuela, focusing more on the attitudes and behavior of political elites and parties. Levine recognizes the importance of oil in Venezuelan politics, but assigns it a less decisive role than Karl does. Karl (1986a) criticized Levine's book (1973) for understating the importance of oil in the construction of Venezuelan democracy; Levine's recent article (1989) pays more attention to oil than his book did.

Seligson's two chapters in *Authoritarians and Democrats* argue that the rapid economic growth much of Latin America experienced in the 1960s and 1970s helps explain why the 1980s have been a decade of democracy. Essentially following Lipset (1959), Seligson affirms that a minimal level of economic development is a necessary but not sufficient condition for democracy. Operationally, he focuses on two measures that indicate a crucial threshold below which democracy does not work: a per capita income of $250 in 1957 dollars and a literary rate of 50 percent.

The high correlation between level of economic development and democracy has been noted by many authors (Lipset 1959; Dahl 1971; Bollen 1979; Huntington 1984) and is beyond dispute. Nevertheless, the manner in which Seligson formulates his arguments is debatable. Despite the strong correlation between per capita GNP or literacy and democracy, the case of India suggests that there is no *necessary* minimal threshold. Conversely, the fact that three of the countries with the highest literacy rates and GNPs per capita in Latin America — Argentina, Chile, and Uruguay — suffered authoritarian involutions in the 1960s and 1970s is troublesome for his argument. Seligson does not claim that economic development and literacy are sufficient conditions for democracy, but in Latin America the fit between GNP or literacy and democracy is weak. This weak correlation prompted O'Donnell's formulation (1973) that at a certain stage in industrialization, the more developed countries might be subject to greater pressures toward authoritarianism than the intermediate ones. O'Donnell's book has been criticized on other scores, (see Cammack 1985; Collier 1979; Linz 1975; Remmer and Merkx 1982), but his argument about the weak correlation between modernization and democracy in Latin America has endured. Coulter (1975) showed that on a global level, this correlation was strong, but that in Latin America it did not exist. Finally, Seligson's own data (Figure 8.5) contradict his assertion that Central America has reached the minimal threshold of a per capita income of $250 in 1957 dollars that is allegedly necessary for democracy.[11] Today, only Guatemala and Costa Rica are above the threshold; with the protracted wars, both El Salvador and Nicaragua have slipped below it.

The level of aggregate development is an important factor in supporting democracy, but it is only one of several such factors. The sequence of economic development also appears to matter,[12] as do degrees of inequality (see Dahl 1971 and Stephens 1987). Political arrangements (the party system, the electoral regime, a presidential or parliamentary system) can have a decisive impact on prospects for democracy (González 1988; Linz 1985; A. Valenzuela 1985). Lijphart (1984) makes apparent that no single institutional arrangement is necessary for democracy, but it still seems plausible that some arrangements are more conducive than others. In a different vein, Sartori (1976) calls attention to the crucial importance of party systems in the functioning of democracy. Levine (1973), Rustow (1955 and 1970), Dahl (1971) and Linz (1978) have underscored the fundamental weight of elite values and/or behavior in the consolidation of democratic regimes, a point I discussed earlier. Hartlyn (1988) emphasized elite pacts in this same process.

This is not to argue that socioeconomic conditions are not important in assessing prospects for democracy; there is massive evidence that they are. Unfortunately, the best explanations of what makes democracy work are not very parsimonious. Socioeconomic conditions, political arrangements and institutions, and cultural patterns and ideas all weigh in making democracy viable.[13] This is not to make the vapid argument that everything matters; such a perspective leads nowhere. Dahl's *Polyarchy* (1971) exemplifies a clear formulation, with reasonably parsimonious yet not simplistic explanations. This is what we should strive for.

The Methodology of Studying Democratic Transitions

How should we study democratic transitions? Here I focus on a controversial methodological issue: whether studying transitions requires a different method from studying a stable regime type. This issue emerges most conspicuously in differences between O'Donnell and Schmitter (1986) and Levine (1988). Central to O'Donnell and Schmitter's argument is the contention that studying democratic transitions requires a different method from studying democratic processes. Central to Levine's criticism (1988) of their argument is the assertion that this contention is wrong. I agree with O'Donnell and Schmitter on one issue and with Levine on another.

O'Donnell and Schmitter begin their discussion of transitions by underscoring the high level of uncertainty and indeterminacy. They insist on

> the high degree of indeterminacy embedded in situations where unexpected events (fortuna), insufficient information, hurried and audacious choices, confusion about motives and interests, plasticity, and even indefinition of political identities, as well as the talents of specific individuals (virtù) are frequently deci-

sive in determining the outcomes. . . . The short-term political calculations we stress here cannot be 'deduced' from or 'im-
puted' to such structures. (1986:5)

Elsewhere, the authors claim that this indeterminacy, this uncertainty, the importance of choice, distinguishes transitions from
"normal" political circumstances. Under most conditions, choice is
less of an element of politics; political life is more closely bounded
by structural factors. They argue that there is an asymmetry between
the processes that lead to the demise of democratic governments
and those that lead to transitions from authoritarian rule to democracy. "Hope, opportunity, choice, incorporation of new actors, shap-
ing and renewal of political identities, inventiveness—these and many
other characteristics of the politics of the transition stand in sharp
contrast to the mode and tone of politics in the periods preceding
the breakdown of democratic regimes" (p. 19).

Levine takes O'Donnell and Schmitter to task for distinguishing so sharply between the study of transitions and the study of democracy. He argues that the proper study of transitions must be
rooted in an understanding of democracy. "[P]redominant or exclusive attention to transitions will not suffice. Full understanding
requires that study of transitions to democracy be rooted in consideration of democracy's own characteristic motivations, organizational resources, and operative patterns of leadership and legitimacy
. . . [O'Donnell and Schmitter] reveal an empirical focus more concerned with transitions than with either authoritarianism or democracy" (1988:377, 385).

Levine's assertion that O'Donnell and Schmitter are primarily
concerned with transitions rather than authoritarianism or democracy is indisputable, as the authors themselves recognize. The question is whether such a focus is warranted. I think it is, for two principal reasons. First, transition processes constitute an interesting and
important subject in their own right; there is no reason not to focus
on them. Second, O'Donnell and Schmitter's claim that transition
processes are different from political processes under an institutionalized authoritarian regime or a consolidated democratic regime is
compelling. In a consolidated democratic regime the rules of the
game are widely known and accepted. The rules of the game are
often not as clear in authoritarian regimes; many such regimes use
uncertainty about the rules as a means of reinforcing fear. Never-

theless, in a stable authoritarian regime, the major political actors attempt to conform to what they perceive as the dominant rules of the game. In contrast, in a transition period the rules are in constant flux; they are neither widely known nor widely accepted. Sharp change in the rules is unusual in consolidated democracies; it is common in transition processes.

The dominant actors in democratic politics are not always important in transition periods, and conversely the actors who are important in transition periods are not always central to democratic politics. For example, parties and elections are essential in understanding democratic politics, but they may be secondary during some phases of transitions. Among recent transitions in Latin America, the Brazilian case is the only one in which parties and elections played a major role from the beginning of the transition. By the time elections are called, parties invariably become important actors, but in numerous cases they appear relatively late on the scene of transition politics. Conversely, the military has consistently been a dominant force in transition politics and has remained an unfortunately obtrusive actor in the new democracies, but in consolidated democracies becomes considerably less conspicuous.

The other question revolves around the more specific issue of choice and leadership in politics. I agree with Levine that not only transitions, but all politics — democratic, transitional, authoritarian — involves choice. O'Donnell and Schmitter are generally right in suggesting that there is a big difference between analyzing transitional politics and stable democracies, but on this particular issue they overstate the differences. There is nothing extraordinary about the fact that the choices, leadership abilities, and predilections of political leaders can affect the outcome of transition processes. Linz (1978) compellingly argued that this is also the case in processes of democratic breakdown. It is equally true in new democracies, in which the battles to define the rules are ongoing. Only in well-institutionalized democracies does the element of choice become slightly less important, and then only in specific ways: radical change (whether substantive or in the rules of the game) is less likely. In highly institutionalized political systems, choice, strategies, and leadership are of crucial importance, but choice is usually less comprehensive in the sense that it does not involve making the basic rules of the game — as it does during transition periods. Leadership is generally a residual category for analysis because it is difficult to formulate nontautological, rigorous arguments about it. In terms of impact on politics, however, it is very far from being residual.

None of this is to imply that choices are not bounded by structural factors; they obviously are. But it is simply not clear that what O'Donnell and Schmitter term "normal" political processes (p. 5) involve radically less choice and radically more determination by structural factors.

Conclusion

In the past decades, the volume of literature analyzing democratic transitions and democratic processes in Latin America has far outstripped anything produced in the past. Latin Americans and Latin Americanists have produced works on democracy that have received attention throughout the entire Western world, and in many countries beyond the West. They did groundbreaking work on transitions to democracy, and have also contributed important works on democratic processes.

One of the results of the quantity and quality of work on these subjects is that a rich debate has emerged on several important issues. Until now, however, these debates have generally been inchoate. Because the transition phase is over and democratic governments are now in place, it is predictable that fewer people will write about democratic transitions as they turn their attention to the new democratic processes. But it would be unfortunate to simply forget about the interesting issues in the transitions literature, especially because, as I have implied throughout this chapter, they have strong implications for the analysis of democratic consolidation as well. It is precisely at this point when a considerable amount has been written that an overview of the issues and debates can be most valuable. That is what I hoped to do in this effort to flush out several debates in the literature and to challenge influential writings on some issues.

NOTES

The author wishes to thank Caroline Domingo, Jonathan Hartlyn, Daniel Levine, Juan Linz, Guillermo O'Donnell, Timothy Power, William C. Smith, and J. Samuel Valenzuela for helpful comments.

1. This point can be obscured by those who speak of cycles of authoritarianism and democracy in Latin America. It is true that Latin America has experienced several cycles of authoritarianism and democracy in the past; see Chalmers (1977) for one explanation of this phenomenon. However, until the 1980s, authoritarian regimes and oligarchic predemocratic regimes consistently prevailed except for short interregnums.

2. The current longevity of the new democracies in Latin America owes more to this change among intellectuals than is generally recognized. Latin American intellectuals have considerable influence in parties of the left and center-left, as well as in a wide amalgam of social movements. Their commitment to democracy helps explain the current longevity of democratic governments as much as this longevity explains the interest of intellectuals in democracy. At other points in Latin American history, it is doubtful that democratic governments could have withstood such dismal public policy performances.

3. Although I agree with Schumpeter's critique of idealized conceptions of democracy, I do not agree with all aspects of his own conception. Schumpeter wrote (p. 287) that democracy "forces upon the men at or near the helm a short-run view and makes it extremely difficult for them to serve such long-run interests of the nation as may require consistent work for far-off ends." In itself, this statement is unobjectionable, but there is no evidence that democracy holds a monopoly on myopic politicians; authoritarian leaders can be equally, if not more, short-sighted. Also, Schumpeter generally understates the importance of mechanisms of accountability in democratic politics. For a discussion of Schumpeter's definition of democracy, see J.S. Valenzuela (1985:22–35).

4. This requirement cannot be applied to regimes usually considered democratic in the period before women won the right to vote. It creates a troublesome issue in a case like Switzerland in which women won the suffrage late: was Switzerland not a democracy because women could not vote?

5. Linz (1978:16–23) properly insists that "the relationships between these variables [legitimacy, efficacy, and effectiveness] are far from fully transitive and lineal, since perception of the efficacy and effectiveness of a regime tends to be biased by the initial commitments to its legitimacy" (18).

6. Weber is not consistent on this point. At times he seems to imply that obedience through tradition does not constitute legitimacy. He affirms that "an order which is adhered to from motives of pure expediency is generally much less stable than one upheld on a purely customary basis through the fact that the corresponding behavior has become habitual. . . . But even this type of order is in turn much less stable than an order which enjoys the prestige of being considered binding, or, as it may be expressed, of 'legitimacy'" (31). Elsewhere, however, he argues that "ac-

tors may ascribe legitimacy to a social order by virtue of tradition: valid is that which has always been" (36). Here, as in most of his work, he argues that unquestioning adherence to tradition constitutes a form of legitimacy.

7. O'Donnell and Schmitter are somewhat inconsistent on this point. Elsewhere (p. 11) they agree with Przeworski's argument that uncertainty is a central feature of democracy. "As Adam Przeworski argues in his chapter, democracy institutionalizes uncertainty."

8. I emphasize contemporary transitions. By this, I exclude the generally protracted transitions from oligarchic regimes to modern mass democracies that occurred in the United States, Canada, and northern Europe during the nineteenth and early twentieth centuries. The reason for excluding these cases is that they would be impossible to reproduce in the contemporary setting. See Therborn (1977) for a broader typology of paths to democracy.

9. Stepan's discussion (1986) of three paths in which warfare and conquest play a major role usefully disaggregates the category of transitions initiated with regime defeats.

10. The new wave of institutionalism in Latin America has some precursors, especially in the study of Venezuelan politics, where attention to institutions is well established. However, even in Chile and Uruguay, political institutions had never received widespread scholarly attention until recently.

11. Seligson uses 1957 dollars for his minimum threshold, while Figure 8.5 reports 1950 dollars. Even if the table were adjusted to 1957 dollars, it appears unlikely that El Salvador and Nicaragua would reach the minimum threshold of $250 per capita.

12. Bollen (1979) argues that sequence is not too important, but he takes only one year (1965) and shows that at that particular juncture, there was a strong positive correlation between democracy and GNP, and a very weak correlation between democracy and timing of development. This approach has two problems. First, because he focuses on one year, the method does not allow him to examine the question of *stable* democracy. Second, if we wish to test the hypothesis that a certain level of GNP per capita is crucial for democracy, then we should compare the GNPs (in fixed dollars) of nondemocratic countries with those of established democracies at the period of democratic instauration, not at the present. Collier (1975) argued that timing of development had an independent impact on democracy; the late developing countries within Latin America were less likely to be democratic.

13. I am aware that emphasizing cultural patterns runs counter to some trends in the transitions literature and in democratic theory in general. At a minimum, what I have in mind is something akin to Dahl's (1971)

analysis of the beliefs of political elites, Hirschman's (1979) emphasis on how ideology affects development models and politics, and Weber's insistence (1958) on the importance of ideas. Broader cultural patterns also have their importance, but their impact is more difficult to weigh. See Scott (1985) and DaMatta (1985) for interesting contributions to this question.

REFERENCES

Baloyra, Enrique, ed. 1987a. *Comparing New Democracies: Transition and Consolidation in Mediterranean Europe and the Southern Cone.* Boulder: Westview.

Baloyra, Enrique. 1987b. "Democratic Transition in Comparative Perspective." In Baloyra, ed., *Comparing New Democracies,* pp. 9–52.

Barry, Brian. 1978. *Sociologists, Economists and Democracy.* Chicago: University of Chicago Press.

Bollen, Kenneth. 1979. "Political Democracy and the Timing of Development." *American Sociological Review* 44 (August), pp. 572–587.

Bresser Pereira, Luis Carlos. 1984. "Os limites da 'Abertura' e a sociedade civil." *CEDEC Cadernos Contribuições* no. 4.

Cammack, Paul. 1985. "The Political Economy of Contemporary Military Regimes in Latin America: From Bureaucratic-Authoritarianism to Restructuring." In Philip O'Brien and Paul Cammack, eds., *Generals in Retreat,* pp. 1–36. Manchester: Manchester University Press.

Cavarozzi, Marcelo. 1983. *Autoritarismo y democracia (1955–1983).* Buenos Aires: Centro Editor.

———. 1986. "Political Cycles in Argentina since 1955." In O'Donnell et al., eds., *Transitions from Authoritarian Rule,* pp. 19–48.

Chalmers, Douglas. 1977. "The Politicized State in Latin America." In James Malloy, ed., *Authoritarianism and Corporatism in Latin America,* pp. 23–46. Pittsburgh: University of Pittsburgh.

Chalmers, Douglas, and Craig Robinson. 1982. "Why Power Contenders Choose Liberalization." *International Studies Quarterly* 26 (March), pp. 3–36.

Collier, David. 1975. "Timing of Economic Growth and Regime Characteristics in Latin America." *Comparative Politics* 7 (April), pp. 331–360.

———, ed. 1979. *The New Authoritarianism in Latin America.* Princeton: Princeton University Press.

Conaghan, Catherine. 1985. "Democracy by Attrition: Parties, Civil Society, and Political Order in Ecuador." Paper for the Conference on Redemocratization in Latin America, University of Pittsburgh, March 28–30.

———. 1987. "Party Politics and Democratization in Ecuador." In Malloy and Seligson, eds., *Authoritarians and Democrats,* pp. 145–163.

Cortázar, René. 1987. "La no transición a la democracia en Chile y el plebiscito de 1988." *Estudios CIEPLAN* 22 (December), pp. 111–128.

Coulter, Phillip. 1975. *Social Mobilization and Liberal Democracy.* Lexington: Heath.

Coutinho, Carlos Nelson. 1980. *A democracia como valor universal.* São Paulo: Livraría Editora Ciências Humanas.

Dahl, Robert. 1956. *A Preface to Democracy Theory.* Chicago: University of Chicago Press.

———. 1961. *Who Governs?* New Haven: Yale University Press.

———. 1971. *Polyarchy.* New Haven: Yale University Press.

DaMatta, Roberto. 1985. *A casa e a rua.* São Paulo: Brasiliense.

Garretón, Manuel Antonio. 1986. "Political Processes in an Authoritarian Regime: The Dynamics of Institutionalization and Opposition in Chile, 1973–1980." In J. Samuel Valenzuela and Arturo Valenzuela, eds., *Military Rule in Chile: Dictatorship and Opposition,* pp. 144–183. Baltimore: Johns Hopkins University Press.

Gillespie, Charles. 1986. "Uruguay's Transition from Collegial Military-Technocratic Rule." In O'Donnell et al., eds., *Transitions from Authoritarian Rule,* pp. 173–195.

González, Luis. 1988. "Political Structures and the Prospects for Democracy in Uruguay." Ph.D. dissertation, Yale University.

Hagopian, Frances, and Scott Mainwaring. 1987. "Democracy in Brazil: Prospects and Problems." *World Policy Journal* IV, pp. 485–514.

Hartlyn, Jonathan. 1988. *The Politics of Coalition Rule in Colombia.* Cambridge University Press.

Hirschman, Albert. 1979. "The Turn to Authoritarianism in Latin America and the Search for Its Economic Determinants." In Collier, ed., *The New Authoritarianism in Latin America,* pp. 61–98.

———. 1987. "The Political Economy of Latin American Development: Seven Exercises in Retrospection." *Latin American Research Review* 22, no. 3, pp. 7–36.

Huntington, Samuel. 1984. "Will More Countries Become Democratic?" *Political Science Quarterly* 99 (Summer), pp. 193–218.

Karl, Terry Lynn. 1986a. "Petroleum and Political Pacts: The Transition to Democracy in Venezuela." In O'Donnell, Schmitter, and Whitehead, eds., *Transitions from Authoritarian Rule,* pp. 196–219.

———. 1986b. "Imposing Consent? Electoralism vs. Democratization in El Salvador." In Paul Drake and Eduardo Silva, eds., *Elections and Democratization in Latin America, 1980–1985,* pp. 9–36. San Diego: University of California.

————. 1986c. "Democracy by Design: The Christian Democratic Party in El Salvador." In Giuseppe Di Palma and Laurence Whitehead, eds., *The Central American Impasse,* pp. 195–217. New York: St. Martin's Press.

Kaufman, Robert. 1986. "Liberalization and Democratization in South America: Perpsectives from the 1970s." In O'Donnell et al., eds., *Transitions from Authoritarian Rule,* pp. 85–107.

Lamounier, Bolívar. 1979a. "O discurso e o processo (da Distensão às opções do regime brasileiro." In Henrique Rattner, ed., *Brasil 1990: Caminhos alternativos do desenvolvimento,* pp. 88–120. São Paulo: Brasiliense.

————. 1979b. "Representação política: a importância de certos formalismos." In Lamounier, Francisco Weffort, and Maria Victória Benevides, eds., *Direito, cidadania e participação,* pp. 230–257. São Paulo: Tao.

Levine, Daniel. 1973. *Conflict and Political Change in Venezuela.* Princeton: Princeton University Press.

————. 1978. "Venezuela since 1958: The Consolidation of Democratic Politics." In Juan Linz and Alfred Stepan, eds., *The Breakdown of Democratic Regimes,* pp. 82–109. Baltimore: Johns Hopkins University Press.

————. 1988. "Paradigm Lost: From Dependency to Democracy." *World Politics* 40, pp. 377–394.

————. 1989. "Venezuela: The Nature, Sources, and Future Prospects of Democracy." In Larry Diamond, Juan Linz, and Seymour Martin Lipset, eds., *Democracy in Developing Countries,* Vol. 4, pp. 247–289. Boulder: Lynne Rienner.

Lijphart, Arend. 1977. *Democracy in Plural Societies: A Comparative Exploration.* New Haven: Yale University Press.

————. 1984. *Democracies.* New Haven: Yale University Press.

Linz, Juan. 1973. "The Future of an Authoritarian Situation or the Institutionalization of an Authoritarian Regime." In Alfred Stepan, ed., *Authoritarian Brazil: Origins, Policies, and Future,* pp. 233–254. New Haven: Yale University Press.

————. 1975. "Totalitarian and Authoritarian Regimes." In Fred Greenstein and Nelson Polsby, eds., *Handbook of Political Science,* pp. 175–411. Reading, MA: Addison-Wesley.

————. 1978. *The Breakdown of Democratic Regimes: Crisis, Breakdown, and Reequilibration.* Baltimore: Johns Hopkins University Press.

————. 1981. "Some Comparative Thoughts on the Transition to Democracy in Portugal and Spain." In Jorge Braga de Macedo and Simon Serfaty, eds., *Portugal Since the Revolution: Economic and Political Perspectives,* pp. 25–45. Boulder: Westview.

————. 1985. "Democracy: Presidential or Parliamentary. Does It Make a Difference?" Unpublished paper.

Linz, Juan J., and Alfred Stepan. 1989. "Political Crafting of Democratic Consolidation or Destruction: European and South American Comparisons." In Robert A. Pastor, ed., *Democracy in the Americas: Stopping the Pendulum,* pp. 41–61. New York: Holmes and Meier.

Lipset, Seymour Martin. 1959. "Some Social Requisites of Democracy: Economic Development and Political Legitimacy." *American Political Science Review* 53, pp. 69–105.

López-Pintor, Rafael. 1987. "Mass and Elite Perspectives in the Process of Transition to Democracy." In Baloyra, ed., *Comparing New Democracies,* pp. 79–106.

Mainwaring, Scott, and Donald Share. 1986. "Transitions through Transaction: Democratization in Brazil and Spain." In Wayne Selcher, ed., *Political Liberalization in Brazil,* pp. 175–215. Boulder: Westview.

Mainwaring, Scott, and Eduardo Viola. 1985. "Transitions to Democracy: Brazil and Argentina in the 1980s." *Journal of International Affairs* 38 (Winter), pp. 193–219.

Malloy, James. 1987. "The Politics of Transition in Latin America." In Malloy and Seligson, eds., *Authoritarians and Democrats,* pp. 235–258.

Malloy, James and Eduardo Gamarra. 1987. "The Transition to Democracy in Bolivia." In Malloy and Seligson, eds., *Authoritarians and Democrats,* pp. 93–120.

Malloy, James, and Mitchell Seligson, eds. 1987. *Authoritarians and Democrats: Regime Transition in Latin America.* Pittsburgh: University of Pittsburgh Press.

March, James, and Johan Olsen. 1984. "The New Institutionalism: Organizational Factors in Political Life." *American Political Science Review* 78 (September), pp. 734–749.

Martins, Luciano. 1986. "The 'Liberalization' of Authoritarian Rule in Brazil." In O'Donnell, Schmitter, and Whitehead, eds., *Transitions from Authoritarian Rule,* Part II, pp. 72–94.

McDonough, Peter, et al. 1981. "The Spanish Public in Political Transition." *British Journal of Political Science* 11, pp. 49–79.

Michels, Robert. 1959. *Political Parties.* New York: Dover.

Moisés, José Alvaro. 1986. "Sociedade civil, cultura política e democracia: Descaminhos da transição política." In Maria de Lourdes Covre, ed., *A cidadania que não temos,* pp. 119–150. São Paulo: Brasiliense.

Morlino, Leonardo. 1987. "Democratic Establishments: A Dimensional Analysis." In Baloyra, ed., *Comparing New Democracies,* pp. 53–78.

Nun, José, and Juan Carlos Portantiero, eds. 1987. *Ensayos sobre la transición democrática en la Argentina.* Buenos Aires: Puntosur.

O'Donnell, Guillermo. 1973. *Modernization and Bureaucratic-Authoritarianism.* Berkeley: Institute of International Studies.

————. 1979a. "Notas para el estudio de procesos de democratización política a partir del estado burocrático-autoritario." *Estudios CEDES* 2, no. 5.

————. 1979b. "Tensions in the Bureaucratic-Authoritarian State and the Question of Democracy." In Collier, ed., *The New Authoritarianism in Latin America,* pp. 285–318.

————. 1982. *El estado burocrático-autoritario, 1966–1973: Triunfos, derrotas y crisis.* Buenos Aires: Editorial del Belgrano.

————. 1984. "Y a mi que me importa?: Notas sobre sociabilidad y política en Argentina y Brasil." Kellogg Institute Working Paper no. 9, University of Notre Dame (January).

————. 1986. "Introduction to the Latin American Cases." In O'Donnell et al., eds., *Transitions from Authoritarian Rule,* Part II, pp. 3–18.

————. 1989. "Transitions to Democracy: Some Navigation Instruments." In Robert Pastor, ed., *Democracy in the Americas: Stopping of the Pendulum,* pp. 62–75. New York: Holmes and Meier.

O'Donnell, Guillermo, and Philippe Schmitter. 1986. "Tentative Conclusions about Uncertain Democracies." In O'Donnell et al., eds., *Transitions from Authoritarian Rule,* Part 4, pp. 1–78.

O'Donnell, Guillermo, Philippe Schmitter, and Laurence Whitehead, eds. 1986. *Transitions from Authoritarian Rule: Prospects for Democracy.* Baltimore: Johns Hopkins University Press.

Ollier, María Matilde. 1986. *El fenómeno insurreccional y la cultura política (1969–1973).* Buenos Aires: Centro Editor.

Packenham, Robert. 1986. "The Changing Political Discourse in Brazil." In Wayne Selcher, ed., *Political Liberalization in Brazil: Dynamics, Dilemmas, and Future Prospects,* pp. 135–173. Boulder: Westview.

Peeler, John. 1985. *Latin American Democracies.* Chapel Hill: University of North Carolina Press.

Pizzorno, Alessandro. 1985. "On the Rationality of Democratic Choice." *Telos* 64 (Spring), pp. 41–69.

Przeworski, Adam. 1985. *Capitalism and Social Democracy.* Cambridge University Press.

————. 1986. "Some Problems in the Study of the Transition to Democracy." In O'Donnell et al., eds., *Transitions from Authoritarian Rule,* pp. 47–63.

————. 1988. "Democracy as a Contingent Outcome of Conflicts." In Jon Elster and Rune Slagstad, eds., *Constitutionalism and Democracy,* pp. 59–80. Cambridge: Cambridge University Press.

Reis, Fábio Wanderley. 1988. "Partidos, ideologia e consolidação democrática." In Fábio Wanderley Reis and Guillermo O'Donnell, eds., *A democracia no Brasil: Dilemas e perspectivas,* pp. 296–326. São Paulo: Vértice.

Remmer, Karen, and Gilbert Merkx. 1982. "Bureaucratic-Authoritarianism

Revisited." *Latin American Research Review* 17, no. 2, pp. 3–40.

Rustow, Dankwart. 1955. *The Politics of Compromise: A Study of Parties and Cabinet Government in Sweden.* Princeton: Princeton University Press.

———. 1970. "Transitions to Democracy." *Comparative Politics* 2 (April), pp. 337–363.

Sahlins, Marshall. 1976. *Culture and Practical Reason.* Chicago: University of Chicago Press.

Santos, Wanderley Guilherme. 1986. *Sessenta e quatro: Anatomia da crise.* São Paulo: Vértice.

Sartori, Giovanni. 1976. *Parties and Party Systems: A Framework for Analysis.* Cambridge: Cambridge University Press.

———. 1987. *The Theory of Democracy Revisited.* Chatham, N.J.: Chatham House.

Schumpeter, Joseph. 1950. *Capitalism, Socialism, and Democracy.* New York: Harper & Row.

Scott, James. 1985. *Weapons of the Weak: Everyday Forms of Peasant Resistance.* New Haven: Yale University Press.

Seligson, Mitchell. 1987a. "Democratization in Latin America: The Current Cycle." In Malloy and Seligson, eds., *Authoritarians and Democrats,* pp. 3–12.

———. 1987b. "Development, Democratization, and Decay: Central America at the Crossroads." In Malloy and Seligson, *Authoritarians and Democrats,* pp. 167–192.

Serra, José. 1979. "Three Mistaken Theses Regarding the Connection between Industrialization and Authoritarian Regimes." In Collier, ed., *The New Authoritarianism in Latin America,* pp. 99–163.

Share, Donald. 1987. "Transitions to Democracy and Transition through Transaction." *Comparative Political Studies* 19 (January), pp. 525–548.

Smith, William. 1987. "The Political Transition in Brazil: From Authoritarian Liberalization and Elite Conciliation to Democratization." In Enrique Baloyra, *Comparing New Democracies,* pp. 179–240.

Stepan, Alfred. 1971. *The Military in Politics: Changing Patterns in Brazil.* Princeton: Princeton University Press.

———. 1986. "Paths toward Redemocratization: Theoretical and Comparative Considerations." In O'Donnell et al., eds., *Transitions to Democracy,* pp. 65–84.

———. 1988. *Rethinking Military Politics: Brazil and the Southern Cone.* Princeton: Princeton University Press.

Stephens, John. 1987. "Democratic Transition and Breakdown in Europe, 1870–1939: A Test of the Moore Thesis." Kellogg Institute Working Paper no. 101 (November).

Therborn, Goran. 1977. "The Rule of Capital and the Rise of Democracy." *New Left Review* 103 (May–June), pp. 3–41.

Valenzuela, Arturo. 1985. "Origins and Characteristics of the Chilean Party System." Working Paper no. 164, Latin American Program, Woodrow Wilson Center (May).

Valenzuela, Arturo, and J. Samuel Valenzuela. 1983. "Los orígenes de la democracia: Reflexiones teóricas sobre el caso de Chile." *Estudios Públicos* 12 (Spring), pp. 5–39.

Valenzuela, J. Samuel. 1985. *Democratización vía reforma: La expansión del sufragio en Chile*. Buenos Aires: IDES.

Viola, Eduardo. 1982. "Democracia e autoritarismo na Argentina contemporânea." Ph.D. thesis, University of São Paulo.

Weber, Max. 1958. *The Protestant Ethic and the Spirit of Capitalism*. New York: Charles Scribner's Sons.

———. 1978. *Economy and Society*. Berkeley: University of California Press.

Weffort, Francisco. 1984. *Por que Democracia?* São Paulo: Brasiliense.

Whitehead, Laurence. 1985. "The Consolidation of Democracy: A Discussion Note." Unpublished paper.

Contributors

Felipe Agüero is an Assistant Professor of Political Science at the Ohio State University. He is coauthor of a book on the Chilean military and has published articles on military politics and democratization in Spain and Latin America.

Catherine M. Conaghan is an Associate Professor of Political Studies at Queen's University in Kingston, Canada. She is the author of *Restructuring Domination: Industrialists and the State in Ecuador* (University of Pittsburgh Press, 1988). Her work on regime transition and comparative economic policy making includes contributions to the *Latin American Research Review* and the *Journal of Latin American Studies*.

Frances Hagopian is an Assistant Professor of Political Science at Tufts University. She taught at Harvard University from 1987 until 1991. She is the author of *Traditional Politics and Regime Change in Brazil* (Cambridge University Press, forthcoming), and several articles on Brazil and Latin American democratization. Her current research focuses on the reorganization of political representation occasioned by the retreat of the state from the economy.

Scott Mainwaring is a Senior Fellow of the Kellogg Institute and an Associate Professor of Government and International Studies at the University of Notre Dame. He is the author of *The Catholic Church and Politics in Brazil, 1916–1985* (Stanford University Press, 1986) and the coeditor of *The Progressive Church in Latin America* (Kellogg Institute/University of Notre Dame Press, 1989) and of *A Igreja nas Bases em Tempo de Transição* (L & PM, 1986).

Guillermo O'Donnell is Academic Director of the Kellogg Institute and Helen Kellogg Professor of Government and International Studies and Sociology at the University of Notre Dame and Senior Researcher at CEBRAP, São Paulo. He is the author and editor of many works, including *Transitions from Authoritarian Rule* (Johns Hopkins University Press, 1986), *Bureaucratic Authoritarianism* (University of California Press, 1988), *A democracia no Brasil* (Vértice, 1988), and *Modernization and Bureaucratic-Authoritarianism* (Institute of International Studies, University of California, 1973).

Adam Przeworski is the Martin A. Ryerson Distinguished Service Professor of Political Science at the University of Chicago. He is the author of many books, including *Capitalism and Social Democracy* (Cambridge University Press, 1985), *The Logic of Comparative Social Inquiry* (Wiley-Interscience, 1970), and *Paper Stones: A History of Electoral Socialism* (University of Chicago Press, 1986).

J. Samuel Valenzuela is a Senior Fellow of the Kellogg Institute and Professor and Chair of Sociology at the University of Notre Dame. He is the author of *Democratización vía reforma: La expansión del sufragio en Chile,* coeditor of *Military Rule in Chile: Dictatorship and Oppositions* and of *Chile: Politics and Society,* and editor of *Labor Movements in Transitions to Democracy* (forthcoming). His articles on comparative labor, development theory, and political change have appeared in English, Spanish, Italian, and French publications.

Index

Acción Democrática Nacionalista (ADN) (Bolivia), 213, 215, 228
Acción Popular (AP) (Peru), 201, 221–22
Accountability: lack in Brazilian politics, 47; uncertainty in electoral policies, 228; as viewed in a democracy, 38, 54 n.29, 59, 61, 63
"Acordo de Minas" ("Minas Agreement") (Brazil), 260, 261, 264, 288 n.29
ADN. See Acción Democrática Nacionalista
Agrarian reform: in 1988 Brazilian constitution, 272, 274, 277; proposed by military regimes, 205
Alfonsín, Raúl (Argentina), 9, 88, 90, 160
Alliances: between liberalization factions and opposition, 301; state management of external economic, 200
Amnesty: laws absolving military, 97 n.13, 157, 182 n.8; pardons for convicted military, 161, 185 n.26
Anderson, Charles, 6, 69, 99 n.27
Anticommunism: in authoritarian regimes, 92, 174, 325; and democratic divisions, 124, 135–36, 144 n.40
Antidemocratic attitudes, of business elites, 233–34, 242 n.72, 309
APRA (Peru), 167, 171, 187 n.37, 228
ARENA. See National Renovating Alliance
Argentina, 295, 300; effect of external defeat on military, 24, 35, 168, 192

Argentina (cont.)
n.64, 301; inflationary strategies in, 129–30; military coups attempts, 88, 100 n.30; military role in, 159–62, 168; military tutelage, 90, 131–32, 147 n.62
Armed forces: as bulwarks against communism, 92; Franquist sentiment in Spain, 90–91; need for in South America, 178–79, 197–98 n.92; place in a democratized regime, 117, 118, 142 n.26; refounding during transitional period, 90–91; Sandinista control of, 78; splits in Bolivian, 212; during transitional period, 32, 33. See also Amnesty; Coups, military; Military; Officers, military
Asamblea Popular (Bolivia), 202, 233
Association of Exporters (ADEX) (Peru), 206–7, 214–15, 220, 222, 238 n.34
Austerity measures: formulated for Bolivia, 216; policy making in central Andean states, 215–16, 219, 223
Authoritarian actors: role in liberalization, 299–300; in transitional democracies, 17, 22, 33–34, 244, 302; view of democracy as second-best solution, 309
Authoritarian regimes, 14, 21, 74, 294; attitudes of elites towards democratization, 73–78; extrication from, 64, 116–22, 322; legitimacy of rule,